D&B

Industry & Financial Consulting Services

INDUSTRY NORMS
AND KEY BUSINESS RATIOS

One Year
Desk-Top Edition
SIC #0100-8999

ISBN 978-1-59274-801-3

To obtain reprint permission, please send your correspondence to

Mergent Inc.
444 Madison Avenue Suite 502
New York, NY 10022
Telephone: 800.342.5647
www.mergentbusinesspress.com

Manufactured in the United States of America.

CONTENTS

INDUSTRY NORMS AND KEY BUSINESS RATIOS

APPENDIX - SIC Numbers Appearing in This Directory

CONTENTS

The Desk-Top Edition of The D&B Industry Norms and Key Business Ratios is made possible through over one million financial statements in the D&B Financial Information Base. This file consists of U.S. corporations, partnerships and proprietorships both public and privately owned, in all size ranges, and includes over 800 different lines of business as defined by the U.S. Standard Industrial Classification (SIC) code numbers. Our data is collected weekly, maintained daily, and constantly edited and updated. All of these factors combine to make this financial information unequaled anywhere for scope and timeliness*.

It should be noted that only general data is supplied in the Desk-Top Edition. However, for more detailed asset/geographical breakdowns of this data, an expanded set of Industry Norms and Key Business Ratios are also published by D&B for the Corporate Marketplace in the following five segments:

1. **Agriculture, Mining, Construction/ Transportation/Communication/Utilities**
2. **Manufacturing**
3. **Wholesaling**
4. **Retailing**
5. **Finance/Real Estate/Services**

All five segments are available in two other formats. The formats are as follows:

1. **Industry Norms and Key Business Ratios, Three Year Edition.**
   Directories and electronic file versions available.

2. **Industry Norms and Key Business Ratios, One Year Edition.**
   Directories and electronic file versions available.

Note that the Industry Norms contain "typical" balance sheets and income statements, and "common-size" financial figures, <u>as well as Key Business Ratios</u>. The Key Business Ratios books contain fourteen indicators of performance.

*To provide the most current information available, fiscal years January 1 - December 31 were utilized to calculate the Norms.

INDUSTRY NORM FORMAT

At the top of each industry norm will be identifying information: SIC code number and short title. Beside the year date, in parenthesis, is the number of companies in the sample. The "typical" balance-sheet figures are in the first column and the "common-size" balance-sheet figures are in the second. The respective income statements begin with the item "Net Sales", and the respective Key Business Ratios begin with the item "Ratios." The latter are further broken down, or refined, into the median, and the upper quartile and lower quartile.

THE COMMON - SIZE FINANCIAL STATEMENT

The common-size balance-sheet and income statement present each item of the financial statement as a percentage of its respective aggregate total. Common-size percentages are computed for all statement items of all the individual companies used in the industry sample. An average for each statement item is then determined and presented as the industry norm.

This enables the analyst to examine the current composition of assets, liabilities and sales of a particular industry.

THE TYPICAL FINANCIAL STATEMENT

The typical balance-sheet figures are the result of translating the common-size percentages into dollar figures. They permit, for example, a quick check of the relative size of assets and liabilities between one's own company and that company's own line of business.

After the common-size percentages have been computed for the particular sample, the actual financial statements are then sequenced by both *total assets* and *total sales*, with the median, or mid-point figure in both these groups serving as the "typical" amount. We then compute the typical balance-sheet and income statement dollar figures by multiplying the common-size percentages for each statement item by their respective total amounts.

(For example, if the median total assets for an SIC category are $669,599, and the common-size figure for cash is 9.2 percent, then by multiplying the two we derive a cash figure of $61,603 for the typical balance sheet.)

KEY BUSINESS RATIOS

The Fourteen Key Business Ratios are broken down into median figures, with upper and lower quartiles, giving the analyst an even more refined set of figures to work with. These ratios cover all those critical areas of business performance with indicators of solvency, efficiency and profitability.

They provide a profound and well-documented insight into all aspects for everyone interested in the financial workings of business—business executives and managers, credit executives, bankers, lenders, investors, academicians and students.

In the ratio tables appearing in this book, the figures are broken down into the median—which is the midpoint of all companies in the sample—and the upper quartile and lower quartile—which are mid-points of the upper and lower halves.

Upper quartile figures are not always the highest numerical value, nor are lower quartile figures always the lowest numerical value. The quartile listings reflect *judgmental ranking*, thus the upper quartile represents the best condition in any given ratio and is not necessarily the highest numerical value. (For example, see the items Total Liabilities-to-Net Worth or Collection Period, where a lower numerical value represents a better condition.)

Each of the fourteen ratios is calculated individually for every concern in the sample. These individual figures are then sequenced for each ratio according to condition (best to worst), and the figure that falls in the middle of this series becomes the median (or mid-point) for that ratio in that line of business. The figure halfway between the median and the best condition of the series becomes the upper quartile; and the number halfway between the medianand the least favorable condition of the series is the lower quartile.

In a statistical sense, each median is considered the *typical* ratio figure for a concern in a given category.

SOLVENCY RATIOS

Quick Ratio

Cash + Accounts Receivable
Current Liabilities

The Quick Ratio is computed by dividing cash plus accounts receivable by total current liabilities. Current liabilities are all the liabilities that fall due within one year. This ratio reveals the protection afforded short-term creditors in cash or near-cash assets. It shows the number of dollars of liquid assets available to cover each dollar of current debt. Any time this ratio is as much as 1 to 1 (1.0) the business is said to be in a liquid condition. The larger the ratio the greater the liquidity.

Current Ratio

Current Assets
Current Liabilities

Total current assets are divided by total current liabilities. Current assets include cash, accounts and notes receivable (less reserves for bad debts), advances on inventories, merchandise inventories and marketable securities. This ratio measures the degree to which current assets cover current liabilities. The higher the ratio the more assurance exists that the retirement of current liabilities can be made. The current ratio measures the margin of safety available to cover any possible shrinkage in the value of current assets. Normally a ratio of 2 to 1 (2.0) or better is considered good.

Current Liabilities to Net Worth

Current Liabilities
Net Worth

Current Liabilities to Net Worth is derived by dividing current liabilities by net worth. This contrasts the funds that creditors temporarily are risking with the funds permanently invested by the owners. The smaller the net worth and the larger the liabilities, the less security for the creditors. Care should be exercised when selling any firm with current liabilities exceeding two-thirds (66.6 percent) of net worth.

Current Liabilities to Inventory

Current Liabilities
Inventory

Dividing current liabilities by inventory yields another indication of the extent to which the business relies on funds from disposal of unsold inventories to meet its debts. This ratio combines with Net Sales to Inventory to indicate how management controls inventory. It is possible to have decreasing liquidity while maintaining consistent sales-to-inventory ratios. Large increases in sales with corresponding increases in inventory levels can cause an inappropriate rise in current liabilities if growth isn't made wisely.

Total Liabilities to Net Worth

Total Liabilities
Net Worth

Obtained by dividing total current plus long-term and deferred liabilities by net worth. The effect of long-term (funded) debt on a business can be determined by comparing this ratio with Current Liabilities to Net Worth. The difference will pinpoint the relative size of long-term debt, which, if sizable, can burden a firm with substantial interest charges. In general, total liabilities shouldn't exceed net worth (100 percent) since in such cases creditors have more at stake than owners.

Fixed Assets to Net Worth

Fixed Assets
Net Worth

Fixed assets are divided by net worth. The proportion of net worth that consists of fixed assets will vary greatly from industry to industry but generally a smaller proportion is desirable. A high ratio is unfavorable because heavy investment in fixed assets indicates that either the concern has a low net working capital and is overtrading or has utilized large funded debt to supplement working capital. Also, the larger the fixed assets, the bigger the annual depreciation charge that must be deducted from the income statement. Normally, fixed assets above 75 percent of net worth indicate possible over-investment and should be examined with care.

EFFICIENCY RATIOS

Collection Period

Accounts Receivable
Sales   x 365

Accounts receivable are divided by sales and then multiplied by 365 days to obtain this figure. The quality of the receivables of a company can be determined by this relationship when compared with selling terms and industry norms. In some industries where credit sales are not the normal way of doing business, the percentage of cash sales should be taken into consideration. Generally, where most sales are for credit, any collection period more than one-third over normal selling terms (40.0 for 30-day terms) is indicative of some slow-turning receivables. When comparing the collection period of one concern with that of another, allowances should be made for possible variations in selling terms.

Sales to Inventory

Annual Net Sales
Inventory

Obtained by dividing annual net sales by inventory. Inventory control is a prime management objective since poor controls allow inventory to become costly to store, obsolete or insufficient to meet demands. The sales-to-inventory relationship is a guide to the rapidity at which merchandise is being moved and the effect on the flow of funds into the business. This ratio varies widely between lines of business and a company's figure is only meaningful when compared with industry norms. Individual figures that are outside either the upper or lower quartiles for a given industry should be examined with care. Although low figures are usually the biggest problem, as they indicate excessively high inventories, extremely high turnovers might reflect insufficient merchandise to meet customer demand and result in lost sales.

Asset to Sales

Total Assets
Net Sales

Assets to sales is calculated by dividing total assets by annual net sales. This ratio ties in sales and the total investment that is used to generate those sales. While figures vary greatly from in-

dustry to industry, by comparing a company's ratio with industry norms it can be determined whether a firm is overtrading (handling an excessive volume of sales in relation to investment) or undertrading (not generating sufficient sales to warrant the assets invested). Abnormally low percentages (above the upper quartile) can indicate overtrading which may lead to financial difficulties if not corrected. Extremely high percentages (below the lower quartile) can be the result of overly conservative or poor sales management, indicating a more aggressive sales policy may need to be followed.

Sales to Net Working Capital

Sales
Net Working Capital

Net sales are divided by net working capital (net working capital is current assets minus current liabilities.). This relationship indicates whether a company is overtrading or conversely carrying more liquid assets than needed for its volume. Each industry can vary substantially and it is necessary to compare a company with its peers to see if it is either overtrading on its available funds or being overly conservative. Companies with substantial sales gains often reach a level where their working capital becomes strained. Even if they maintain an adequate total investment for the volume being generated (Assets to Sales), that investment may be so centered in fixed assets or other noncurrent items that it will be difficult to continue meeting all current obligations without additional investment or reducing sales.

Accounts Payable to Sales

Accounts Payable
Annual Net Sales

Computed by dividing accounts payable by annual net sales. This ratio measures how the company is paying its suppliers in relation to the volume being transacted. An increasing percentage, or one larger than the industry norm, indicates the firm may be using suppliers to help finance operations. This ratio is especially important to short-term creditors since a high percentage could indicate potential problems in paying vendors.

PROFITABILITY RATIOS

Return on Sales (Profit Margin)

Net Profit After Taxes
Annual Net Sales

Obtained by dividing net profit after taxes by annual net sales. This reveals the profits earned per dollar of sales and therefore measures the efficiency of the operation. Return must be adequate for the firm to be able to achieve satisfactory profits for its owners. This ratio is an indicator of the firm's ability to withstand adverse conditions such as falling prices, rising costs and declining sales.

Return on Assets

Net Profit After Taxes
Total Assets

Net profit after taxes divided by total assets. This ratio is the key indicator of profitability for a firm. It matches operating profits with the assets available to earn a return. Companies efficiently using their assets will have a relatively high return while less well-run businesses will be relatively low.

Return on Net Worth (Return on Equity)

Net Profit After Taxes
Net Worth

Obtained by dividing net profit after tax by net worth. This ratio is used to analyze the ability of the firm's management to realize an adequate return on the capital invested by the owners of the firm. Tendency is to look increasingly to this ratio as a final criterion of profitability. Generally, a relationship of at least 10 percent is regarded as a desirable objective for providing dividends plus funds for future growth.

Using Industry Norms for Financial Analysis

The principal purpose of financial analysis is to identify irregularities that require explanations to completely understand an industry's or company's current status and future potential. These irregularities can be identified by comparing the industry norms with the figures of specific companies (*comparative analysis*). D&B's Industry Norms are specifically formatted to accommodate this analysis.

Relative Position

Common-size and typical balance sheets provide an excellent picture of the makeup of the industry's assets and liabilities. Are assets concentrated in inventories or accounts receivable? Are payables to the trade or bank loans more important as a method for financing operations? The answers to these and other important questions are clearly shown by the Industry Norms, its common-size balance sheet approach and is then further crystallized by the typical balance sheets.

Financial Ratio Trends

Key Business Ratio changes indicate trends in the important *relationships* between key financial items, such as the relationship between Net Profits and Net Sales (a common indicator of profitability). Ratios that reflect short and long-term liquidity, efficiency in managing assets and controlling debt, and different measures of profitability are all included in the Key Business Ratios sections of the Industry Norms.

Comparative Analysis

Comparing a company with its peers is a reliable method for evaluating financial status. The key to this technique is the composition of the peer group and the timeliness of the data. The D&B Industry Norms are unique in scope of sample size and in level of detail.

Sample Size

The number of firms in the sample must be representative or they will be unduly influenced by irregular figures from relatively few companies. The more than one million companies used as a basis for the Industry Norms allow for more than adequate sample sizes in most cases.

Key Business Ratios Analysis

Valuable insights into an industry's performance can be obtained by equating two related statement items in the form of a financial ratio. For really effective ratio analysis, the items compared must be meaningful and the comparison should reflect the combined effort of two potentially diverse trends. While dozens of different ratios can be computed from financial statements, the fourteen included in the Industry Norms and Key Business Ratio books are those most commonly used and were rated as the most significant as shown in a survey of financial analysts. Many of the other ratios in existence are variations on these fourteen.

The fourteen Key Business Ratios are categorized into three major groups:

Solvency, or liquidity, measurements are significant in evaluating a company's ability to meet short and long-term obligations. These figures are of prime interest to credit managers of commercial companies and financial institutions.

Efficiency ratios indicate how effectively a company uses and controls its assets. This is critical information for evaluating how a company is managed. Studying these ratios is useful for credit, marketing and investment purposes.

Profitability ratios show how successfully a business is earning a return to its owners. Those interested in mergers and acquisitions consider this key data for selecting candidates.

APPLICATIONS BY FUNCTIONAL AREAS

Recent research efforts have revealed that the use of financial analysis (via Industry Norms) is very useful in several functional areas. To follow are only a few of the more widely used applications of this unique data.

Credit

Industry Norm data has proven to be an invaluable tool in determining minimum acceptable standards for risk. The credit worthiness of an existing or potential account is immediately visible by ranking its solvency status and comparing its solvency trends to that of the industry. Short term solvency gauges, such as the quick and current ratios, are ideal indicators when evaluating an account. Balance sheet comparisons supplement this qualification by allowing a comparison of the make-up of current assets and liability items. Moreover, leverage ratios such as current liability to net worth and total liability to net worth provide valuable benchmarks to spot potential problem accounts while profitability and collection period figures provide cash flow comparisons for an overall evaluation of accounts.

In addition to evaluating individual accounts against industry standards, internal credit polices also benefit from Industry Norm data. Are receivables growing at an excessive rate as compared to the industry? If so, how does your firm's collections stack up to the industry?

Finance

Here exists a unique opportunity for financial executives to rank their firm, or their firm's subsidiaries and divisions, against its peers. Determine the efficiency of management via ratio quartile breakdowns which provides you the opportunity to pinpoint your firm's profitability position versus the industry. For example, are returns on sales and gross profit margins comparatively low thereby indicating that pricing per unit may be too low or that the cost of goods is unnecessarily high?

In much the same way, matching the firm's growth and efficiency trends to that of the industry reveals conditions which prove to be vital in projecting budgets. If asset expansion exceeds the industry standard while asset utilization (as indicated by the asset to sales ratio) is sub par, should growth be slowed?

Investment executives have also utilized this diverse information when identifying optimal investment opportunities. By uncovering which industries exhibit the strongest sales growth while maintaining adequate returns, risk is minimized.

Corporate Planning

Corporate plans, competitive strategies and merger/acquisition decisions dictate a comprehensive analysis of the industry in question. Industry Norm data provides invaluable information in scrutinizing the performance of today's highly competitive, and sometimes unstable, markets. Does the liquidity of an industry provide a sufficient cushion to endure the recent record-high interest levels or is it too volatile to risk an entry? Are the profitability and equity statuses of an acquisition candidate among the best in the industry thereby qualifying it as an ideal acquisition target?

Industry Norm data provides these all-important benchmarks for setting strategic goals and measuring overall corporate performance.

Marketing and Sales

Attaining an in-depth knowledge of a potential or existing customer base is a key factor when developing successful marketing strategies and sales projections. Industry Norm data provides a competitive edge when determining market potential and market candidates. Identify those industries that meet or exceed your qualifications and take it one step further by focusing in on the specific region or size category that exhibits the greatest potential. For example, isolate the industries which have experienced the strongest growth trends in sales and inventory turnover and then fine tune marketing and sales strategies by identifying the particular *segment* which is the most attractive (such as firms with assets of $1 million or more).

You can also utilize this information from a different perspective by examining the industries of existing accounts. If an account's industry shows signs of faltering profitability and stagnating sales, should precautionary measures be taken? Will the next sale be profitable for your company or will it be written-off? Industry Norm data assist in answering these and many other important questions.

FINAL NOTE

The SIC categories in this directory reflect those appearing in the 1987 edition of the Standard Industrial Classification Manual

The D&B Financial Information Base includes over one million U.S. companies and is the most extensive and complete source of financial information of its kind. This compilation of data should be regarded only as a source of financial information, to be used in conjunction with other sources of data, when performing financial analysis. When utilizing these figures, remember:

- Because of the size of this database, and in order to facilitate the many calculations and rankings, many of the very large group samples have been randomly reduced.

- On the other hand, some of the samples from our file are very small, and, therefore, may not present a true picture of an entire line of business. In these small groups there is a chance that a few extreme variations might have an undue influence on the overall figures in a particular category.

- The companies composing our database are organized by principal line of business without consideration for multiple-operation functions.

- Within the primary SIC numbers, no allowance has been made for differing accounting methods, terms of sale, or fiscal-year closing date, all of which might have had an effect on the composite data.

- Therefore, D&B advises users that the Industry Norms and Key Business Ratios be used as yardsticks and not as absolutes.

	SIC 01 AGRICULTURL CROPS (NO BREAKDOWN) 2013 (66 Establishments) $	%	SIC 0181 ORNMNTL NURS PRDCTS (NO BREAKDOWN) 2013 (18 Establishments) $	%	SIC 02 AGRICULTURAL PRD LVSK (NO BREAKDOWN) 2013 (17 Establishments) $	%	SIC 07 AGRICULTURAL SERVICES (NO BREAKDOWN) 2013 (142 Establishments) $	%
Cash	592,374	8.7	598,285	17.4	2,353,441	12.5	367,992	15.6
Accounts Receivable	980,481	14.4	195,990	5.7	1,732,132	9.2	582,653	24.7
Notes Receivable	20,427	0.3	24,069	0.7	56,483	0.3	2,359	0.1
Inventory	1,075,805	15.8	1,010,895	29.4	3,370,127	17.9	183,996	7.8
Other Current	640,035	9.4	381,664	11.1	1,242,617	6.6	217,021	9.2
Total Current	**3,309,122**	**48.6**	**2,210,903**	**64.3**	**8,754,800**	**46.5**	**1,354,021**	**57.4**
Fixed Assets	2,859,735	42.0	921,496	26.8	7,210,943	38.3	799,674	33.9
Other Non-current	640,036	9.4	306,019	8.9	2,861,784	15.2	205,226	8.7
Total Assets	**6,808,893**	**100.0**	**3,438,418**	**100.0**	**18,827,527**	**100.0**	**2,358,921**	**100.0**
Accounts Payable	1,130,276	16.6	306,019	8.9	790,756	4.2	273,635	11.6
Bank Loans	129,369	1.9	99,714	2.9	0	0.0	37,743	1.6
Notes Payable	258,738	3.8	89,399	2.6	658,963	3.5	58,973	2.5
Other Current	2,873,353	42.2	756,452	22.0	1,543,858	8.2	448,195	19.0
Total Current	**4,391,736**	**64.5**	**1,251,584**	**36.4**	**2,993,577**	**15.9**	**818,546**	**34.7**
Other Long Term	1,579,663	23.2	419,487	12.2	2,052,200	10.9	412,811	17.5
Deferred Credits	0	0.0	0	0.0	0	0.0	0	0.0
Net Worth	837,494	12.3	1,767,347	51.4	13,781,750	73.2	1,127,564	47.8
Total Liab & Net Worth	**6,808,893**	**100.0**	**3,438,418**	**100.0**	**18,827,527**	**100.0**	**2,358,921**	**100.0**
Net Sales	10,964,401	100.0	6,064,229	100.0	42,025,730	100.0	5,725,536	100.0
Gross Profit	3,738,861	34.1	2,813,802	46.4	14,835,083	35.3	2,364,646	41.3
Net Profit After Tax	526,291	4.8	345,661	5.7	2,563,570	6.1	320,630	5.6
Working Capital	(1,082,614)	—	959,319	—	5,761,223	—	535,475	—

RATIOS	UQ	MED	LQ	UQ	MED	LQ	UQ	MED	LQ	UQ	MED	LQ
SOLVENCY												
Quick Ratio (times)	1.8	0.8	0.2	2.6	1.2	0.2	6.4	1.2	0.7	2.5	1.2	0.6
Current Ratio (times)	3.8	1.5	0.9	3.9	2.1	1.3	6.9	3.2	1.7	3.7	1.8	1.2
Curr Liab To Nw (%)	10.1	47.3	144.4	21.0	47.3	74.1	3.9	18.9	47.7	15.5	54.7	114.8
Curr Liab To Inv (%)	66.5	195.0	604.2	35.4	68.8	384.0	72.9	85.2	135.0	182.4	466.6	999.9
Total Liab To Nw (%)	21.0	84.3	209.6	38.0	70.8	121.1	4.4	22.3	100.2	37.1	85.0	176.3
Fixed Assets To Nw (%)	35.3	58.3	96.4	36.7	50.5	60.0	29.4	56.7	72.7	32.0	59.7	105.3
EFFICIENCY												
Coll Period (days)	13.5	27.9	34.2	11.0	21.2	30.3	9.1	17.5	23.0	15.7	31.8	59.1
Sales To Inv (times)	32.8	14.1	4.4	17.7	7.1	2.9	17.3	9.1	6.8	163.7	44.2	16.1
Assets To Sales (%)	30.8	62.1	116.5	33.9	56.7	81.0	38.2	44.8	97.6	29.1	41.2	56.4
Sales To Nwc (times)	21.5	6.1	3.4	6.3	5.1	3.6	9.8	4.9	4.3	14.8	7.9	5.0
Acct Pay To Sales (%)	2.1	4.7	8.0	2.2	5.6	7.7	0.6	2.3	3.0	1.5	3.9	7.7
PROFITABILITY												
Return On Sales (%)	7.5	2.2	0.2	8.3	3.0	0.6	9.4	4.9	0.8	8.4	3.1	0.3
Return On Assets (%)	15.5	5.4	0.2	20.7	2.9	0.6	10.5	6.8	2.0	18.3	6.2	0.9
Return On Nw (%)	34.8	13.9	4.0	29.8	12.9	0.8	13.6	11.0	3.8	34.4	14.7	2.5

Balance Sheet

	SIC 0723 CROP PREP SVCS,MRKT (NO BREAKDOWN) 2013 (32 Establishments) $	%	SIC 0781 LNDSCPE CNSLNG,PLNG (NO BREAKDOWN) 2013 (27 Establishments) $	%	SIC 0782 LAWN GARDEN SVCS (NO BREAKDOWN) 2013 (45 Establishments) $	%	SIC 08 FORESTRY (NO BREAKDOWN) 2013 (11 Establishments) $	%
Cash	1,359,291	12.7	133,909	15.8	325,862	18.7	1,288,890	25.2
Accounts Receivable	2,054,991	19.2	275,445	32.5	569,823	32.7	414,286	8.1
Notes Receivable	42,812	0.4	848	0.1	0	0.0	0	0.0
Inventory	1,477,024	13.8	38,986	4.6	87,129	5.0	143,210	2.8
Other Current	899,058	8.4	81,361	9.6	115,010	6.6	311,993	6.1
Total Current	**5,833,176**	**54.5**	**530,549**	**62.6**	**1,097,824**	**63.0**	**2,158,379**	**42.2**
Fixed Assets	4,184,903	39.1	235,611	27.8	543,684	31.2	2,250,442	44.0
Other Non-current	684,997	6.4	81,363	9.6	101,070	5.8	705,821	13.8
Total Assets	**10,703,076**	**100.0**	**847,523**	**100.0**	**1,742,578**	**100.0**	**5,114,642**	**100.0**
Accounts Payable	1,348,588	12.6	96,618	11.4	236,991	13.6	225,044	4.4
Bank Loans	0	0.0	22,036	2.6	59,248	3.4	112,522	2.2
Notes Payable	139,140	1.3	44,071	5.2	38,337	2.2	15,344	0.3
Other Current	2,429,598	22.7	194,930	23.0	270,099	15.5	951,324	18.6
Total Current	**3,917,326**	**36.6**	**357,655**	**42.2**	**604,675**	**34.7**	**1,304,234**	**25.5**
Other Long Term	1,626,867	15.2	153,401	18.1	254,416	14.6	3,247,797	63.5
Deferred Credits	0	0.0	848	0.1	0	0.0	0	0.0
Net Worth	5,158,883	48.2	335,619	39.6	883,487	50.7	562,611	11.0
Total Liab & Net Worth	**10,703,076**	**100.0**	**847,523**	**100.0**	**1,742,578**	**100.0**	**5,114,642**	**100.0**
Net Sales	24,948,895	100.0	2,648,509	100.0	4,302,662	100.0	4,287,210	100.0
Gross Profit	5,738,246	23.0	1,393,116	52.6	1,746,881	40.6	1,933,532	45.1
Net Profit After Tax	1,372,189	5.5	198,638	7.5	163,501	3.8	437,295	10.2
Working Capital	1,915,850	---	172,894	---	493,149	---	854,145	---

RATIOS

	SIC 0723 UQ	MED	LQ	SIC 0781 UQ	MED	LQ	SIC 0782 UQ	MED	LQ	SIC 08 UQ	MED	LQ
SOLVENCY												
Quick Ratio (times)	1.4	0.7	0.5	2.0	1.2	0.9	3.2	1.6	0.9	2.4	1.2	0.6
Current Ratio (times)	2.5	1.4	1.1	2.2	1.5	1.3	4.0	2.2	1.3	2.6	2.4	1.7
Curr Liab To Nw (%)	32.6	79.1	155.2	34.3	97.2	171.5	11.3	42.5	97.9	8.2	28.1	75.3
Curr Liab To Inv (%)	164.0	271.4	683.3	318.1	999.9	999.9	258.1	940.3	999.9	175.4	203.2	208.1
Total Liab To Nw (%)	65.0	113.2	247.8	71.5	123.8	213.6	33.0	64.3	133.7	48.4	64.9	233.4
Fixed Assets To Nw (%)	58.3	85.4	115.5	19.3	44.1	96.6	19.3	50.0	88.5	29.4	64.2	143.5
EFFICIENCY												
Coll Period (days)	15.7	29.2	38.3	17.9	53.3	80.1	21.5	34.4	82.9	7.7	13.1	37.2
Sales To Inv (times)	52.7	22.2	10.7	320.4	116.5	17.0	298.3	76.6	28.6	16.1	15.7	15.7
Assets To Sales (%)	30.7	42.9	61.1	28.0	32.0	44.0	25.7	40.5	51.1	53.5	119.3	182.0
Sales To Nwc (times)	17.3	8.7	6.6	25.1	8.2	4.8	10.4	7.7	5.1	9.3	7.1	5.7
Acct Pay To Sales (%)	1.1	2.5	7.0	3.5	4.7	8.1	2.4	4.0	7.4	2.3	4.0	4.7
PROFITABILITY												
Return On Sales (%)	6.9	2.0	0.5	9.0	5.3	0.9	6.4	2.6	0.3	17.2	12.4	3.4
Return On Assets (%)	10.8	4.3	1.7	26.5	11.8	1.8	18.3	5.6	0.9	24.1	6.4	2.0
Return On Nw (%)	26.0	10.0	4.2	58.5	27.3	3.9	34.0	14.4	1.8	100.0	16.4	5.5

SIC 10 — METAL MINING (NO BREAKDOWN) — 2013 (67 Establishments)

	$	%
Cash	615,339	24.7
Accounts Receivable	22,421	0.9
Notes Receivable	4,983	0.2
Inventory	82,211	3.3
Other Current	219,231	8.8
Total Current	**944,185**	**37.9**
Fixed Assets	829,587	33.3
Other Non-current	717,481	28.8
Total Assets	**2,491,253**	**100.0**
Accounts Payable	6,263,010	251.4
Bank Loans	0	0.0
Notes Payable	5,104,577	204.9
Other Current	4,967,559	199.4
Total Current	**16,335,146**	**655.7**
Other Long Term	383,653	15.4
Deferred Credits	19,930	0.8
Net Worth	(14,247,476)	(571.9)
Total Liab & Net Worth	**2,491,253**	**100.0**
Net Sales	721,684	100.0
Gross Profit	108,253	15.0
Net Profit After Tax	(187,638)	(26.0)
Working Capital	(15,390,961)	---

RATIOS	UQ	MED	LQ
SOLVENCY			
Quick Ratio (times)	1.9	0.2	0.0
Current Ratio (times)	3.0	0.5	0.1
Curr Liab To Nw (%)	9.1	16.3	80.9
Curr Liab To Inv (%)	96.1	195.2	999.9
Total Liab To Nw (%)	20.4	73.7	159.6
Fixed Assets To Nw (%)	19.4	87.0	129.5
EFFICIENCY			
Coll Period (days)	6.6	15.0	39.8
Sales To Inv (times)	11.9	5.3	3.2
Assets To Sales (%)	135.8	345.2	710.3
Sales To Nwc (times)	3.8	1.9	1.2
Acct Pay To Sales (%)	8.4	15.2	44.1
PROFITABILITY			
Return On Sales (%)	0.1	(58.8)	(999.9)
Return On Assets (%)	(16.2)	)(84.7	(438.0)
Return On Nw (%)	(13.4)	)(38.1	(186.6)

SIC 1041 — GOLD ORES (NO BREAKDOWN) — 2013 (28 Establishments)

	$	%
Cash	480,034	31.0
Accounts Receivable	15,485	1.0
Notes Receivable	0	0.0
Inventory	41,809	2.7
Other Current	147,108	9.5
Total Current	**684,436**	**44.2**
Fixed Assets	480,034	31.0
Other Non-current	384,027	24.8
Total Assets	**1,548,497**	**100.0**
Accounts Payable	7,342,973	474.2
Bank Loans	0	0.0
Notes Payable	5,365,542	346.5
Other Current	(843,931)	(54.5)
Total Current	**11,864,584**	**766.2**
Other Long Term	126,977	8.2
Deferred Credits	0	0.0
Net Worth	(10,443,064)	(674.4)
Total Liab & Net Worth	**1,548,497**	**100.0**
Net Sales	343,805	100.0
Gross Profit	69,105	20.1
Net Profit After Tax	(58,103)	(16.9)
Working Capital	(11,180,148)	---

RATIOS	UQ	MED	LQ
Quick Ratio	1.9	0.1	0.0
Current Ratio	3.7	0.5	0.0
Curr Liab To Nw	8.4	19.4	112.8
Curr Liab To Inv	152.9	204.8	999.9
Total Liab To Nw	18.1	67.6	133.3
Fixed Assets To Nw	25.9	82.7	129.5
Coll Period	8.3	11.0	15.9
Sales To Inv	16.8	5.3	3.5
Assets To Sales	73.1	450.4	583.4
Sales To Nwc	4.5	2.9	1.5
Acct Pay To Sales	6.1	12.8	25.4
Return On Sales	0.5	(19.6)	(999.9)
Return On Assets	(16.5)	)(83.3	(502.8)
Return On Nw	(1.9)	)(40.1	(308.0)

SIC 1081 — METAL MINING SVCS (NO BREAKDOWN) — 2013 (26 Establishments)

	$	%
Cash	438,551	26.3
Accounts Receivable	5,002	0.3
Notes Receivable	8,337	0.5
Inventory	13,340	0.8
Other Current	175,088	10.5
Total Current	**640,318**	**38.4**
Fixed Assets	446,889	26.8
Other Non-current	580,288	34.8
Total Assets	**1,667,495**	**100.0**
Accounts Payable	2,141,064	128.4
Bank Loans	0	0.0
Notes Payable	2,524,587	151.4
Other Current	9,326,300	559.3
Total Current	**13,991,951**	**839.1**
Other Long Term	256,794	15.4
Deferred Credits	18,342	1.1
Net Worth	(12,599,592)	(755.6)
Total Liab & Net Worth	**1,667,495**	**100.0**
Net Sales	205,483	100.0
Gross Profit	11,713	5.7
Net Profit After Tax	0	0.0
Working Capital	(13,351,633)	---

RATIOS	UQ	MED	LQ
Quick Ratio	0.4	0.1	0.0
Current Ratio	0.7	0.3	0.0
Curr Liab To Nw	6.7	30.0	274.3
Curr Liab To Inv	579.9	999.9	999.9
Total Liab To Nw	16.3	46.8	351.3
Fixed Assets To Nw	1.8	6.2	111.0
Coll Period	1.8	8.8	294.2
Sales To Inv	11.9	9.3	3.7
Assets To Sales	135.8	811.5	999.9
Sales To Nwc	0.8	0.8	0.8
Acct Pay To Sales	44.1	83.7	110.6
Return On Sales	(242.2)	)(999.9	(999.9)
Return On Assets	(83.4)	)(224.3	(457.9)
Return On Nw	(38.1)	)(131.6	(459.5)

SIC 12 — BITUMINOUS & LIGNITE (NO BREAKDOWN) — 2013 (19 Establishments)

	$	%
Cash	34,002,666	8.1
Accounts Receivable	22,248,658	5.3
Notes Receivable	419,786	0.1
Inventory	18,890,370	4.5
Other Current	16,371,654	3.9
Total Current	**91,933,134**	**21.9**
Fixed Assets	252,291,386	60.1
Other Non-current	75,561,480	18.0
Total Assets	**419,786,000**	**100.0**
Accounts Payable	281,676,406	67.1
Bank Loans	0	0.0
Notes Payable	0	0.0
Other Current	311,900,998	74.3
Total Current	**593,577,404**	**141.4**
Other Long Term	210,312,786	50.1
Deferred Credits	1,259,358	0.3
Net Worth	(385,363,548)	(91.8)
Total Liab & Net Worth	**419,786,000**	**100.0**
Net Sales	248,100,473	100.0
Gross Profit	62,521,319	25.2
Net Profit After Tax	7,443,014	3.0
Working Capital	(501,644,270)	---

RATIOS	UQ	MED	LQ
Quick Ratio	1.1	0.8	0.6
Current Ratio	1.8	1.5	1.0
Curr Liab To Nw	23.7	30.7	87.1
Curr Liab To Inv	154.3	356.6	444.2
Total Liab To Nw	122.3	166.3	450.4
Fixed Assets To Nw	151.1	188.6	250.4
Coll Period	23.0	28.7	34.0
Sales To Inv	20.6	16.6	8.9
Assets To Sales	124.7	169.2	216.8
Sales To Nwc	26.3	6.6	4.9
Acct Pay To Sales	4.7	6.6	8.3
Return On Sales	8.0	3.7	(6.8)
Return On Assets	6.0	1.7	(7.2)
Return On Nw	59.2	12.6	(3.3)

	SIC 13 OIL,GAS EXTRACTION (NO BREAKDOWN) 2013 (219 Establishments)		SIC 1311 CRUDE PTRLM,NAT GAS (NO BREAKDOWN) 2013 (107 Establishments)		SIC 1382 OIL GAS EXPLOR SVCS (NO BREAKDOWN) 2013 (49 Establishments)		SIC 1389 OIL GAS FLD SVC,NEC (NO BREAKDOWN) 2013 (42 Establishments)	
	$	%	$	%	$	%	$	%
Cash	25,704,230	11.9	102,286,158	11.4	9,953,240	14.2	3,576,146	14.1
Accounts Receivable	20,088,180	9.3	54,732,067	6.1	4,345,781	6.2	4,971,096	19.6
Notes Receivable	216,002	0.1	0	0.0	140,186	0.2	0	0.0
Inventory	3,024,027	1.4	6,280,729	0.7	420,559	0.6	887,696	3.5
Other Current	11,880,106	5.5	35,889,880	4.0	5,327,087	7.6	2,130,470	8.4
Total Current	**60,912,545**	**28.2**	**199,188,834**	**22.2**	**20,186,853**	**28.8**	**11,565,408**	**45.6**
Fixed Assets	127,657,142	59.1	576,032,574	64.2	42,616,689	60.8	10,424,084	41.1
Other Non-current	27,432,246	12.7	122,025,592	13.6	7,289,696	10.4	3,373,244	13.3
Total Assets	**216,001,933**	**100.0**	**897,247,000**	**100.0**	**70,093,238**	**100.0**	**25,362,736**	**100.0**
Accounts Payable	125,281,121	58.0	274,557,582	30.6	128,410,812	183.2	1,800,754	7.1
Bank Loans	0	0.0	0	0.0	0	0.0	25,363	0.1
Notes Payable	20,736,186	9.6	23,328,422	2.6	19,626,107	28.0	126,814	0.5
Other Current	45,792,410	21.2	188,421,870	21.0	22,289,649	31.8	3,601,508	14.2
Total Current	**191,809,717**	**88.8**	**486,307,874**	**54.2**	**170,326,568**	**243.0**	**5,554,439**	**21.9**
Other Long Term	1,944,017	0.9	380,432,728	42.4	(89,298,785)	(127.4)	6,036,331	23.8
Deferred Credits	432,004	0.2	2,691,741	0.3	210,280	0.3	25,363	0.1
Net Worth	21,816,195	10.1	27,814,657	3.1	(11,144,825)	(15.9)	13,746,603	54.2
Total Liab & Net Worth	**216,001,933**	**100.0**	**897,247,000**	**100.0**	**70,093,238**	**100.0**	**25,362,736**	**100.0**
Net Sales	80,060,020	100.0	246,564,166	100.0	17,272,853	100.0	26,952,961	100.0
Gross Profit	35,946,949	44.9	130,432,444	52.9	10,605,532	61.4	9,810,878	36.4
Net Profit After Tax	1,361,020	1.7	4,684,719	1.9	380,003	2.2	700,777	2.6
Working Capital	(130,897,172)	—	(287,119,040)	—	(150,139,715)	—	6,010,969	—

RATIOS	UQ	MED	LQ	UQ	MED	LQ	UQ	MED	LQ	UQ	MED	LQ
SOLVENCY												
Quick Ratio (times)	1.7	0.8	0.4	1.2	0.7	0.4	1.0	0.6	0.1	3.0	1.8	1.0
Current Ratio (times)	2.2	1.2	0.6	1.5	1.0	0.7	1.5	0.8	0.2	3.6	2.3	1.6
Curr Liab To Nw (%)	13.7	24.1	45.6	12.8	22.1	43.2	20.4	28.8	67.5	13.9	24.7	56.0
Curr Liab To Inv (%)	408.3	932.6	999.9	695.1	999.9	999.9	999.9	999.9	999.9	152.1	290.0	718.6
Total Liab To Nw (%)	43.7	98.3	154.5	60.1	109.3	181.0	35.7	81.5	141.0	26.3	67.8	121.3
Fixed Assets To Nw (%)	72.7	138.8	204.7	107.3	161.6	225.1	35.5	129.8	182.6	51.1	77.4	108.4
EFFICIENCY												
Coll Period (days)	38.7	58.4	83.2	36.2	50.7	77.6	44.2	63.9	98.2	44.2	65.5	82.5
Sales To Inv (times)	93.6	33.0	14.7	137.6	35.0	18.6	187.8	48.8	25.7	44.1	25.5	11.7
Assets To Sales (%)	136.1	269.8	495.6	232.5	363.9	500.7	211.0	405.8	672.3	60.1	94.1	174.1
Sales To Nwc (times)	10.8	5.9	3.4	14.2	8.0	3.4	12.0	5.2	0.9	7.7	5.1	3.5
Acct Pay To Sales (%)	5.1	12.4	26.6	6.9	14.9	27.6	9.5	16.9	41.2	3.3	5.9	11.2
PROFITABILITY												
Return On Sales (%)	13.7	3.1	(25.9)	15.7	5.9	(27.8)	15.8	(0.5)	(154.4)	9.0	2.7	(2.6)
Return On Assets (%)	5.9	1.0	(12.5)	5.1	1.6	(6.6)	4.4	(11.5)	(68.9)	10.9	3.0	(2.4)
Return On Nw (%)	14.2	4.6	(8.5)	13.8	4.9	(7.0)	14.2	(0.1)	(29.9)	18.2	8.3	(3.5)

	SIC 14 NONMETALLIC MINERALS (NO BREAKDOWN) 2013 (43 Establishments) $	%	SIC 1422 CRUSHED BRKN LMSTNE (NO BREAKDOWN) 2013 (14 Establishments) $	%	SIC 1442 CNSTR SAND,GRAVEL (NO BREAKDOWN) 2013 (10 Establishments) $	%	SIC 15 GEN'L BLDG CONTRS (NO BREAKDOWN) 2013 (1190 Establishments) $	%
Cash	1,384,596	15.5	1,664,753	18.2	910,621	10.2	1,003,851	26.7
Accounts Receivable	768,228	8.6	695,171	7.6	857,055	9.6	977,533	26.0
Notes Receivable	0	0.0	0	0.0	0	0.0	15,039	0.4
Inventory	1,143,408	12.8	1,454,372	15.9	562,442	6.3	86,474	2.3
Other Current	795,026	8.9	594,555	6.5	607,081	6.8	1,045,208	27.8
Total Current	**4,091,258**	**45.8**	**4,408,851**	**48.2**	**2,937,199**	**32.9**	**3,128,105**	**83.2**
Fixed Assets	3,010,380	33.7	3,631,356	39.7	2,785,429	31.2	424,851	11.3
Other Non-current	1,831,240	20.5	1,106,786	12.1	3,205,028	35.9	206,785	5.5
Total Assets	**8,932,878**	**100.0**	**9,146,993**	**100.0**	**8,927,656**	**100.0**	**3,759,741**	**100.0**
Accounts Payable	1,563,254	17.5	1,326,314	14.5	330,323	3.7	936,176	24.9
Bank Loans	0	0.0	0	0.0	0	0.0	11,279	0.3
Notes Payable	875,422	9.8	9,147	0.1	17,855	0.2	45,117	1.2
Other Current	5,198,935	58.2	6,448,630	70.5	1,053,464	11.8	1,000,091	26.6
Total Current	**7,637,611**	**85.5**	**7,784,091**	**85.1**	**1,401,642**	**15.7**	**1,992,663**	**53.0**
Other Long Term	3,278,366	36.7	1,399,490	15.3	1,383,787	15.5	195,506	5.2
Deferred Credits	8,933	0.1	18,294	0.2	0	0.0	0	0.0
Net Worth	(1,992,032)	(22.3)	(54,882)	(0.6)	6,142,227	68.8	1,571,572	41.8
Total Liab & Net Worth	**8,932,878**	**100.0**	**9,146,993**	**100.0**	**8,927,656**	**100.0**	**3,759,741**	**100.0**
Net Sales	6,371,525	100.0	6,913,827	100.0	5,151,561	100.0	11,156,501	100.0
Gross Profit	1,911,458	30.0	2,253,908	32.6	1,468,195	28.5	1,706,945	15.3
Net Profit After Tax	471,493	7.4	414,830	6.0	412,125	8.0	301,226	2.7
Working Capital	(3,546,353)	---	(3,375,240)	---	1,535,557	---	1,135,442	---

RATIOS	UQ	MED	LQ	UQ	MED	LQ	UQ	MED	LQ	UQ	MED	LQ
SOLVENCY												
Quick Ratio (times)	4.1	1.5	0.5	7.5	2.1	0.7	3.8	1.4	0.6	1.8	1.1	0.6
Current Ratio (times)	6.1	3.8	1.2	22.9	5.1	2.0	5.8	2.9	1.0	2.7	1.6	1.3
Curr Liab To Nw (%)	3.5	17.3	47.2	2.6	7.3	9.2	2.8	18.1	51.1	41.9	110.8	245.2
Curr Liab To Inv (%)	67.1	94.4	174.7	53.7	95.8	174.7	82.1	130.4	270.3	378.9	999.9	999.9
Total Liab To Nw (%)	7.9	37.1	109.7	3.5	10.7	56.8	5.0	40.3	105.6	49.4	124.9	265.7
Fixed Assets To Nw (%)	31.5	58.7	91.4	29.4	32.9	69.9	14.9	45.4	77.1	5.8	15.0	33.2
EFFICIENCY												
Coll Period (days)	28.1	44.5	68.3	20.1	29.2	41.4	59.5	74.5	83.2	28.5	46.4	70.7
Sales To Inv (times)	10.2	6.6	3.7	10.2	6.7	3.4	10.0	8.7	5.5	571.6	164.2	24.1
Assets To Sales (%)	102.3	140.2	216.0	107.2	132.3	219.9	138.2	173.3	241.1	24.9	33.7	47.3
Sales To Nwc (times)	4.2	2.7	1.8	4.8	2.1	1.6	4.1	3.2	2.4	17.3	9.4	4.8
Acct Pay To Sales (%)	4.3	5.9	8.8	2.8	4.1	5.5	5.0	6.8	10.4	3.8	7.8	13.3
PROFITABILITY												
Return On Sales (%)	11.4	5.4	0.0	9.4	6.3	0.8	10.0	4.8	(0.6)	4.4	1.6	0.3
Return On Assets (%)	6.4	2.0	(21.0)	6.4	2.0	0.3	7.0	3.0	0.6	12.9	4.9	1.0
Return On Nw (%)	17.2	2.8	(4.2)	10.8	3.3	0.7	17.4	3.9	0.7	32.6	11.3	2.2

Balance Sheet / Income Data

	SIC 1521 SNGL-FAM HSNG CNSTR (NO BREAKDOWN) 2013 (120 Establishments) $	%	SIC 1522 RSDNTL CNSTR, NEC (NO BREAKDOWN) 2013 (39 Establishments) $	%	SIC 1531 OPERATIVE BUILDERS (NO BREAKDOWN) 2013 (14 Establishments) $	%	SIC 1541 INDL BLDNGS, WRHSES (NO BREAKDOWN) 2013 (211 Establishments) $	%
Cash	379,681	24.4	406,891	18.0	3,744,169	17.2	1,126,326	26.4
Accounts Receivable	261,420	16.8	443,059	19.6	1,915,621	8.8	1,186,056	27.8
Notes Receivable	1,556	0.1	6,782	0.3	1,131,958	5.2	21,332	0.5
Inventory	141,602	9.1	54,252	2.4	4,244,843	19.5	38,397	0.9
Other Current	315,883	20.3	901,941	39.9	5,442,107	25.0	1,198,855	28.1
Total Current	**1,100,142**	**70.7**	**1,812,925**	**80.2**	**16,478,698**	**75.7**	**3,570,966**	**83.7**
Fixed Assets	314,326	20.2	316,471	14.0	3,330,569	15.3	494,901	11.6
Other Non-current	141,603	9.1	131,109	5.8	1,959,159	9.0	200,520	4.7
Total Assets	**1,556,071**	**100.0**	**2,260,505**	**100.0**	**21,768,426**	**100.0**	**4,266,387**	**100.0**
Accounts Payable	180,504	11.6	481,488	21.3	2,655,748	12.2	972,736	22.8
Bank Loans	9,336	0.6	6,782	0.3	761,895	3.5	4,266	0.1
Notes Payable	91,808	5.9	47,471	2.1	348,295	1.6	25,598	0.6
Other Current	505,724	32.5	592,251	26.2	6,661,138	30.6	998,336	23.4
Total Current	**787,372**	**50.6**	**1,127,992**	**49.9**	**10,427,076**	**47.9**	**2,000,936**	**46.9**
Other Long Term	182,060	11.7	194,403	8.6	2,285,685	10.5	166,389	3.9
Deferred Credits	1,556	0.1	0	0.0	65,305	0.3	0	0.0
Net Worth	585,083	37.6	938,110	41.5	8,990,360	41.3	2,099,062	49.2
Total Liab & Net Worth	**1,556,071**	**100.0**	**2,260,505**	**100.0**	**21,768,426**	**100.0**	**4,266,387**	**100.0**
Net Sales	4,160,618	100.0	6,403,697	100.0	18,308,180	100.0	12,154,949	100.0
Gross Profit	998,548	24.0	1,095,032	17.1	4,705,202	25.7	1,920,482	15.8
Net Profit After Tax	187,228	4.5	160,092	2.5	1,684,353	9.2	437,578	3.6
Working Capital	312,770	—	684,933	—	6,051,622	—	1,570,030	—

RATIOS

	SIC 1521 UQ	MED	LQ	SIC 1522 UQ	MED	LQ	SIC 1531 UQ	MED	LQ	SIC 1541 UQ	MED	LQ
SOLVENCY												
Quick Ratio (times)	2.4	1.1	0.4	2.1	0.8	0.4	1.1	0.6	0.2	1.9	1.2	0.7
Current Ratio (times)	3.6	1.9	1.2	4.5	1.7	1.2	2.1	1.6	1.2	2.9	1.7	1.3
Curr Liab To Nw (%)	18.8	53.2	179.5	21.7	110.8	289.7	62.8	122.3	200.9	37.5	101.7	217.0
Curr Liab To Inv (%)	117.6	265.2	694.8	262.3	648.0	999.9	73.6	93.1	115.6	940.9	999.9	999.9
Total Liab To Nw (%)	29.1	76.0	227.2	31.5	118.7	355.1	62.8	124.1	229.0	40.6	121.5	232.9
Fixed Assets To Nw (%)	5.8	19.7	50.6	4.0	10.6	44.1	2.6	8.8	118.0	6.3	15.6	34.8
EFFICIENCY												
Coll Period (days)	14.6	29.6	50.4	30.5	39.4	67.2	0.0	13.1	31.4	33.4	47.1	79.8
Sales To Inv (times)	67.0	15.7	4.6	173.9	80.0	20.2	3.8	1.6	0.9	515.1	249.9	78.4
Assets To Sales (%)	20.9	37.4	74.9	21.1	35.3	63.5	54.7	118.9	145.3	27.4	35.1	47.6
Sales To Nwc (times)	16.8	7.1	3.2	18.3	9.3	4.8	5.7	3.1	2.6	15.7	9.4	4.5
Acct Pay To Sales (%)	1.6	4.3	7.1	3.7	8.5	15.5	3.0	5.9	8.1	3.6	6.8	12.2
PROFITABILITY												
Return On Sales (%)	6.4	2.3	0.2	6.0	2.0	(1.3)	15.6	3.3	1.8	4.8	2.1	0.7
Return On Assets (%)	18.1	5.4	0.1	18.1	6.2	(3.8)	11.6	5.3	2.7	12.9	5.5	1.7
Return On Nw (%)	42.1	11.0	1.4	40.0	10.7	(1.6)	24.8	13.2	8.9	33.0	11.3	3.8

	SIC 1542 NONRESID CONSTR,NEC (NO BREAKDOWN) 2013 (806 Establishments) $	%	SIC 16 HEAVY CONSTR CONTRS (NO BREAKDOWN) 2013 (569 Establishments) $	%	SIC 1611 HIGHWAY,ST CONSTR (NO BREAKDOWN) 2013 (192 Establishments) $	%	SIC 1622 BRDGE,TNNEL,ELV HGY (NO BREAKDOWN) 2013 (41 Establishments) $	%
Cash	1,136,559	27.6	1,085,075	21.2	933,650	20.4	1,839,122	27.0
Accounts Receivable	1,132,441	27.5	1,100,430	21.5	929,074	20.3	960,431	14.1
Notes Receivable	12,354	0.3	10,237	0.2	13,730	0.3	0	0.0
Inventory	57,652	1.4	117,720	2.3	118,995	2.6	217,970	3.2
Other Current	1,173,621	28.5	1,049,247	20.5	874,153	19.1	1,764,195	25.9
Total Current	**3,512,627**	**85.3**	**3,362,709**	**65.7**	**2,869,602**	**62.7**	**4,781,718**	**70.2**
Fixed Assets	399,443	9.7	1,463,828	28.6	1,432,513	31.3	1,730,137	25.4
Other Non-current	205,898	5.0	291,741	5.7	274,603	6.0	299,709	4.4
Total Assets	**4,117,968**	**100.0**	**5,118,278**	**100.0**	**4,576,718**	**100.0**	**6,811,564**	**100.0**
Accounts Payable	1,144,795	27.8	624,430	12.2	631,587	13.8	667,533	9.8
Bank Loans	12,354	0.3	15,355	0.3	18,307	0.4	0	0.0
Notes Payable	28,826	0.7	71,656	1.4	73,227	1.6	20,435	0.3
Other Current	1,087,143	26.4	936,645	18.3	901,614	19.7	1,348,690	19.8
Total Current	**2,273,118**	**55.2**	**1,648,086**	**32.2**	**1,624,735**	**35.5**	**2,036,658**	**29.9**
Other Long Term	177,073	4.3	731,913	14.3	782,619	17.1	633,475	9.3
Deferred Credits	0	0.0	10,237	0.2	0	0.0	0	0.0
Net Worth	1,667,777	40.5	2,728,042	53.3	2,169,364	47.4	4,141,431	60.8
Total Liab & Net Worth	**4,117,968**	**100.0**	**5,118,278**	**100.0**	**4,576,718**	**100.0**	**6,811,564**	**100.0**
Net Sales	12,554,780	100.0	10,752,685	100.0	10,193,136	100.0	13,760,735	100.0
Gross Profit	1,720,005	13.7	2,096,774	19.5	1,702,254	16.7	1,940,264	14.1
Net Profit After Tax	263,650	2.1	376,344	3.5	173,283	1.7	206,411	1.5
Working Capital	1,239,509	—	1,714,623	—	1,244,867	—	2,745,060	—

RATIOS	UQ	MED	LQ	UQ	MED	LQ	UQ	MED	LQ	UQ	MED	LQ
SOLVENCY												
Quick Ratio (times)	1.8	1.1	0.7	2.5	1.4	0.8	2.3	1.4	0.8	2.1	1.2	0.8
Current Ratio (times)	2.5	1.6	1.3	3.8	2.2	1.5	3.3	2.1	1.4	4.0	2.0	1.6
Curr Liab To Nw (%)	48.4	121.8	255.1	20.9	49.8	98.0	23.4	51.9	111.9	21.7	46.5	86.2
Curr Liab To Inv (%)	586.3	999.9	999.9	285.2	865.1	999.9	199.4	791.2	999.9	385.9	999.9	999.9
Total Liab To Nw (%)	56.3	133.9	278.8	31.3	76.4	154.1	33.1	80.1	160.9	30.1	65.3	106.5
Fixed Assets To Nw (%)	5.9	14.9	30.6	20.8	47.0	85.1	26.6	53.5	87.8	22.6	38.3	71.5
EFFICIENCY												
Coll Period (days)	29.6	49.1	70.7	30.7	49.3	70.8	23.4	40.4	68.6	22.3	41.6	56.9
Sales To Inv (times)	999.9	293.6	41.6	223.2	68.8	25.8	193.1	64.7	24.2	116.4	61.4	33.0
Assets To Sales (%)	24.9	32.8	44.4	36.6	47.6	71.3	34.7	44.9	65.9	42.0	49.5	82.4
Sales To Nwc (times)	17.5	9.8	5.4	10.9	6.4	3.8	12.9	6.8	4.5	9.2	5.4	3.0
Acct Pay To Sales (%)	4.3	8.7	14.2	2.6	5.4	8.7	2.4	4.9	9.5	2.8	4.8	7.7
PROFITABILITY												
Return On Sales (%)	4.0	1.5	0.3	6.9	2.8	0.3	5.1	2.5	0.0	7.2	1.5	(0.7)
Return On Assets (%)	12.2	4.6	0.9	14.0	5.4	0.5	11.5	4.9	0.1	14.6	3.5	(1.6)
Return On Nw (%)	31.3	11.2	1.9	25.6	11.1	1.5	23.0	9.8	0.5	21.3	6.5	(3.0)

SIC 1623 WTER,SWER,UTIL LNES (NO BREAKDOWN) 2013 (194 Establishments)
SIC 1629 HEAVY CONSTR,NEC (NO BREAKDOWN) 2013 (142 Establishments)
SIC 17 SPECIAL TRADE CONTRS (NO BREAKDOWN) 2013 (2187 Establishments)
SIC 1711 PLBNG,HTNG,AIR-COND (NO BREAKDOWN) 2013 (554 Establishments)

	SIC 1623 $	%	SIC 1629 $	%	SIC 17 $	%	SIC 1711 $	%
Cash	910,258	20.5	1,502,149	21.5	453,759	20.2	447,096	20.8
Accounts Receivable	1,092,310	24.6	1,467,215	21.0	743,537	33.1	715,783	33.3
Notes Receivable	8,881	0.2	6,987	0.1	4,493	0.2	2,149	0.1
Inventory	79,925	1.8	153,708	2.2	125,795	5.6	154,764	7.2
Other Current	874,736	19.7	1,544,069	22.1	458,252	20.4	421,302	19.6
Total Current	**2,966,110**	**66.8**	**4,674,128**	**66.9**	**1,785,836**	**79.5**	**1,741,094**	**81.0**
Fixed Assets	1,252,160	28.2	1,844,499	26.4	350,428	15.6	292,332	13.6
Other Non-current	222,015	5.0	468,111	6.7	110,070	4.9	116,073	5.4
Total Assets	**4,440,285**	**100.0**	**6,986,738**	**100.0**	**2,246,334**	**100.0**	**2,149,499**	**100.0**
Accounts Payable	546,155	12.3	754,568	10.8	381,877	17.0	556,720	25.9
Bank Loans	8,881	0.2	20,960	0.3	15,724	0.7	12,897	0.6
Notes Payable	62,164	1.4	90,828	1.3	107,824	4.8	262,239	12.2
Other Current	732,647	16.5	1,292,546	18.5	536,874	23.9	414,853	19.3
Total Current	**1,349,847**	**30.4**	**2,158,902**	**30.9**	**1,042,299**	**46.4**	**1,246,709**	**58.0**
Other Long Term	559,475	12.6	999,104	14.3	213,402	9.5	167,661	7.8
Deferred Credits	13,321	0.3	20,960	0.3	2,246	0.1	4,299	0.2
Net Worth	2,517,642	56.7	3,807,772	54.5	988,387	44.0	730,830	34.0
Total Liab & Net Worth	**4,440,285**	**100.0**	**6,986,738**	**100.0**	**2,246,334**	**100.0**	**2,149,499**	**100.0**
Net Sales	9,024,970	100.0	13,182,525	100.0	6,137,525	100.0	6,513,633	100.0
Gross Profit	1,931,344	21.4	2,913,338	22.1	1,638,719	26.7	1,726,113	26.5
Net Profit After Tax	460,273	5.1	593,214	4.5	227,088	3.7	162,841	2.5
Working Capital	1,616,263	—	2,515,226	—	743,537	—	494,385	—

RATIOS

	SIC 1623 UQ	MED	LQ	SIC 1629 UQ	MED	LQ	SIC 17 UQ	MED	LQ	SIC 1711 UQ	MED	LQ
SOLVENCY												
Quick Ratio (times)	2.8	1.4	0.9	2.5	1.5	0.9	2.7	1.5	0.9	2.3	1.4	0.9
Current Ratio (times)	4.2	2.3	1.5	3.9	2.2	1.6	3.9	2.2	1.5	3.4	2.1	1.5
Curr Liab To Nw (%)	18.7	46.7	92.3	20.9	53.1	110.5	26.6	59.8	131.2	33.4	71.1	149.9
Curr Liab To Inv (%)	467.8	999.9	999.9	324.3	869.7	999.9	249.8	769.8	999.9	247.6	753.7	999.9
Total Liab To Nw (%)	31.4	73.4	153.9	29.9	80.4	166.1	32.1	74.0	161.2	39.0	84.5	178.9
Fixed Assets To Nw (%)	21.2	46.2	86.8	15.3	39.2	76.2	9.2	20.8	44.1	9.8	20.3	40.9
EFFICIENCY												
Coll Period (days)	39.4	53.9	73.7	35.4	52.2	68.3	35.4	56.6	77.4	31.0	48.6	71.9
Sales To Inv (times)	243.2	67.8	26.4	247.5	70.7	25.8	201.0	65.1	25.1	162.4	62.0	24.0
Assets To Sales (%)	36.8	49.2	67.5	37.2	53.0	78.0	27.9	36.6	48.0	25.1	33.0	45.1
Sales To Nwc (times)	10.4	6.3	3.4	10.8	6.2	3.7	11.0	6.4	4.1	13.2	7.5	4.6
Acct Pay To Sales (%)	2.7	5.2	8.1	2.7	5.7	8.6	2.4	4.5	7.8	2.9	4.9	8.3
PROFITABILITY												
Return On Sales (%)	9.5	3.6	1.5	6.9	2.7	0.3	6.6	2.6	0.5	5.3	1.9	0.5
Return On Assets (%)	19.8	7.1	2.1	12.0	5.4	0.7	17.3	6.5	1.3	15.1	5.4	1.2
Return On Nw (%)	32.3	14.1	3.3	23.7	10.3	1.6	34.1	13.5	2.9	28.5	10.6	2.8

Balance Sheet

	SIC 1721 PNTNG,PAPER HANGING (83 Est.) $	%	SIC 1731 ELECTRICAL WORK (643 Est.) $	%	SIC 1741 MSNRY,OTHER STNWRK (49 Est.) $	%	SIC 1742 PLSTRNG,DWALL,INSUL (68 Est.) $	%
Cash	268,986	19.9	523,719	21.3	312,994	14.6	436,377	17.9
Accounts Receivable	454,167	33.6	860,571	35.0	791,061	36.9	1,011,713	41.5
Notes Receivable	4,055	0.3	4,918	0.2	10,719	0.5	0	0.0
Inventory	22,979	1.7	115,562	4.7	83,608	3.9	82,887	3.4
Other Current	262,227	19.4	533,553	21.7	555,243	25.9	538,769	22.1
Total Current	**1,012,414**	**74.9**	**2,038,323**	**82.9**	**1,753,625**	**81.8**	**2,069,746**	**84.9**
Fixed Assets	262,227	19.4	312,264	12.7	280,837	13.1	263,289	10.8
Other Non-current	77,046	5.7	108,186	4.4	109,334	5.1	104,828	4.3
Total Assets	**1,351,687**	**100.0**	**2,458,773**	**100.0**	**2,143,796**	**100.0**	**2,437,863**	**100.0**
Accounts Payable	116,245	8.6	383,569	15.6	295,844	13.8	297,419	12.2
Bank Loans	21,627	1.6	9,835	0.4	0	0.0	21,941	0.9
Notes Payable	27,034	2.0	81,140	3.3	47,164	2.2	56,071	2.3
Other Current	324,405	24.0	742,549	30.2	679,583	31.7	580,211	23.8
Total Current	**489,311**	**36.2**	**1,217,093**	**49.5**	**1,022,591**	**47.7**	**955,642**	**39.2**
Other Long Term	127,058	9.4	248,335	10.1	87,895	4.1	143,834	5.9
Deferred Credits	1,352	0.1	2,459	0.1	0	0.0	0	0.0
Net Worth	733,966	54.3	990,886	40.3	1,033,310	48.2	1,338,387	54.9
Total Liab & Net Worth	**1,351,687**	**100.0**	**2,458,773**	**100.0**	**2,143,796**	**100.0**	**2,437,863**	**100.0**
Net Sales	3,387,687	100.0	6,681,448	100.0	5,778,426	100.0	6,299,388	100.0
Gross Profit	999,368	29.5	1,737,176	26.0	1,282,811	22.2	1,448,859	23.0
Net Profit After Tax	172,772	5.1	280,621	4.2	92,455	1.6	176,383	2.8
Working Capital	523,103	---	821,230	---	731,034	---	1,114,104	---

RATIOS

	SIC 1721 UQ	MED	LQ	SIC 1731 UQ	MED	LQ	SIC 1741 UQ	MED	LQ	SIC 1742 UQ	MED	LQ
SOLVENCY												
Quick Ratio (times)	3.2	1.8	1.1	2.9	1.5	0.9	2.8	1.4	0.5	2.4	1.7	1.1
Current Ratio (times)	4.5	2.5	1.7	3.9	2.2	1.5	3.3	2.0	1.3	3.8	2.1	1.6
Curr Liab To Nw (%)	19.9	46.9	88.5	28.5	62.1	134.2	31.5	63.9	151.0	34.1	68.0	137.6
Curr Liab To Inv (%)	482.4	999.9	999.9	347.7	999.9	999.9	359.3	906.5	999.9	315.3	751.4	999.9
Total Liab To Nw (%)	24.2	61.0	112.3	31.5	73.5	159.4	35.7	79.4	160.4	35.2	74.1	144.8
Fixed Assets To Nw (%)	11.9	24.4	47.5	7.5	17.5	35.2	7.1	19.2	40.0	6.3	11.0	28.2
EFFICIENCY												
Coll Period (days)	38.4	61.7	81.2	41.3	60.4	80.5	49.3	59.1	91.1	51.1	57.3	91.6
Sales To Inv (times)	377.8	190.0	48.8	289.9	98.3	37.2	212.9	97.7	34.2	162.7	36.7	24.5
Assets To Sales (%)	29.9	39.9	48.2	28.8	36.8	46.6	27.3	37.1	46.6	29.6	38.7	45.2
Sales To Nwc (times)	10.2	5.9	3.6	10.1	6.1	4.0	10.2	6.4	3.9	8.5	5.7	3.6
Acct Pay To Sales (%)	2.2	3.3	5.0	2.8	4.9	7.8	2.0	4.7	8.8	2.2	4.0	6.0
PROFITABILITY												
Return On Sales (%)	10.5	3.6	0.4	6.6	3.0	0.6	5.3	2.4	0.5	5.0	1.5	0.1
Return On Assets (%)	25.5	8.5	1.4	17.0	7.8	1.5	15.7	6.1	1.3	14.7	3.9	0.2
Return On Nw (%)	43.4	16.3	3.0	34.3	15.0	3.7	35.1	18.8	3.2	25.3	8.5	0.2

SIC 1721 PNTNG,PAPER HANGING (NO BREAKDOWN) 2013 (83 Establishments)
SIC 1731 ELECTRICAL WORK (NO BREAKDOWN) 2013 (643 Establishments)
SIC 1741 MSNRY,OTHER STNWRK (NO BREAKDOWN) 2013 (49 Establishments)
SIC 1742 PLSTRNG,DWALL,INSUL (NO BREAKDOWN) 2013 (68 Establishments)

SIC 1743 TRZ,TILE,MRBL,MSAIC
(NO BREAKDOWN)
2013 (11 Establishments)

	$	%
Cash	427,673	19.5
Accounts Receivable	866,313	39.5
Notes Receivable	24,125	1.1
Inventory	105,273	4.8
Other Current	480,311	21.9
Total Current	**1,903,695**	**86.8**
Fixed Assets	225,899	10.3
Other Non-current	63,603	2.9
Total Assets	**2,193,197**	**100.0**
Accounts Payable	414,514	18.9
Bank Loans	0	0.0
Notes Payable	76,762	3.5
Other Current	434,253	19.8
Total Current	**925,529**	**42.2**
Other Long Term	100,887	4.6
Deferred Credits	0	0.0
Net Worth	1,166,781	53.2
Total Liab & Net Worth	**2,193,197**	**100.0**
Net Sales	6,143,409	100.0
Gross Profit	1,554,282	25.3
Net Profit After Tax	380,891	6.2
Working Capital	978,166	—

RATIOS	UQ	MED	LQ
SOLVENCY			
Quick Ratio (times)	3.1	1.4	1.2
Current Ratio (times)	5.7	2.3	1.6
Curr Liab To Nw (%)	18.7	62.7	112.5
Curr Liab To Inv (%)	95.7	749.0	999.9
Total Liab To Nw (%)	27.1	67.0	112.5
Fixed Assets To Nw (%)	6.8	21.4	25.0
EFFICIENCY			
Coll Period (days)	47.1	59.5	141.6
Sales To Inv (times)	248.1	114.3	23.3
Assets To Sales (%)	32.1	35.7	57.3
Sales To Nwc (times)	5.5	4.7	4.2
Acct Pay To Sales (%)	2.0	5.2	19.9
PROFITABILITY			
Return On Sales (%)	6.2	5.0	3.4
Return On Assets (%)	21.3	16.4	10.6
Return On Nw (%)	40.1	23.9	10.7

SIC 1751 CARPENTRY WORK
(NO BREAKDOWN)
2013 (21 Establishments)

	$	%
Cash	253,668	15.3
Accounts Receivable	530,548	32.0
Notes Receivable	1,658	0.1
Inventory	167,454	10.1
Other Current	311,699	18.8
Total Current	**1,265,027**	**76.3**
Fixed Assets	303,407	18.3
Other Non-current	89,530	5.4
Total Assets	**1,657,964**	**100.0**
Accounts Payable	283,512	17.1
Bank Loans	71,292	4.3
Notes Payable	38,133	2.3
Other Current	310,040	18.7
Total Current	**702,977**	**42.4**
Other Long Term	477,493	28.8
Deferred Credits	0	0.0
Net Worth	477,494	28.8
Total Liab & Net Worth	**1,657,964**	**100.0**
Net Sales	4,433,059	100.0
Gross Profit	1,196,926	27.0
Net Profit After Tax	93,094	2.1
Working Capital	562,050	—

RATIOS	UQ	MED	LQ
SOLVENCY			
Quick Ratio (times)	2.2	1.1	0.7
Current Ratio (times)	3.2	1.8	1.4
Curr Liab To Nw (%)	33.4	102.7	285.3
Curr Liab To Inv (%)	84.5	229.4	685.6
Total Liab To Nw (%)	46.3	159.2	427.4
Fixed Assets To Nw (%)	9.4	26.9	75.3
EFFICIENCY			
Coll Period (days)	34.7	48.6	68.7
Sales To Inv (times)	78.3	27.0	14.4
Assets To Sales (%)	20.8	37.4	50.5
Sales To Nwc (times)	15.3	10.4	4.3
Acct Pay To Sales (%)	3.6	5.6	9.6
PROFITABILITY			
Return On Sales (%)	3.4	2.4	0.4
Return On Assets (%)	14.3	5.8	1.5
Return On Nw (%)	65.5	30.4	7.2

SIC 1752 FLR LAYING WORK,NEC
(NO BREAKDOWN)
2013 (67 Establishments)

	$	%
Cash	280,723	15.1
Accounts Receivable	710,174	38.2
Notes Receivable	1,859	0.1
Inventory	180,332	9.7
Other Current	403,423	21.7
Total Current	**1,576,511**	**84.8**
Fixed Assets	197,064	10.6
Other Non-current	85,518	4.6
Total Assets	**1,859,093**	**100.0**
Accounts Payable	271,428	14.6
Bank Loans	40,900	2.2
Notes Payable	44,618	2.4
Other Current	488,941	26.3
Total Current	**845,887**	**45.5**
Other Long Term	100,391	5.4
Deferred Credits	0	0.0
Net Worth	912,815	49.1
Total Liab & Net Worth	**1,859,093**	**100.0**
Net Sales	5,404,340	100.0
Gross Profit	1,507,811	27.9
Net Profit After Tax	199,961	3.7
Working Capital	730,624	—

RATIOS	UQ	MED	LQ
SOLVENCY			
Quick Ratio (times)	2.3	1.2	0.7
Current Ratio (times)	3.4	1.9	1.4
Curr Liab To Nw (%)	31.2	78.1	176.4
Curr Liab To Inv (%)	171.1	421.2	999.9
Total Liab To Nw (%)	40.4	95.2	205.5
Fixed Assets To Nw (%)	7.1	16.1	32.5
EFFICIENCY			
Coll Period (days)	34.0	62.1	76.7
Sales To Inv (times)	145.1	35.7	15.3
Assets To Sales (%)	26.4	34.4	40.2
Sales To Nwc (times)	10.7	7.2	4.3
Acct Pay To Sales (%)	2.2	4.3	7.4
PROFITABILITY			
Return On Sales (%)	6.7	2.5	0.6
Return On Assets (%)	21.9	8.1	1.5
Return On Nw (%)	36.4	20.9	4.0

SIC 1761 RRNF,SDNG,SHT MTLWK
(NO BREAKDOWN)
2013 (193 Establishments)

	$	%
Cash	472,064	21.0
Accounts Receivable	692,360	30.8
Notes Receivable	0	0.0
Inventory	139,371	6.2
Other Current	532,757	23.7
Total Current	**1,836,552**	**81.7**
Fixed Assets	321,453	14.3
Other Non-current	89,917	4.0
Total Assets	**2,247,922**	**100.0**
Accounts Payable	316,957	14.1
Bank Loans	15,735	0.7
Notes Payable	35,967	1.6
Other Current	420,362	18.7
Total Current	**789,021**	**35.1**
Other Long Term	211,304	9.4
Deferred Credits	0	0.0
Net Worth	1,247,597	55.5
Total Liab & Net Worth	**2,247,922**	**100.0**
Net Sales	6,226,931	100.0
Gross Profit	1,724,860	27.7
Net Profit After Tax	217,943	3.5
Working Capital	1,047,531	—

RATIOS	UQ	MED	LQ
SOLVENCY			
Quick Ratio (times)	3.6	1.5	0.7
Current Ratio (times)	4.9	2.6	1.6
Curr Liab To Nw (%)	21.3	48.9	109.5
Curr Liab To Inv (%)	242.3	634.2	999.9
Total Liab To Nw (%)	25.0	58.2	128.5
Fixed Assets To Nw (%)	8.7	20.3	41.9
EFFICIENCY			
Coll Period (days)	31.1	53.7	76.2
Sales To Inv (times)	112.7	59.9	25.2
Assets To Sales (%)	27.2	36.1	48.0
Sales To Nwc (times)	10.4	5.9	3.7
Acct Pay To Sales (%)	2.3	4.4	7.6
PROFITABILITY			
Return On Sales (%)	6.6	2.3	0.4
Return On Assets (%)	17.4	5.6	0.9
Return On Nw (%)	34.3	11.0	2.3

SIC 1794 EXCAVATION WORK (NO BREAKDOWN) — 2013 (97 Establishments)

	$	%
Cash	510,526	16.1
Accounts Receivable	707,127	22.3
Notes Receivable	6,342	0.2
Inventory	50,736	1.6
Other Current	551,748	17.4
Total Current	**1,826,479**	**57.6**
Fixed Assets	1,182,772	37.3
Other Non-current	161,720	5.1
Total Assets	**3,170,971**	**100.0**
Accounts Payable	358,320	11.3
Bank Loans	31,710	1.0
Notes Payable	50,736	1.6
Other Current	564,432	17.8
Total Current	**1,005,198**	**31.7**
Other Long Term	443,936	14.0
Deferred Credits	3,171	0.1
Net Worth	1,718,666	54.2
Total Liab & Net Worth	**3,170,971**	**100.0**
Net Sales	5,592,541	100.0
Gross Profit	1,420,505	25.4
Net Profit After Tax	173,369	3.1
Working Capital	821,281	—

RATIOS	UQ	MED	LQ
SOLVENCY			
Quick Ratio (times)	2.3	1.3	0.9
Current Ratio (times)	3.6	1.8	1.4
Curr Liab To Nw (%)	13.8	54.9	102.1
Curr Liab To Inv (%)	165.1	979.0	999.9
Total Liab To Nw (%)	29.8	79.4	159.9
Fixed Assets To Nw (%)	35.9	61.9	106.4
EFFICIENCY			
Coll Period (days)	30.7	55.5	73.4
Sales To Inv (times)	156.4	68.1	31.2
Assets To Sales (%)	42.1	56.7	70.4
Sales To Nwc (times)	11.8	7.0	4.0
Acct Pay To Sales (%)	2.4	5.7	10.5
PROFITABILITY			
Return On Sales (%)	7.2	2.8	0.5
Return On Assets (%)	11.8	5.2	0.9
Return On Nw (%)	23.8	9.2	2.5

SIC 1795 WRCKNG,DMLTN WORK (NO BREAKDOWN) — 2013 (18 Establishments)

	$	%
Cash	1,632,603	24.5
Accounts Receivable	1,146,154	17.2
Notes Receivable	0	0.0
Inventory	406,485	6.1
Other Current	1,812,523	27.2
Total Current	**4,997,765**	**75.0**
Fixed Assets	1,499,330	22.5
Other Non-current	166,592	2.5
Total Assets	**6,663,687**	**100.0**
Accounts Payable	546,422	8.2
Bank Loans	73,301	1.1
Notes Payable	13,327	0.2
Other Current	1,499,330	22.5
Total Current	**2,132,380**	**32.0**
Other Long Term	1,032,871	15.5
Deferred Credits	0	0.0
Net Worth	3,498,436	52.5
Total Liab & Net Worth	**6,663,687**	**100.0**
Net Sales	15,679,264	100.0
Gross Profit	4,625,383	29.5
Net Profit After Tax	1,207,303	7.7
Working Capital	2,865,385	—

RATIOS	UQ	MED	LQ
SOLVENCY			
Quick Ratio (times)	3.3	1.2	0.7
Current Ratio (times)	5.7	2.4	1.6
Curr Liab To Nw (%)	22.4	58.4	97.5
Curr Liab To Inv (%)	124.2	241.3	874.5
Total Liab To Nw (%)	26.9	78.4	137.4
Fixed Assets To Nw (%)	18.1	39.0	77.5
EFFICIENCY			
Coll Period (days)	47.1	70.1	78.8
Sales To Inv (times)	279.9	25.0	12.4
Assets To Sales (%)	33.5	42.5	61.4
Sales To Nwc (times)	11.5	6.7	5.8
Acct Pay To Sales (%)	1.6	3.3	7.7
PROFITABILITY			
Return On Sales (%)	12.2	6.1	0.8
Return On Assets (%)	34.0	10.0	1.2
Return On Nw (%)	59.1	15.2	6.5

SIC 1796 INSTL BLDG EQPT.NEC (NO BREAKDOWN) — 2013 (24 Establishments)

	$	%
Cash	773,264	22.8
Accounts Receivable	1,132,764	33.4
Notes Receivable	16,958	0.5
Inventory	250,972	7.4
Other Current	630,819	18.6
Total Current	**2,804,777**	**82.7**
Fixed Assets	403,589	11.9
Other Non-current	183,142	5.4
Total Assets	**3,391,508**	**100.0**
Accounts Payable	318,802	9.4
Bank Loans	30,524	0.9
Notes Payable	61,047	1.8
Other Current	552,815	16.3
Total Current	**963,188**	**28.4**
Other Long Term	328,977	9.7
Deferred Credits	0	0.0
Net Worth	2,099,343	61.9
Total Liab & Net Worth	**3,391,508**	**100.0**
Net Sales	7,638,532	100.0
Gross Profit	2,581,824	33.8
Net Profit After Tax	565,251	7.4
Working Capital	1,841,589	—

RATIOS	UQ	MED	LQ
SOLVENCY			
Quick Ratio (times)	3.9	2.1	1.0
Current Ratio (times)	5.7	3.2	2.0
Curr Liab To Nw (%)	19.6	43.3	102.1
Curr Liab To Inv (%)	129.7	248.3	999.9
Total Liab To Nw (%)	19.6	46.3	149.4
Fixed Assets To Nw (%)	6.6	13.2	47.4
EFFICIENCY			
Coll Period (days)	38.2	48.2	67.2
Sales To Inv (times)	75.5	38.4	7.1
Assets To Sales (%)	37.8	44.4	62.6
Sales To Nwc (times)	6.2	4.2	2.9
Acct Pay To Sales (%)	1.5	3.8	6.7
PROFITABILITY			
Return On Sales (%)	14.7	7.9	0.8
Return On Assets (%)	24.7	13.7	1.3
Return On Nw (%)	34.0	20.6	3.4

SIC 1799 SPCL TRD CNTRS.NEC (NO BREAKDOWN) — 2013 (174 Establishments)

	$	%
Cash	293,143	19.6
Accounts Receivable	493,558	33.0
Notes Receivable	5,983	0.4
Inventory	118,155	7.9
Other Current	231,822	15.5
Total Current	**1,142,661**	**76.4**
Fixed Assets	275,196	18.4
Other Non-current	77,772	5.2
Total Assets	**1,495,629**	**100.0**
Accounts Payable	171,997	11.5
Bank Loans	13,461	0.9
Notes Payable	17,948	1.2
Other Current	321,560	21.5
Total Current	**524,966**	**35.1**
Other Long Term	131,615	8.8
Deferred Credits	0	0.0
Net Worth	839,048	56.1
Total Liab & Net Worth	**1,495,629**	**100.0**
Net Sales	4,097,614	100.0
Gross Profit	1,339,920	32.7
Net Profit After Tax	196,685	4.8
Working Capital	617,695	—

RATIOS	UQ	MED	LQ
SOLVENCY			
Quick Ratio (times)	3.3	1.7	1.0
Current Ratio (times)	4.5	2.6	1.5
Curr Liab To Nw (%)	17.1	44.9	121.4
Curr Liab To Inv (%)	136.4	357.0	999.9
Total Liab To Nw (%)	24.8	58.4	146.9
Fixed Assets To Nw (%)	11.6	25.0	55.1
EFFICIENCY			
Coll Period (days)	33.2	57.5	80.3
Sales To Inv (times)	94.1	35.6	13.9
Assets To Sales (%)	27.8	36.5	48.5
Sales To Nwc (times)	10.7	5.9	4.2
Acct Pay To Sales (%)	1.6	4.2	7.0
PROFITABILITY			
Return On Sales (%)	9.7	3.6	0.6
Return On Assets (%)	25.6	9.4	1.5
Return On Nw (%)	43.4	15.5	4.1

SIC 1771 CONCRETE WORK (NO BREAKDOWN) 2013 (91 Establishments)

	$	%
Cash	488,438	20.7
Accounts Receivable	568,665	24.1
Notes Receivable	9,438	0.4
Inventory	61,350	2.6
Other Current	523,833	22.2
Total Current	**1,651,724**	**70.0**
Fixed Assets	575,744	24.4
Other Non-current	132,138	5.6
Total Assets	**2,359,606**	**100.0**
Accounts Payable	358,660	15.2
Bank Loans	14,158	0.6
Notes Payable	18,877	0.8
Other Current	802,266	34.0
Total Current	**1,193,961**	**50.6**
Other Long Term	311,468	13.2
Deferred Credits	0	0.0
Net Worth	854,177	36.2
Total Liab & Net Worth	**2,359,606**	**100.0**
Net Sales	6,819,671	100.0
Gross Profit	1,459,410	21.4
Net Profit After Tax	184,131	2.7
Working Capital	457,763	—

RATIOS	UQ	MED	LQ
SOLVENCY			
Quick Ratio (times)	2.5	1.3	0.7
Current Ratio (times)	4.3	2.0	1.4
Curr Liab To Nw (%)	27.2	55.0	120.7
Curr Liab To Inv (%)	436.7	999.9	999.9
Total Liab To Nw (%)	38.9	78.6	168.2
Fixed Assets To Nw (%)	13.8	36.1	79.0
EFFICIENCY			
Coll Period (days)	27.8	50.8	76.3
Sales To Inv (times)	328.3	153.0	34.5
Assets To Sales (%)	30.4	34.6	44.4
Sales To Nwc (times)	13.5	7.8	4.6

SIC 1781 WATER WELL DRILLING (NO BREAKDOWN) 2013 (14 Establishments)

	$	%
Cash	378,703	13.1
Accounts Receivable	491,446	17.0
Notes Receivable	20,236	0.7
Inventory	242,832	8.4
Other Current	370,030	12.8
Total Current	**1,503,247**	**52.0**
Fixed Assets	1,167,907	40.4
Other Non-current	219,706	7.6
Total Assets	**2,890,860**	**100.0**
Accounts Payable	156,106	5.4
Bank Loans	0	0.0
Notes Payable	43,363	1.5
Other Current	381,594	13.2
Total Current	**581,063**	**20.1**
Other Long Term	263,068	9.1
Deferred Credits	2,891	0.1
Net Worth	2,043,838	70.7
Total Liab & Net Worth	**2,890,860**	**100.0**
Net Sales	4,975,663	100.0
Gross Profit	1,587,236	31.9
Net Profit After Tax	442,834	8.9
Working Capital	922,184	—

RATIOS	UQ	MED	LQ
SOLVENCY			
Quick Ratio (times)	5.2	1.3	0.7
Current Ratio (times)	21.2	2.1	1.5
Curr Liab To Nw (%)	3.9	34.3	58.4
Curr Liab To Inv (%)	58.5	200.2	509.2
Total Liab To Nw (%)	6.8	42.4	84.7
Fixed Assets To Nw (%)	41.5	63.2	80.8
EFFICIENCY			
Coll Period (days)	34.3	42.0	83.2
Sales To Inv (times)	30.1	22.1	15.1
Assets To Sales (%)	48.0	58.1	71.0

SIC 1791 STRUCT STEEL ERCTN (NO BREAKDOWN) 2013 (33 Establishments)

	$	%
Cash	634,787	18.8
Accounts Receivable	1,141,265	33.8
Notes Receivable	3,377	0.1
Inventory	77,660	2.3
Other Current	688,810	20.4
Total Current	**2,545,899**	**75.4**
Fixed Assets	729,329	21.6
Other Non-current	101,296	3.0
Total Assets	**3,376,524**	**100.0**
Accounts Payable	685,434	20.3
Bank Loans	37,142	1.1
Notes Payable	10,130	0.3
Other Current	803,612	23.8
Total Current	**1,536,318**	**45.5**
Other Long Term	614,528	18.2
Deferred Credits	0	0.0
Net Worth	1,225,678	36.3
Total Liab & Net Worth	**3,376,524**	**100.0**
Net Sales	8,724,868	100.0
Gross Profit	1,997,995	22.9
Net Profit After Tax	436,243	5.0
Working Capital	1,009,581	—

RATIOS	UQ	MED	LQ
SOLVENCY			
Quick Ratio (times)	2.5	1.4	1.0
Current Ratio (times)	3.4	2.1	1.4
Curr Liab To Nw (%)	31.5	51.4	173.5
Curr Liab To Inv (%)	161.9	999.9	999.9
Total Liab To Nw (%)	36.2	58.7	234.5
Fixed Assets To Nw (%)	12.6	31.0	76.6
EFFICIENCY			
Coll Period (days)	41.4	58.4	74.8
Sales To Inv (times)	354.6	189.4	41.1
Assets To Sales (%)	29.3	38.7	61.2

SIC 1793 GLASS,GLAZING WORK (NO BREAKDOWN) 2013 (47 Establishments)

	$	%
Cash	393,669	22.9
Accounts Receivable	661,846	38.5
Notes Receivable	0	0.0
Inventory	91,111	5.3
Other Current	302,558	17.6
Total Current	**1,449,184**	**84.3**
Fixed Assets	199,413	11.6
Other Non-current	70,483	4.1
Total Assets	**1,719,080**	**100.0**
Accounts Payable	233,795	13.6
Bank Loans	0	0.0
Notes Payable	24,067	1.4
Other Current	290,525	16.9
Total Current	**548,387**	**31.9**
Other Long Term	147,840	8.6
Deferred Credits	0	0.0
Net Worth	1,022,853	59.5
Total Liab & Net Worth	**1,719,080**	**100.0**
Net Sales	4,559,894	100.0
Gross Profit	1,158,213	25.4
Net Profit After Tax	155,036	3.4
Working Capital	900,797	—

RATIOS	UQ	MED	LQ
SOLVENCY			
Quick Ratio (times)	3.8	2.2	1.3
Current Ratio (times)	5.4	2.8	1.8
Curr Liab To Nw (%)	19.7	45.7	82.0
Curr Liab To Inv (%)	293.8	690.8	999.9
Total Liab To Nw (%)	21.0	55.0	112.1
Fixed Assets To Nw (%)	7.8	13.6	24.3
EFFICIENCY			
Coll Period (days)	42.0	63.0	78.3
Sales To Inv (times)	231.6	79.4	29.9
Assets To Sales (%)	29.5	37.7	47.2

SIC 20 — FOOD,KINDRED PRODUCT (NO BREAKDOWN) 2013 (262 Establishments)

Item	$	%
Cash	1,457,580	11.6
Accounts Receivable	2,073,283	16.5
Notes Receivable	50,261	0.4
Inventory	3,040,814	24.2
Other Current	841,879	6.7
Total Current	**7,463,817**	**59.4**
Fixed Assets	3,455,471	27.5
Other Non-current	1,646,061	13.1
Total Assets	**12,565,349**	**100.0**
Accounts Payable	2,563,331	20.4
Bank Loans	100,523	0.8
Notes Payable	1,495,277	11.9
Other Current	6,219,847	49.5
Total Current	**10,378,978**	**82.6**
Other Long Term	2,814,638	22.4
Deferred Credits	25,131	0.2
Net Worth	(653,398)	(5.2)
Total Liab & Net Worth	**12,565,349**	**100.0**
Net Sales	25,333,365	100.0
Gross Profit	7,169,342	28.3
Net Profit After Tax	1,064,001	4.2
Working Capital	(2,915,161)	—

RATIOS	UQ	MED	LQ
SOLVENCY			
Quick Ratio (times)	1.7	1.0	0.6
Current Ratio (times)	3.6	2.1	1.3
Curr Liab To Nw (%)	22.6	48.5	105.2
Curr Liab To Inv (%)	63.2	121.2	228.3
Total Liab To Nw (%)	39.8	94.5	215.8
Fixed Assets To Nw (%)	28.9	51.7	105.3
EFFICIENCY			
Coll Period (days)	19.7	28.1	39.5
Sales To Inv (times)	16.6	9.4	5.9
Assets To Sales (%)	31.6	49.6	80.3
Sales To Nwc (times)	12.8	6.6	4.4
Acct Pay To Sales (%)	2.7	5.2	8.3
PROFITABILITY			
Return On Sales (%)	7.2	3.1	0.6
Return On Assets (%)	12.6	5.6	1.5
Return On Nw (%)	27.4	13.7	6.0

SIC 2033 — CANNED FRTS,VGTBLS (NO BREAKDOWN) 2013 (11 Establishments)

Item	$	%
Cash	2,391,737	8.0
Accounts Receivable	3,049,465	10.2
Notes Receivable	0	0.0
Inventory	10,105,089	33.8
Other Current	388,656	1.3
Total Current	**15,934,947**	**53.3**
Fixed Assets	11,719,511	39.2
Other Non-current	2,242,254	7.5
Total Assets	**29,896,712**	**100.0**
Accounts Payable	896,901	3.0
Bank Loans	418,554	1.4
Notes Payable	29,897	0.1
Other Current	7,354,591	24.6
Total Current	**8,699,943**	**29.1**
Other Long Term	8,998,911	30.1
Deferred Credits	0	0.0
Net Worth	12,197,858	40.8
Total Liab & Net Worth	**29,896,712**	**100.0**
Net Sales	46,933,614	100.0
Gross Profit	13,047,545	27.8
Net Profit After Tax	3,707,756	7.9
Working Capital	7,235,004	—

RATIOS	UQ	MED	LQ
SOLVENCY			
Quick Ratio (times)	1.2	0.6	0.4
Current Ratio (times)	3.3	2.2	1.7
Curr Liab To Nw (%)	33.5	52.6	110.9
Curr Liab To Inv (%)	38.3	71.9	128.7
Total Liab To Nw (%)	60.7	120.9	364.3
Fixed Assets To Nw (%)	25.7	65.3	158.5
EFFICIENCY			
Coll Period (days)	21.2	27.0	36.3
Sales To Inv (times)	6.4	2.9	2.7
Assets To Sales (%)	27.0	63.7	87.3
Sales To Nwc (times)	10.6	4.3	3.1
Acct Pay To Sales (%)	1.9	3.6	5.7
PROFITABILITY			
Return On Sales (%)	11.7	4.1	2.4
Return On Assets (%)	17.0	6.1	3.4
Return On Nw (%)	101.0	13.8	11.3

SIC 2048 — PREPARED FEEDS, NEC (NO BREAKDOWN) 2013 (22 Establishments)

Item	$	%
Cash	855,560	12.4
Accounts Receivable	1,283,339	18.6
Notes Receivable	20,699	0.3
Inventory	1,966,407	28.5
Other Current	407,081	5.9
Total Current	**4,533,086**	**65.7**
Fixed Assets	1,814,614	26.3
Other Non-current	551,974	8.0
Total Assets	**6,899,674**	**100.0**
Accounts Payable	952,155	13.8
Bank Loans	0	0.0
Notes Payable	158,693	2.3
Other Current	965,954	14.0
Total Current	**2,076,802**	**30.1**
Other Long Term	1,179,844	17.1
Deferred Credits	6,900	0.1
Net Worth	3,636,128	52.7
Total Liab & Net Worth	**6,899,674**	**100.0**
Net Sales	19,435,701	100.0
Gross Profit	3,964,883	20.4
Net Profit After Tax	408,150	2.1
Working Capital	2,456,284	—

RATIOS	UQ	MED	LQ
SOLVENCY			
Quick Ratio (times)	1.9	1.0	0.6
Current Ratio (times)	4.8	2.0	1.5
Curr Liab To Nw (%)	22.6	57.7	107.7
Curr Liab To Inv (%)	55.6	109.1	145.6
Total Liab To Nw (%)	30.4	99.5	179.7
Fixed Assets To Nw (%)	34.2	50.3	83.2
EFFICIENCY			
Coll Period (days)	10.1	15.7	27.1
Sales To Inv (times)	15.8	9.0	7.8
Assets To Sales (%)	30.4	35.5	46.2
Sales To Nwc (times)	18.6	10.2	5.5
Acct Pay To Sales (%)	1.7	4.2	6.9
PROFITABILITY			
Return On Sales (%)	5.1	1.4	0.2
Return On Assets (%)	13.8	6.1	0.6
Return On Nw (%)	23.2	15.5	1.5

SIC 2051 — BRD,CKE,RLTD PRDCTS (NO BREAKDOWN) 2013 (13 Establishments)

Item	$	%
Cash	927,669	12.8
Accounts Receivable	1,239,308	17.1
Notes Receivable	210,175	2.9
Inventory	840,700	11.6
Other Current	514,567	7.1
Total Current	**3,732,419**	**51.5**
Fixed Assets	2,768,513	38.2
Other Non-current	746,483	10.3
Total Assets	**7,247,415**	**100.0**
Accounts Payable	789,968	10.9
Bank Loans	14,495	0.2
Notes Payable	36,237	0.5
Other Current	1,804,606	24.9
Total Current	**2,645,306**	**36.5**
Other Long Term	2,036,524	28.1
Deferred Credits	21,742	0.3
Net Worth	2,543,843	35.1
Total Liab & Net Worth	**7,247,415**	**100.0**
Net Sales	15,789,575	100.0
Gross Profit	4,547,398	28.8
Net Profit After Tax	600,004	3.8
Working Capital	1,087,113	—

RATIOS	UQ	MED	LQ
SOLVENCY			
Quick Ratio (times)	1.9	0.8	0.6
Current Ratio (times)	3.5	1.9	1.1
Curr Liab To Nw (%)	13.9	43.2	104.8
Curr Liab To Inv (%)	197.5	233.2	401.3
Total Liab To Nw (%)	34.5	121.6	225.6
Fixed Assets To Nw (%)	27.9	45.6	141.8
EFFICIENCY			
Coll Period (days)	15.3	25.1	32.9
Sales To Inv (times)	32.7	26.3	23.1
Assets To Sales (%)	25.5	45.9	71.0
Sales To Nwc (times)	32.0	8.0	3.6
Acct Pay To Sales (%)	2.4	3.7	6.4
PROFITABILITY			
Return On Sales (%)	6.8	2.7	0.3
Return On Assets (%)	12.2	4.6	1.1
Return On Nw (%)	24.0	17.6	13.1

SIC 2064 CNDY CNFCTNR PRDCTS (NO BREAKDOWN) 2013 (11 Establishments)
SIC 2086 BOTL,CND SFT DRNKS (NO BREAKDOWN) 2013 (18 Establishments)
SIC 2099 FOOD PRPRTNS,NEC (NO BREAKDOWN) 2013 (31 Establishments)
SIC 22 TEXTILE MILL PDTS (NO BREAKDOWN) 2013 (42 Establishments)

	SIC 2064 $	%	SIC 2086 $	%	SIC 2099 $	%	SIC 22 $	%
Cash	343,909	19.9	1,252,474	16.3	829,434	9.4	797,170	8.5
Accounts Receivable	205,654	11.9	1,075,744	14.0	1,950,052	22.1	2,082,021	22.2
Notes Receivable	0	0.0	0	0.0	61,766	0.7	0	0.0
Inventory	637,701	36.9	1,344,680	17.5	2,144,175	24.3	2,766,649	29.5
Other Current	58,760	3.4	1,045,009	13.6	758,843	8.6	675,249	7.2
Total Current	**1,246,024**	**72.1**	**4,717,907**	**61.4**	**5,744,270**	**65.1**	**6,321,089**	**67.4**
Fixed Assets	373,289	21.6	1,390,784	18.1	2,082,408	23.6	1,978,857	21.1
Other Non-current	108,875	6.3	1,575,197	20.5	997,086	11.3	1,078,525	11.5
Total Assets	**1,728,188**	**100.0**	**7,683,888**	**100.0**	**8,823,764**	**100.0**	**9,378,471**	**100.0**
Accounts Payable	84,681	4.9	4,564,229	59.4	1,676,515	19.0	1,406,771	15.0
Bank Loans	0	0.0	23,052	0.3	8,824	0.1	84,406	0.9
Notes Payable	8,641	0.5	1,813,398	23.6	150,004	1.7	28,135	0.3
Other Current	190,101	11.0	19,040,674	247.8	1,879,462	21.3	2,691,621	28.7
Total Current	**283,423**	**16.4**	**25,441,353**	**331.1**	**3,714,805**	**42.1**	**4,210,933**	**44.9**
Other Long Term	214,295	12.4	1,659,720	21.6	2,197,117	24.9	1,519,313	16.2
Deferred Credits	12,097	0.7	99,891	1.3	8,824	0.1	0	0.0
Net Worth	1,218,373	70.5	(19,517,076)	(254.0)	2,903,018	32.9	3,648,225	38.9
Total Liab & Net Worth	**1,728,188**	**100.0**	**7,683,888**	**100.0**	**8,823,764**	**100.0**	**9,378,471**	**100.0**
Net Sales	3,592,906	100.0	15,125,764	100.0	23,719,796	100.0	17,432,102	100.0
Gross Profit	1,379,676	38.4	5,520,904	36.5	7,708,934	32.5	4,950,717	28.4
Net Profit After Tax	330,547	9.2	(75,629)	(0.5)	1,518,067	6.4	383,506	2.2
Working Capital	962,601	---	(20,723,446)	---	2,029,465	---	2,110,156	---

RATIOS

	SIC 2064 UQ	MED	LQ	SIC 2086 UQ	MED	LQ	SIC 2099 UQ	MED	LQ	SIC 22 UQ	MED	LQ
SOLVENCY												
Quick Ratio (times)	2.9	2.1	1.2	1.6	1.1	0.4	1.4	1.0	0.4	1.9	1.2	0.7
Current Ratio (times)	6.4	4.7	3.6	3.7	1.7	1.1	3.1	2.1	1.3	3.3	2.3	1.7
Curr Liab To Nw (%)	10.5	19.7	34.1	23.1	55.8	90.2	28.4	52.7	171.2	28.6	61.6	86.3
Curr Liab To Inv (%)	28.1	36.2	86.8	120.7	200.9	411.3	63.1	150.1	342.2	72.2	95.1	139.2
Total Liab To Nw (%)	24.9	35.4	48.4	34.4	97.4	317.8	39.2	129.4	289.4	47.5	88.3	135.5
Fixed Assets To Nw (%)	18.1	28.9	38.6	19.1	64.6	103.2	15.2	45.6	131.0	9.3	26.6	57.1
EFFICIENCY												
Coll Period (days)	16.1	27.0	43.3	21.4	25.1	42.4	16.8	29.9	35.8	25.9	45.8	52.6
Sales To Inv (times)	9.7	8.4	6.3	27.2	18.3	8.0	27.5	11.1	6.2	11.9	6.5	4.7
Assets To Sales (%)	26.4	48.1	56.1	31.5	50.8	116.0	24.5	37.2	58.6	36.0	53.8	81.4
Sales To Nwc (times)	6.0	5.1	3.5	22.0	10.2	5.6	13.4	7.5	5.3	8.6	5.0	3.6
Acct Pay To Sales (%)	1.7	2.2	4.6	4.6	5.4	12.1	3.6	6.9	10.2	4.9	7.7	11.1
PROFITABILITY												
Return On Sales (%)	12.1	10.4	3.3	8.1	2.4	(4.1)	6.7	4.1	0.5	7.5	4.2	0.3
Return On Assets (%)	21.6	7.9	6.8	14.5	6.1	(34.3)	14.0	7.5	2.0	12.7	5.9	0.7
Return On Nw (%)	101.4	9.8	8.9	29.3	14.4	10.1	37.7	20.0	8.5	23.7	12.4	2.6

SIC 23 APPAREL,RELATED PDTS
(NO BREAKDOWN)
2013 (103 Establishments)

	$	%
Cash	905,164	13.8
Accounts Receivable	1,206,886	18.4
Notes Receivable	13,118	0.2
Inventory	2,203,878	33.6
Other Current	596,884	9.1
Total Current	**4,925,930**	**75.1**
Fixed Assets	885,487	13.5
Other Non-current	747,744	11.4
Total Assets	**6,559,161**	**100.0**
Accounts Payable	813,336	12.4
Bank Loans	52,473	0.8
Notes Payable	65,592	1.0
Other Current	1,324,950	20.2
Total Current	**2,256,351**	**34.4**
Other Long Term	918,283	14.0
Deferred Credits	0	0.0
Net Worth	3,384,527	51.6
Total Liab & Net Worth	**6,559,161**	**100.0**
Net Sales	13,277,654	100.0
Gross Profit	4,912,732	37.0
Net Profit After Tax	345,219	2.6
Working Capital	2,669,579	—

RATIOS	UQ	MED	LQ
SOLVENCY			
Quick Ratio (times)	2.3	1.3	0.5
Current Ratio (times)	5.0	2.6	1.5
Curr Liab To Nw (%)	18.7	41.2	106.1
Curr Liab To Inv (%)	43.9	95.6	143.0
Total Liab To Nw (%)	23.8	67.2	167.0
Fixed Assets To Nw (%)	7.8	17.3	37.9
EFFICIENCY			
Coll Period (days)	20.8	33.8	55.1
Sales To Inv (times)	11.4	6.9	4.6
Assets To Sales (%)	35.0	49.4	71.2
Sales To Nwc (times)	7.5	4.4	3.0
Acct Pay To Sales (%)	2.2	5.1	8.2
PROFITABILITY			
Return On Sales (%)	6.1	3.4	0.8
Return On Assets (%)	11.7	6.2	1.4
Return On Nw (%)	19.9	13.3	2.9

SIC 24 LUMBER,WOOD PRODUCTS
(NO BREAKDOWN)
2013 (143 Establishments)

	$	%
Cash	440,544	16.0
Accounts Receivable	498,365	18.1
Notes Receivable	30,287	1.1
Inventory	578,213	21.0
Other Current	200,998	7.3
Total Current	**1,748,407**	**63.5**
Fixed Assets	798,485	29.0
Other Non-current	206,505	7.5
Total Assets	**2,753,397**	**100.0**
Accounts Payable	209,258	7.6
Bank Loans	11,014	0.4
Notes Payable	44,054	1.6
Other Current	492,858	17.9
Total Current	**757,184**	**27.5**
Other Long Term	322,148	11.7
Deferred Credits	2,753	0.1
Net Worth	1,671,312	60.7
Total Liab & Net Worth	**2,753,397**	**100.0**
Net Sales	6,602,871	100.0
Gross Profit	1,617,703	24.5
Net Profit After Tax	171,675	2.6
Working Capital	991,223	—

RATIOS	UQ	MED	LQ
Quick Ratio (times)	4.1	1.3	0.6
Current Ratio (times)	6.3	2.7	1.4
Curr Liab To Nw (%)	8.9	28.3	62.5
Curr Liab To Inv (%)	52.8	109.5	231.0
Total Liab To Nw (%)	12.3	43.0	110.3
Fixed Assets To Nw (%)	17.9	44.6	80.3
Coll Period (days)	16.1	27.4	39.4
Sales To Inv (times)	24.1	12.0	7.1
Assets To Sales (%)	30.7	41.7	71.4
Sales To Nwc (times)	10.5	6.8	3.8
Acct Pay To Sales (%)	1.6	2.6	4.3
Return On Sales (%)	5.6	2.6	0.0
Return On Assets (%)	13.6	5.0	0.0
Return On Nw (%)	25.6	9.0	0.5

SIC 2421 SAWML PLNG,MLL,GNRL
(NO BREAKDOWN)
2013 (24 Establishments)

	$	%
Cash	1,038,489	18.9
Accounts Receivable	692,326	12.6
Notes Receivable	120,882	2.2
Inventory	1,368,168	24.9
Other Current	357,152	6.5
Total Current	**3,577,017**	**65.1**
Fixed Assets	1,582,459	28.8
Other Non-current	335,174	6.1
Total Assets	**5,494,650**	**100.0**
Accounts Payable	285,722	5.2
Bank Loans	0	0.0
Notes Payable	49,452	0.9
Other Current	890,133	16.2
Total Current	**1,225,307**	**22.3**
Other Long Term	626,390	11.4
Deferred Credits	0	0.0
Net Worth	3,642,953	66.3
Total Liab & Net Worth	**5,494,650**	**100.0**
Net Sales	10,063,462	100.0
Gross Profit	2,505,802	24.9
Net Profit After Tax	573,617	5.7
Working Capital	2,351,710	—

RATIOS	UQ	MED	LQ
Quick Ratio (times)	3.8	1.3	0.6
Current Ratio (times)	8.5	3.4	1.6
Curr Liab To Nw (%)	8.7	23.1	53.3
Curr Liab To Inv (%)	35.1	58.9	131.9
Total Liab To Nw (%)	8.9	38.8	109.5
Fixed Assets To Nw (%)	13.0	49.5	88.3
Coll Period (days)	13.0	20.4	31.4
Sales To Inv (times)	12.8	8.3	5.1
Assets To Sales (%)	37.5	54.6	71.8
Sales To Nwc (times)	9.6	5.7	3.3
Acct Pay To Sales (%)	1.7	2.1	3.7
Return On Sales (%)	7.9	3.3	0.5
Return On Assets (%)	18.4	4.9	0.7
Return On Nw (%)	37.7	7.8	1.3

SIC 2431 MILLWORK
(NO BREAKDOWN)
2013 (38 Establishments)

	$	%
Cash	343,202	22.5
Accounts Receivable	283,714	18.6
Notes Receivable	0	0.0
Inventory	282,188	18.5
Other Current	140,331	9.2
Total Current	**1,049,435**	**68.8**
Fixed Assets	346,253	22.7
Other Non-current	129,654	8.5
Total Assets	**1,525,342**	**100.0**
Accounts Payable	118,977	7.8
Bank Loans	0	0.0
Notes Payable	19,829	1.3
Other Current	263,884	17.3
Total Current	**402,690**	**26.4**
Other Long Term	207,447	13.6
Deferred Credits	0	0.0
Net Worth	915,205	60.0
Total Liab & Net Worth	**1,525,342**	**100.0**
Net Sales	4,067,579	100.0
Gross Profit	1,126,719	27.7
Net Profit After Tax	61,014	1.5
Working Capital	646,745	—

RATIOS	UQ	MED	LQ
Quick Ratio (times)	4.1	1.7	0.7
Current Ratio (times)	8.1	3.2	1.4
Curr Liab To Nw (%)	7.5	26.6	79.8
Curr Liab To Inv (%)	66.9	140.1	234.3
Total Liab To Nw (%)	9.6	39.8	158.9
Fixed Assets To Nw (%)	18.4	42.8	74.7
Coll Period (days)	21.9	33.3	48.8
Sales To Inv (times)	29.0	18.0	10.1
Assets To Sales (%)	30.6	37.5	74.0
Sales To Nwc (times)	9.5	7.1	3.9
Acct Pay To Sales (%)	1.8	3.5	4.7
Return On Sales (%)	6.3	2.5	(2.1)
Return On Assets (%)	19.7	5.6	(4.0)
Return On Nw (%)	28.4	10.8	(4.4)

SIC 2434 WOOD KTCHN CABINETS
(NO BREAKDOWN)
2013 (11 Establishments)

	$	%
Cash	156,100	19.3
Accounts Receivable	268,524	33.2
Notes Receivable	0	0.0
Inventory	96,248	11.9
Other Current	70,366	8.7
Total Current	**591,238**	**73.1**
Fixed Assets	136,688	16.9
Other Non-current	80,881	10.0
Total Assets	**808,807**	**100.0**
Accounts Payable	75,219	9.3
Bank Loans	10,514	1.3
Notes Payable	21,029	2.6
Other Current	253,966	31.4
Total Current	**360,728**	**44.6**
Other Long Term	221,613	27.4
Deferred Credits	0	0.0
Net Worth	226,466	28.0
Total Liab & Net Worth	**808,807**	**100.0**
Net Sales	1,846,591	100.0
Gross Profit	677,699	36.7
Net Profit After Tax	120,028	6.5
Working Capital	230,510	---

RATIOS	UQ	MED	LQ
SOLVENCY			
Quick Ratio (times)	2.0	1.5	1.0
Current Ratio (times)	2.7	2.6	1.6
Curr Liab To Nw (%)	34.0	52.4	86.4
Curr Liab To Inv (%)	138.2	243.0	999.9
Total Liab To Nw (%)	38.4	82.3	271.0
Fixed Assets To Nw (%)	5.9	25.7	56.5
EFFICIENCY			
Coll Period (days)	22.3	39.5	44.5
Sales To Inv (times)	45.1	21.5	15.0
Assets To Sales (%)	19.1	43.8	72.0
Sales To Nwc (times)	6.2	5.1	3.4
Acct Pay To Sales (%)	2.0	2.4	4.3
PROFITABILITY			
Return On Sales (%)	8.7	5.6	1.5
Return On Assets (%)	27.5	10.9	3.3
Return On Nw (%)	52.5	28.7	10.9

SIC 2448 WOOD PALLETS,SKIDS
(NO BREAKDOWN)
2013 (10 Establishments)

	$	%
Cash	228,429	11.1
Accounts Receivable	454,800	22.1
Notes Receivable	135,823	6.6
Inventory	353,962	17.2
Other Current	82,316	4.0
Total Current	**1,255,330**	**61.0**
Fixed Assets	726,445	35.3
Other Non-current	76,143	3.7
Total Assets	**2,057,918**	**100.0**
Accounts Payable	170,807	8.3
Bank Loans	0	0.0
Notes Payable	133,765	6.5
Other Current	185,212	9.0
Total Current	**489,784**	**23.8**
Other Long Term	246,951	12.0
Deferred Credits	0	0.0
Net Worth	1,321,183	64.2
Total Liab & Net Worth	**2,057,918**	**100.0**
Net Sales	5,444,228	100.0
Gross Profit	484,536	8.9
Net Profit After Tax	(342,986)	(6.3)
Working Capital	765,546	---

RATIOS	UQ	MED	LQ
SOLVENCY			
Quick Ratio (times)	2.8	1.5	0.5
Current Ratio (times)	5.2	2.2	1.6
Curr Liab To Nw (%)	14.8	26.5	73.2
Curr Liab To Inv (%)	101.0	139.0	172.2
Total Liab To Nw (%)	17.7	27.2	197.5
Fixed Assets To Nw (%)	30.4	64.6	98.5
EFFICIENCY			
Coll Period (days)	28.8	31.8	38.3
Sales To Inv (times)	19.8	16.8	15.4
Assets To Sales (%)	21.9	37.8	57.4
Sales To Nwc (times)	17.6	13.5	8.7
Acct Pay To Sales (%)	1.3	4.0	4.9
PROFITABILITY			
Return On Sales (%)	3.3	1.8	0.0
Return On Assets (%)	13.4	4.8	0.0
Return On Nw (%)	24.5	8.7	(0.2)

SIC 25 FURNITURE,FIXTURES
(NO BREAKDOWN)
2013 (101 Establishments)

	$	%
Cash	751,015	15.4
Accounts Receivable	1,072,878	22.0
Notes Receivable	14,630	0.3
Inventory	1,316,714	27.0
Other Current	385,262	7.9
Total Current	**3,540,499**	**72.6**
Fixed Assets	902,193	18.5
Other Non-current	434,028	8.9
Total Assets	**4,876,720**	**100.0**
Accounts Payable	609,590	12.5
Bank Loans	58,521	1.2
Notes Payable	121,918	2.5
Other Current	1,209,426	24.8
Total Current	**1,999,455**	**41.0**
Other Long Term	629,097	12.9
Deferred Credits	0	0.0
Net Worth	2,248,168	46.1
Total Liab & Net Worth	**4,876,720**	**100.0**
Net Sales	11,008,397	100.0
Gross Profit	3,214,452	29.2
Net Profit After Tax	374,285	3.4
Working Capital	1,541,044	---

RATIOS	UQ	MED	LQ
SOLVENCY			
Quick Ratio (times)	2.1	1.1	0.6
Current Ratio (times)	4.2	2.3	1.5
Curr Liab To Nw (%)	22.1	49.2	96.4
Curr Liab To Inv (%)	57.2	130.5	224.8
Total Liab To Nw (%)	27.3	66.1	152.9
Fixed Assets To Nw (%)	14.5	29.9	52.7
EFFICIENCY			
Coll Period (days)	21.2	36.5	48.9
Sales To Inv (times)	19.1	9.6	5.3
Assets To Sales (%)	29.0	44.3	61.7
Sales To Nwc (times)	11.6	6.1	3.7
Acct Pay To Sales (%)	2.8	5.0	7.6
PROFITABILITY			
Return On Sales (%)	5.6	2.9	0.9
Return On Assets (%)	13.8	5.7	2.0
Return On Nw (%)	26.5	10.1	4.3

SIC 2511 WOOD HSHLD FURNTR
(NO BREAKDOWN)
2013 (12 Establishments)

	$	%
Cash	1,050,032	13.9
Accounts Receivable	1,314,428	17.4
Notes Receivable	0	0.0
Inventory	2,659,073	35.2
Other Current	679,876	9.0
Total Current	**5,703,409**	**75.5**
Fixed Assets	1,367,307	18.1
Other Non-current	483,468	6.4
Total Assets	**7,554,184**	**100.0**
Accounts Payable	634,551	8.4
Bank Loans	0	0.0
Notes Payable	211,517	2.8
Other Current	1,080,249	14.3
Total Current	**1,926,317**	**25.5**
Other Long Term	309,721	4.1
Deferred Credits	0	0.0
Net Worth	5,318,146	70.4
Total Liab & Net Worth	**7,554,184**	**100.0**
Net Sales	13,513,746	100.0
Gross Profit	3,108,162	23.0
Net Profit After Tax	351,357	2.6
Working Capital	3,777,092	---

RATIOS	UQ	MED	LQ
SOLVENCY			
Quick Ratio (times)	3.4	2.1	0.6
Current Ratio (times)	6.1	4.7	2.1
Curr Liab To Nw (%)	14.5	25.3	52.5
Curr Liab To Inv (%)	37.1	51.7	98.9
Total Liab To Nw (%)	17.3	28.1	72.4
Fixed Assets To Nw (%)	9.9	22.0	39.2
EFFICIENCY			
Coll Period (days)	23.0	34.5	47.1
Sales To Inv (times)	10.2	5.3	3.7
Assets To Sales (%)	35.4	55.9	71.4
Sales To Nwc (times)	5.3	4.6	2.4
Acct Pay To Sales (%)	2.2	5.8	6.2
PROFITABILITY			
Return On Sales (%)	4.0	3.0	1.6
Return On Assets (%)	11.9	6.1	2.3
Return On Nw (%)	16.6	9.3	4.8

	SIC 2512 UPHLSTRD HSHLD FURN (NO BREAKDOWN) 2013 (14 Establishments)		SIC 2515 MATTRESSES,BDSPRNGS (NO BREAKDOWN) 2013 (13 Establishments)		SIC 2541 WD PARTNS,FXTRS (NO BREAKDOWN) 2013 (22 Establishments)		SIC 26 PAPER,ALLIED PDTS (NO BREAKDOWN) 2013 (84 Establishments)	
	$	%	$	%	$	%	$	%
Cash	1,476,881	15.5	708,117	18.7	359,673	16.3	1,120,694	10.1
Accounts Receivable	2,505,934	26.3	639,956	16.9	586,950	26.6	2,563,171	23.1
Notes Receivable	0	0.0	0	0.0	4,413	0.2	11,096	0.1
Inventory	2,963,291	31.1	1,136,017	30.0	425,870	19.3	2,319,059	20.9
Other Current	285,849	3.0	261,283	6.9	302,301	13.7	532,606	4.8
Total Current	**7,231,955**	**75.9**	**2,745,373**	**72.5**	**1,679,207**	**76.1**	**6,546,626**	**59.0**
Fixed Assets	1,495,938	15.7	677,823	17.9	450,142	20.4	3,273,313	29.5
Other Non-current	800,374	8.4	363,526	9.6	77,231	3.5	1,276,038	11.5
Total Assets	**9,528,267**	**100.0**	**3,786,722**	**100.0**	**2,206,580**	**100.0**	**11,095,977**	**100.0**
Accounts Payable	867,072	9.1	473,340	12.5	240,517	10.9	1,153,982	10.4
Bank Loans	0	0.0	0	0.0	119,155	5.4	188,632	1.7
Notes Payable	228,678	2.4	265,071	7.0	66,197	3.0	77,672	0.7
Other Current	1,419,712	14.9	855,799	22.6	900,286	40.8	1,520,148	13.7
Total Current	**2,515,462**	**26.4**	**1,594,210**	**42.1**	**1,326,155**	**60.1**	**2,940,434**	**26.5**
Other Long Term	609,810	6.4	374,885	9.9	368,498	16.7	3,195,641	28.8
Deferred Credits	0	0.0	0	0.0	0	0.0	55,480	0.5
Net Worth	6,402,995	67.2	1,817,627	48.0	511,927	23.2	4,904,422	44.2
Total Liab & Net Worth	**9,528,267**	**100.0**	**3,786,722**	**100.0**	**2,206,580**	**100.0**	**11,095,977**	**100.0**
Net Sales	22,632,463	100.0	9,258,489	100.0	6,215,718	100.0	21,462,238	100.0
Gross Profit	4,707,552	20.8	3,416,382	36.9	1,765,264	28.4	4,914,853	22.9
Net Profit After Tax	927,931	4.1	101,843	1.1	298,354	4.8	772,641	3.6
Working Capital	4,716,493	---	1,151,163	---	353,052	---	3,606,192	---

RATIOS	UQ	MED	LQ	UQ	MED	LQ	UQ	MED	LQ	UQ	MED	LQ
SOLVENCY												
Quick Ratio (times)	3.3	1.8	1.1	1.9	0.9	0.3	2.1	1.7	0.7	2.2	1.1	0.8
Current Ratio (times)	4.2	3.6	1.8	3.6	2.6	1.5	5.0	2.6	1.8	4.0	2.2	1.5
Curr Liab To Nw (%)	22.1	28.7	76.7	33.0	43.8	97.0	18.2	43.5	85.4	20.1	42.9	94.9
Curr Liab To Inv (%)	38.4	108.3	161.0	69.7	138.3	248.6	62.8	104.5	470.8	70.1	121.4	197.7
Total Liab To Nw (%)	27.3	40.2	93.3	33.9	47.6	127.6	21.0	60.6	115.6	37.7	116.5	209.0
Fixed Assets To Nw (%)	10.9	20.9	36.6	11.0	39.1	49.8	16.2	30.2	39.6	21.0	59.2	105.7
EFFICIENCY												
Coll Period (days)	28.9	38.9	53.7	11.7	16.4	42.3	26.5	35.1	49.9	30.7	40.2	48.2
Sales To Inv (times)	13.2	9.9	6.4	16.8	10.0	5.7	33.5	19.8	7.5	12.5	9.6	7.4
Assets To Sales (%)	33.3	42.1	53.4	22.8	40.9	73.5	28.7	35.5	50.0	30.1	51.7	93.6
Sales To Nwc (times)	8.8	4.3	3.1	10.4	8.2	4.5	6.6	5.4	3.6	10.8	6.2	3.7
Acct Pay To Sales (%)	2.1	3.5	4.6	3.3	5.8	7.8	2.8	3.6	5.2	2.7	6.1	9.5
PROFITABILITY												
Return On Sales (%)	6.0	4.3	2.5	5.3	2.2	(0.5)	4.6	3.1	0.4	5.2	2.9	0.2
Return On Assets (%)	17.7	8.0	6.1	15.7	3.7	(0.9)	24.7	4.3	2.0	8.5	4.8	0.6
Return On Nw (%)	28.3	12.6	9.2	28.0	14.3	3.4	22.6	5.4	3.2	21.5	11.3	3.2

	SIC 2653 CRRGTD SLD FBR BXS (NO BREAKDOWN) 2013 (14 Establishments)		SIC 2673 BAGS:PLSTC,LMND,CTD (NO BREAKDOWN) 2013 (12 Establishments)		SIC 2679 CNVTD PPR PRDTS,NEC (NO BREAKDOWN) 2013 (12 Establishments)		SIC 27 PRINTING,PUBLISHING (NO BREAKDOWN) 2013 (169 Establishments)	
	$	%	$	%	$	%	$	%
Cash	742,049	9.1	702,967	19.7	517,867	12.0	625,113	17.9
Accounts Receivable	2,095,678	25.7	752,924	21.1	966,685	22.4	848,617	24.3
Notes Receivable	0	0.0	0	0.0	8,631	0.2	6,985	0.2
Inventory	1,810,274	22.2	909,931	25.5	1,091,837	25.3	398,117	11.4
Other Current	489,264	6.0	164,144	4.6	194,201	4.5	261,918	7.5
Total Current	**5,137,265**	**63.0**	**2,529,966**	**70.9**	**2,779,221**	**64.4**	**2,140,750**	**61.3**
Fixed Assets	2,364,773	29.0	724,377	20.3	1,251,512	29.0	820,679	23.5
Other Non-current	652,351	8.0	314,015	8.8	284,827	6.6	530,822	15.2
Total Assets	**8,154,389**	**100.0**	**3,568,358**	**100.0**	**4,315,560**	**100.0**	**3,492,251**	**100.0**
Accounts Payable	1,157,923	14.2	474,592	13.3	233,040	5.4	680,989	19.5
Bank Loans	464,800	5.7	17,842	0.5	38,840	0.9	24,446	0.7
Notes Payable	57,081	0.7	7,137	0.2	51,787	1.2	80,322	2.3
Other Current	1,410,709	17.3	403,224	11.3	504,921	11.7	1,169,904	33.5
Total Current	**3,090,513**	**37.9**	**902,795**	**25.3**	**828,588**	**19.2**	**1,955,661**	**56.0**
Other Long Term	1,369,938	16.8	977,730	27.4	880,374	20.4	674,004	19.3
Deferred Credits	122,316	1.5	0	0.0	56,102	1.3	10,477	0.3
Net Worth	3,571,622	43.8	1,687,833	47.3	2,550,496	59.1	852,109	24.4
Total Liab & Net Worth	**8,154,389**	**100.0**	**3,568,358**	**100.0**	**4,315,560**	**100.0**	**3,492,251**	**100.0**
Net Sales	25,562,348	100.0	8,337,285	100.0	9,123,805	100.0	6,614,112	100.0
Gross Profit	5,700,404	22.3	2,092,659	25.1	1,906,875	20.9	2,817,612	42.6
Net Profit After Tax	562,372	2.2	441,876	5.3	392,324	4.3	132,282	2.0
Working Capital	2,046,752	---	1,627,171	---	1,950,633	---	185,089	---

RATIOS	UQ	MED	LQ	UQ	MED	LQ	UQ	MED	LQ	UQ	MED	LQ
SOLVENCY												
Quick Ratio (times)	1.5	1.0	0.6	4.4	1.2	0.8	3.5	1.5	1.2	3.1	1.3	0.8
Current Ratio (times)	3.3	1.9	1.1	8.1	2.3	1.7	7.0	3.0	2.3	4.1	2.0	1.2
Curr Liab To Nw (%)	28.8	44.1	212.5	25.9	50.4	112.9	11.2	20.1	44.1	16.8	42.9	87.7
Curr Liab To Inv (%)	92.3	168.8	214.8	40.1	136.4	207.1	39.6	65.8	121.3	165.6	266.5	635.6
Total Liab To Nw (%)	37.3	136.5	241.7	29.3	58.1	188.5	27.3	35.3	56.7	26.3	66.1	167.9
Fixed Assets To Nw (%)	32.3	55.8	100.0	19.9	21.0	89.5	19.4	34.7	70.6	12.5	32.8	74.0
EFFICIENCY												
Coll Period (days)	29.8	35.4	40.2	27.7	30.5	41.3	32.2	40.5	48.2	28.5	42.0	59.5
Sales To Inv (times)	17.1	11.6	9.8	11.5	9.9	8.4	12.7	9.5	6.4	49.3	22.5	10.5
Assets To Sales (%)	24.4	31.9	44.4	25.5	42.8	80.4	34.1	47.3	58.1	36.1	52.8	89.6
Sales To Nwc (times)	15.2	7.5	6.5	12.4	7.6	3.1	7.5	4.9	3.5	12.0	6.1	3.3
Acct Pay To Sales (%)	2.1	8.3	10.0	2.3	4.6	7.5	1.4	2.7	4.4	2.8	4.5	6.9
PROFITABILITY												
Return On Sales (%)	3.4	1.2	0.6	5.6	1.0	0.1	4.2	3.6	0.7	5.9	2.6	0.1
Return On Assets (%)	6.1	3.8	2.1	8.2	3.5	0.2	13.3	8.6	2.5	9.8	3.8	0.1
Return On Nw (%)	21.0	13.8	4.6	12.1	8.9	0.9	23.3	16.0	6.1	24.5	9.2	1.7

	SIC 2711 NEWSPAPERS (NO BREAKDOWN) 2013 (11 Establishments)		SIC 2731 BOOK PUBLISHING (NO BREAKDOWN) 2013 (24 Establishments)		SIC 2741 MISC PUBLISHING (NO BREAKDOWN) 2013 (12 Establishments)		SIC 2752 COMMRCL PRTNG,LITH (NO BREAKDOWN) 2013 (68 Establishments)	
	$	%	$	%	$	%	$	%
Cash	99,353,232	14.4	995,237	19.5	1,707,644	21.2	456,073	18.0
Accounts Receivable	106,252,762	15.4	1,071,794	21.0	1,860,687	23.1	727,183	28.7
Notes Receivable	2,759,812	0.4	40,830	0.8	0	0.0	2,534	0.1
Inventory	10,349,295	1.5	1,173,869	23.0	193,318	2.4	222,969	8.8
Other Current	67,615,394	9.8	546,105	10.7	1,296,843	16.1	124,153	4.9
Total Current	**286,330,495**	**41.5**	**3,827,835**	**75.0**	**5,058,492**	**62.8**	**1,532,912**	**60.5**
Fixed Assets	189,047,122	27.4	505,274	9.9	716,888	8.9	767,723	30.3
Other Non-current	214,575,383	31.1	770,671	15.1	2,279,544	28.3	233,104	9.2
Total Assets	**689,953,000**	**100.0**	**5,103,780**	**100.0**	**8,054,924**	**100.0**	**2,533,739**	**100.0**
Accounts Payable	26,908,167	3.9	444,029	8.7	1,385,447	17.2	250,840	9.9
Bank Loans	0	0.0	0	0.0	0	0.0	40,540	1.6
Notes Payable	2,759,812	0.4	91,868	1.8	16,110	0.2	32,939	1.3
Other Current	287,710,401	41.7	1,929,229	37.8	2,086,225	25.9	392,729	15.5
Total Current	**317,378,380**	**46.0**	**2,465,126**	**48.3**	**3,487,782**	**43.3**	**717,048**	**28.3**
Other Long Term	275,291,247	39.9	699,217	13.7	1,868,742	23.2	418,067	16.5
Deferred Credits	0	0.0	51,038	1.0	0	0.0	2,534	0.1
Net Worth	97,283,373	14.1	1,888,399	37.0	2,698,400	33.5	1,396,090	55.1
Total Liab & Net Worth	**689,953,000**	**100.0**	**5,103,780**	**100.0**	**8,054,924**	**100.0**	**2,533,739**	**100.0**
Net Sales	451,244,604	100.0	6,363,815	100.0	14,008,563	100.0	5,077,633	100.0
Gross Profit	185,010,288	41.0	3,767,378	59.2	7,088,333	50.6	2,015,820	39.7
Net Profit After Tax	17,147,295	3.8	57,274	0.9	(952,582)	(6.8)	137,096	2.7
Working Capital	(31,047,885)	—	1,362,709	—	1,570,710	—	815,864	—

RATIOS	UQ	MED	LQ	UQ	MED	LQ	UQ	MED	LQ	UQ	MED	LQ
SOLVENCY												
Quick Ratio (times)	1.7	1.0	0.8	3.0	1.3	0.7	1.8	0.9	0.6	3.7	2.2	1.1
Current Ratio (times)	2.7	1.4	1.2	5.9	2.1	1.4	2.9	1.3	1.1	4.6	2.7	1.5
Curr Liab To Nw (%)	25.9	34.8	41.2	15.2	51.1	114.4	15.3	128.7	337.9	14.7	31.7	55.8
Curr Liab To Inv (%)	563.7	967.8	999.9	71.3	151.6	337.1	411.3	804.9	930.8	177.4	295.9	557.9
Total Liab To Nw (%)	70.4	76.1	203.9	34.7	65.0	177.1	26.3	208.8	377.3	20.3	44.2	109.4
Fixed Assets To Nw (%)	28.1	68.3	106.6	4.0	6.4	22.4	4.0	10.2	55.0	17.8	46.1	72.9
EFFICIENCY												
Coll Period (days)	32.2	41.6	48.9	25.6	59.5	79.1	17.9	50.4	71.9	33.2	42.3	55.7
Sales To Inv (times)	104.3	46.5	30.7	9.3	6.6	3.9	58.0	39.4	24.3	55.8	27.7	15.5
Assets To Sales (%)	60.7	152.9	172.8	62.6	80.2	101.1	38.5	57.5	124.0	34.5	49.9	76.8
Sales To Nwc (times)	10.3	5.1	2.5	6.8	2.5	1.5	13.1	5.8	4.7	9.3	6.0	3.7
Acct Pay To Sales (%)	2.5	3.4	4.9	1.1	4.6	8.1	2.2	5.9	15.1	3.0	4.1	5.4
PROFITABILITY												
Return On Sales (%)	6.9	5.1	2.1	9.2	5.6	0.9	2.9	0.2	(21.7)	4.7	2.3	0.6
Return On Assets (%)	5.6	2.5	0.9	13.1	5.1	1.4	8.1	0.4	(18.5)	9.1	4.5	0.8
Return On Nw (%)	14.3	7.7	1.8	21.4	10.7	3.8	42.9	0.9	(35.0)	21.0	9.2	1.8

SIC 2759 COMMRCL PRTNG,NEC
(NO BREAKDOWN)
2013 (28 Establishments)

	$	%
Cash	256,281	12.4
Accounts Receivable	574,565	27.8
Notes Receivable	2,067	0.1
Inventory	367,887	17.8
Other Current	117,806	5.7
Total Current	**1,318,606**	**63.8**
Fixed Assets	597,300	28.9
Other Non-current	150,875	7.3
Total Assets	**2,066,781**	**100.0**
Accounts Payable	1,486,016	71.9
Bank Loans	10,334	0.5
Notes Payable	188,077	9.1
Other Current	1,864,236	90.2
Total Current	**3,548,663**	**171.7**
Other Long Term	442,291	21.4
Deferred Credits	0	0.0
Net Worth	(1,924,173)	(93.1)
Total Liab & Net Worth	**2,066,781**	**100.0**
Net Sales	5,725,155	100.0
Gross Profit	2,135,483	37.3
Net Profit After Tax	183,205	3.2
Working Capital	(2,230,057)	—

RATIOS	UQ	MED	LQ
SOLVENCY			
Quick Ratio (times)	1.4	0.9	0.6
Current Ratio (times)	2.5	1.4	1.1
Curr Liab To Nw (%)	46.5	72.7	122.6
Curr Liab To Inv (%)	179.6	258.9	422.1
Total Liab To Nw (%)	63.8	107.7	204.5
Fixed Assets To Nw (%)	26.3	74.6	108.3
EFFICIENCY			
Coll Period (days)	15.7	31.6	45.5
Sales To Inv (times)	39.6	23.1	13.5
Assets To Sales (%)	18.1	36.1	40.9
Sales To Nwc (times)	39.9	12.4	7.6
Acct Pay To Sales (%)	2.9	6.1	8.8
PROFITABILITY			
Return On Sales (%)	4.7	2.8	(0.1)
Return On Assets (%)	15.4	5.4	0.2
Return On Nw (%)	39.8	17.4	5.2

SIC 28 CHEMICALS,ALLIED PDT
(NO BREAKDOWN)
2013 (541 Establishments)

	$	%
Cash	14,282,351	29.8
Accounts Receivable	4,505,171	9.4
Notes Receivable	143,782	0.3
Inventory	5,415,791	11.3
Other Current	7,380,813	15.4
Total Current	**31,727,908**	**66.2**
Fixed Assets	7,908,013	16.5
Other Non-current	8,291,432	17.3
Total Assets	**47,927,353**	**100.0**
Accounts Payable	38,581,519	80.5
Bank Loans	47,927	0.1
Notes Payable	21,183,890	44.2
Other Current	21,471,455	44.8
Total Current	**81,284,791**	**169.6**
Other Long Term	30,385,942	63.4
Deferred Credits	1,389,893	2.9
Net Worth	(65,133,273)	(135.9)
Total Liab & Net Worth	**47,927,353**	**100.0**
Net Sales	35,111,614	100.0
Gross Profit	15,659,780	44.6
Net Profit After Tax	280,893	0.8
Working Capital	(49,556,883)	—

RATIOS	UQ	MED	LQ
SOLVENCY			
Quick Ratio (times)	3.2	1.4	0.8
Current Ratio (times)	5.4	2.7	1.6
Curr Liab To Nw (%)	13.2	28.3	62.0
Curr Liab To Inv (%)	94.5	179.8	402.8
Total Liab To Nw (%)	23.0	61.9	153.8
Fixed Assets To Nw (%)	3.9	21.5	56.4
EFFICIENCY			
Coll Period (days)	28.5	45.6	64.6
Sales To Inv (times)	12.4	8.0	5.0
Assets To Sales (%)	59.7	136.5	333.6
Sales To Nwc (times)	5.8	2.6	0.8
Acct Pay To Sales (%)	4.4	8.4	18.1
PROFITABILITY			
Return On Sales (%)	8.2	1.1	(138.7)
Return On Assets (%)	7.7	(2.5)	(59.1)
Return On Nw (%)	16.7	4.2	(42.7)

SIC 2819 IND INORG CHEM,NEC
(NO BREAKDOWN)
2013 (17 Establishments)

	$	%
Cash	44,636,892	14.1
Accounts Receivable	42,737,450	13.5
Notes Receivable	0	0.0
Inventory	55,716,972	17.6
Other Current	27,541,912	8.7
Total Current	**170,633,226**	**53.9**
Fixed Assets	71,229,083	22.5
Other Non-current	74,711,395	23.6
Total Assets	**316,573,704**	**100.0**
Accounts Payable	78,193,705	24.7
Bank Loans	0	0.0
Notes Payable	36,405,976	11.5
Other Current	26,592,191	8.4
Total Current	**141,191,872**	**44.6**
Other Long Term	87,690,916	27.7
Deferred Credits	633,147	0.2
Net Worth	87,057,769	27.5
Total Liab & Net Worth	**316,573,704**	**100.0**
Net Sales	317,845,084	100.0
Gross Profit	107,749,483	33.9
Net Profit After Tax	12,713,803	4.0
Working Capital	29,441,354	—

RATIOS	UQ	MED	LQ
SOLVENCY			
Quick Ratio (times)	2.8	1.5	1.1
Current Ratio (times)	4.4	2.2	2.1
Curr Liab To Nw (%)	14.2	31.3	85.2
Curr Liab To Inv (%)	100.3	122.0	192.2
Total Liab To Nw (%)	33.9	93.9	341.4
Fixed Assets To Nw (%)	25.5	41.8	111.4
EFFICIENCY			
Coll Period (days)	35.4	43.8	58.1
Sales To Inv (times)	10.4	8.1	5.6
Assets To Sales (%)	52.7	99.6	138.5
Sales To Nwc (times)	5.9	3.8	2.1
Acct Pay To Sales (%)	5.9	8.1	9.4
PROFITABILITY			
Return On Sales (%)	13.9	3.1	0.4
Return On Assets (%)	13.8	4.8	0.3
Return On Nw (%)	35.3	12.9	3.5

SIC 2833 MEDCNLS,BOTANICALS
(NO BREAKDOWN)
2013 (16 Establishments)

	$	%
Cash	4,645,833	23.5
Accounts Receivable	(533,777)	(2.7)
Notes Receivable	0	0.0
Inventory	3,538,741	17.9
Other Current	3,024,733	15.3
Total Current	**10,675,530**	**54.0**
Fixed Assets	3,756,205	19.0
Other Non-current	5,337,765	27.0
Total Assets	**19,769,500**	**100.0**
Accounts Payable	15,262,054	77.2
Bank Loans	0	0.0
Notes Payable	0	0.0
Other Current	134,254,675	679.1
Total Current	**149,516,729**	**756.3**
Other Long Term	10,576,682	53.5
Deferred Credits	0	0.0
Net Worth	(140,323,911)	(709.8)
Total Liab & Net Worth	**19,769,500**	**100.0**
Net Sales	20,172,959	100.0
Gross Profit	9,824,231	48.7
Net Profit After Tax	161,384	0.8
Working Capital	(138,841,199)	—

RATIOS	UQ	MED	LQ
SOLVENCY			
Quick Ratio (times)	1.5	1.0	0.7
Current Ratio (times)	3.0	2.3	1.5
Curr Liab To Nw (%)	15.8	29.5	50.1
Curr Liab To Inv (%)	64.8	114.4	202.9
Total Liab To Nw (%)	39.5	56.9	139.0
Fixed Assets To Nw (%)	18.8	35.2	52.0
EFFICIENCY			
Coll Period (days)	19.7	29.9	38.0
Sales To Inv (times)	9.4	6.3	4.3
Assets To Sales (%)	71.3	98.0	160.6
Sales To Nwc (times)	6.5	4.3	3.0
Acct Pay To Sales (%)	6.8	8.2	22.9
PROFITABILITY			
Return On Sales (%)	9.6	2.8	(201.4)
Return On Assets (%)	11.8	2.7	(52.4)
Return On Nw (%)	20.8	9.1	3.9

	SIC 2834 PHRMCTCL PREPRTNS (NO BREAKDOWN) 2013 (239 Establishments)		SIC 2835 DGNOSTIC SUBSTANCES (NO BREAKDOWN) 2013 (23 Establishments)		SIC 2836 BIOL PRD,EXC DGNSTC (NO BREAKDOWN) 2013 (29 Establishments)		SIC 2842 POLISHES,SANT GOODS (NO BREAKDOWN) 2013 (17 Establishments)	
	$	%	$	%	$	%	$	%
Cash	27,627,726	43.8	16,678,719	34.8	22,820,422	46.7	1,057,631	11.4
Accounts Receivable	2,838,465	4.5	4,265,534	8.9	2,443,300	5.0	1,475,116	15.9
Notes Receivable	189,231	0.3	0	0.0	0	0.0	0	0.0
Inventory	2,775,388	4.4	3,738,334	7.8	2,247,836	4.6	2,031,764	21.9
Other Current	13,750,786	21.8	8,578,996	17.9	8,649,282	17.7	964,856	10.4
Total Current	**47,181,596**	**74.8**	**33,261,583**	**69.4**	**36,160,840**	**74.0**	**5,529,367**	**59.6**
Fixed Assets	4,478,467	7.1	4,648,953	9.7	3,420,620	7.0	2,180,203	23.5
Other Non-current	11,416,937	18.1	10,016,817	20.9	9,284,540	19.0	1,567,891	16.9
Total Assets	**63,077,000**	**100.0**	**47,927,353**	**100.0**	**48,866,000**	**100.0**	**9,277,461**	**100.0**
Accounts Payable	58,220,071	92.3	5,847,137	12.2	3,371,754	6.9	2,913,123	31.4
Bank Loans	0	0.0	0	0.0	0	0.0	46,387	0.5
Notes Payable	8,389,241	13.3	10,831,582	22.6	977,320	2.0	241,214	2.6
Other Current	21,572,334	34.2	17,253,847	36.0	51,993,424	106.4	2,653,354	28.6
Total Current	**88,181,646**	**139.8**	**33,932,566**	**70.8**	**56,342,498**	**115.3**	**5,854,078**	**63.1**
Other Long Term	60,301,612	95.6	8,243,505	17.2	16,565,574	33.9	2,829,625	30.5
Deferred Credits	3,847,697	6.1	527,201	1.1	684,124	1.4	0	0.0
Net Worth	(89,253,955)	(141.5)	5,224,081	10.9	(24,726,196)	(50.6)	593,758	6.4
Total Liab & Net Worth	**63,077,000**	**100.0**	**47,927,353**	**100.0**	**48,866,000**	**100.0**	**9,277,461**	**100.0**
Net Sales	21,345,854	100.0	30,960,822	100.0	15,361,836	100.0	15,036,404	100.0
Gross Profit	12,572,708	58.9	19,629,161	63.4	11,168,055	72.7	6,405,508	42.6
Net Profit After Tax	(1,280,751)	(6.0)	557,295	1.8	15,362	0.1	842,039	5.6
Working Capital	(41,000,050)	---	(670,983)	---	(20,181,658)	---	(324,711)	---

RATIOS	UQ	MED	LQ	UQ	MED	LQ	UQ	MED	LQ	UQ	MED	LQ
SOLVENCY												
Quick Ratio (times)	4.3	2.0	1.0	5.0	3.2	2.5	4.9	2.8	1.0	1.8	1.1	0.5
Current Ratio (times)	7.6	3.5	1.7	8.6	5.8	3.3	9.2	3.5	2.0	4.2	2.5	1.2
Curr Liab To Nw (%)	10.2	23.5	60.6	10.2	11.9	19.2	8.3	24.9	53.9	20.9	37.2	49.8
Curr Liab To Inv (%)	195.0	412.5	790.9	68.5	153.3	188.6	95.8	263.2	366.4	69.3	122.8	239.4
Total Liab To Nw (%)	17.1	55.3	136.2	14.3	21.4	54.0	14.2	46.7	110.2	23.6	69.9	78.3
Fixed Assets To Nw (%)	0.6	4.1	20.3	10.5	14.6	19.5	1.6	9.4	19.0	12.0	37.3	105.4
EFFICIENCY												
Coll Period (days)	31.4	55.5	89.8	44.4	55.9	69.6	21.9	39.8	59.9	31.6	38.0	46.0
Sales To Inv (times)	12.5	7.5	4.4	8.8	6.3	5.0	9.9	6.8	5.8	10.2	6.7	5.1
Assets To Sales (%)	156.0	295.5	999.9	93.7	154.8	328.3	176.9	318.1	929.8	43.3	61.7	76.7
Sales To Nwc (times)	2.2	0.8	0.2	2.1	1.5	0.8	1.0	0.5	0.1	8.6	4.8	3.2
Acct Pay To Sales (%)	5.7	14.0	84.9	3.0	4.4	8.6	12.5	22.0	63.2	3.6	6.4	9.2
PROFITABILITY												
Return On Sales (%)	3.3	(100.1)	(999.9)	5.9	(2.3)	(11.9)	13.0	(110.0)	(603.7)	7.4	4.0	1.0
Return On Assets (%)	(2.9)	)(42.6	(89.6)	5.8	(2.0)	(19.4)	(10.3)	)(47.1	(74.9)	11.0	7.7	1.7
Return On Nw (%)	4.0	(36.8)	(103.7)	10.5	(3.4)	(15.6)	15.2	(27.3)	(124.9)	22.5	13.3	7.3

	SIC 2844 TOILET PREPARATIONS (NO BREAKDOWN) 2013 (23 Establishments)		SIC 2851 PAINTS,ALLIED PRDTS (NO BREAKDOWN) 2013 (21 Establishments)		SIC 2869 IND ORG CHEM, NEC (NO BREAKDOWN) 2013 (47 Establishments)		SIC 2873 NITROGENOUS FRTLZRS (NO BREAKDOWN) 2013 (10 Establishments)	
	$	%	$	%	$	%	$	%
Cash	3,108,798	11.8	869,671	16.6	10,325,932	17.3	4,668,802	12.9
Accounts Receivable	4,873,964	18.5	927,300	17.7	6,625,309	11.1	6,586,991	18.2
Notes Receivable	0	0.0	15,717	0.3	1,134,062	1.9	108,577	0.3
Inventory	6,665,474	25.3	1,273,073	24.3	5,252,497	8.8	6,044,107	16.7
Other Current	2,766,304	10.5	440,075	8.4	3,999,061	6.7	1,447,690	4.0
Total Current	**17,414,540**	**66.1**	**3,525,836**	**67.3**	**27,336,861**	**45.8**	**18,856,167**	**52.1**
Fixed Assets	2,924,378	11.1	832,998	15.9	26,143,111	43.8	14,151,174	39.1
Other Non-current	6,006,831	22.8	880,149	16.8	6,207,497	10.4	3,184,919	8.8
Total Assets	**26,345,749**	**100.0**	**5,238,983**	**100.0**	**59,687,469**	**100.0**	**36,192,260**	**100.0**
Accounts Payable	3,240,527	12.3	812,042	15.5	99,797,448	167.2	44,588,864	123.2
Bank Loans	0	0.0	0	0.0	0	0.0	108,577	0.3
Notes Payable	158,074	0.6	529,137	10.1	5,670,310	9.5	19,218,090	53.1
Other Current	8,246,220	31.3	11,028,060	210.5	(15,279,992)	(25.6)	291,420,078	805.2
Total Current	**11,644,821**	**44.2**	**12,369,239**	**236.1**	**90,187,766**	**151.1**	**355,335,609**	**981.8**
Other Long Term	6,270,288	23.8	644,395	12.3	97,469,636	163.3	(114,258,965)	(315.7)
Deferred Credits	0	0.0	10,478	0.2	119,375	0.2	0	0.0
Net Worth	8,430,640	32.0	(7,785,129)	(148.6)	(128,089,308)	(214.6)	(204,884,384)	(566.1)
Total Liab & Net Worth	**26,345,749**	**100.0**	**5,238,983**	**100.0**	**59,687,469**	**100.0**	**36,192,260**	**100.0**
Net Sales	35,844,556	100.0	9,979,015	100.0	101,509,301	100.0	59,920,960	100.0
Gross Profit	20,503,086	57.2	3,103,474	31.1	22,129,028	21.8	20,433,047	34.1
Net Profit After Tax	1,541,316	4.3	(149,685)	(1.5)	710,565	0.7	10,606,010	17.7
Working Capital	5,769,719	—	(8,843,403)	—	(62,850,905)	—	(336,479,442)	—

RATIOS	UQ	MED	LQ	UQ	MED	LQ	UQ	MED	LQ	UQ	MED	LQ
SOLVENCY												
Quick Ratio (times)	1.5	0.9	0.8	2.9	1.2	0.7	2.1	1.2	0.4	2.3	1.5	0.7
Current Ratio (times)	3.2	2.2	1.6	3.7	2.4	1.3	3.6	1.9	1.0	3.9	2.8	1.4
Curr Liab To Nw (%)	24.2	51.4	93.7	16.7	41.2	62.4	11.4	26.8	43.3	12.8	24.2	99.5
Curr Liab To Inv (%)	72.2	107.5	228.7	63.1	111.5	198.7	92.5	148.1	465.3	82.8	162.8	188.3
Total Liab To Nw (%)	37.5	65.2	167.5	16.7	58.3	196.3	18.8	49.9	139.1	24.8	62.3	120.3
Fixed Assets To Nw (%)	6.9	20.7	45.2	9.6	23.1	52.6	46.8	77.6	123.4	39.6	57.7	75.4
EFFICIENCY												
Coll Period (days)	42.0	51.7	59.5	25.9	38.0	62.1	10.4	21.2	56.6	8.4	21.9	28.5
Sales To Inv (times)	8.5	5.5	4.5	8.3	7.4	6.7	34.2	19.5	6.9	14.4	10.0	9.8
Assets To Sales (%)	57.3	73.5	117.8	32.3	52.5	98.1	42.1	58.8	136.1	27.7	60.4	130.5
Sales To Nwc (times)	6.1	4.4	3.0	5.2	4.8	4.2	19.1	8.9	1.6	9.6	6.6	3.9
Acct Pay To Sales (%)	4.7	7.7	11.1	3.1	7.9	18.3	1.4	3.7	10.4	3.5	5.0	8.2
PROFITABILITY												
Return On Sales (%)	10.1	3.0	(0.4)	6.0	2.5	(1.1)	8.6	2.5	(13.6)	28.0	6.1	3.1
Return On Assets (%)	17.4	4.0	(0.3)	7.4	4.0	(5.4)	15.3	0.9	(17.2)	20.0	15.0	10.2
Return On Nw (%)	32.2	12.5	4.7	25.8	12.1	5.6	24.6	10.5	(7.2)	28.2	25.3	14.3

SIC 2879 AGRCLTRL CHEM,NEC
(NO BREAKDOWN)
2013 (12 Establishments)

	$	%
Cash	3,709,139	9.9
Accounts Receivable	3,671,673	9.8
Notes Receivable	0	0.0
Inventory	10,640,360	28.4
Other Current	5,470,044	14.6
Total Current	**23,491,216**	**62.7**
Fixed Assets	7,156,017	19.1
Other Non-current	6,818,822	18.2
Total Assets	**37,466,055**	**100.0**
Accounts Payable	224,009,543	597.9
Bank Loans	0	0.0
Notes Payable	288,601,022	770.3
Other Current	(237,384,925)	(633.6)
Total Current	**275,225,640**	**734.6**
Other Long Term	5,170,316	13.8
Deferred Credits	74,932	0.2
Net Worth	(243,004,833)	(648.6)
Total Liab & Net Worth	**37,466,055**	**100.0**
Net Sales	42,672,044	100.0
Gross Profit	14,081,775	33.0
Net Profit After Tax	2,090,930	4.9
Working Capital	(251,734,424)	—

RATIOS	UQ	MED	LQ
SOLVENCY			
Quick Ratio (times)	1.4	0.7	0.2
Current Ratio (times)	4.2	2.1	1.4
Curr Liab To Nw (%)	28.1	41.7	82.1
Curr Liab To Inv (%)	65.7	123.9	298.2
Total Liab To Nw (%)	40.4	63.6	121.2
Fixed Assets To Nw (%)	22.5	41.2	62.7
EFFICIENCY			
Coll Period (days)	35.8	38.7	61.0
Sales To Inv (times)	9.9	4.8	3.0
Assets To Sales (%)	40.1	87.8	140.8
Sales To Nwc (times)	7.1	3.0	2.6
Acct Pay To Sales (%)	4.4	10.0	14.3
PROFITABILITY			
Return On Sales (%)	11.2	4.3	(9.6)
Return On Assets (%)	8.5	6.1	(20.6)
Return On Nw (%)	20.4	14.5	6.0

SIC 2891 ADHESIVES,SEALANTS
(NO BREAKDOWN)
2013 (11 Establishments)

	$	%
Cash	2,724,848	12.2
Accounts Receivable	4,154,277	18.6
Notes Receivable	0	0.0
Inventory	4,868,991	21.8
Other Current	982,732	4.4
Total Current	**12,730,848**	**57.0**
Fixed Assets	6,722,781	30.1
Other Non-current	2,881,192	12.9
Total Assets	**22,334,821**	**100.0**
Accounts Payable	2,367,491	10.6
Bank Loans	0	0.0
Notes Payable	22,335	0.1
Other Current	3,037,536	13.6
Total Current	**5,427,362**	**24.3**
Other Long Term	2,925,861	13.1
Deferred Credits	0	0.0
Net Worth	13,981,598	62.6
Total Liab & Net Worth	**22,334,821**	**100.0**
Net Sales	39,883,609	100.0
Gross Profit	13,121,707	32.9
Net Profit After Tax	1,395,926	3.5
Working Capital	7,303,486	—

RATIOS	UQ	MED	LQ
SOLVENCY			
Quick Ratio (times)	3.3	1.3	0.9
Current Ratio (times)	4.9	2.6	1.5
Curr Liab To Nw (%)	14.9	38.8	66.1
Curr Liab To Inv (%)	73.8	133.2	153.4
Total Liab To Nw (%)	26.2	61.3	98.0
Fixed Assets To Nw (%)	32.7	46.7	71.7
EFFICIENCY			
Coll Period (days)	29.2	45.6	54.4
Sales To Inv (times)	12.5	10.8	8.3
Assets To Sales (%)	49.9	56.0	61.3
Sales To Nwc (times)	13.4	7.1	4.2
Acct Pay To Sales (%)	2.5	4.7	9.7
PROFITABILITY			
Return On Sales (%)	5.2	4.2	0.6
Return On Assets (%)	6.8	5.2	1.2
Return On Nw (%)	15.8	10.0	3.0

SIC 2899 CHEM PRPRTNS, NEC
(NO BREAKDOWN)
2013 (20 Establishments)

	$	%
Cash	2,153,489	13.3
Accounts Receivable	3,011,646	18.6
Notes Receivable	32,383	0.2
Inventory	3,108,795	19.2
Other Current	1,764,889	10.9
Total Current	**10,071,202**	**62.2**
Fixed Assets	3,837,419	23.7
Other Non-current	2,283,022	14.1
Total Assets	**16,191,643**	**100.0**
Accounts Payable	1,700,123	10.5
Bank Loans	420,983	2.6
Notes Payable	210,491	1.3
Other Current	9,245,428	57.1
Total Current	**11,577,025**	**71.5**
Other Long Term	5,148,942	31.8
Deferred Credits	16,192	0.1
Net Worth	(550,516)	(3.4)
Total Liab & Net Worth	**16,191,643**	**100.0**
Net Sales	28,208,437	100.0
Gross Profit	11,424,417	40.5
Net Profit After Tax	(535,960)	(1.9)
Working Capital	(1,505,823)	—

RATIOS	UQ	MED	LQ
SOLVENCY			
Quick Ratio (times)	2.6	1.1	0.8
Current Ratio (times)	3.9	2.4	1.5
Curr Liab To Nw (%)	24.8	37.9	80.5
Curr Liab To Inv (%)	87.7	145.6	262.1
Total Liab To Nw (%)	30.0	104.6	189.1
Fixed Assets To Nw (%)	27.8	62.4	96.1
EFFICIENCY			
Coll Period (days)	38.3	51.5	68.6
Sales To Inv (times)	13.4	8.7	5.7
Assets To Sales (%)	45.3	57.4	133.1
Sales To Nwc (times)	9.0	4.6	2.8
Acct Pay To Sales (%)	4.0	6.3	10.7
PROFITABILITY			
Return On Sales (%)	7.1	3.6	0.8
Return On Assets (%)	10.1	5.3	0.9
Return On Nw (%)	14.9	12.8	3.8

SIC 29 PETRO RFNG RLTD IND
(NO BREAKDOWN)
2013 (49 Establishments)

	$	%
Cash	22,919,100	12.5
Accounts Receivable	34,470,326	18.8
Notes Receivable	183,353	0.1
Inventory	23,652,511	12.9
Other Current	13,201,401	7.2
Total Current	**94,426,691**	**51.5**
Fixed Assets	60,689,776	33.1
Other Non-current	28,236,331	15.4
Total Assets	**183,352,798**	**100.0**
Accounts Payable	34,470,326	18.8
Bank Loans	0	0.0
Notes Payable	1,650,175	0.9
Other Current	70,774,180	38.6
Total Current	**106,894,681**	**58.3**
Other Long Term	45,838,200	25.0
Deferred Credits	183,353	0.1
Net Worth	30,436,564	16.6
Total Liab & Net Worth	**183,352,798**	**100.0**
Net Sales	445,031,063	100.0
Gross Profit	89,006,213	20.0
Net Profit After Tax	8,010,559	1.8
Working Capital	(12,467,990)	—

RATIOS	UQ	MED	LQ
SOLVENCY			
Quick Ratio (times)	1.4	0.9	0.6
Current Ratio (times)	2.6	1.6	1.1
Curr Liab To Nw (%)	36.5	60.0	106.2
Curr Liab To Inv (%)	116.5	239.5	481.0
Total Liab To Nw (%)	68.2	125.4	212.7
Fixed Assets To Nw (%)	34.9	82.7	118.5
EFFICIENCY			
Coll Period (days)	12.8	25.2	49.3
Sales To Inv (times)	30.0	17.6	11.3
Assets To Sales (%)	26.0	41.2	83.1
Sales To Nwc (times)	24.5	11.5	5.4
Acct Pay To Sales (%)	4.5	6.9	10.3
PROFITABILITY			
Return On Sales (%)	5.9	2.1	0.1
Return On Assets (%)	13.0	5.5	0.0
Return On Nw (%)	29.6	13.5	2.5

SIC 30 — RUBBER & PLASTICS (NO BREAKDOWN) — 2013 (156 Establishments)
SIC 3069 — FBRTD RBBR PRDS,NEC (NO BREAKDOWN) — 2013 (18 Establishments)
SIC 3089 — PLSTCS PRODUCTS,NEC (NO BREAKDOWN) — 2013 (94 Establishments)
SIC 31 — LEATHER,LEATHER PDTS (NO BREAKDOWN) — 2013 (14 Establishments)

	SIC 30 $	SIC 30 %	SIC 3069 $	SIC 3069 %	SIC 3089 $	SIC 3089 %	SIC 31 $	SIC 31 %
Cash	1,122,075	17.4	474,253	20.0	981,760	16.2	29,771,485	12.5
Accounts Receivable	1,341,331	20.8	578,588	24.4	1,296,892	21.4	38,583,844	16.2
Notes Receivable	0	0.0	0	0.0	0	0.0	0	0.0
Inventory	1,386,472	21.5	441,055	18.6	1,339,314	22.1	75,262,314	31.6
Other Current	335,332	5.2	118,564	5.0	327,253	5.4	16,910,203	7.1
Total Current	**4,185,210**	**64.9**	**1,612,460**	**68.0**	**3,945,219**	**65.1**	**160,527,846**	**67.4**
Fixed Assets	1,618,625	25.1	545,391	23.0	1,454,459	24.0	23,817,188	10.0
Other Non-current	644,870	10.0	213,413	9.0	660,567	10.9	53,826,845	22.6
Total Assets	**6,448,705**	**100.0**	**2,371,264**	**100.0**	**6,060,245**	**100.0**	**238,171,879**	**100.0**
Accounts Payable	4,694,657	72.8	123,306	5.2	4,914,859	81.1	21,435,469	9.0
Bank Loans	19,346	0.3	4,743	0.2	30,301	0.5	0	0.0
Notes Payable	90,282	1.4	42,683	1.8	90,904	1.5	0	0.0
Other Current	870,575	13.5	260,838	11.0	(812,073)	(13.4)	30,009,657	12.6
Total Current	**5,674,860**	**88.0**	**431,570**	**18.2**	**4,223,991**	**69.7**	**51,445,126**	**21.6**
Other Long Term	986,652	15.3	177,845	7.5	987,820	16.3	32,391,375	13.6
Deferred Credits	0	0.0	2,371	0.1	6,060	0.1	0	0.0
Net Worth	(212,807)	(3.3)	1,759,478	74.2	842,374	13.9	154,335,378	64.8
Total Liab & Net Worth	**6,448,705**	**100.0**	**2,371,264**	**100.0**	**6,060,245**	**100.0**	**238,171,879**	**100.0**
Net Sales	12,377,553	100.0	5,619,109	100.0	11,721,944	100.0	361,963,342	100.0
Gross Profit	3,552,358	28.7	2,084,689	37.1	3,399,364	29.0	142,975,520	39.5
Net Profit After Tax	705,521	5.7	466,386	8.3	750,204	6.4	21,717,801	6.0
Working Capital	(1,489,650)	--	1,180,890	--	(278,772)	--	109,082,720	--

RATIOS

	SIC 30 UQ	SIC 30 MED	SIC 30 LQ	SIC 3069 UQ	SIC 3069 MED	SIC 3069 LQ	SIC 3089 UQ	SIC 3089 MED	SIC 3089 LQ	SIC 31 UQ	SIC 31 MED	SIC 31 LQ
SOLVENCY												
Quick Ratio (times)	2.7	1.3	0.8	5.0	2.5	1.7	2.7	1.1	0.7	1.9	1.7	0.8
Current Ratio (times)	4.7	2.6	1.5	6.4	4.2	2.8	4.5	2.2	1.4	4.7	3.7	2.9
Curr Liab To Nw (%)	14.8	35.2	80.0	12.7	24.7	41.1	14.5	43.9	90.9	22.6	24.5	30.8
Curr Liab To Inv (%)	74.4	120.2	184.0	40.4	98.0	152.2	71.7	124.6	197.3	40.1	75.8	105.5
Total Liab To Nw (%)	23.3	55.0	137.0	12.7	26.9	57.7	25.0	65.9	166.2	29.7	40.2	51.7
Fixed Assets To Nw (%)	19.3	41.9	73.1	11.3	33.8	47.5	19.8	43.2	72.2	4.8	16.0	28.8
EFFICIENCY												
Coll Period (days)	34.7	44.2	53.0	34.4	40.2	45.7	34.9	47.0	54.6	22.6	34.1	53.7
Sales To Inv (times)	14.8	8.8	6.0	23.6	14.3	6.9	15.5	8.8	5.9	8.7	5.7	4.1
Assets To Sales (%)	40.0	52.1	76.6	31.5	42.2	63.1	39.9	51.7	76.1	40.2	65.8	88.6
Sales To Nwc (times)	8.4	5.3	3.1	5.3	4.7	2.8	9.3	5.3	3.3	4.9	3.8	3.1
Acct Pay To Sales (%)	2.7	4.9	7.9	1.5	2.9	3.7	3.0	5.1	8.2	4.6	5.0	7.5
PROFITABILITY												
Return On Sales (%)	9.1	3.5	1.5	8.2	4.0	2.6	9.8	4.1	1.8	11.7	3.5	2.6
Return On Assets (%)	15.6	7.4	2.0	20.7	10.8	6.7	17.8	8.5	2.0	15.1	8.2	3.9
Return On Nw (%)	27.5	12.6	5.3	26.0	14.3	8.5	36.3	14.0	7.7	19.6	13.4	7.1

SIC 32 — STONE CLAY,GLASS PDT (NO BREAKDOWN) — 2013 (90 Establishments)

	$	%
Cash	914,371	16.0
Accounts Receivable	1,205,826	21.1
Notes Receivable	11,430	0.2
Inventory	840,078	14.7
Other Current	400,036	7.0
Total Current	**3,371,741**	**59.0**
Fixed Assets	1,725,874	30.2
Other Non-current	617,201	10.8
Total Assets	**5,714,816**	**100.0**
Accounts Payable	554,337	9.7
Bank Loans	11,430	0.2
Notes Payable	57,148	1.0
Other Current	754,356	13.2
Total Current	**1,377,271**	**24.1**
Other Long Term	1,251,545	21.9
Deferred Credits	17,144	0.3
Net Worth	3,068,856	53.7
Total Liab & Net Worth	**5,714,816**	**100.0**
Net Sales	9,524,693	100.0
Gross Profit	2,819,309	29.6
Net Profit After Tax	457,185	4.8
Working Capital	1,994,470	---

RATIOS	UQ	MED	LQ
SOLVENCY			
Quick Ratio (times)	2.6	1.5	1.1
Current Ratio (times)	4.5	3.0	1.8
Curr Liab To Nw (%)	17.5	29.2	60.6
Curr Liab To Inv (%)	72.9	170.8	320.0
Total Liab To Nw (%)	29.5	52.4	113.9
Fixed Assets To Nw (%)	22.9	49.5	86.4
EFFICIENCY			
Coll Period (days)	33.5	44.5	60.3
Sales To Inv (times)	23.7	12.2	6.2
Assets To Sales (%)	39.8	60.0	98.2
Sales To Nwc (times)	8.1	4.6	3.1
Acct Pay To Sales (%)	3.0	4.6	9.2
PROFITABILITY			
Return On Sales (%)	7.9	3.5	0.9
Return On Assets (%)	13.0	4.5	1.1
Return On Nw (%)	18.2	9.2	2.5

SIC 3272 — CONCRETE PRDCTS,NEC (NO BREAKDOWN) — 2013 (21 Establishments)

	$	%
Cash	715,680	14.6
Accounts Receivable	1,387,243	28.3
Notes Receivable	19,608	0.4
Inventory	465,682	9.5
Other Current	622,545	12.7
Total Current	**3,210,758**	**65.5**
Fixed Assets	1,264,695	25.8
Other Non-current	426,467	8.7
Total Assets	**4,901,920**	**100.0**
Accounts Payable	416,663	8.5
Bank Loans	0	0.0
Notes Payable	29,412	0.6
Other Current	946,070	19.3
Total Current	**1,392,145**	**28.4**
Other Long Term	607,838	12.4
Deferred Credits	24,510	0.5
Net Worth	2,877,427	58.7
Total Liab & Net Worth	**4,901,920**	**100.0**
Net Sales	9,784,271	100.0
Gross Profit	3,248,378	33.2
Net Profit After Tax	469,645	4.8
Working Capital	1,818,613	---

RATIOS	UQ	MED	LQ
SOLVENCY			
Quick Ratio (times)	3.5	1.8	1.2
Current Ratio (times)	4.9	3.2	1.8
Curr Liab To Nw (%)	17.8	27.7	47.4
Curr Liab To Inv (%)	148.4	222.5	351.2
Total Liab To Nw (%)	29.4	53.4	80.7
Fixed Assets To Nw (%)	12.5	37.9	68.0
EFFICIENCY			
Coll Period (days)	29.6	56.9	82.5
Sales To Inv (times)	36.8	23.1	13.3
Assets To Sales (%)	38.2	50.1	67.3
Sales To Nwc (times)	8.8	7.4	4.0
Acct Pay To Sales (%)	2.8	3.4	5.3
PROFITABILITY			
Return On Sales (%)	6.2	2.3	0.3
Return On Assets (%)	16.3	4.4	1.0
Return On Nw (%)	24.2	8.5	2.3

SIC 3273 — READY-MIX CONCRETE (NO BREAKDOWN) — 2013 (14 Establishments)

	$	%
Cash	521,342	20.8
Accounts Receivable	528,861	21.1
Notes Receivable	0	0.0
Inventory	182,971	7.3
Other Current	57,648	2.3
Total Current	**1,290,822**	**51.5**
Fixed Assets	887,283	35.4
Other Non-current	328,345	13.1
Total Assets	**2,506,450**	**100.0**
Accounts Payable	228,087	9.1
Bank Loans	0	0.0
Notes Payable	42,610	1.7
Other Current	160,412	6.4
Total Current	**431,109**	**17.2**
Other Long Term	541,393	21.6
Deferred Credits	20,052	0.8
Net Worth	1,513,896	60.4
Total Liab & Net Worth	**2,506,450**	**100.0**
Net Sales	5,925,414	100.0
Gross Profit	1,647,265	27.8
Net Profit After Tax	94,807	1.6
Working Capital	859,713	---

RATIOS	UQ	MED	LQ
SOLVENCY			
Quick Ratio (times)	3.2	1.9	1.4
Current Ratio (times)	3.7	2.5	2.2
Curr Liab To Nw (%)	15.2	31.3	40.0
Curr Liab To Inv (%)	151.5	320.5	458.1
Total Liab To Nw (%)	33.4	53.4	125.5
Fixed Assets To Nw (%)	49.5	60.5	92.3
EFFICIENCY			
Coll Period (days)	27.7	35.2	40.5
Sales To Inv (times)	85.0	26.9	22.3
Assets To Sales (%)	39.6	42.3	64.8
Sales To Nwc (times)	8.9	5.3	4.6
Acct Pay To Sales (%)	3.4	4.6	6.1
PROFITABILITY			
Return On Sales (%)	2.6	1.4	(1.3)
Return On Assets (%)	6.9	2.5	(1.7)
Return On Nw (%)	13.4	3.6	(2.8)

SIC 33 — PRIMARY METAL INDS (NO BREAKDOWN) — 2013 (112 Establishments)

	$	%
Cash	4,598,393	12.1
Accounts Receivable	6,992,597	18.4
Notes Receivable	228,019	0.6
Inventory	8,208,701	21.6
Other Current	2,318,199	6.1
Total Current	**22,345,909**	**58.8**
Fixed Assets	11,819,010	31.1
Other Non-current	3,838,327	10.1
Total Assets	**38,003,246**	**100.0**
Accounts Payable	3,800,325	10.0
Bank Loans	114,010	0.3
Notes Payable	684,058	1.8
Other Current	3,724,318	9.8
Total Current	**8,322,711**	**21.9**
Other Long Term	8,284,708	21.8
Deferred Credits	38,003	0.1
Net Worth	21,357,824	56.2
Total Liab & Net Worth	**38,003,246**	**100.0**
Net Sales	53,300,485	100.0
Gross Profit	11,779,407	22.1
Net Profit After Tax	1,545,714	2.9
Working Capital	14,023,198	---

RATIOS	UQ	MED	LQ
SOLVENCY			
Quick Ratio (times)	2.2	1.3	0.9
Current Ratio (times)	4.8	2.7	1.9
Curr Liab To Nw (%)	16.3	31.0	66.4
Curr Liab To Inv (%)	55.7	101.3	154.2
Total Liab To Nw (%)	32.0	68.0	130.7
Fixed Assets To Nw (%)	27.2	51.6	77.4
EFFICIENCY			
Coll Period (days)	34.5	46.4	56.2
Sales To Inv (times)	12.2	7.7	4.5
Assets To Sales (%)	50.6	71.3	113.9
Sales To Nwc (times)	6.7	4.0	2.6
Acct Pay To Sales (%)	4.1	5.8	8.5
PROFITABILITY			
Return On Sales (%)	6.2	3.0	(0.1)
Return On Assets (%)	8.4	3.3	0.0
Return On Nw (%)	14.1	7.0	0.0

SIC 3312 BLST FRNCS,STL MLLS
(NO BREAKDOWN)
2013 (22 Establishments)

	$	%
Cash	40,318,388	8.8
Accounts Receivable	58,644,928	12.8
Notes Receivable	0	0.0
Inventory	80,178,613	17.5
Other Current	24,282,665	5.3
Total Current	**203,424,594**	**44.4**
Fixed Assets	202,050,104	44.1
Other Non-current	52,688,802	11.5
Total Assets	**458,163,500**	**100.0**
Accounts Payable	32,071,445	7.0
Bank Loans	0	0.0
Notes Payable	0	0.0
Other Current	62,768,400	13.7
Total Current	**94,839,845**	**20.7**
Other Long Term	123,704,144	27.0
Deferred Credits	1,374,491	0.3
Net Worth	238,245,020	52.0
Total Liab & Net Worth	**458,163,500**	**100.0**
Net Sales	562,163,804	100.0
Gross Profit	83,762,407	14.9
Net Profit After Tax	12,929,767	2.3
Working Capital	108,584,749	---

RATIOS	UQ	MED	LQ
SOLVENCY			
Quick Ratio (times)	1.8	1.2	0.7
Current Ratio (times)	3.3	2.6	1.9
Curr Liab To Nw (%)	17.0	32.3	41.8
Curr Liab To Inv (%)	74.2	101.3	135.2
Total Liab To Nw (%)	34.4	77.1	130.4
Fixed Assets To Nw (%)	60.7	74.0	96.0
EFFICIENCY			
Coll Period (days)	33.6	43.7	53.5
Sales To Inv (times)	9.5	7.3	4.1
Assets To Sales (%)	53.8	81.5	149.5
Sales To Nwc (times)	8.1	4.3	2.6
Acct Pay To Sales (%)	5.6	8.1	10.1
PROFITABILITY			
Return On Sales (%)	4.3	3.0	1.1
Return On Assets (%)	5.1	2.3	1.6
Return On Nw (%)	9.2	6.1	3.3

SIC 34 FABRICATED METAL PDT
(NO BREAKDOWN)
2013 (492 Establishments)

	$	%
Cash	683,984	17.6
Accounts Receivable	932,705	24.0
Notes Receivable	11,659	0.3
Inventory	746,164	19.2
Other Current	369,195	9.5
Total Current	**2,743,707**	**70.6**
Fixed Assets	866,638	22.3
Other Non-current	275,925	7.1
Total Assets	**3,886,270**	**100.0**
Accounts Payable	439,149	11.3
Bank Loans	27,204	0.7
Notes Payable	38,863	1.0
Other Current	683,983	17.6
Total Current	**1,189,199**	**30.6**
Other Long Term	551,849	14.2
Deferred Credits	7,773	0.2
Net Worth	2,137,449	55.0
Total Liab & Net Worth	**3,886,270**	**100.0**
Net Sales	7,590,371	100.0
Gross Profit	2,390,967	31.5
Net Profit After Tax	379,519	5.0
Working Capital	1,554,508	---

RATIOS	UQ	MED	LQ
SOLVENCY			
Quick Ratio (times)	3.2	1.5	0.8
Current Ratio (times)	5.6	2.8	1.6
Curr Liab To Nw (%)	14.8	37.1	94.5
Curr Liab To Inv (%)	55.2	131.1	276.4
Total Liab To Nw (%)	21.1	54.6	131.8
Fixed Assets To Nw (%)	15.2	31.6	60.2
EFFICIENCY			
Coll Period (days)	32.5	42.7	58.0
Sales To Inv (times)	25.9	12.0	5.7
Assets To Sales (%)	36.9	51.2	71.8
Sales To Nwc (times)	8.5	4.7	2.8
Acct Pay To Sales (%)	1.9	4.1	6.7
PROFITABILITY			
Return On Sales (%)	8.5	3.9	0.9
Return On Assets (%)	16.0	7.2	1.7
Return On Nw (%)	27.5	12.3	3.7

SIC 3429 HAEDWARE, NEC
(NO BREAKDOWN)
2013 (12 Establishments)

	$	%
Cash	986,516	23.1
Accounts Receivable	679,030	15.9
Notes Receivable	0	0.0
Inventory	1,140,258	26.7
Other Current	298,945	7.0
Total Current	**3,104,749**	**72.7**
Fixed Assets	649,136	15.2
Other Non-current	516,746	12.1
Total Assets	**4,270,631**	**100.0**
Accounts Payable	303,215	7.1
Bank Loans	0	0.0
Notes Payable	0	0.0
Other Current	1,268,377	29.7
Total Current	**1,571,592**	**36.8**
Other Long Term	555,182	13.0
Deferred Credits	21,353	0.5
Net Worth	2,122,504	49.7
Total Liab & Net Worth	**4,270,631**	**100.0**
Net Sales	6,510,108	100.0
Gross Profit	2,122,295	32.6
Net Profit After Tax	299,465	4.6
Working Capital	1,533,157	---

RATIOS	UQ	MED	LQ
SOLVENCY			
Quick Ratio (times)	4.4	2.8	0.9
Current Ratio (times)	9.0	6.8	2.1
Curr Liab To Nw (%)	9.1	14.5	31.8
Curr Liab To Inv (%)	20.9	42.3	57.2
Total Liab To Nw (%)	13.7	23.5	90.0
Fixed Assets To Nw (%)	13.2	23.1	33.6
EFFICIENCY			
Coll Period (days)	34.7	47.7	54.0
Sales To Inv (times)	5.5	4.9	4.0
Assets To Sales (%)	61.8	65.6	87.1
Sales To Nwc (times)	3.3	2.6	1.9
Acct Pay To Sales (%)	1.4	3.8	12.1
PROFITABILITY			
Return On Sales (%)	7.9	7.2	4.8
Return On Assets (%)	13.4	8.0	3.1
Return On Nw (%)	17.3	10.7	7.7

SIC 3433 HTNG EQPT,EXC ELEC
(NO BREAKDOWN)
2013 (12 Establishments)

	$	%
Cash	2,214,322	23.7
Accounts Receivable	2,858,997	30.6
Notes Receivable	93,431	1.0
Inventory	1,849,940	19.8
Other Current	411,098	4.4
Total Current	**7,427,788**	**79.5**
Fixed Assets	1,130,519	12.1
Other Non-current	784,822	8.4
Total Assets	**9,343,129**	**100.0**
Accounts Payable	4,634,192	49.6
Bank Loans	0	0.0
Notes Payable	0	0.0
Other Current	5,129,378	54.9
Total Current	**9,763,570**	**104.5**
Other Long Term	868,911	9.3
Deferred Credits	0	0.0
Net Worth	(1,289,352)	(13.8)
Total Liab & Net Worth	**9,343,129**	**100.0**
Net Sales	14,220,896	100.0
Gross Profit	3,853,863	27.1
Net Profit After Tax	(412,406)	(2.9)
Working Capital	(2,335,782)	---

RATIOS	UQ	MED	LQ
SOLVENCY			
Quick Ratio (times)	2.3	1.1	0.8
Current Ratio (times)	3.8	1.8	1.4
Curr Liab To Nw (%)	26.8	67.0	198.1
Curr Liab To Inv (%)	55.5	145.8	999.9
Total Liab To Nw (%)	26.8	95.0	198.1
Fixed Assets To Nw (%)	14.7	21.0	28.5
EFFICIENCY			
Coll Period (days)	43.5	55.1	78.7
Sales To Inv (times)	72.3	10.1	4.6
Assets To Sales (%)	46.9	65.7	83.6
Sales To Nwc (times)	6.9	4.8	2.7
Acct Pay To Sales (%)	4.3	8.9	12.7
PROFITABILITY			
Return On Sales (%)	7.6	3.1	(5.4)
Return On Assets (%)	10.8	5.5	(12.1)
Return On Nw (%)	26.5	13.7	6.5

	SIC 3441 FBRCTED STRCTRL MTL (NO BREAKDOWN) 2013 (93 Establishments) $	%	SIC 3442 MTL DOORS,SASH,TRIM (NO BREAKDOWN) 2013 (16 Establishments) $	%	SIC 3443 FBRCT PLT WK BLR SH (NO BREAKDOWN) 2013 (45 Establishments) $	%	SIC 3444 SHEET METALWORK (NO BREAKDOWN) 2013 (68 Establishments) $	%
Cash	504,403	15.6	828,086	20.9	881,356	23.1	551,642	19.4
Accounts Receivable	908,572	28.1	986,572	24.9	717,294	18.8	679,600	23.9
Notes Receivable	0	0.0	3,962	0.1	7,631	0.2	17,061	0.6
Inventory	452,669	14.0	836,010	21.1	663,878	17.4	486,241	17.1
Other Current	462,370	14.3	372,441	9.4	404,431	10.6	307,100	10.8
Total Current	**2,328,014**	**72.0**	**3,027,071**	**76.4**	**2,674,590**	**70.1**	**2,041,644**	**71.8**
Fixed Assets	724,271	22.4	570,547	14.4	751,632	19.7	676,757	23.8
Other Non-current	181,068	5.6	364,517	9.2	389,170	10.2	125,115	4.4
Total Assets	**3,233,353**	**100.0**	**3,962,135**	**100.0**	**3,815,392**	**100.0**	**2,843,516**	**100.0**
Accounts Payable	397,702	12.3	316,971	8.0	267,077	7.0	281,508	9.9
Bank Loans	9,700	0.3	23,773	0.6	7,631	0.2	17,061	0.6
Notes Payable	22,633	0.7	47,546	1.2	26,708	0.7	36,966	1.3
Other Current	653,138	20.2	606,206	15.3	770,709	20.2	417,997	14.7
Total Current	**1,083,173**	**33.5**	**994,496**	**25.1**	**1,072,125**	**28.1**	**753,532**	**26.5**
Other Long Term	378,302	11.7	320,933	8.1	339,570	8.9	386,718	13.6
Deferred Credits	16,167	0.5	0	0.0	0	0.0	0	0.0
Net Worth	1,755,711	54.3	2,646,706	66.8	2,403,697	63.0	1,703,266	59.9
Total Liab & Net Worth	**3,233,353**	**100.0**	**3,962,135**	**100.0**	**3,815,392**	**100.0**	**2,843,516**	**100.0**
Net Sales	7,698,460	100.0	8,746,435	100.0	7,525,428	100.0	5,756,105	100.0
Gross Profit	2,240,252	29.1	2,912,563	33.3	2,129,696	28.3	1,899,515	33.0
Net Profit After Tax	277,145	3.6	384,843	4.4	391,322	5.2	305,074	5.3
Working Capital	1,244,841	—	2,032,575	—	1,602,465	—	1,288,112	—

RATIOS	UQ	MED	LQ	UQ	MED	LQ	UQ	MED	LQ	UQ	MED	LQ
SOLVENCY												
Quick Ratio (times)	2.5	1.4	0.8	5.2	1.6	1.0	3.0	1.8	0.8	4.0	1.8	0.8
Current Ratio (times)	3.6	2.2	1.6	6.1	3.5	2.8	5.8	2.7	1.5	7.9	3.3	1.8
Curr Liab To Nw (%)	29.1	56.7	103.3	13.5	36.9	49.3	14.6	28.3	72.3	9.8	25.8	87.0
Curr Liab To Inv (%)	114.9	241.7	886.7	68.0	106.1	175.2	62.9	178.6	432.9	57.5	130.9	324.8
Total Liab To Nw (%)	33.0	73.6	123.8	13.5	41.8	116.2	16.3	39.3	97.4	13.6	42.7	146.4
Fixed Assets To Nw (%)	22.8	36.9	58.3	2.9	20.5	50.6	12.5	23.6	45.1	11.7	35.1	65.6
EFFICIENCY												
Coll Period (days)	35.8	46.7	57.1	29.4	39.4	56.4	25.2	37.6	51.5	31.4	38.0	52.4
Sales To Inv (times)	47.5	20.5	12.4	15.7	13.7	8.2	31.1	15.5	6.4	31.4	15.8	8.8
Assets To Sales (%)	31.9	42.0	54.3	30.7	45.3	91.1	37.1	50.7	68.8	29.2	49.4	66.0
Sales To Nwc (times)	10.3	6.5	4.1	6.7	3.5	3.2	7.1	4.2	3.0	9.4	5.5	3.0
Acct Pay To Sales (%)	2.8	4.6	6.9	2.0	2.8	5.1	1.9	2.9	5.6	1.4	3.9	6.4
PROFITABILITY												
Return On Sales (%)	6.5	2.9	0.9	8.7	1.6	0.6	8.5	4.5	0.8	8.7	4.1	1.1
Return On Assets (%)	14.4	6.9	1.8	16.2	4.4	1.4	16.9	7.1	1.9	17.3	8.3	3.3
Return On Nw (%)	25.5	11.7	2.8	22.9	5.6	3.3	28.7	9.7	4.6	47.3	13.8	4.4

SIC 3446 ARCHTCTRL METALWORK
(NO BREAKDOWN)
2013 (14 Establishments)

	$	%
Cash	400,353	17.3
Accounts Receivable	777,565	33.6
Notes Receivable	0	0.0
Inventory	136,537	5.9
Other Current	641,028	27.7
Total Current	**1,955,483**	**84.5**
Fixed Assets	333,242	14.4
Other Non-current	25,456	1.1
Total Assets	**2,314,181**	**100.0**
Accounts Payable	289,273	12.5
Bank Loans	6,943	0.3
Notes Payable	0	0.0
Other Current	335,555	14.5
Total Current	**631,771**	**27.3**
Other Long Term	224,476	9.7
Deferred Credits	0	0.0
Net Worth	1,457,934	63.0
Total Liab & Net Worth	**2,314,181**	**100.0**
Net Sales	5,332,214	100.0
Gross Profit	1,535,678	28.8
Net Profit After Tax	319,933	6.0
Working Capital	1,323,712	—

RATIOS	UQ	MED	LQ
SOLVENCY			
Quick Ratio (times)	3.6	1.9	1.4
Current Ratio (times)	4.6	3.2	2.2
Curr Liab To Nw (%)	23.7	37.0	95.3
Curr Liab To Inv (%)	141.6	419.9	999.9
Total Liab To Nw (%)	27.4	44.2	123.9
Fixed Assets To Nw (%)	11.6	21.5	38.3
EFFICIENCY			
Coll Period (days)	40.4	65.0	112.1
Sales To Inv (times)	261.3	28.9	14.2
Assets To Sales (%)	30.3	43.4	71.0
Sales To Nwc (times)	7.1	3.7	1.9
Acct Pay To Sales (%)	3.7	5.5	7.6
PROFITABILITY			
Return On Sales (%)	12.1	5.6	1.3
Return On Assets (%)	19.4	11.6	5.4
Return On Nw (%)	41.8	19.9	12.3

SIC 3448 PREFBRCTD MTL BLDGS
(NO BREAKDOWN)
2013 (11 Establishments)

	$	%
Cash	451,837	13.1
Accounts Receivable	572,557	16.6
Notes Receivable	0	0.0
Inventory	1,024,393	29.7
Other Current	510,472	14.8
Total Current	**2,559,259**	**74.2**
Fixed Assets	793,301	23.0
Other Non-current	96,576	2.8
Total Assets	**3,449,136**	**100.0**
Accounts Payable	334,566	9.7
Bank Loans	0	0.0
Notes Payable	72,432	2.1
Other Current	576,006	16.7
Total Current	**983,004**	**28.5**
Other Long Term	424,243	12.3
Deferred Credits	0	0.0
Net Worth	2,041,889	59.2
Total Liab & Net Worth	**3,449,136**	**100.0**
Net Sales	7,039,053	100.0
Gross Profit	1,724,568	24.5
Net Profit After Tax	323,796	4.6
Working Capital	1,576,255	—

RATIOS	UQ	MED	LQ
SOLVENCY			
Quick Ratio (times)	1.7	1.2	0.7
Current Ratio (times)	4.6	2.2	1.7
Curr Liab To Nw (%)	25.6	48.4	78.2
Curr Liab To Inv (%)	50.3	127.1	175.0
Total Liab To Nw (%)	36.1	80.4	107.9
Fixed Assets To Nw (%)	19.2	28.2	71.8
EFFICIENCY			
Coll Period (days)	30.9	37.6	39.1
Sales To Inv (times)	12.3	11.8	10.7
Assets To Sales (%)	29.2	49.0	59.0
Sales To Nwc (times)	9.4	7.9	3.4
Acct Pay To Sales (%)	2.3	3.6	6.0
PROFITABILITY			
Return On Sales (%)	7.7	5.0	0.6
Return On Assets (%)	17.0	6.7	2.0
Return On Nw (%)	37.1	8.6	2.9

SIC 3451 SCREW MACHINE PRDTS
(NO BREAKDOWN)
2013 (22 Establishments)

	$	%
Cash	428,574	14.5
Accounts Receivable	638,427	21.6
Notes Receivable	0	0.0
Inventory	774,388	26.2
Other Current	103,449	3.5
Total Current	**1,944,838**	**65.8**
Fixed Assets	839,413	28.4
Other Non-current	171,430	5.8
Total Assets	**2,955,681**	**100.0**
Accounts Payable	221,676	7.5
Bank Loans	29,557	1.0
Notes Payable	2,956	0.1
Other Current	567,490	19.2
Total Current	**821,679**	**27.8**
Other Long Term	750,744	25.4
Deferred Credits	5,911	0.2
Net Worth	1,377,347	46.6
Total Liab & Net Worth	**2,955,681**	**100.0**
Net Sales	4,618,252	100.0
Gross Profit	1,611,770	34.9
Net Profit After Tax	290,950	6.3
Working Capital	1,123,159	—

RATIOS	UQ	MED	LQ
SOLVENCY			
Quick Ratio (times)	3.8	1.3	0.7
Current Ratio (times)	7.1	2.6	1.3
Curr Liab To Nw (%)	13.7	41.8	107.4
Curr Liab To Inv (%)	40.6	93.0	162.3
Total Liab To Nw (%)	21.7	86.8	121.6
Fixed Assets To Nw (%)	22.3	41.4	93.2
EFFICIENCY			
Coll Period (days)	36.1	45.3	54.4
Sales To Inv (times)	8.9	5.3	4.0
Assets To Sales (%)	47.2	64.0	79.1
Sales To Nwc (times)	10.8	3.9	2.2
Acct Pay To Sales (%)	2.9	3.7	6.2
PROFITABILITY			
Return On Sales (%)	10.8	4.3	1.0
Return On Assets (%)	15.2	9.1	1.4
Return On Nw (%)	24.8	12.5	2.4

SIC 3469 METAL STAMPINGS,NEC
(NO BREAKDOWN)
2013 (35 Establishments)

	$	%
Cash	581,619	14.8
Accounts Receivable	939,237	23.9
Notes Receivable	0	0.0
Inventory	911,728	23.2
Other Current	322,249	8.2
Total Current	**2,754,833**	**70.1**
Fixed Assets	1,108,221	28.2
Other Non-current	66,807	1.7
Total Assets	**3,929,861**	**100.0**
Accounts Payable	554,110	14.1
Bank Loans	7,860	0.2
Notes Payable	110,036	2.8
Other Current	664,147	16.9
Total Current	**1,336,153**	**34.0**
Other Long Term	727,024	18.5
Deferred Credits	0	0.0
Net Worth	1,866,684	47.5
Total Liab & Net Worth	**3,929,861**	**100.0**
Net Sales	8,308,374	100.0
Gross Profit	2,542,362	30.6
Net Profit After Tax	240,943	2.9
Working Capital	1,418,680	—

RATIOS	UQ	MED	LQ
SOLVENCY			
Quick Ratio (times)	2.6	1.5	0.7
Current Ratio (times)	3.9	2.5	1.6
Curr Liab To Nw (%)	21.5	46.8	100.5
Curr Liab To Inv (%)	79.1	107.3	249.8
Total Liab To Nw (%)	35.2	77.5	172.6
Fixed Assets To Nw (%)	31.1	57.9	88.9
EFFICIENCY			
Coll Period (days)	28.8	43.8	52.9
Sales To Inv (times)	17.9	10.0	5.3
Assets To Sales (%)	39.3	47.3	71.1
Sales To Nwc (times)	8.9	6.4	3.6
Acct Pay To Sales (%)	2.7	4.8	8.7
PROFITABILITY			
Return On Sales (%)	6.6	1.2	0.2
Return On Assets (%)	10.4	3.8	0.1
Return On Nw (%)	20.2	10.5	0.5

	SIC 3471 PLATING,POLISHING (NO BREAKDOWN) 2013 (17 Establishments)		SIC 3479 MTL CTNG,ALLD SVCS (NO BREAKDOWN) 2013 (18 Establishments)		SIC 3496 MISC FBRCTD WRE PRD (NO BREAKDOWN) 2013 (20 Establishments)		SIC 3499 FBRCTD MTL PRDS,NEC (NO BREAKDOWN) 2013 (18 Establishments)	
	$	%	$	%	$	%	$	%
Cash	598,284	20.8	543,702	19.5	693,219	17.8	1,013,379	25.5
Accounts Receivable	906,056	31.5	925,688	33.2	798,370	20.5	1,013,379	25.5
Notes Receivable	11,505	0.4	36,247	1.3	7,789	0.2	11,922	0.3
Inventory	149,571	5.2	376,409	13.5	1,074,878	27.6	739,171	18.6
Other Current	290,514	10.1	64,129	2.3	159,673	4.1	103,324	2.6
Total Current	**1,955,930**	**68.0**	**1,946,175**	**69.8**	**2,733,929**	**70.2**	**2,881,175**	**72.5**
Fixed Assets	773,743	26.9	663,595	23.8	876,259	22.5	743,145	18.7
Other Non-current	146,694	5.1	178,446	6.4	284,298	7.3	349,715	8.8
Total Assets	**2,876,367**	**100.0**	**2,788,216**	**100.0**	**3,894,486**	**100.0**	**3,974,035**	**100.0**
Accounts Payable	186,964	6.5	337,374	12.1	331,031	8.5	588,157	14.8
Bank Loans	17,258	0.6	36,247	1.3	109,046	2.8	107,299	2.7
Notes Payable	14,382	0.5	0	0.0	27,261	0.7	15,896	0.4
Other Current	204,222	7.1	499,091	17.9	366,082	9.4	886,210	22.3
Total Current	**422,826**	**14.7**	**872,712**	**31.3**	**833,420**	**21.4**	**1,597,562**	**40.2**
Other Long Term	310,648	10.8	373,621	13.4	471,233	12.1	727,248	18.3
Deferred Credits	17,258	0.6	5,576	0.2	27,261	0.7	0	0.0
Net Worth	2,125,635	73.9	1,536,307	55.1	2,562,572	65.8	1,649,225	41.5
Total Liab & Net Worth	**2,876,367**	**100.0**	**2,788,216**	**100.0**	**3,894,486**	**100.0**	**3,974,035**	**100.0**
Net Sales	5,662,140	100.0	6,767,515	100.0	8,791,165	100.0	9,114,759	100.0
Gross Profit	2,230,883	39.4	2,240,047	33.1	2,654,932	30.2	3,199,280	35.1
Net Profit After Tax	271,783	4.8	527,866	7.8	439,558	5.0	364,590	4.0
Working Capital	1,533,104	—	1,073,463	—	1,900,509	—	1,283,613	—

RATIOS	UQ	MED	LQ	UQ	MED	LQ	UQ	MED	LQ	UQ	MED	LQ
SOLVENCY												
Quick Ratio (times)	11.1	4.0	2.7	3.4	1.8	1.0	7.1	2.1	0.8	3.3	1.5	1.0
Current Ratio (times)	11.7	5.3	3.0	4.6	2.1	1.4	15.2	3.5	2.0	5.3	2.7	1.2
Curr Liab To Nw (%)	5.5	15.3	35.8	20.5	58.7	139.6	6.4	23.4	96.0	12.6	23.7	132.7
Curr Liab To Inv (%)	58.3	169.4	357.5	117.5	164.9	761.9	16.2	56.9	102.6	62.6	166.2	228.4
Total Liab To Nw (%)	8.8	22.2	46.8	24.2	114.7	236.4	13.0	41.4	107.8	46.2	55.8	164.8
Fixed Assets To Nw (%)	12.4	41.1	51.8	9.9	36.0	108.5	12.9	27.0	62.7	9.9	36.5	65.6
EFFICIENCY												
Coll Period (days)	40.0	54.2	64.6	34.2	52.6	61.7	33.4	38.7	42.4	21.9	34.5	59.9
Sales To Inv (times)	48.1	39.4	20.3	122.2	13.6	9.1	9.3	5.0	4.5	17.1	9.6	7.1
Assets To Sales (%)	34.9	50.8	62.6	25.4	41.2	54.5	37.5	44.3	74.1	30.0	43.6	75.2
Sales To Nwc (times)	5.5	4.0	3.2	13.2	6.7	3.8	6.1	3.5	2.7	6.8	5.3	2.5
Acct Pay To Sales (%)	1.4	2.7	4.3	1.5	2.7	5.6	1.7	4.3	5.8	3.1	4.3	8.4
PROFITABILITY												
Return On Sales (%)	8.6	4.3	1.2	8.5	4.2	2.4	8.7	2.4	0.5	9.1	2.7	0.8
Return On Assets (%)	14.0	7.3	5.1	20.0	12.9	3.3	9.3	6.3	1.2	12.7	5.2	1.5
Return On Nw (%)	23.1	10.5	6.3	50.9	26.5	6.9	12.5	7.6	1.6	48.6	16.8	10.5

	SIC 35 MACHINERY EX ELECTRL (NO BREAKDOWN) 2013 (674 Establishments) $	%	SIC 3523 FARM MCHNRY,EQPMT (NO BREAKDOWN) 2013 (30 Establishments) $	%	SIC 3531 CONSTR MACHINERY (NO BREAKDOWN) 2013 (30 Establishments) $	%	SIC 3533 OIL,GAS FLD MCHNRY (NO BREAKDOWN) 2013 (20 Establishments) $	%
Cash	819,852	18.7	646,856	16.8	1,365,369	15.0	2,936,033	19.0
Accounts Receivable	920,690	21.0	492,843	12.8	1,511,008	16.6	2,951,486	19.1
Notes Receivable	17,537	0.4	100,109	2.6	18,205	0.2	15,453	0.1
Inventory	876,847	20.0	1,432,325	37.2	2,375,742	26.1	2,920,581	18.9
Other Current	372,660	8.5	277,224	7.2	828,324	9.1	1,483,469	9.6
Total Current	**3,007,586**	**68.6**	**2,949,357**	**76.6**	**6,098,648**	**67.0**	**10,307,022**	**66.7**
Fixed Assets	890,000	20.3	627,605	16.3	1,738,570	19.1	2,688,788	17.4
Other Non-current	486,650	11.1	273,374	7.1	1,265,241	13.9	2,456,997	15.9
Total Assets	**4,384,236**	**100.0**	**3,850,336**	**100.0**	**9,102,459**	**100.0**	**15,452,807**	**100.0**
Accounts Payable	442,808	10.1	331,129	8.6	673,582	7.4	741,735	4.8
Bank Loans	30,690	0.7	19,252	0.5	182,049	2.0	46,358	0.3
Notes Payable	109,606	2.5	103,959	2.7	118,332	1.3	108,170	0.7
Other Current	977,684	22.3	669,958	17.4	1,356,267	14.9	2,611,524	16.9
Total Current	**1,560,788**	**35.6**	**1,124,298**	**29.2**	**2,330,230**	**25.6**	**3,507,787**	**22.7**
Other Long Term	705,862	16.1	581,401	15.1	1,401,778	15.4	1,668,903	10.8
Deferred Credits	35,074	0.8	11,551	0.3	0	0.0	0	0.0
Net Worth	2,082,512	47.5	2,133,086	55.4	5,370,451	59.0	10,276,117	66.5
Total Liab & Net Worth	**4,384,236**	**100.0**	**3,850,336**	**100.0**	**9,102,459**	**100.0**	**15,452,807**	**100.0**
Net Sales	7,405,804	100.0	5,869,415	100.0	15,454,090	100.0	17,480,551	100.0
Gross Profit	2,629,060	35.5	1,778,433	30.3	4,296,237	27.8	6,869,857	39.3
Net Profit After Tax	333,261	4.5	346,295	5.9	324,536	2.1	2,412,316	13.8
Working Capital	1,446,798	—	1,825,059	—	3,768,418	—	6,799,235	—

RATIOS	UQ	MED	LQ	UQ	MED	LQ	UQ	MED	LQ	UQ	MED	LQ
SOLVENCY												
Quick Ratio (times)	2.9	1.4	0.7	2.4	0.7	0.4	1.9	1.3	0.8	3.2	1.3	0.8
Current Ratio (times)	4.7	2.6	1.6	4.2	3.3	2.0	4.0	2.8	2.1	5.8	2.9	2.1
Curr Liab To Nw (%)	16.6	36.9	82.5	24.9	34.1	75.5	21.1	37.9	85.7	15.8	27.8	50.5
Curr Liab To Inv (%)	67.5	134.8	322.9	42.3	63.3	130.2	41.9	79.0	129.0	48.1	93.6	201.4
Total Liab To Nw (%)	24.4	56.4	131.3	26.6	50.1	97.5	29.1	61.0	137.4	25.5	53.8	63.4
Fixed Assets To Nw (%)	12.4	27.3	55.6	14.5	22.1	40.1	16.0	27.4	50.3	9.6	24.3	49.8
EFFICIENCY												
Coll Period (days)	30.3	45.3	62.4	16.8	30.2	54.4	13.5	35.8	60.6	50.6	67.9	92.2
Sales To Inv (times)	19.2	8.4	5.4	7.6	5.6	2.8	8.8	5.9	3.4	7.7	5.8	3.3
Assets To Sales (%)	40.4	59.2	91.1	52.4	65.6	76.7	42.0	58.9	91.6	60.4	88.4	135.8
Sales To Nwc (times)	6.9	4.2	2.7	5.2	3.4	2.6	4.5	3.8	3.2	5.1	2.6	2.3
Acct Pay To Sales (%)	2.2	4.4	7.7	1.2	3.8	6.7	2.8	5.0	7.0	1.7	5.6	10.0
PROFITABILITY												
Return On Sales (%)	9.1	4.4	0.5	11.3	6.4	1.1	5.7	2.0	0.4	13.6	8.0	4.7
Return On Assets (%)	14.6	6.4	1.1	25.0	7.9	1.8	6.4	3.4	0.5	16.8	6.7	4.5
Return On Nw (%)	28.5	12.6	3.0	41.6	16.6	6.7	13.6	6.2	2.1	23.7	10.5	6.9

	SIC 3535 CNVYRS,CNVYNG EQPMT (NO BREAKDOWN) 2013 (13 Establishments)		SIC 3537 INDL TRUCKS,TRCTORS (NO BREAKDOWN) 2013 (10 Establishments)		SIC 3541 MACH TLS,MTL CTTNG (NO BREAKDOWN) 2013 (12 Establishments)		SIC 3542 MACH TLS,MTL FRMNG (NO BREAKDOWN) 2013 (12 Establishments)	
	$	%	$	%	$	%	$	%
Cash	567,863	18.1	7,257,686	6.0	1,532,622	14.7	943,511	15.6
Accounts Receivable	900,423	28.7	18,144,214	15.0	3,221,634	30.9	1,088,666	18.0
Notes Receivable	0	0.0	5,564,226	4.6	0	0.0	0	0.0
Inventory	495,704	15.8	35,804,582	29.6	2,700,334	25.9	937,462	15.5
Other Current	602,374	19.2	3,991,726	3.3	448,317	4.3	659,248	10.9
Total Current	**2,566,364**	**81.8**	**70,762,434**	**58.5**	**7,902,907**	**75.8**	**3,628,887**	**60.0**
Fixed Assets	373,346	11.9	18,507,098	15.3	1,428,362	13.7	1,632,999	27.0
Other Non-current	197,654	6.3	31,691,893	26.2	1,094,730	10.5	786,259	13.0
Total Assets	**3,137,364**	**100.0**	**120,961,425**	**100.0**	**10,425,999**	**100.0**	**6,048,145**	**100.0**
Accounts Payable	313,736	10.0	14,878,255	12.3	719,394	6.9	320,552	5.3
Bank Loans	0	0.0	0	0.0	0	0.0	254,022	4.2
Notes Payable	0	0.0	5,322,303	4.4	0	0.0	247,974	4.1
Other Current	931,798	29.7	20,321,519	16.8	3,106,948	29.8	1,155,195	19.1
Total Current	**1,245,534**	**39.7**	**40,522,077**	**33.5**	**3,826,342**	**36.7**	**1,977,743**	**32.7**
Other Long Term	320,011	10.2	20,079,597	16.6	1,397,083	13.4	876,981	14.5
Deferred Credits	0	0.0	120,961	0.1	0	0.0	0	0.0
Net Worth	1,571,819	50.1	60,238,790	49.8	5,202,574	49.9	3,193,421	52.8
Total Liab & Net Worth	**3,137,364**	**100.0**	**120,961,425**	**100.0**	**10,425,999**	**100.0**	**6,048,145**	**100.0**
Net Sales	6,747,019	100.0	200,932,600	100.0	15,749,243	100.0	8,790,908	100.0
Gross Profit	2,078,082	30.8	49,831,285	24.8	5,748,474	36.5	3,472,409	39.5
Net Profit After Tax	182,170	2.7	12,256,889	6.1	1,511,927	9.6	712,064	8.1
Working Capital	1,320,830	—	30,240,357	—	4,076,565	—	1,651,144	—

RATIOS	UQ	MED	LQ	UQ	MED	LQ	UQ	MED	LQ	UQ	MED	LQ
SOLVENCY												
Quick Ratio (times)	1.9	1.0	0.6	0.9	0.9	0.1	6.5	1.7	1.0	2.0	0.8	0.5
Current Ratio (times)	2.8	2.4	1.4	2.5	1.5	1.0	9.9	2.9	2.1	3.1	2.3	1.7
Curr Liab To Nw (%)	43.5	70.7	97.1	14.9	75.3	135.2	11.0	29.0	77.4	23.3	62.4	137.1
Curr Liab To Inv (%)	144.3	350.4	382.9	48.1	100.3	204.7	48.7	106.0	281.9	79.0	103.4	411.3
Total Liab To Nw (%)	63.1	73.2	247.6	53.3	136.3	195.3	17.8	50.5	80.4	33.5	101.9	260.2
Fixed Assets To Nw (%)	7.8	16.7	27.9	13.0	35.9	73.0	9.7	23.9	42.0	17.7	48.1	103.3
EFFICIENCY												
Coll Period (days)	36.5	58.8	103.3	18.4	51.1	57.9	44.2	50.6	62.7	32.1	48.9	67.2
Sales To Inv (times)	27.6	11.9	8.8	8.4	5.2	3.0	15.3	7.3	3.4	14.0	7.9	3.2
Assets To Sales (%)	30.3	46.5	62.6	48.7	60.2	106.8	32.3	66.2	80.6	52.2	68.8	104.7
Sales To Nwc (times)	8.9	6.0	3.5	8.1	5.9	2.8	5.0	4.4	2.6	5.3	4.8	3.8
Acct Pay To Sales (%)	2.5	3.8	9.6	4.2	6.7	11.5	1.0	2.0	4.9	2.9	3.8	6.9
PROFITABILITY												
Return On Sales (%)	8.2	4.1	0.4	9.2	5.0	4.0	13.2	4.6	2.8	11.8	5.7	2.5
Return On Assets (%)	25.2	13.7	0.7	12.6	6.3	5.7	29.4	8.1	5.0	14.6	8.3	3.1
Return On Nw (%)	57.3	44.0	1.8	32.6	16.7	10.4	45.9	22.9	13.7	61.9	22.7	10.3

	SIC 3544 SPCL DIES,TLS,FXTRS (NO BREAKDOWN) 2013 (43 Establishments)		SIC 3545 MACHINE TOOL,ACCS (NO BREAKDOWN) 2013 (22 Establishments)		SIC 3549 MTLWRKNG MCHNRY,NEC (NO BREAKDOWN) 2013 (10 Establishments)		SIC 3556 FOOD PRDCTS MCHNRY (NO BREAKDOWN) 2013 (11 Establishments)	
	$	%	$	%	$	%	$	%
Cash	346,911	20.8	396,588	14.6	566,235	18.9	2,186,899	14.9
Accounts Receivable	438,642	26.3	654,642	24.1	769,959	25.7	2,891,403	19.7
Notes Receivable	3,336	0.2	13,582	0.5	0	0.0	0	0.0
Inventory	266,855	16.0	695,387	25.6	593,198	19.8	3,361,072	22.9
Other Current	40,028	2.4	206,443	7.6	275,627	9.2	1,482,394	10.1
Total Current	**1,095,772**	**65.7**	**1,966,642**	**72.4**	**2,205,019**	**73.6**	**9,921,768**	**67.6**
Fixed Assets	446,982	26.8	603,031	22.2	635,141	21.2	2,920,757	19.9
Other Non-current	125,088	7.5	146,683	5.4	155,790	5.2	1,834,647	12.5
Total Assets	**1,667,842**	**100.0**	**2,716,356**	**100.0**	**2,995,950**	**100.0**	**14,677,172**	**100.0**
Accounts Payable	115,081	6.9	201,010	7.4	434,413	14.5	1,585,135	10.8
Bank Loans	1,668	0.1	13,582	0.5	0	0.0	0	0.0
Notes Payable	33,357	2.0	160,265	5.9	170,769	5.7	0	0.0
Other Current	385,271	23.1	342,261	12.6	605,182	20.2	3,537,198	24.1
Total Current	**535,377**	**32.1**	**717,118**	**26.4**	**1,210,364**	**40.4**	**5,122,333**	**34.9**
Other Long Term	231,830	13.9	581,300	21.4	2,441,699	81.5	1,878,678	12.8
Deferred Credits	0	0.0	0	0.0	0	0.0	0	0.0
Net Worth	900,635	54.0	1,417,938	52.2	(656,113)	(21.9)	7,676,161	52.3
Total Liab & Net Worth	**1,667,842**	**100.0**	**2,716,356**	**100.0**	**2,995,950**	**100.0**	**14,677,172**	**100.0**
Net Sales	3,176,842	100.0	5,315,765	100.0	5,885,953	100.0	26,209,236	100.0
Gross Profit	1,042,004	32.8	1,849,886	34.8	2,248,434	38.2	8,911,140	34.0
Net Profit After Tax	193,787	6.1	430,577	8.1	559,166	9.5	917,323	3.5
Working Capital	560,395	---	1,249,524	---	994,655	---	4,799,435	---

RATIOS	UQ	MED	LQ	UQ	MED	LQ	UQ	MED	LQ	UQ	MED	LQ
SOLVENCY												
Quick Ratio (times)	4.2	1.9	1.0	2.8	2.1	1.3	1.8	1.3	0.5	1.4	0.8	0.8
Current Ratio (times)	5.3	2.6	1.8	5.8	3.3	1.7	4.0	2.0	1.3	2.8	2.4	1.6
Curr Liab To Nw (%)	12.1	33.2	67.7	14.6	23.3	102.3	29.8	36.9	120.9	36.8	43.4	142.3
Curr Liab To Inv (%)	79.8	143.6	378.0	42.4	104.2	225.5	81.7	437.1	537.7	89.0	160.0	508.0
Total Liab To Nw (%)	26.9	50.0	107.9	18.6	50.4	130.6	29.8	36.9	266.2	48.6	71.3	170.0
Fixed Assets To Nw (%)	25.4	37.2	67.4	14.6	23.5	52.1	15.0	20.2	42.4	23.6	42.6	69.4
EFFICIENCY												
Coll Period (days)	37.6	46.0	57.7	36.3	54.8	60.4	15.0	36.5	39.4	32.9	47.1	55.1
Sales To Inv (times)	31.5	15.1	8.6	16.7	8.8	4.6	22.3	13.2	8.3	16.5	7.2	4.9
Assets To Sales (%)	35.2	52.5	61.5	41.3	51.1	65.1	27.0	50.9	65.1	42.8	56.0	75.2
Sales To Nwc (times)	7.9	4.8	3.1	6.0	3.7	2.5	9.8	7.2	3.0	7.9	5.2	3.4
Acct Pay To Sales (%)	1.9	2.8	4.6	2.2	4.3	5.5	1.8	3.4	8.4	3.3	5.4	9.4
PROFITABILITY												
Return On Sales (%)	9.6	5.7	2.3	10.6	8.0	1.4	10.5	1.7	1.0	5.9	3.2	0.3
Return On Assets (%)	19.3	9.1	4.9	25.4	8.0	2.8	31.3	7.9	1.9	8.7	5.6	0.8
Return On Nw (%)	34.3	15.4	8.6	33.1	13.7	4.5	38.5	21.3	2.5	19.1	15.2	1.4

SIC 3559 SPEC IND MCHNRY,NEC (NO BREAKDOWN) 2013 (34 Establishments) · SIC 3561 PUMPS,PUMPING EQPMT (NO BREAKDOWN) 2013 (10 Establishments) · SIC 3564 BLOWERS AND FANS (NO BREAKDOWN) 2013 (11 Establishments) · SIC 3569 GNRL IND MCHNRY,NEC (NO BREAKDOWN) 2013 (15 Establishments)

	SIC 3559 $	%	SIC 3561 $	%	SIC 3564 $	%	SIC 3569 $	%
Cash	4,362,055	19.4	32,875,274	14.1	1,117,099	17.9	1,355,069	19.5
Accounts Receivable	4,496,964	20.0	43,367,382	18.6	1,697,492	27.2	1,257,782	18.1
Notes Receivable	0	0.0	0	0.0	0	0.0	55,593	0.8
Inventory	4,586,903	20.4	53,160,017	22.8	1,191,989	19.1	1,646,930	23.7
Other Current	2,675,694	11.9	10,258,951	4.4	449,335	7.2	597,619	8.6
Total Current	**16,121,616**	**71.7**	**139,661,624**	**59.9**	**4,455,915**	**71.4**	**4,912,993**	**70.7**
Fixed Assets	3,665,026	16.3	34,740,538	14.9	1,160,785	18.6	1,167,444	16.8
Other Non-current	2,698,178	12.0	58,755,808	25.2	624,078	10.0	868,634	12.5
Total Assets	**22,484,820**	**100.0**	**233,157,970**	**100.0**	**6,240,778**	**100.0**	**6,949,071**	**100.0**
Accounts Payable	3,485,147	15.5	24,947,903	10.7	505,503	8.1	701,856	10.1
Bank Loans	269,818	1.2	0	0.0	0	0.0	34,745	0.5
Notes Payable	3,125,390	13.9	466,316	0.2	493,021	7.9	20,847	0.3
Other Current	6,138,356	27.3	24,015,271	10.3	848,746	13.6	1,320,324	19.0
Total Current	**13,018,711**	**57.9**	**49,429,490**	**21.2**	**1,847,270**	**29.6**	**2,077,772**	**29.9**
Other Long Term	1,551,452	6.9	40,103,170	17.2	961,081	15.4	437,792	6.3
Deferred Credits	22,485	0.1	0	0.0	43,685	0.7	0	0.0
Net Worth	7,892,172	35.1	143,625,310	61.6	3,388,742	54.3	4,433,507	63.8
Total Liab & Net Worth	**22,484,820**	**100.0**	**233,157,970**	**100.0**	**6,240,778**	**100.0**	**6,949,071**	**100.0**
Net Sales	26,895,718	100.0	275,600,437	100.0	11,578,438	100.0	13,925,994	100.0
Gross Profit	9,547,980	35.5	100,594,160	36.5	4,040,875	34.9	5,013,358	36.0
Net Profit After Tax	(53,791)	(0.2)	26,182,042	9.5	219,990	1.9	724,152	5.2
Working Capital	3,102,905	---	90,232,134	---	2,608,645	---	2,835,221	---

RATIOS	SIC 3559 UQ	MED	LQ	SIC 3561 UQ	MED	LQ	SIC 3564 UQ	MED	LQ	SIC 3569 UQ	MED	LQ
SOLVENCY												
Quick Ratio (times)	1.9	1.4	0.8	1.8	1.6	1.1	3.1	2.0	1.5	2.1	1.7	1.1
Current Ratio (times)	4.8	2.6	1.5	3.3	3.1	2.4	5.5	3.5	2.6	3.5	2.8	2.2
Curr Liab To Nw (%)	15.5	40.4	94.3	23.0	35.2	50.2	14.3	27.0	56.6	23.7	40.2	59.3
Curr Liab To Inv (%)	75.8	155.3	225.0	62.0	93.2	146.9	62.0	102.6	454.4	67.4	134.8	479.7
Total Liab To Nw (%)	23.2	59.5	122.4	34.6	48.5	118.5	20.1	34.2	150.6	31.3	57.0	95.7
Fixed Assets To Nw (%)	8.8	17.8	33.1	13.6	22.1	38.2	14.7	24.5	48.9	14.9	18.3	40.3
EFFICIENCY												
Coll Period (days)	31.8	64.1	85.4	42.0	59.9	77.4	38.3	44.6	54.4	19.6	36.0	58.6
Sales To Inv (times)	9.1	5.6	4.3	8.8	7.7	4.7	25.0	11.9	7.1	20.6	10.6	5.5
Assets To Sales (%)	45.7	83.6	191.1	60.9	84.6	127.6	38.2	53.9	57.0	39.7	49.9	90.2
Sales To Nwc (times)	6.0	3.0	1.0	4.2	3.5	2.9	5.5	3.7	3.1	6.7	3.9	2.1
Acct Pay To Sales (%)	4.1	5.7	11.3	5.0	7.7	11.8	0.7	2.3	7.8	2.9	5.4	9.2
PROFITABILITY												
Return On Sales (%)	9.9	2.7	(8.0)	9.9	6.5	5.7	11.1	2.7	1.5	10.3	5.4	0.2
Return On Assets (%)	13.2	1.8	(3.8)	13.8	9.9	8.5	34.1	4.6	3.5	11.3	6.6	0.6
Return On Nw (%)	30.4	3.6	(4.5)	26.0	15.1	11.4	42.0	14.9	4.2	22.7	9.5	1.2

	SIC 3571 ELECTRNC COMPUTERS (NO BREAKDOWN) 2013 (20 Establishments)		SIC 3572 COMPTR STRGE DVCES (NO BREAKDOWN) 2013 (15 Establishments)		SIC 3577 CMPTR PRPRL EQP,NEC (NO BREAKDOWN) 2013 (45 Establishments)		SIC 3585 RRFGRTN,HTNG EQPMT (NO BREAKDOWN) 2013 (20 Establishments)	
	$	%	$	%	$	%	$	%
Cash	1,888,495	24.9	5,589,734	17.8	17,745,218	30.2	2,139,171	15.5
Accounts Receivable	2,381,476	31.4	8,573,019	27.3	9,342,681	15.9	2,981,038	21.6
Notes Receivable	22,753	0.3	62,806	0.2	0	0.0	0	0.0
Inventory	1,114,895	14.7	4,396,420	14.0	8,578,814	14.6	3,132,850	22.7
Other Current	948,039	12.5	3,517,136	11.2	7,991,224	13.6	814,265	5.9
Total Current	**6,355,658**	**83.8**	**22,139,115**	**70.5**	**43,657,937**	**74.3**	**9,067,324**	**65.7**
Fixed Assets	606,745	8.0	4,396,420	14.0	4,113,130	7.0	2,691,215	19.5
Other Non-current	621,915	8.2	4,867,465	15.5	10,987,933	18.7	2,042,563	14.8
Total Assets	**7,584,318**	**100.0**	**31,403,000**	**100.0**	**58,759,000**	**100.0**	**13,801,102**	**100.0**
Accounts Payable	1,425,852	18.8	5,558,331	17.7	7,403,634	12.6	1,725,138	12.5
Bank Loans	22,753	0.3	0	0.0	0	0.0	13,801	0.1
Notes Payable	30,337	0.4	0	0.0	352,554	0.6	96,608	0.7
Other Current	2,237,374	29.5	15,670,097	49.9	13,632,088	23.2	2,511,800	18.2
Total Current	**3,716,316**	**49.0**	**21,228,428**	**67.6**	**21,388,276**	**36.4**	**4,347,347**	**31.5**
Other Long Term	470,227	6.2	4,365,017	13.9	11,575,523	19.7	3,450,275	25.0
Deferred Credits	45,506	0.6	439,642	1.4	940,144	1.6	1,738,939	12.6
Net Worth	3,352,269	44.2	5,369,913	17.1	24,855,057	42.3	4,264,541	30.9
Total Liab & Net Worth	**7,584,318**	**100.0**	**31,403,000**	**100.0**	**58,759,000**	**100.0**	**13,801,102**	**100.0**
Net Sales	15,637,769	100.0	40,003,822	100.0	61,656,873	100.0	25,092,913	100.0
Gross Profit	5,160,464	33.0	14,721,406	36.8	32,308,201	52.4	7,276,945	29.0
Net Profit After Tax	625,511	4.0	(2,120,203)	(5.3)	986,510	1.6	953,531	3.8
Working Capital	2,639,342	---	910,687	---	22,269,661	---	4,719,977	---

RATIOS	UQ	MED	LQ	UQ	MED	LQ	UQ	MED	LQ	UQ	MED	LQ
SOLVENCY												
Quick Ratio (times)	2.0	1.2	0.7	1.5	1.0	0.8	2.3	1.6	0.9	2.2	1.7	0.7
Current Ratio (times)	2.8	1.8	1.3	2.3	1.7	1.3	4.1	2.7	1.7	3.8	2.6	1.4
Curr Liab To Nw (%)	36.6	64.7	258.4	27.3	49.9	121.3	23.3	40.3	63.8	21.8	40.7	78.0
Curr Liab To Inv (%)	137.8	389.3	752.9	183.0	314.9	756.4	122.2	293.9	569.7	63.1	120.5	186.6
Total Liab To Nw (%)	55.6	69.2	305.8	43.8	77.8	126.7	29.8	47.1	105.1	33.1	47.3	126.7
Fixed Assets To Nw (%)	1.5	8.1	33.4	8.3	14.2	31.4	4.8	9.7	14.1	8.8	26.7	55.8
EFFICIENCY												
Coll Period (days)	36.9	56.8	74.1	39.1	50.4	68.5	32.7	44.9	62.3	31.0	44.0	52.9
Sales To Inv (times)	46.1	12.7	7.2	15.2	8.2	6.4	34.9	13.5	7.6	10.0	8.4	7.5
Assets To Sales (%)	28.5	48.5	99.6	40.4	78.5	149.8	49.0	95.3	141.7	45.4	55.0	72.8
Sales To Nwc (times)	14.9	4.2	2.7	10.8	4.7	1.8	5.2	2.4	1.6	9.1	5.0	4.2
Acct Pay To Sales (%)	4.2	6.5	11.5	6.2	9.2	13.0	3.4	6.0	10.2	2.4	4.4	10.0
PROFITABILITY												
Return On Sales (%)	6.2	2.7	0.6	6.9	0.6	(12.8)	9.4	3.3	(6.4)	9.5	5.0	(0.4)
Return On Assets (%)	12.4	5.1	2.6	6.9	4.2	(32.7)	12.9	4.1	(5.0)	14.5	6.7	(0.4)
Return On Nw (%)	25.1	10.0	6.3	18.5	12.4	(0.4)	19.0	9.1	(2.3)	23.2	15.6	(0.7)

SIC 3589 SVC IND MCHNRY,NEC
(NO BREAKDOWN)
2013 (20 Establishments)

	$	%
Cash	724,433	16.6
Accounts Receivable	1,051,738	24.1
Notes Receivable	8,728	0.2
Inventory	947,000	21.7
Other Current	519,323	11.9
Total Current	**3,251,222**	**74.5**
Fixed Assets	977,549	22.4
Other Non-current	135,286	3.1
Total Assets	**4,364,057**	**100.0**
Accounts Payable	680,793	15.6
Bank Loans	0	0.0
Notes Payable	109,101	2.5
Other Current	3,277,407	75.1
Total Current	**4,067,301**	**93.2**
Other Long Term	392,765	9.0
Deferred Credits	4,364	0.1
Net Worth	(100,373)	(2.3)
Total Liab & Net Worth	**4,364,057**	**100.0**
Net Sales	7,992,778	100.0
Gross Profit	3,348,974	41.9
Net Profit After Tax	(415,624)	(5.2)
Working Capital	(816,079)	---

RATIOS	UQ	MED	LQ
SOLVENCY			
Quick Ratio (times)	2.3	0.8	0.4
Current Ratio (times)	4.2	2.0	0.9
Curr Liab To Nw (%)	21.0	44.2	169.4
Curr Liab To Inv (%)	179.5	271.5	417.5
Total Liab To Nw (%)	23.6	82.0	192.0
Fixed Assets To Nw (%)	17.7	49.7	90.1
EFFICIENCY			
Coll Period (days)	33.6	52.2	65.3
Sales To Inv (times)	18.8	10.8	4.4
Assets To Sales (%)	36.6	54.6	82.7
Sales To Nwc (times)	8.2	3.9	2.5
Acct Pay To Sales (%)	4.4	7.8	10.8
PROFITABILITY			
Return On Sales (%)	4.9	2.0	(1.0)
Return On Assets (%)	8.0	3.8	(2.7)
Return On Nw (%)	12.9	6.8	2.5

SIC 3599 IND MACHINERY,NEC
(NO BREAKDOWN)
2013 (167 Establishments)

	$	%
Cash	399,397	21.2
Accounts Receivable	418,236	22.2
Notes Receivable	7,536	0.4
Inventory	292,012	15.5
Other Current	126,224	6.7
Total Current	**1,243,405**	**66.0**
Fixed Assets	536,925	28.5
Other Non-current	103,617	5.5
Total Assets	**1,883,947**	**100.0**
Accounts Payable	135,644	7.2
Bank Loans	28,259	1.5
Notes Payable	11,304	0.6
Other Current	303,316	16.1
Total Current	**478,523**	**25.4**
Other Long Term	295,779	15.7
Deferred Credits	9,420	0.5
Net Worth	1,100,225	58.4
Total Liab & Net Worth	**1,883,947**	**100.0**
Net Sales	3,813,658	100.0
Gross Profit	1,342,408	35.2
Net Profit After Tax	209,751	5.5
Working Capital	764,882	---

RATIOS	UQ	MED	LQ
SOLVENCY			
Quick Ratio (times)	6.3	2.1	1.0
Current Ratio (times)	8.5	3.5	1.9
Curr Liab To Nw (%)	8.7	23.2	57.0
Curr Liab To Inv (%)	61.2	105.7	380.9
Total Liab To Nw (%)	13.4	42.7	82.9
Fixed Assets To Nw (%)	17.0	40.7	69.9
EFFICIENCY			
Coll Period (days)	29.2	42.7	58.4
Sales To Inv (times)	43.2	12.5	6.5
Assets To Sales (%)	33.9	49.4	71.1
Sales To Nwc (times)	6.5	4.4	2.8
Acct Pay To Sales (%)	1.6	2.9	4.7
PROFITABILITY			
Return On Sales (%)	8.5	4.2	0.4
Return On Assets (%)	15.7	7.9	1.0
Return On Nw (%)	29.9	13.5	2.7

SIC 36 ELECTRICAL EQUIPMENT
(NO BREAKDOWN)
2013 (511 Establishments)

	$	%
Cash	4,737,712	19.6
Accounts Receivable	4,520,164	18.7
Notes Receivable	24,172	0.1
Inventory	4,979,432	20.6
Other Current	2,562,231	10.6
Total Current	**16,823,711**	**69.6**
Fixed Assets	3,480,768	14.4
Other Non-current	3,867,520	16.0
Total Assets	**24,171,999**	**100.0**
Accounts Payable	8,581,060	35.5
Bank Loans	72,516	0.3
Notes Payable	918,536	3.8
Other Current	19,579,319	81.0
Total Current	**29,151,431**	**120.6**
Other Long Term	9,523,767	39.4
Deferred Credits	72,516	0.3
Net Worth	(14,575,715)	(60.3)
Total Liab & Net Worth	**24,171,999**	**100.0**
Net Sales	28,879,330	100.0
Gross Profit	10,367,679	35.9
Net Profit After Tax	259,914	0.9
Working Capital	(12,327,720)	---

RATIOS	UQ	MED	LQ
SOLVENCY			
Quick Ratio (times)	2.5	1.4	0.8
Current Ratio (times)	5.0	2.8	1.7
Curr Liab To Nw (%)	15.8	31.1	70.8
Curr Liab To Inv (%)	70.7	132.1	271.1
Total Liab To Nw (%)	21.5	53.9	109.3
Fixed Assets To Nw (%)	7.4	19.2	40.5
EFFICIENCY			
Coll Period (days)	38.7	50.6	64.2
Sales To Inv (times)	11.2	7.0	4.6
Assets To Sales (%)	53.8	83.7	130.2
Sales To Nwc (times)	4.7	2.9	1.8
Acct Pay To Sales (%)	3.7	7.1	11.3
PROFITABILITY			
Return On Sales (%)	7.7	2.5	(5.1)
Return On Assets (%)	9.7	2.9	(5.9)
Return On Nw (%)	17.2	6.7	(4.1)

SIC 3612 TRNSFRMRS,EXC ELEC
(NO BREAKDOWN)
2013 (11 Establishments)

	$	%
Cash	1,328,303	19.3
Accounts Receivable	1,844,482	26.8
Notes Receivable	0	0.0
Inventory	1,789,423	26.0
Other Current	468,003	6.8
Total Current	**5,430,211**	**78.9**
Fixed Assets	1,073,654	15.6
Other Non-current	378,532	5.5
Total Assets	**6,882,397**	**100.0**
Accounts Payable	825,888	12.0
Bank Loans	0	0.0
Notes Payable	61,942	0.9
Other Current	867,181	12.6
Total Current	**1,755,011**	**25.5**
Other Long Term	736,417	10.7
Deferred Credits	6,882	0.1
Net Worth	4,384,087	63.7
Total Liab & Net Worth	**6,882,397**	**100.0**
Net Sales	11,264,152	100.0
Gross Profit	4,595,774	40.8
Net Profit After Tax	934,925	8.3
Working Capital	3,675,200	---

RATIOS	UQ	MED	LQ
SOLVENCY			
Quick Ratio (times)	3.4	2.1	1.4
Current Ratio (times)	4.8	3.3	2.4
Curr Liab To Nw (%)	27.8	40.1	48.9
Curr Liab To Inv (%)	63.6	69.4	118.9
Total Liab To Nw (%)	31.9	49.5	96.7
Fixed Assets To Nw (%)	18.3	21.4	36.6
EFFICIENCY			
Coll Period (days)	37.1	40.2	51.5
Sales To Inv (times)	12.3	7.7	6.4
Assets To Sales (%)	33.7	61.1	68.9
Sales To Nwc (times)	7.0	5.3	2.7
Acct Pay To Sales (%)	3.0	3.7	9.1
PROFITABILITY			
Return On Sales (%)	10.9	6.2	6.0
Return On Assets (%)	20.4	17.0	11.6
Return On Nw (%)	36.5	28.6	19.8

SIC 3613 SWTCHGR,BRD APPRTUS
(NO BREAKDOWN)
2013 (14 Establishments)

	$	%
Cash	1,094,957	21.7
Accounts Receivable	1,503,674	29.8
Notes Receivable	10,092	0.2
Inventory	832,571	16.5
Other Current	640,827	12.7
Total Current	**4,082,121**	**80.9**
Fixed Assets	539,910	10.7
Other Non-current	423,854	8.4
Total Assets	**5,045,885**	**100.0**
Accounts Payable	373,395	7.4
Bank Loans	0	0.0
Notes Payable	10,092	0.2
Other Current	797,250	15.8
Total Current	**1,180,737**	**23.4**
Other Long Term	277,524	5.5
Deferred Credits	0	0.0
Net Worth	3,587,624	71.1
Total Liab & Net Worth	**5,045,885**	**100.0**
Net Sales	10,011,677	100.0
Gross Profit	2,963,456	29.6
Net Profit After Tax	740,864	7.4
Working Capital	2,901,384	---

RATIOS	UQ	MED	LQ
SOLVENCY			
Quick Ratio (times)	4.2	2.5	1.7
Current Ratio (times)	7.7	4.0	2.7
Curr Liab To Nw (%)	14.3	25.8	38.8
Curr Liab To Inv (%)	74.6	214.2	379.2
Total Liab To Nw (%)	16.8	30.2	59.4
Fixed Assets To Nw (%)	8.8	14.2	21.4
EFFICIENCY			
Coll Period (days)	43.4	52.9	68.3
Sales To Inv (times)	50.1	9.6	6.0
Assets To Sales (%)	38.3	50.4	64.7
Sales To Nwc (times)	4.6	3.7	2.4
Acct Pay To Sales (%)	2.3	3.4	4.6
PROFITABILITY			
Return On Sales (%)	10.7	5.5	3.5
Return On Assets (%)	13.8	10.2	7.7
Return On Nw (%)	22.0	13.0	11.1

SIC 3621 MOTORS,GENERATORS
(NO BREAKDOWN)
2013 (21 Establishments)

	$	%
Cash	1,337,352	19.1
Accounts Receivable	819,216	11.7
Notes Receivable	0	0.0
Inventory	1,470,387	21.0
Other Current	756,199	10.8
Total Current	**4,383,154**	**62.6**
Fixed Assets	1,379,363	19.7
Other Non-current	1,239,327	17.7
Total Assets	**7,001,844**	**100.0**
Accounts Payable	1,372,361	19.6
Bank Loans	0	0.0
Notes Payable	315,083	4.5
Other Current	3,640,959	52.0
Total Current	**5,328,403**	**76.1**
Other Long Term	2,632,693	37.6
Deferred Credits	7,002	0.1
Net Worth	(966,254)	(13.8)
Total Liab & Net Worth	**7,001,844**	**100.0**
Net Sales	5,948,890	100.0
Gross Profit	1,463,427	24.6
Net Profit After Tax	148,722	2.5
Working Capital	(945,249)	---

RATIOS	UQ	MED	LQ
SOLVENCY			
Quick Ratio (times)	1.4	1.0	0.4
Current Ratio (times)	3.3	2.1	0.7
Curr Liab To Nw (%)	29.7	43.3	79.1
Curr Liab To Inv (%)	69.4	113.3	252.6
Total Liab To Nw (%)	37.0	62.5	120.6
Fixed Assets To Nw (%)	10.7	27.3	46.2
EFFICIENCY			
Coll Period (days)	40.2	50.4	63.5
Sales To Inv (times)	6.8	5.9	3.4
Assets To Sales (%)	73.1	117.7	149.9
Sales To Nwc (times)	4.0	2.7	1.5
Acct Pay To Sales (%)	6.2	9.8	13.5
PROFITABILITY			
Return On Sales (%)	8.1	2.2	(148.9)
Return On Assets (%)	8.2	2.0	(143.1)
Return On Nw (%)	18.2	7.1	(62.5)

SIC 3625 RELAYS,IND CONTROLS
(NO BREAKDOWN)
2013 (19 Establishments)

	$	%
Cash	458,191	12.1
Accounts Receivable	1,079,211	28.5
Notes Receivable	0	0.0
Inventory	923,956	24.4
Other Current	443,044	11.7
Total Current	**2,904,402**	**76.7**
Fixed Assets	507,418	13.4
Other Non-current	374,884	9.9
Total Assets	**3,786,704**	**100.0**
Accounts Payable	420,324	11.1
Bank Loans	0	0.0
Notes Payable	34,080	0.9
Other Current	711,901	18.8
Total Current	**1,166,305**	**30.8**
Other Long Term	897,448	23.7
Deferred Credits	15,147	0.4
Net Worth	1,707,804	45.1
Total Liab & Net Worth	**3,786,704**	**100.0**
Net Sales	7,775,573	100.0
Gross Profit	2,503,735	32.2
Net Profit After Tax	575,392	7.4
Working Capital	1,738,097	---

RATIOS	UQ	MED	LQ
SOLVENCY			
Quick Ratio (times)	2.9	1.5	0.9
Current Ratio (times)	6.0	2.5	2.0
Curr Liab To Nw (%)	18.1	40.1	103.7
Curr Liab To Inv (%)	67.5	96.4	195.5
Total Liab To Nw (%)	40.1	59.1	126.1
Fixed Assets To Nw (%)	13.0	25.1	42.9
EFFICIENCY			
Coll Period (days)	37.2	51.5	62.8
Sales To Inv (times)	12.4	7.7	6.5
Assets To Sales (%)	37.1	48.7	79.3
Sales To Nwc (times)	6.4	3.7	2.8
Acct Pay To Sales (%)	1.5	6.6	8.6
PROFITABILITY			
Return On Sales (%)	11.9	5.6	3.6
Return On Assets (%)	18.8	10.2	6.6
Return On Nw (%)	36.4	18.7	12.8

SIC 3648 LGHTNG EQPMNT,NEC
(NO BREAKDOWN)
2013 (11 Establishments)

	$	%
Cash	519,077	12.4
Accounts Receivable	916,756	21.9
Notes Receivable	16,744	0.4
Inventory	1,201,411	28.7
Other Current	305,585	7.3
Total Current	**2,959,573**	**70.7**
Fixed Assets	661,404	15.8
Other Non-current	565,124	13.5
Total Assets	**4,186,101**	**100.0**
Accounts Payable	322,330	7.7
Bank Loans	16,744	0.4
Notes Payable	230,236	5.5
Other Current	602,798	14.4
Total Current	**1,172,108**	**28.0**
Other Long Term	686,521	16.4
Deferred Credits	0	0.0
Net Worth	2,327,472	55.6
Total Liab & Net Worth	**4,186,101**	**100.0**
Net Sales	5,415,396	100.0
Gross Profit	2,241,974	41.4
Net Profit After Tax	146,216	2.7
Working Capital	1,787,465	---

RATIOS	UQ	MED	LQ
SOLVENCY			
Quick Ratio (times)	2.8	1.0	0.6
Current Ratio (times)	5.3	3.1	2.1
Curr Liab To Nw (%)	14.6	21.6	92.4
Curr Liab To Inv (%)	42.9	61.5	120.8
Total Liab To Nw (%)	19.4	32.6	143.3
Fixed Assets To Nw (%)	4.1	17.6	48.4
EFFICIENCY			
Coll Period (days)	21.8	31.4	71.4
Sales To Inv (times)	8.4	5.0	2.9
Assets To Sales (%)	61.2	77.3	90.1
Sales To Nwc (times)	3.8	3.3	2.2
Acct Pay To Sales (%)	1.5	4.4	11.2
PROFITABILITY			
Return On Sales (%)	14.2	3.9	0.7
Return On Assets (%)	18.9	6.3	1.4
Return On Nw (%)	30.9	17.6	3.6

	SIC 3651 HSHLD AUDIO,VDEO EQ (NO BREAKDOWN) 2013 (12 Establishments) $	%	SIC 3661 TLPHNE,TLGPH APPTUS (NO BREAKDOWN) 2013 (26 Establishments) $	%	SIC 3663 RDIO,TV CMMNCTNS EQ (NO BREAKDOWN) 2013 (43 Establishments) $	%	SIC 3669 CMMNCTNS EQPMNT.NEC (NO BREAKDOWN) 2013 (12 Establishments) $	%
Cash	3,228,814	15.8	49,390,449	22.2	4,256,508	18.8	6,338,216	27.2
Accounts Receivable	4,536,689	22.2	43,161,023	19.4	4,460,277	19.7	4,474,035	19.2
Notes Receivable	0	0.0	667,439	0.3	113,205	0.5	0	0.0
Inventory	5,844,563	28.6	30,702,171	13.8	4,007,457	17.7	3,611,851	15.5
Other Current	1,961,811	9.6	30,924,650	13.9	1,879,203	8.3	3,681,759	15.8
Total Current	**15,571,877**	**76.2**	**154,845,732**	**69.6**	**14,716,650**	**65.0**	**18,105,861**	**77.7**
Fixed Assets	2,452,264	12.0	16,241,004	7.3	2,037,690	9.0	1,444,740	6.2
Other Non-current	2,411,393	11.8	51,392,764	23.1	5,886,660	26.0	3,751,665	16.1
Total Assets	**20,435,534**	**100.0**	**222,479,500**	**100.0**	**22,641,000**	**100.0**	**23,302,266**	**100.0**
Accounts Payable	2,350,086	11.5	351,962,569	158.2	11,275,218	49.8	32,646,475	140.1
Bank Loans	0	0.0	0	0.0	0	0.0	0	0.0
Notes Payable	0	0.0	4,672,070	2.1	3,056,535	13.5	6,944,075	29.8
Other Current	4,189,285	20.5	246,284,806	110.7	20,490,105	90.5	63,125,839	270.9
Total Current	**6,539,371**	**32.0**	**602,919,445**	**271.0**	**34,821,858**	**153.8**	**102,716,389**	**440.8**
Other Long Term	1,880,069	9.2	122,808,684	55.2	5,524,404	24.4	3,145,805	13.5
Deferred Credits	0	0.0	1,334,877	0.6	407,538	1.8	326,232	1.4
Net Worth	12,016,094	58.8	(504,583,506)	(226.8)	(18,112,800)	(80.0)	(82,886,160)	(355.7)
Total Liab & Net Worth	**20,435,534**	**100.0**	**222,479,500**	**100.0**	**22,641,000**	**100.0**	**23,302,266**	**100.0**
Net Sales	27,138,823	100.0	221,814,058	100.0	25,699,205	100.0	38,901,947	100.0
Gross Profit	7,788,842	28.7	87,838,367	39.6	10,331,080	40.2	15,755,289	40.5
Net Profit After Tax	488,499	1.8	(1,774,512)	(0.8)	0	0.0	505,725	1.3
Working Capital	9,032,506	---	(448,073,713)	---	(20,105,208)	---	(84,610,528)	---

RATIOS	3651 UQ	MED	LQ	3661 UQ	MED	LQ	3663 UQ	MED	LQ	3669 UQ	MED	LQ
SOLVENCY												
Quick Ratio (times)	1.9	1.2	0.7	2.8	1.5	1.0	2.0	1.3	0.6	2.2	1.3	0.9
Current Ratio (times)	3.1	2.1	1.9	4.8	2.8	1.7	3.7	2.1	1.2	4.2	2.1	1.6
Curr Liab To Nw (%)	31.0	51.4	107.6	16.0	33.7	59.5	21.6	41.4	88.9	27.9	41.7	117.9
Curr Liab To Inv (%)	85.1	117.2	186.3	105.7	153.5	374.2	104.7	222.4	690.6	83.9	329.1	499.6
Total Liab To Nw (%)	36.2	75.6	119.0	18.3	40.3	79.1	40.8	89.3	129.7	31.1	81.5	184.1
Fixed Assets To Nw (%)	5.2	17.9	25.9	3.7	11.8	16.9	5.5	13.7	27.9	9.2	13.5	16.9
EFFICIENCY												
Coll Period (days)	31.8	61.3	79.8	50.7	59.1	64.6	38.3	56.9	66.8	46.4	64.6	69.6
Sales To Inv (times)	8.9	6.4	4.7	13.2	8.4	6.1	13.9	8.9	4.1	18.1	11.0	5.4
Assets To Sales (%)	42.2	75.3	92.2	78.8	100.3	128.8	52.7	88.1	139.0	58.6	59.9	148.0
Sales To Nwc (times)	6.1	4.2	2.2	3.1	2.5	1.8	5.9	3.0	1.9	6.1	3.1	2.4
Acct Pay To Sales (%)	6.8	9.3	11.1	6.2	8.3	10.3	5.1	7.2	17.0	5.8	7.4	8.4
PROFITABILITY												
Return On Sales (%)	7.1	4.3	2.2	3.5	(0.7)	(7.7)	8.0	1.6	(5.3)	1.4	0.4	(5.2)
Return On Assets (%)	11.3	4.6	3.5	3.7	(1.0)	(4.9)	9.3	1.0	(7.7)	4.1	1.2	(3.0)
Return On Nw (%)	17.1	7.9	5.1	5.1	0.7	(3.7)	30.3	4.2	(5.4)	11.9	0.8	(6.6)

Balance Sheet

	SIC 3672 PRINTED CIRCT BRDS (NO BREAKDOWN) 2013 (33 Establishments) $	%	SIC 3674 SMCNDCTRS,RLTD DVCS (NO BREAKDOWN) 2013 (118 Establishments) $	%	SIC 3678 ELEC CONNECTORS (NO BREAKDOWN) 2013 (10 Establishments) $	%	SIC 3679 ELEC COMPONENTS,NEC (NO BREAKDOWN) 2013 (53 Establishments) $	%
Cash	2,817,566	15.1	61,416,036	21.6	1,609,841	17.1	1,015,154	23.8
Accounts Receivable	4,272,997	22.9	34,404,354	12.1	2,080,555	22.1	976,765	22.9
Notes Receivable	0	0.0	0	0.0	65,900	0.7	0	0.0
Inventory	4,459,591	23.9	38,100,689	13.4	2,814,869	29.9	1,143,114	26.8
Other Current	1,380,793	7.4	46,915,027	16.5	847,284	9.0	277,248	6.5
Total Current	**12,930,947**	**69.3**	**180,836,106**	**63.6**	**7,418,449**	**78.8**	**3,412,281**	**80.0**
Fixed Assets	3,806,513	20.4	45,493,360	16.0	847,285	9.0	588,618	13.8
Other Non-current	1,921,915	10.3	58,004,034	20.4	1,148,542	12.2	264,452	6.2
Total Assets	**18,659,375**	**100.0**	**284,333,500**	**100.0**	**9,414,276**	**100.0**	**4,265,351**	**100.0**
Accounts Payable	3,489,303	18.7	51,180,030	18.0	1,261,513	13.4	584,353	13.7
Bank Loans	149,275	0.8	0	0.0	225,943	2.4	8,531	0.2
Notes Payable	317,209	1.7	7,108,338	2.5	131,800	1.4	93,838	2.2
Other Current	2,873,544	15.4	323,855,856	113.9	687,242	7.3	1,053,541	24.7
Total Current	**6,829,331**	**36.6**	**382,144,224**	**134.4**	**2,306,498**	**24.5**	**1,740,263**	**40.8**
Other Long Term	3,060,138	16.4	215,240,460	75.7	1,242,684	13.2	371,085	8.7
Deferred Credits	0	0.0	568,667	0.2	0	0.0	8,531	0.2
Net Worth	8,769,906	47.0	(313,619,851)	(110.3)	5,865,094	62.3	2,145,472	50.3
Total Liab & Net Worth	**18,659,375**	**100.0**	**284,333,500**	**100.0**	**9,414,276**	**100.0**	**4,265,351**	**100.0**
Net Sales	30,047,303	100.0	222,483,177	100.0	12,687,704	100.0	7,204,985	100.0
Gross Profit	6,790,690	22.6	91,218,103	41.0	4,389,946	34.6	2,637,025	36.6
Net Profit After Tax	(60,095)	(0.2)	(5,339,596)	(2.4)	1,141,893	9.0	28,820	0.4
Working Capital	6,101,616	—	(201,308,118)	—	5,111,951	—	1,672,018	—

RATIOS

	SIC 3672 UQ	MED	LQ	SIC 3674 UQ	MED	LQ	SIC 3678 UQ	MED	LQ	SIC 3679 UQ	MED	LQ
SOLVENCY												
Quick Ratio (times)	1.3	1.1	0.7	2.6	1.7	1.0	5.7	2.1	0.8	3.3	1.6	0.9
Current Ratio (times)	3.4	1.9	1.4	5.6	3.3	2.0	9.8	3.1	2.5	5.6	3.1	1.6
Curr Liab To Nw (%)	23.8	66.2	132.9	12.9	22.1	47.9	10.2	31.7	55.9	16.7	27.8	77.4
Curr Liab To Inv (%)	85.6	139.3	218.4	102.8	158.6	278.4	32.3	98.3	203.1	53.9	100.1	154.5
Total Liab To Nw (%)	41.1	112.4	178.0	18.4	34.6	76.2	13.9	56.1	114.2	18.9	40.7	112.5
Fixed Assets To Nw (%)	14.8	48.0	90.6	8.3	19.0	42.8	2.6	17.4	25.2	7.1	17.9	39.0
EFFICIENCY												
Coll Period (days)	40.9	50.8	60.8	38.7	48.2	61.2	42.0	54.4	76.3	38.2	48.6	60.8
Sales To Inv (times)	9.8	8.6	5.6	11.1	7.2	4.9	9.5	6.0	3.3	10.0	5.6	4.7
Assets To Sales (%)	47.1	62.1	95.5	88.7	127.8	191.4	62.1	74.2	117.2	36.9	59.2	91.4
Sales To Nwc (times)	9.7	4.7	2.9	3.2	2.0	1.3	3.1	2.8	1.9	5.6	3.2	1.9
Acct Pay To Sales (%)	4.4	9.0	14.1	4.8	7.1	11.5	2.2	8.9	11.8	3.7	6.7	10.5
PROFITABILITY												
Return On Sales (%)	3.7	1.5	(2.4)	8.4	1.9	(11.8)	13.8	7.4	2.0	7.8	2.6	(5.6)
Return On Assets (%)	6.7	2.3	(2.5)	6.3	1.1	(9.7)	13.2	9.7	2.2	12.2	5.0	(11.4)
Return On Nw (%)	15.4	4.2	(2.2)	11.1	3.0	(10.6)	22.2	14.6	10.8	30.2	9.6	(11.7)

Balance Sheet / Income

	SIC 3691 STORAGE BATTERIES (NO BREAKDOWN) 2013 (11 Establishments) $	%	SIC 3699 ELEC EQPT,SPPLS,NEC (NO BREAKDOWN) 2013 (41 Establishments) $	%	SIC 37 TRANSPORTATION EQPT (NO BREAKDOWN) 2013 (210 Establishments) $	%	SIC 3711 MTR VHCL,CAR BODIES (NO BREAKDOWN) 2013 (18 Establishments) $	%
Cash	14,267,837	17.9	1,211,460	24.4	2,300,261	14.9	8,326,546	14.0
Accounts Receivable	17,695,307	22.2	769,575	15.5	2,439,203	15.8	6,363,860	10.7
Notes Receivable	0	0.0	0	0.0	46,314	0.3	59,475	0.1
Inventory	18,332,975	23.0	1,047,615	21.1	3,828,623	24.8	14,452,504	24.3
Other Current	2,949,218	3.7	461,745	9.3	1,219,602	7.9	2,616,914	4.4
Total Current	**53,245,337**	**66.8**	**3,490,395**	**70.3**	**9,834,003**	**63.7**	**31,819,299**	**53.5**
Fixed Assets	12,514,248	15.7	705,030	14.2	3,118,475	20.2	11,300,312	19.0
Other Non-current	13,949,003	17.5	769,575	15.5	2,485,517	16.1	16,355,715	27.5
Total Assets	**79,708,588**	**100.0**	**4,965,000**	**100.0**	**15,437,995**	**100.0**	**59,475,326**	**100.0**
Accounts Payable	9,325,905	11.7	5,173,530	104.2	9,262,797	60.0	157,550,139	264.9
Bank Loans	1,115,920	1.4	79,440	1.6	154,380	1.0	1,784,260	3.0
Notes Payable	79,709	0.1	178,740	3.6	1,373,982	8.9	178,426	0.3
Other Current	61,774,155	77.5	9,800,910	197.4	9,448,052	61.2	113,954,724	191.6
Total Current	**72,295,689**	**90.7**	**15,232,620**	**306.8**	**20,239,211**	**131.1**	**273,467,549**	**459.8**
Other Long Term	14,188,129	17.8	4,230,180	85.2	2,377,452	15.4	44,368,593	74.6
Deferred Credits	0	0.0	4,965	0.1	15,438	0.1	416,327	0.7
Net Worth	(6,775,230)	(8.5)	(14,502,765)	(292.1)	(7,194,106)	(46.6)	(258,777,143)	(435.1)
Total Liab & Net Worth	**79,708,588**	**100.0**	**4,965,000**	**100.0**	**15,437,995**	**100.0**	**59,475,326**	**100.0**
Net Sales	89,359,404	100.0	5,045,732	100.0	24,740,377	100.0	93,514,664	100.0
Gross Profit	25,467,430	28.5	1,993,064	39.5	6,234,575	25.2	15,803,978	16.9
Net Profit After Tax	3,038,220	3.4	(10,091)	(0.2)	766,952	3.1	4,301,675	4.6
Working Capital	(19,050,352)	--	(11,742,225)	--	(10,405,208)	--	(241,648,250)	--

RATIOS

	SIC 3691 UQ	MED	LQ	SIC 3699 UQ	MED	LQ	SIC 37 UQ	MED	LQ	SIC 3711 UQ	MED	LQ
SOLVENCY												
Quick Ratio (times)	1.4	1.1	0.9	2.5	1.3	0.3	2.0	1.0	0.6	1.0	0.7	0.4
Current Ratio (times)	2.4	2.1	1.4	4.5	2.3	0.9	3.7	2.2	1.5	1.9	1.4	0.8
Curr Liab To Nw (%)	38.0	58.3	96.5	19.2	31.6	75.5	22.2	42.5	90.2	37.8	61.4	148.4
Curr Liab To Inv (%)	101.8	152.7	187.0	69.6	209.6	768.1	67.5	111.3	237.4	102.2	183.2	350.7
Total Liab To Nw (%)	68.1	91.9	177.9	19.2	56.7	107.9	36.4	77.2	189.8	47.6	140.8	224.9
Fixed Assets To Nw (%)	13.9	32.0	68.0	6.8	17.4	32.6	15.7	32.5	64.9	17.2	31.1	53.5
EFFICIENCY												
Coll Period (days)	39.1	58.6	65.7	38.7	57.9	86.5	19.7	39.1	54.8	8.8	29.2	46.2
Sales To Inv (times)	8.8	6.8	3.1	14.7	6.7	3.8	10.5	6.3	4.3	9.7	5.9	4.5
Assets To Sales (%)	40.6	89.2	123.3	55.2	98.4	160.2	43.4	62.4	94.8	47.7	63.6	93.8
Sales To Nwc (times)	8.9	4.3	3.2	3.6	2.2	1.5	7.4	4.9	3.1	9.8	6.5	4.7
Acct Pay To Sales (%)	6.2	7.5	8.9	3.3	6.6	15.2	3.2	6.4	9.9	5.1	7.5	15.1
PROFITABILITY												
Return On Sales (%)	7.2	2.8	(7.5)	7.9	1.5	(82.3)	8.0	3.8	0.2	5.7	3.8	(1.3)
Return On Assets (%)	9.8	2.7	(8.8)	10.2	1.6	(50.6)	11.8	5.5	0.0	12.3	5.9	(2.4)
Return On Nw (%)	31.2	9.3	(6.5)	20.6	6.4	(5.5)	23.7	13.0	2.4	31.4	16.4	0.0

SIC 3713 TRUCK,BUS BODIES (NO BREAKDOWN) 2013 (12 Establishments)

	$	%
Cash	395,196	7.1
Accounts Receivable	1,174,456	21.1
Notes Receivable	0	0.0
Inventory	2,360,044	42.4
Other Current	372,931	6.7
Total Current	**4,302,627**	**77.3**
Fixed Assets	790,392	14.2
Other Non-current	473,122	8.5
Total Assets	**5,566,141**	**100.0**
Accounts Payable	2,810,901	50.5
Bank Loans	0	0.0
Notes Payable	166,984	3.0
Other Current	9,312,154	167.3
Total Current	**12,290,039**	**220.8**
Other Long Term	233,778	4.2
Deferred Credits	0	0.0
Net Worth	(6,957,676)	(125.0)
Total Liab & Net Worth	**5,566,141**	**100.0**
Net Sales	10,384,591	100.0
Gross Profit	1,661,535	16.0
Net Profit After Tax	311,538	3.0
Working Capital	(7,987,412)	--

RATIOS	UQ	MED	LQ
SOLVENCY			
Quick Ratio (times)	1.6	1.3	0.5
Current Ratio (times)	4.8	2.6	1.1
Curr Liab To Nw (%)	21.7	39.0	187.0
Curr Liab To Inv (%)	44.4	106.6	136.1
Total Liab To Nw (%)	28.9	43.6	211.7
Fixed Assets To Nw (%)	14.5	23.0	36.9
EFFICIENCY			
Coll Period (days)	18.1	32.3	54.0
Sales To Inv (times)	7.6	6.1	4.2
Assets To Sales (%)	32.4	53.6	61.8
Sales To Nwc (times)	15.0	4.3	3.1
Acct Pay To Sales (%)	3.1	6.7	11.4
PROFITABILITY			
Return On Sales (%)	5.6	2.1	0.1
Return On Assets (%)	10.5	6.2	0.3
Return On Nw (%)	24.0	12.1	2.4

SIC 3714 MTR VHCLE PRTS,ACCS (NO BREAKDOWN) 2013 (58 Establishments)

	$	%
Cash	7,742,535	13.2
Accounts Receivable	10,088,758	17.2
Notes Receivable	293,278	0.5
Inventory	12,669,602	21.6
Other Current	3,636,645	6.2
Total Current	**34,430,818**	**58.7**
Fixed Assets	13,842,714	23.6
Other Non-current	10,382,035	17.7
Total Assets	**58,655,567**	**100.0**
Accounts Payable	9,854,135	16.8
Bank Loans	293,278	0.5
Notes Payable	5,513,623	9.4
Other Current	34,313,507	58.5
Total Current	**49,974,543**	**85.2**
Other Long Term	21,233,315	36.2
Deferred Credits	117,311	0.2
Net Worth	(12,669,602)	(21.6)
Total Liab & Net Worth	**58,655,567**	**100.0**
Net Sales	84,518,108	100.0
Gross Profit	20,622,418	24.4
Net Profit After Tax	1,521,326	1.8
Working Capital	(15,543,725)	--

RATIOS	UQ	MED	LQ
SOLVENCY			
Quick Ratio (times)	2.0	1.1	0.7
Current Ratio (times)	3.6	2.1	1.5
Curr Liab To Nw (%)	21.9	45.3	94.0
Curr Liab To Inv (%)	82.6	131.4	252.7
Total Liab To Nw (%)	37.1	74.6	229.1
Fixed Assets To Nw (%)	25.0	44.7	72.4
EFFICIENCY			
Coll Period (days)	36.5	46.4	59.1
Sales To Inv (times)	11.8	7.8	5.2
Assets To Sales (%)	51.8	69.4	93.7
Sales To Nwc (times)	7.6	5.0	3.2
Acct Pay To Sales (%)	5.5	8.6	12.0
PROFITABILITY			
Return On Sales (%)	5.6	2.7	(0.1)
Return On Assets (%)	8.4	3.1	(1.6)
Return On Nw (%)	18.4	9.6	0.3

SIC 3724 AIRCRFT ENG,ENG PRT (NO BREAKDOWN) 2013 (11 Establishments)

	$	%
Cash	2,136,605	14.4
Accounts Receivable	2,374,006	16.0
Notes Receivable	0	0.0
Inventory	2,730,107	18.4
Other Current	2,166,280	14.6
Total Current	**9,406,998**	**63.4**
Fixed Assets	1,691,479	11.4
Other Non-current	3,739,060	25.2
Total Assets	**14,837,537**	**100.0**
Accounts Payable	994,115	6.7
Bank Loans	0	0.0
Notes Payable	14,838	0.1
Other Current	3,130,720	21.1
Total Current	**4,139,673**	**27.9**
Other Long Term	2,181,118	14.7
Deferred Credits	0	0.0
Net Worth	8,516,746	57.4
Total Liab & Net Worth	**14,837,537**	**100.0**
Net Sales	16,075,338	100.0
Gross Profit	3,906,307	24.3
Net Profit After Tax	1,221,726	7.6
Working Capital	5,267,325	--

RATIOS	UQ	MED	LQ
SOLVENCY			
Quick Ratio (times)	1.8	1.1	1.0
Current Ratio (times)	2.8	2.6	1.7
Curr Liab To Nw (%)	24.3	42.3	77.1
Curr Liab To Inv (%)	73.7	125.4	330.3
Total Liab To Nw (%)	47.8	86.1	145.5
Fixed Assets To Nw (%)	13.5	23.3	39.3
EFFICIENCY			
Coll Period (days)	26.7	47.6	74.1
Sales To Inv (times)	11.1	6.3	4.7
Assets To Sales (%)	24.3	92.3	116.3
Sales To Nwc (times)	9.0	4.8	3.6
Acct Pay To Sales (%)	2.8	5.4	7.0
PROFITABILITY			
Return On Sales (%)	12.3	9.5	1.0
Return On Assets (%)	12.1	8.4	2.6
Return On Nw (%)	22.5	13.4	6.3

SIC 3728 AIRCRFT PRT,EQP,NEC (NO BREAKDOWN) 2013 (40 Establishments)

	$	%
Cash	1,050,615	15.8
Accounts Receivable	1,256,748	18.9
Notes Receivable	46,546	0.7
Inventory	1,635,767	24.6
Other Current	571,854	8.6
Total Current	**4,561,530**	**68.6**
Fixed Assets	1,283,346	19.3
Other Non-current	804,584	12.1
Total Assets	**6,649,460**	**100.0**
Accounts Payable	585,152	8.8
Bank Loans	152,938	2.3
Notes Payable	139,639	2.1
Other Current	744,739	11.2
Total Current	**1,622,468**	**24.4**
Other Long Term	1,502,778	22.6
Deferred Credits	0	0.0
Net Worth	3,524,214	53.0
Total Liab & Net Worth	**6,649,460**	**100.0**
Net Sales	9,445,256	100.0
Gross Profit	3,041,372	32.2
Net Profit After Tax	491,153	5.2
Working Capital	2,939,062	--

RATIOS	UQ	MED	LQ
SOLVENCY			
Quick Ratio (times)	2.8	1.6	0.8
Current Ratio (times)	5.3	3.4	2.1
Curr Liab To Nw (%)	17.7	34.0	51.3
Curr Liab To Inv (%)	42.4	74.9	96.5
Total Liab To Nw (%)	20.3	70.4	143.0
Fixed Assets To Nw (%)	17.0	31.4	74.4
EFFICIENCY			
Coll Period (days)	33.6	45.3	56.9
Sales To Inv (times)	8.2	4.5	3.6
Assets To Sales (%)	44.2	70.4	112.5
Sales To Nwc (times)	5.0	3.2	2.2
Acct Pay To Sales (%)	3.0	4.7	7.9
PROFITABILITY			
Return On Sales (%)	10.1	5.8	1.1
Return On Assets (%)	10.8	5.6	2.3
Return On Nw (%)	21.3	10.1	4.4

SIC 38 INSTRUMENTS RLTD PDTS (NO BREAKDOWN) 2013 (402 Establishments) | SIC 3812 SEARCH.NVGTN EQPMNT (NO BREAKDOWN) 2013 (23 Establishments) | SIC 3821 LBRTRY APPTUS.FURN (NO BREAKDOWN) 2013 (12 Establishments) | SIC 3823 PROC CNTL INSTRMNTS (NO BREAKDOWN) 2013 (36 Establishments)

	SIC 38 $	SIC 38 %	SIC 3812 $	SIC 3812 %	SIC 3821 $	SIC 3821 %	SIC 3823 $	SIC 3823 %
Cash	4,091,116	22.3	5,753,536	18.6	1,208,644	29.6	1,257,610	23.1
Accounts Receivable	2,806,909	15.3	5,784,469	18.7	734,986	18.0	1,012,621	18.6
Notes Receivable	18,346	0.1	0	0.0	0	0.0	0	0.0
Inventory	3,430,666	18.7	5,970,066	19.3	845,234	20.7	952,735	17.5
Other Current	2,109,768	11.5	4,052,221	13.1	322,579	7.9	860,183	15.8
Total Current	**12,456,805**	**67.9**	**21,560,292**	**69.7**	**3,111,443**	**76.2**	**4,083,149**	**75.0**
Fixed Assets	2,403,301	13.1	4,361,551	14.1	265,412	6.5	571,641	10.5
Other Non-current	3,485,704	19.0	5,011,144	16.2	706,403	17.3	789,408	14.5
Total Assets	**18,345,810**	**100.0**	**30,932,987**	**100.0**	**4,083,258**	**100.0**	**5,444,198**	**100.0**
Accounts Payable	11,264,327	61.4	2,691,170	8.7	204,163	5.0	402,871	7.4
Bank Loans	36,692	0.2	30,933	0.1	16,333	0.4	59,886	1.1
Notes Payable	1,375,936	7.5	185,598	0.6	4,083	0.1	54,442	1.0
Other Current	12,383,421	67.5	20,477,637	66.2	824,818	20.2	778,520	14.3
Total Current	**25,060,376**	**136.6**	**23,385,338**	**75.6**	**1,049,397**	**25.7**	**1,295,719**	**23.8**
Other Long Term	1,577,740	8.6	6,001,000	19.4	261,329	6.4	408,315	7.5
Deferred Credits	165,112	0.9	0	0.0	0	0.0	16,333	0.3
Net Worth	(8,457,418)	(46.1)	1,546,649	5.0	2,772,532	67.9	3,723,831	68.4
Total Liab & Net Worth	**18,345,810**	**100.0**	**30,932,987**	**100.0**	**4,083,258**	**100.0**	**5,444,198**	**100.0**
Net Sales	17,708,311	100.0	32,872,462	100.0	6,131,018	100.0	8,480,059	100.0
Gross Profit	8,340,614	47.1	12,524,408	38.1	2,930,627	47.8	3,510,744	41.4
Net Profit After Tax	(265,625)	(1.5)	2,268,200	6.9	349,468	5.7	517,284	6.1
Working Capital	(12,603,571)	—	(1,825,046)	—	2,062,046	—	2,787,430	—

RATIOS	SIC 38 UQ	SIC 38 MED	SIC 38 LQ	SIC 3812 UQ	SIC 3812 MED	SIC 3812 LQ	SIC 3821 UQ	SIC 3821 MED	SIC 3821 LQ	SIC 3823 UQ	SIC 3823 MED	SIC 3823 LQ
SOLVENCY												
Quick Ratio (times)	3.0	1.6	0.8	2.2	1.2	0.7	6.3	2.8	1.9	3.7	2.1	1.2
Current Ratio (times)	5.2	3.0	1.7	4.8	1.9	1.5	12.6	5.4	3.1	6.3	4.0	2.2
Curr Liab To Nw (%)	15.4	27.6	55.9	21.4	50.0	88.8	5.5	14.7	31.9	10.6	24.8	61.3
Curr Liab To Inv (%)	77.9	148.8	286.1	126.4	148.8	555.8	37.7	90.2	144.2	52.5	97.7	337.7
Total Liab To Nw (%)	22.0	46.0	102.4	39.8	121.4	177.9	10.1	14.7	41.8	21.2	31.6	92.5
Fixed Assets To Nw (%)	6.9	15.8	32.0	17.4	28.7	44.7	4.1	5.1	16.6	4.7	9.6	32.5
EFFICIENCY												
Coll Period (days)	39.8	52.6	69.4	42.0	51.8	68.8	43.1	48.9	62.8	35.8	52.8	68.3
Sales To Inv (times)	9.5	6.5	4.1	22.1	7.6	4.7	8.4	6.7	4.8	13.4	8.8	5.7
Assets To Sales (%)	63.3	103.6	166.0	57.4	94.1	114.9	53.8	66.6	93.6	43.7	64.2	139.4
Sales To Nwc (times)	4.4	2.3	1.5	6.3	2.8	1.7	4.7	2.6	1.6	4.7	3.1	1.8
Acct Pay To Sales (%)	3.3	5.3	9.1	2.3	5.5	7.5	2.5	3.4	5.7	2.0	2.8	4.4
PROFITABILITY												
Return On Sales (%)	9.3	2.1	(23.5)	9.9	7.0	3.4	22.5	3.1	(1.0)	11.0	6.0	2.4
Return On Assets (%)	9.1	2.7	(26.8)	13.2	7.9	3.7	30.5	5.4	(1.4)	16.7	8.1	2.3
Return On Nw (%)	16.7	6.1	(16.0)	22.6	18.4	7.4	53.2	9.1	(1.4)	24.3	11.7	3.2

SIC 3825 INSTRMNTS MEAS ELEC
(NO BREAKDOWN)
2013 (25 Establishments)

SIC 3826 ANALYTCL INSTRMNTS
(NO BREAKDOWN)
2013 (31 Establishments)

SIC 3827 OPTCL INSTRMNTS,LNS
(NO BREAKDOWN)
2013 (18 Establishments)

SIC 3829 MEAS,CTLNG DVCS,NEC
(NO BREAKDOWN)
2013 (39 Establishments)

	SIC 3825 $	%	SIC 3826 $	%	SIC 3827 $	%	SIC 3829 $	%
Cash	9,615,351	27.1	18,147,998	30.7	2,474,974	23.3	1,209,049	19.9
Accounts Receivable	4,506,087	12.7	8,098,618	13.7	1,391,509	13.1	1,184,746	19.5
Notes Receivable	0	0.0	0	0.0	0	0.0	24,302	0.4
Inventory	7,486,491	21.1	9,044,442	15.3	2,411,241	22.7	1,336,637	22.0
Other Current	5,428,593	15.3	7,743,934	13.1	1,657,065	15.6	662,243	10.9
Total Current	**27,036,522**	**76.2**	**43,034,992**	**72.8**	**7,934,789**	**74.7**	**4,416,977**	**72.7**
Fixed Assets	2,980,404	8.4	6,029,628	10.2	1,603,953	15.1	783,755	12.9
Other Non-current	5,464,074	15.4	10,049,380	17.0	1,083,465	10.2	874,890	14.4
Total Assets	**35,481,000**	**100.0**	**59,114,000**	**100.0**	**10,622,207**	**100.0**	**6,075,622**	**100.0**
Accounts Payable	82,990,059	233.9	13,241,536	22.4	764,799	7.2	534,655	8.8
Bank Loans	0	0.0	0	0.0	0	0.0	0	0.0
Notes Payable	7,699,377	21.7	2,423,674	4.1	0	0.0	48,605	0.8
Other Current	31,400,685	88.5	41,025,116	69.4	4,057,683	38.2	1,227,275	20.2
Total Current	**122,090,121**	**344.1**	**56,690,326**	**95.9**	**4,822,482**	**45.4**	**1,810,535**	**29.8**
Other Long Term	3,335,214	9.4	12,236,598	20.7	2,825,507	26.6	565,033	9.3
Deferred Credits	0	0.0	591,140	1.0	21,244	0.2	243,025	4.0
Net Worth	(89,944,335)	(253.5)	(10,404,064)	(17.6)	2,952,974	27.8	3,457,029	56.9
Total Liab & Net Worth	**35,481,000**	**100.0**	**59,114,000**	**100.0**	**10,622,207**	**100.0**	**6,075,622**	**100.0**
Net Sales	36,578,351	100.0	38,560,992	100.0	12,111,981	100.0	7,973,257	100.0
Gross Profit	13,936,352	38.1	19,241,935	49.9	4,820,568	39.8	3,579,992	44.9
Net Profit After Tax	(2,341,014)	(6.4)	154,244	0.4	(666,159)	(5.5)	0	0.0
Working Capital	(95,053,599)	—	(13,655,334)	—	3,112,307	—	2,606,442	—

RATIOS	UQ	MED	LQ	UQ	MED	LQ	UQ	MED	LQ	UQ	MED	LQ
SOLVENCY												
Quick Ratio (times)	2.0	1.4	0.9	3.1	1.8	1.3	2.9	1.8	0.7	3.2	1.8	1.0
Current Ratio (times)	4.2	3.1	1.8	5.0	4.3	2.5	5.8	3.2	1.9	6.3	3.3	1.9
Curr Liab To Nw (%)	19.1	30.3	62.4	18.9	25.4	31.4	14.2	32.3	61.6	16.1	23.6	49.8
Curr Liab To Inv (%)	74.9	110.3	180.6	89.4	174.9	229.7	53.4	91.6	148.7	59.9	118.8	223.3
Total Liab To Nw (%)	23.3	56.1	101.0	24.4	45.0	96.9	16.6	53.1	102.5	17.5	30.3	64.7
Fixed Assets To Nw (%)	7.3	13.9	22.8	7.1	13.3	29.8	3.2	17.4	43.0	5.1	9.8	24.5
EFFICIENCY												
Coll Period (days)	40.4	48.2	60.6	41.6	54.0	69.7	37.8	48.9	66.5	29.2	45.3	69.0
Sales To Inv (times)	8.5	5.0	4.0	9.0	5.7	4.1	6.7	4.9	2.9	9.6	7.3	4.6
Assets To Sales (%)	66.0	97.0	158.0	53.0	153.3	243.4	68.8	87.7	146.1	56.1	76.2	128.4
Sales To Nwc (times)	3.4	2.0	1.5	4.4	1.7	0.7	4.2	1.6	1.3	4.6	2.5	1.8
Acct Pay To Sales (%)	3.7	5.8	8.7	5.2	6.5	21.1	2.5	4.8	7.9	3.8	5.0	6.8
PROFITABILITY												
Return On Sales (%)	8.5	3.3	(20.8)	8.8	(1.2)	(141.5)	6.0	2.6	(20.4)	10.8	6.8	(0.3)
Return On Assets (%)	8.1	3.4	(24.4)	7.6	(0.5)	(35.2)	6.0	3.0	(32.7)	14.2	7.7	(0.7)
Return On Nw (%)	13.7	4.5	(27.1)	11.8	7.9	(26.9)	11.9	6.0	(10.2)	22.5	10.9	3.5

Balance Sheet

	SIC 3841 SRGL,MDCL INSTRMNTS (NO BREAKDOWN) 2013 (109 Establishments) $	%	SIC 3842 SRGCL APPL,SUPPLS (NO BREAKDOWN) 2013 (23 Establishments) $	%	SIC 3845 ELECTROMDCL EQPT (NO BREAKDOWN) 2013 (42 Establishments) $	%	SIC 3861 PHTGRPH EQPT,SUPPLS (NO BREAKDOWN) 2013 (13 Establishments) $	%
Cash	8,910,396	26.4	10,452,010	11.8	4,256,659	12.7	3,122,402	22.3
Accounts Receivable	3,847,671	11.4	12,666,418	14.3	5,597,339	16.7	3,052,393	21.8
Notes Receivable	101,255	0.3	0	0.0	0	0.0	0	0.0
Inventory	5,130,228	15.2	22,764,123	25.7	6,870,985	20.5	2,156,278	15.4
Other Current	3,003,883	8.9	6,908,955	7.8	4,591,829	13.7	1,722,222	12.3
Total Current	**20,993,433**	**62.2**	**52,791,506**	**59.6**	**21,316,812**	**63.6**	**10,053,295**	**71.8**
Fixed Assets	5,096,477	15.1	12,754,995	14.4	5,362,720	16.0	2,618,337	18.7
Other Non-current	7,661,590	22.7	23,029,852	26.0	6,837,468	20.4	1,330,171	9.5
Total Assets	**33,751,500**	**100.0**	**88,576,353**	**100.0**	**33,517,000**	**100.0**	**14,001,803**	**100.0**
Accounts Payable	38,274,201	113.4	7,440,414	8.4	29,394,409	87.7	5,698,734	40.7
Bank Loans	0	0.0	1,860,103	2.1	0	0.0	0	0.0
Notes Payable	6,716,549	19.9	1,151,493	1.3	536,272	1.6	56,007	0.4
Other Current	35,135,311	104.1	25,775,718	29.1	42,868,243	127.9	6,832,880	48.8
Total Current	**80,126,061**	**237.4**	**36,227,728**	**40.9**	**72,798,924**	**217.2**	**12,587,621**	**89.9**
Other Long Term	(5,771,506)	(17.1)	16,563,778	18.7	10,893,025	32.5	4,256,548	30.4
Deferred Credits	270,012	0.8	177,153	0.2	536,272	1.6	28,004	0.2
Net Worth	(40,873,067)	(121.1)	35,607,694	40.2	(50,711,221)	(151.3)	(2,870,370)	(20.5)
Total Liab & Net Worth	**33,751,500**	**100.0**	**88,576,353**	**100.0**	**33,517,000**	**100.0**	**14,001,803**	**100.0**
Net Sales	23,652,067	100.0	86,500,345	100.0	28,794,674	100.0	15,202,826	100.0
Gross Profit	12,653,856	53.5	40,568,662	46.9	14,858,052	51.6	4,424,022	29.1
Net Profit After Tax	(1,915,817)	(8.1)	(1,384,006)	(1.6)	(1,842,859)	(6.4)	(942,575)	(6.2)
Working Capital	(59,132,628)	—	16,563,778	—	(51,482,112)	—	(2,534,326)	—

RATIOS

	3841 UQ	MED	LQ	3842 UQ	MED	LQ	3845 UQ	MED	LQ	3861 UQ	MED	LQ
SOLVENCY												
Quick Ratio (times)	3.1	1.7	0.7	2.1	1.3	0.8	2.8	1.7	0.9	4.3	1.6	0.7
Current Ratio (times)	5.1	2.6	1.2	4.8	3.6	2.3	4.9	2.6	1.5	8.6	3.1	1.4
Curr Liab To Nw (%)	15.6	28.0	49.2	16.6	25.7	36.2	18.4	26.1	60.2	8.1	18.0	35.3
Curr Liab To Inv (%)	97.3	190.3	383.8	57.6	87.6	151.5	99.5	182.0	245.1	64.8	154.8	247.2
Total Liab To Nw (%)	25.3	61.0	112.0	26.2	57.8	102.0	24.2	39.2	143.3	10.1	18.8	43.6
Fixed Assets To Nw (%)	8.5	17.6	33.6	15.6	27.0	43.5	7.7	14.9	33.6	10.8	24.4	44.7
EFFICIENCY												
Coll Period (days)	40.9	51.9	71.4	41.1	51.7	65.2	40.4	60.1	85.1	52.6	64.6	70.5
Sales To Inv (times)	9.1	6.2	3.9	7.0	4.9	3.3	10.8	7.8	4.2	8.4	6.8	5.1
Assets To Sales (%)	83.2	142.7	210.3	56.6	102.4	186.8	78.5	116.4	183.4	82.9	92.1	140.2
Sales To Nwc (times)	3.2	1.9	1.2	5.1	3.1	1.8	3.5	2.2	1.4	2.4	2.1	1.4
Acct Pay To Sales (%)	4.1	7.0	16.6	3.1	4.5	6.9	3.8	6.0	9.7	4.8	8.9	12.4
PROFITABILITY												
Return On Sales (%)	6.3	(16.4)	(172.3)	8.6	0.9	(22.3)	6.6	(4.6)	(35.3)	2.7	0.2	(35.1)
Return On Assets (%)	4.4	(15.0)	(65.4)	7.9	1.6	(26.5)	6.6	(4.3)	(62.6)	4.0	0.2	(33.8)
Return On Nw (%)	11.9	(5.3)	(56.8)	12.1	4.6	(31.7)	9.8	(0.4)	(36.8)	4.3	0.2	(1.3)

	SIC 39 MISC MANUFACTURING (NO BREAKDOWN) 2013 (106 Establishments)		SIC 3911 JEWELRY,PREC MTL (NO BREAKDOWN) 2013 (14 Establishments)		SIC 3944 GMES,TYS,CHLRN VHCL (NO BREAKDOWN) 2013 (14 Establishments)		SIC 3949 SPRTG,AHLTC GDS NEC (NO BREAKDOWN) 2013 (16 Establishments)	
	$	%	$	%	$	%	$	%
Cash	834,716	16.1	587,298	10.4	7,110,607	24.2	1,426,552	10.8
Accounts Receivable	1,270,221	24.5	1,225,420	21.7	6,199,744	21.1	3,262,578	24.7
Notes Receivable	0	0.0	0	0.0	29,383	0.1	0	0.0
Inventory	1,218,375	23.5	2,343,544	41.5	5,523,943	18.8	4,279,657	32.4
Other Current	414,766	8.0	248,472	4.4	2,879,503	9.8	713,276	5.4
Total Current	**3,738,078**	**72.1**	**4,404,734**	**78.0**	**21,743,180**	**74.0**	**9,682,063**	**73.3**
Fixed Assets	751,763	14.5	592,945	10.5	2,850,119	9.7	1,320,882	10.0
Other Non-current	694,733	13.4	649,416	11.5	4,789,376	16.3	2,205,872	16.7
Total Assets	**5,184,574**	**100.0**	**5,647,095**	**100.0**	**29,382,675**	**100.0**	**13,208,817**	**100.0**
Accounts Payable	710,287	13.7	615,533	10.9	4,142,957	14.1	2,113,411	16.0
Bank Loans	20,738	0.4	0	0.0	0	0.0	132,088	1.0
Notes Payable	155,537	3.0	124,236	2.2	2,615,058	8.9	383,056	2.9
Other Current	1,363,543	26.3	1,072,948	19.0	4,407,402	15.0	2,007,740	15.2
Total Current	**2,250,105**	**43.4**	**1,812,717**	**32.1**	**11,165,417**	**38.0**	**4,636,295**	**35.1**
Other Long Term	798,425	15.4	796,241	14.1	5,318,264	18.1	1,585,058	12.0
Deferred Credits	10,369	0.2	0	0.0	0	0.0	13,209	0.1
Net Worth	2,125,675	41.0	3,038,137	53.8	12,898,994	43.9	6,974,255	52.8
Total Liab & Net Worth	**5,184,574**	**100.0**	**5,647,095**	**100.0**	**29,382,675**	**100.0**	**13,208,817**	**100.0**
Net Sales	8,713,570	100.0	9,977,200	100.0	38,308,572	100.0	19,833,059	100.0
Gross Profit	3,241,448	37.2	3,761,404	37.7	15,476,663	40.4	7,377,898	37.2
Net Profit After Tax	313,689	3.6	159,635	1.6	153,234	0.4	753,656	3.8
Working Capital	1,487,973	---	2,592,017	---	10,577,763	---	5,045,768	---

RATIOS	UQ	MED	LQ	UQ	MED	LQ	UQ	MED	LQ	UQ	MED	LQ
SOLVENCY												
Quick Ratio (times)	2.9	1.3	0.6	2.9	0.8	0.5	3.9	1.6	0.6	2.1	1.5	0.7
Current Ratio (times)	5.0	2.2	1.5	6.2	3.2	1.5	5.0	2.6	1.7	7.4	2.0	1.8
Curr Liab To Nw (%)	17.6	46.1	100.3	17.3	46.1	108.7	17.6	56.6	106.0	10.5	48.5	72.2
Curr Liab To Inv (%)	71.6	145.1	304.5	36.6	86.9	124.7	83.7	207.6	390.9	42.3	87.5	154.3
Total Liab To Nw (%)	21.0	61.4	156.3	17.3	46.9	139.7	25.7	92.9	182.1	14.9	59.1	133.2
Fixed Assets To Nw (%)	5.9	16.3	40.9	3.4	8.5	45.0	3.0	10.9	39.2	5.6	11.8	22.0
EFFICIENCY												
Coll Period (days)	28.5	42.0	74.1	24.3	34.7	65.2	24.8	51.7	87.6	27.4	38.7	77.8
Sales To Inv (times)	14.6	9.4	4.1	10.6	3.4	2.2	15.2	11.0	4.5	6.0	4.8	3.4
Assets To Sales (%)	35.7	59.5	98.2	32.2	56.6	126.0	52.1	76.7	92.7	39.9	66.6	86.7
Sales To Nwc (times)	6.5	4.2	2.8	6.2	4.4	3.3	4.2	3.6	2.5	8.8	4.3	2.3
Acct Pay To Sales (%)	2.6	4.8	10.1	2.7	4.1	13.4	4.0	4.7	16.3	1.8	6.2	14.3
PROFITABILITY												
Return On Sales (%)	8.6	3.6	0.3	1.7	1.0	0.6	7.9	1.8	(8.5)	15.8	6.0	(1.9)
Return On Assets (%)	17.5	5.9	0.5	4.2	1.6	0.5	8.5	3.5	(12.0)	28.0	9.8	(1.6)
Return On Nw (%)	31.8	13.9	2.4	9.4	5.5	1.9	23.7	13.3	(10.3)	46.3	17.8	6.3

	SIC 3993 SIGNS,ADVT SPCLTIES (NO BREAKDOWN) 2013 (29 Establishments) $	%	SIC 3999 MFG INDUSTRIES, NEC (NO BREAKDOWN) 2013 (17 Establishments) $	%	SIC 41 LOCAL PASSENGER TRAN (NO BREAKDOWN) 2013 (41 Establishments) $	%	SIC 4111 LCL SUBURNAN TRANS (NO BREAKDOWN) 2013 (10 Establishments) $	%
Cash	623,825	21.5	784,897	14.7	678,080	16.3	2,776,160	17.6
Accounts Receivable	925,582	31.9	1,249,428	23.4	669,760	16.1	1,498,496	9.5
Notes Receivable	0	0.0	0	0.0	4,160	0.1	0	0.0
Inventory	403,310	13.9	784,897	14.7	37,440	0.9	141,963	0.9
Other Current	261,135	9.0	373,760	7.0	416,000	10.0	1,608,911	10.2
Total Current	**2,213,852**	**76.3**	**3,192,982**	**59.8**	**1,805,440**	**43.4**	**6,025,530**	**38.2**
Fixed Assets	504,863	17.4	993,135	18.6	1,992,640	47.9	7,555,573	47.9
Other Non-current	182,795	6.3	1,153,318	21.6	361,920	8.7	2,192,536	13.9
Total Assets	**2,901,510**	**100.0**	**5,339,435**	**100.0**	**4,160,000**	**100.0**	**15,773,639**	**100.0**
Accounts Payable	426,522	14.7	368,421	6.9	287,040	6.9	567,851	3.6
Bank Loans	0	0.0	0	0.0	8,320	0.2	0	0.0
Notes Payable	84,144	2.9	0	0.0	99,840	2.4	78,868	0.5
Other Current	783,407	27.0	1,724,638	32.3	694,720	16.7	1,877,063	11.9
Total Current	**1,294,073**	**44.6**	**2,093,059**	**39.2**	**1,089,920**	**26.2**	**2,523,782**	**16.0**
Other Long Term	281,446	9.7	1,201,372	22.5	1,098,240	26.4	5,583,868	35.4
Deferred Credits	2,902	0.1	21,358	0.4	20,800	0.5	0	0.0
Net Worth	1,323,089	45.6	2,023,646	37.9	1,951,040	46.9	7,665,989	48.6
Total Liab & Net Worth	**2,901,510**	**100.0**	**5,339,435**	**100.0**	**4,160,000**	**100.0**	**15,773,639**	**100.0**
Net Sales	6,670,138	100.0	7,488,689	100.0	8,077,670	100.0	15,388,916	100.0
Gross Profit	2,734,757	41.0	2,853,191	38.1	3,045,282	37.7	6,648,012	43.2
Net Profit After Tax	360,187	5.4	284,570	3.8	48,466	0.6	(400,112)	(2.6)
Working Capital	919,779	--	1,099,923	--	715,520	--	3,501,748	--

RATIOS	SIC 3993 UQ	MED	LQ	SIC 3999 UQ	MED	LQ	SIC 41 UQ	MED	LQ	SIC 4111 UQ	MED	LQ
SOLVENCY												
Quick Ratio (times)	2.5	1.4	0.9	4.3	1.2	0.6	2.6	1.4	0.5	1.9	1.4	0.2
Current Ratio (times)	3.4	2.1	1.5	5.8	2.2	1.3	3.3	1.7	1.0	5.9	1.8	1.0
Curr Liab To Nw (%)	32.5	60.9	136.1	9.1	38.2	97.1	16.3	36.2	117.0	11.4	19.0	33.2
Curr Liab To Inv (%)	115.1	240.4	544.4	94.4	269.1	439.6	795.1	999.9	999.9	816.6	999.9	999.9
Total Liab To Nw (%)	35.2	69.7	160.0	10.0	65.9	209.3	22.9	97.3	312.0	14.7	19.8	113.7
Fixed Assets To Nw (%)	11.8	19.1	39.3	13.6	28.6	74.8	51.7	90.2	173.5	58.0	93.8	99.8
EFFICIENCY												
Coll Period (days)	32.5	52.6	68.3	15.9	46.4	101.2	10.6	28.8	52.9	5.5	19.2	71.2
Sales To Inv (times)	32.6	14.3	9.3	20.7	12.8	4.1	176.7	73.5	15.8	15.8	9.6	5.7
Assets To Sales (%)	28.5	43.5	61.8	42.9	71.3	124.1	32.4	51.5	101.1	19.4	102.5	999.9
Sales To Nwc (times)	6.0	4.6	3.8	9.5	6.5	3.2	21.3	10.3	4.7	66.6	10.0	1.4
Acct Pay To Sales (%)	2.6	3.8	7.5	2.6	4.5	6.3	1.2	3.0	6.0	1.1	6.1	38.0
PROFITABILITY												
Return On Sales (%)	9.3	5.5	3.0	8.4	3.0	(1.1)	2.8	(1.8)	(2.4)	3.0	(1.8)	(12.0)
Return On Assets (%)	23.0	15.7	6.9	10.6	4.9	(5.5)	6.0	(0.2)	(1.2)	6.6	(0.2)	(3.0)
Return On Nw (%)	46.3	23.6	11.4	27.0	6.1	(3.1)	22.6	(0.3)	(0.8)	7.3	(0.3)	(2.5)

SIC 4119 — LCL PASS TRANS NEC (NO BREAKDOWN) 2013 (17 Establishments)

	$	%
Cash	481,911	14.6
Accounts Receivable	835,093	25.3
Notes Receivable	0	0.0
Inventory	13,203	0.4
Other Current	389,491	11.8
Total Current	**1,719,698**	**52.1**
Fixed Assets	1,241,087	37.6
Other Non-current	339,978	10.3
Total Assets	**3,300,763**	**100.0**
Accounts Payable	389,490	11.8
Bank Loans	13,203	0.4
Notes Payable	19,805	0.6
Other Current	594,137	18.0
Total Current	**1,016,635**	**30.8**
Other Long Term	831,792	25.2
Deferred Credits	0	0.0
Net Worth	1,452,336	44.0
Total Liab & Net Worth	**3,300,763**	**100.0**
Net Sales	7,896,562	100.0
Gross Profit	2,605,865	33.0
Net Profit After Tax	78,966	1.0
Working Capital	703,063	---

RATIOS	UQ	MED	LQ
SOLVENCY			
Quick Ratio (times)	3.2	1.4	0.8
Curr Ratio (times)	3.3	1.8	1.1
Curr Liab To Nw (%)	18.3	73.3	210.8
Curr Liab To Inv (%)	999.9	999.9	999.9
Total Liab To Nw (%)	53.4	122.9	351.2
Fixed Assets To Nw (%)	35.4	63.4	144.6
EFFICIENCY			
Coll Period (days)	36.5	47.1	56.6
Sales To Inv (times)	520.2	250.8	119.7
Assets To Sales (%)	31.8	41.8	61.2
Sales To Nwc (times)	16.4	10.6	4.7
Acct Pay To Sales (%)	1.1	1.5	3.0
PROFITABILITY			
Return On Sales (%)	1.4	1.1	(2.4)
Return On Assets (%)	4.6	1.5	(6.8)
Return On Nw (%)	28.1	3.5	(9.4)

SIC 42 — TRUCKING & WAREHSNG (NO BREAKDOWN) 2013 (245 Establishments)

	$	%
Cash	437,628	14.1
Accounts Receivable	772,833	24.9
Notes Receivable	18,622	0.6
Inventory	90,009	2.9
Other Current	304,167	9.8
Total Current	**1,623,259**	**52.3**
Fixed Assets	1,257,017	40.5
Other Non-current	223,469	7.2
Total Assets	**3,103,745**	**100.0**
Accounts Payable	263,818	8.5
Bank Loans	34,141	1.1
Notes Payable	62,075	2.0
Other Current	819,389	26.4
Total Current	**1,179,423**	**38.0**
Other Long Term	844,219	27.2
Deferred Credits	0	0.0
Net Worth	1,080,103	34.8
Total Liab & Net Worth	**3,103,745**	**100.0**
Net Sales	9,237,336	100.0
Gross Profit	2,918,998	31.6
Net Profit After Tax	286,357	3.1
Working Capital	443,836	---

RATIOS	UQ	MED	LQ
SOLVENCY			
Quick Ratio (times)	2.5	1.4	0.8
Curr Ratio (times)	3.3	1.8	1.2
Curr Liab To Nw (%)	22.6	48.3	91.5
Curr Liab To Inv (%)	233.7	999.9	999.9
Total Liab To Nw (%)	42.7	95.6	211.1
Fixed Assets To Nw (%)	29.5	78.7	165.5
EFFICIENCY			
Coll Period (days)	22.3	31.8	44.6
Sales To Inv (times)	354.7	108.8	32.9
Assets To Sales (%)	21.8	33.6	54.8
Sales To Nwc (times)	23.4	12.1	6.8
Acct Pay To Sales (%)	1.3	2.7	4.1
PROFITABILITY			
Return On Sales (%)	5.6	2.4	0.7
Return On Assets (%)	15.2	7.2	2.0
Return On Nw (%)	34.4	17.1	5.2

SIC 4212 — LCL TRCKG W/O STRGE (NO BREAKDOWN) 2013 (75 Establishments)

	$	%
Cash	283,187	12.6
Accounts Receivable	469,730	20.9
Notes Receivable	2,248	0.1
Inventory	58,435	2.6
Other Current	265,206	11.8
Total Current	**1,078,806**	**48.0**
Fixed Assets	982,163	43.7
Other Non-current	186,543	8.3
Total Assets	**2,247,512**	**100.0**
Accounts Payable	211,266	9.4
Bank Loans	24,723	1.1
Notes Payable	35,960	1.6
Other Current	854,055	38.0
Total Current	**1,126,004**	**50.1**
Other Long Term	719,203	32.0
Deferred Credits	2,248	0.1
Net Worth	400,057	17.8
Total Liab & Net Worth	**2,247,512**	**100.0**
Net Sales	6,439,862	100.0
Gross Profit	2,279,711	35.4
Net Profit After Tax	264,034	4.1
Working Capital	(47,198)	---

RATIOS	UQ	MED	LQ
SOLVENCY			
Quick Ratio (times)	2.8	1.5	0.7
Curr Ratio (times)	3.5	1.7	1.1
Curr Liab To Nw (%)	14.0	34.7	70.6
Curr Liab To Inv (%)	230.0	620.0	999.9
Total Liab To Nw (%)	41.2	75.9	171.9
Fixed Assets To Nw (%)	37.3	77.9	149.6
EFFICIENCY			
Coll Period (days)	19.7	32.3	46.7
Sales To Inv (times)	286.6	91.9	29.6
Assets To Sales (%)	24.1	34.9	51.3
Sales To Nwc (times)	35.3	12.2	6.7
Acct Pay To Sales (%)	1.4	2.8	4.8
PROFITABILITY			
Return On Sales (%)	5.7	2.7	0.3
Return On Assets (%)	16.2	6.9	1.0
Return On Nw (%)	29.2	17.9	3.1

SIC 4213 — TRCKG, EXCEPT LOCAL (NO BREAKDOWN) 2013 (104 Establishments)

	$	%
Cash	593,443	13.4
Accounts Receivable	1,178,029	26.6
Notes Receivable	26,572	0.6
Inventory	70,859	1.6
Other Current	411,867	9.3
Total Current	**2,280,770**	**51.5**
Fixed Assets	1,868,903	42.2
Other Non-current	279,006	6.3
Total Assets	**4,428,679**	**100.0**
Accounts Payable	283,435	6.4
Bank Loans	39,858	0.9
Notes Payable	97,431	2.2
Other Current	1,040,740	23.5
Total Current	**1,461,464**	**33.0**
Other Long Term	1,315,318	29.7
Deferred Credits	0	0.0
Net Worth	1,651,897	37.3
Total Liab & Net Worth	**4,428,679**	**100.0**
Net Sales	13,180,592	100.0
Gross Profit	3,281,967	24.9
Net Profit After Tax	329,515	2.5
Working Capital	819,306	---

RATIOS	UQ	MED	LQ
SOLVENCY			
Quick Ratio (times)	2.2	1.2	0.8
Curr Ratio (times)	3.0	1.7	1.2
Curr Liab To Nw (%)	27.8	57.6	102.3
Curr Liab To Inv (%)	656.9	999.9	999.9
Total Liab To Nw (%)	49.0	117.1	275.2
Fixed Assets To Nw (%)	24.5	113.4	199.4
EFFICIENCY			
Coll Period (days)	24.8	31.4	41.3
Sales To Inv (times)	548.5	220.5	58.5
Assets To Sales (%)	21.9	33.6	58.6
Sales To Nwc (times)	25.6	13.3	7.6
Acct Pay To Sales (%)	1.1	2.0	3.3
PROFITABILITY			
Return On Sales (%)	4.8	1.8	0.7
Return On Assets (%)	13.3	5.5	2.0
Return On Nw (%)	30.2	12.7	5.9

SIC 4214 — LCL TRCKG WTH STRGE (NO BREAKDOWN) — 2013 (19 Establishments)
SIC 4225 — GNRL WRHSG,STRGE (NO BREAKDOWN) — 2013 (16 Establishments)
SIC 4226 — SPCL WRHSG,STRG,NEC (NO BREAKDOWN) — 2013 (12 Establishments)
SIC 44 — WATER TRANSPORTATION (NO BREAKDOWN) — 2013 (30 Establishments)

	SIC 4214 $	%	SIC 4225 $	%	SIC 4226 $	%	SIC 44 $	%
Cash	193,418	19.4	1,057,950	21.8	1,320,034	13.1	23,047,682	11.9
Accounts Receivable	286,139	28.7	1,349,129	27.8	1,904,476	18.9	7,940,798	4.1
Notes Receivable	24,925	2.5	9,706	0.2	221,685	2.2	0	0.0
Inventory	6,979	0.7	368,827	7.6	241,838	2.4	7,359,764	3.8
Other Current	144,564	14.5	373,679	7.7	846,434	8.4	31,182,158	16.1
Total Current	**656,025**	**65.8**	**3,159,291**	**65.1**	**4,534,467**	**45.0**	**69,530,402**	**35.9**
Fixed Assets	292,121	29.3	1,431,629	29.5	4,141,480	41.1	107,297,612	55.4
Other Non-current	48,853	4.9	262,061	5.4	1,400,646	13.9	16,849,986	8.7
Total Assets	**996,999**	**100.0**	**4,852,981**	**100.0**	**10,076,593**	**100.0**	**193,678,000**	**100.0**
Accounts Payable	94,715	9.5	660,005	13.6	957,276	9.5	3,486,204	1.8
Bank Loans	47,856	4.8	33,971	0.7	0	0.0	0	0.0
Notes Payable	29,910	3.0	29,118	0.6	60,460	0.6	387,356	0.2
Other Current	200,397	20.1	902,655	18.6	1,763,404	17.5	24,790,784	12.8
Total Current	**372,878**	**37.4**	**1,625,749**	**33.5**	**2,781,140**	**27.6**	**28,664,344**	**14.8**
Other Long Term	175,471	17.6	558,092	11.5	3,053,207	30.3	60,040,180	31.0
Deferred Credits	0	0.0	0	0.0	0	0.0	0	0.0
Net Worth	448,650	45.0	2,669,140	55.0	4,242,246	42.1	104,973,476	54.2
Total Liab & Net Worth	**996,999**	**100.0**	**4,852,981**	**100.0**	**10,076,593**	**100.0**	**193,678,000**	**100.0**
Net Sales	4,637,205	100.0	12,072,092	100.0	14,994,930	100.0	77,533,227	100.0
Gross Profit	2,188,761	47.2	3,054,239	25.3	8,622,085	57.5	44,116,406	56.9
Net Profit After Tax	166,939	3.6	603,605	5.0	884,701	5.9	2,946,263	3.8
Working Capital	283,147	—	1,533,542	—	1,753,327	—	40,866,058	—

RATIOS	4214 UQ	MED	LQ	4225 UQ	MED	LQ	4226 UQ	MED	LQ	44 UQ	MED	LQ
SOLVENCY												
Quick Ratio (times)	2.4	1.8	1.2	4.6	1.5	1.0	1.8	1.6	0.7	2.9	1.1	0.5
Current Ratio (times)	3.1	2.0	1.4	4.9	1.8	1.5	2.9	1.9	0.9	12.1	2.5	1.1
Curr Liab To Nw (%)	33.2	58.5	161.3	17.3	46.7	146.7	26.1	51.1	71.2	4.6	16.4	49.4
Curr Liab To Inv (%)	666.2	999.9	999.9	192.2	434.6	999.9	427.0	999.9	999.9	100.0	427.6	999.9
Total Liab To Nw (%)	56.8	107.4	211.1	21.9	69.9	177.7	38.9	118.7	278.6	25.1	69.9	142.9
Fixed Assets To Nw (%)	20.0	64.8	102.9	29.2	55.5	72.9	47.0	65.7	213.3	57.7	120.1	186.0
EFFICIENCY												
Coll Period (days)	15.7	28.5	46.0	36.1	46.0	51.8	24.8	36.5	40.9	9.5	40.5	55.5
Sales To Inv (times)	565.3	361.6	18.9	119.6	46.8	21.3	480.9	149.3	13.3	44.7	21.7	10.1
Assets To Sales (%)	18.8	21.5	41.9	28.0	40.2	48.1	58.2	67.2	92.6	107.2	249.8	358.7
Sales To Nwc (times)	16.7	10.7	5.1	15.8	8.4	4.2	12.3	9.4	4.1	6.2	3.1	0.6
Acct Pay To Sales (%)	1.4	2.3	4.2	3.0	3.5	6.5	3.5	7.2	10.8	2.1	4.8	6.9
PROFITABILITY												
Return On Sales (%)	6.3	2.9	0.8	4.4	4.0	2.4	7.8	4.2	0.7	11.4	6.0	(0.6)
Return On Assets (%)	20.6	15.1	2.7	16.6	9.8	3.4	7.6	4.9	1.5	5.4	2.9	(0.4)
Return On Nw (%)	42.8	35.0	9.2	57.7	20.6	10.5	24.6	10.8	0.9	11.8	4.4	0.5

	SIC 45 TRANS BY AIR (NO BREAKDOWN) 2013 (52 Establishments) $	%	SIC 4522 AIR TRANS,NONSCHED (NO BREAKDOWN) 2013 (19 Establishments) $	%	SIC 4581 ARPTS,FLY FLDS.SVCS (NO BREAKDOWN) 2013 (13 Establishments) $	%	SIC 47 TRANSPORTATION SVS (NO BREAKDOWN) 2013 (134 Establishments) $	%
Cash	3,136,547	11.7	626,346	8.5	2,394,853	16.9	460,791	20.2
Accounts Receivable	3,833,557	14.3	1,179,005	16.0	3,514,340	24.8	992,299	43.5
Notes Receivable	26,808	0.1	7,369	0.1	14,171	0.1	18,249	0.8
Inventory	1,045,516	3.9	324,226	4.4	935,268	6.6	25,093	1.1
Other Current	2,895,274	10.8	1,127,423	15.3	524,316	3.7	266,894	11.7
Total Current	**10,937,702**	**40.8**	**3,264,369**	**44.3**	**7,382,948**	**52.1**	**1,763,326**	**77.3**
Fixed Assets	11,983,217	44.7	3,338,057	45.3	5,880,851	41.5	305,674	13.4
Other Non-current	3,887,173	14.5	766,353	10.4	906,927	6.4	212,146	9.3
Total Assets	**26,808,092**	**100.0**	**7,368,779**	**100.0**	**14,170,726**	**100.0**	**2,281,146**	**100.0**
Accounts Payable	4,959,497	18.5	567,396	7.7	651,853	4.6	823,494	36.1
Bank Loans	134,040	0.5	103,163	1.4	0	0.0	15,968	0.7
Notes Payable	160,849	0.6	58,950	0.8	170,049	1.2	273,738	12.0
Other Current	32,008,862	119.4	1,134,792	15.4	2,394,853	16.9	732,247	32.1
Total Current	**37,263,248**	**139.0**	**1,864,301**	**25.3**	**3,216,755**	**22.7**	**1,845,447**	**80.9**
Other Long Term	8,524,973	31.8	2,380,115	32.3	2,366,511	16.7	280,581	12.3
Deferred Credits	80,424	0.3	7,369	0.1	0	0.0	9,125	0.4
Net Worth	(19,060,553)	(71.1)	3,116,994	42.3	8,587,460	60.6	145,993	6.4
Total Liab & Net Worth	**26,808,092**	**100.0**	**7,368,779**	**100.0**	**14,170,726**	**100.0**	**2,281,146**	**100.0**
Net Sales	35,366,876	100.0	13,545,550	100.0	20,567,091	100.0	12,397,533	100.0
Gross Profit	16,304,130	46.1	6,081,952	44.9	9,645,966	46.9	3,421,719	27.6
Net Profit After Tax	2,475,681	7.0	1,043,007	7.7	2,509,185	12.2	458,709	3.7
Working Capital	(26,325,546)	---	1,400,068	---	4,166,193	---	(82,121)	---

RATIOS	SIC 45 UQ	MED	LQ	SIC 4522 UQ	MED	LQ	SIC 4581 UQ	MED	LQ	SIC 47 UQ	MED	LQ
SOLVENCY												
Quick Ratio (times)	1.7	0.9	0.3	2.3	1.2	0.6	3.1	1.2	1.1	2.3	1.5	0.9
Current Ratio (times)	2.3	1.5	0.9	3.5	1.8	1.2	3.1	2.2	1.6	3.0	1.7	1.2
Curr Liab To Nw (%)	31.6	47.9	105.9	26.1	55.4	125.1	19.2	37.8	41.4	28.3	77.9	174.2
Curr Liab To Inv (%)	329.4	999.9	999.9	227.6	507.8	931.9	133.9	590.8	999.9	269.7	791.7	999.9
Total Liab To Nw (%)	54.3	139.3	244.4	98.8	144.0	285.0	36.1	42.5	147.8	43.0	99.9	214.3
Fixed Assets To Nw (%)	50.3	107.0	188.3	56.1	109.8	214.0	4.5	80.0	107.0	4.8	18.8	50.7
EFFICIENCY												
Coll Period (days)	14.2	35.8	63.5	35.8	47.8	91.3	18.5	39.6	60.3	28.5	35.4	46.4
Sales To Inv (times)	89.4	43.6	15.3	89.4	37.4	18.4	168.7	54.4	12.4	150.9	114.3	15.3
Assets To Sales (%)	41.6	75.8	142.1	38.0	54.4	136.4	32.8	68.9	228.6	12.1	18.4	32.0
Sales To Nwc (times)	16.1	6.8	3.5	16.1	9.4	4.7	14.0	4.9	2.7	27.6	15.4	7.5
Acct Pay To Sales (%)	2.5	4.6	7.4	1.8	4.6	7.8	2.0	3.8	6.6	2.1	4.4	8.2
PROFITABILITY												
Return On Sales (%)	9.8	3.1	0.6	9.3	5.7	2.1	14.2	3.1	0.6	4.7	2.2	0.4
Return On Assets (%)	9.0	2.5	0.7	14.4	7.4	3.4	15.6	2.2	0.7	23.0	9.3	1.4
Return On Nw (%)	23.0	9.3	2.2	46.7	17.0	8.5	25.9	4.6	1.0	65.4	23.1	5.6

Balance Sheet

	SIC 4724 TRAVEL AGENCIES (NO BREAKDOWN) 2013 (13 Establishments) $	%	SIC 4731 FRGT TRANS ARNGMNT (NO BREAKDOWN) 2013 (101 Establishments) $	%	SIC 4789 TRANS SRVCS, NEC (NO BREAKDOWN) 2013 (11 Establishments) $	%	SIC 48 COMMUNICATION (NO BREAKDOWN) 2013 (211 Establishments) $	%
Cash	10,194,208	35.8	351,876	18.2	1,579,224	17.3	13,467,103	16.3
Accounts Receivable	1,850,904	6.5	993,759	51.4	2,702,025	29.6	9,831,811	11.9
Notes Receivable	170,853	0.6	15,467	0.8	0	0.0	743,582	0.9
Inventory	56,951	0.2	11,600	0.6	282,982	3.1	3,056,950	3.7
Other Current	5,609,661	19.7	201,072	10.4	693,763	7.6	7,022,722	8.5
Total Current	**17,882,577**	**62.8**	**1,573,774**	**81.4**	**5,257,994**	**57.6**	**34,122,168**	**41.3**
Fixed Assets	2,050,232	7.2	220,406	11.4	3,222,347	35.3	24,455,597	29.6
Other Non-current	8,542,632	30.0	139,203	7.2	648,121	7.1	24,042,496	29.1
Total Assets	**28,475,441**	**100.0**	**1,933,383**	**100.0**	**9,128,462**	**100.0**	**82,620,261**	**100.0**
Accounts Payable	30,810,427	108.2	543,281	28.1	2,756,796	30.2	20,076,723	24.3
Bank Loans	0	0.0	17,400	0.9	0	0.0	578,342	0.7
Notes Payable	32,917,610	115.6	11,600	0.6	45,642	0.5	41,805,852	50.6
Other Current	7,859,222	27.6	365,410	18.9	14,003,061	153.4	34,039,548	41.2
Total Current	**71,587,259**	**251.4**	**937,691**	**48.5**	**16,805,499**	**184.1**	**96,500,465**	**116.8**
Other Long Term	5,467,284	19.2	224,272	11.6	1,305,370	14.3	30,982,598	37.5
Deferred Credits	427,132	1.5	0	0.0	0	0.0	1,404,544	1.7
Net Worth	(49,006,234)	(172.1)	771,420	39.9	(8,982,407)	(98.4)	(46,267,346)	(56.0)
Total Liab & Net Worth	**28,475,441**	**100.0**	**1,933,383**	**100.0**	**9,128,462**	**100.0**	**82,620,261**	**100.0**
Net Sales	24,213,810	100.0	11,047,903	100.0	12,713,735	100.0	47,868,054	100.0
Gross Profit	14,867,279	61.4	2,253,772	20.4	6,801,848	53.5	23,120,270	48.3
Net Profit After Tax	2,179,243	9.0	309,341	2.8	292,416	2.3	1,053,097	2.2
Working Capital	(53,704,682)	---	636,083	---	(11,547,505)	---	(62,378,297)	---

RATIOS

	SIC 4724 UQ	MED	LQ	SIC 4731 UQ	MED	LQ	SIC 4789 UQ	MED	LQ	SIC 48 UQ	MED	LQ
SOLVENCY												
Quick Ratio (times)	1.3	1.0	0.7	2.7	1.6	1.0	1.6	0.9	0.6	1.9	1.0	0.5
Current Ratio (times)	2.6	1.5	0.8	3.3	1.7	1.2	1.8	1.3	0.9	2.7	1.6	0.8
Curr Liab To Nw (%)	33.9	77.2	154.3	30.6	78.5	184.5	22.2	73.5	82.7	14.8	35.8	85.4
Curr Liab To Inv (%)	999.9	999.9	999.9	476.3	999.9	999.9	219.5	319.9	999.9	299.9	611.2	999.9
Total Liab To Nw (%)	60.8	119.4	244.7	43.0	99.0	204.3	60.5	113.6	274.0	38.9	130.1	309.4
Fixed Assets To Nw (%)	9.4	16.6	28.0	3.6	16.6	47.4	52.2	104.4	165.7	20.0	66.0	174.5
EFFICIENCY												
Coll Period (days)	28.5	35.4	46.7	28.7	36.1	45.9	23.4	33.1	57.3	19.7	36.5	61.7
Sales To Inv (times)	999.9	619.4	238.8	383.4	130.9	15.6	122.9	16.2	15.3	54.0	25.9	14.8
Assets To Sales (%)	23.6	117.6	155.9	12.1	17.5	26.4	11.8	71.8	138.6	66.3	172.6	251.8
Sales To Nwc (times)	19.0	10.3	5.0	30.9	17.9	9.2	8.7	5.2	4.6	12.6	4.7	2.4
Acct Pay To Sales (%)	1.1	2.8	6.0	2.1	4.7	8.2	3.0	4.9	10.4	2.5	5.5	11.5
PROFITABILITY												
Return On Sales (%)	19.5	4.5	1.0	3.9	1.9	0.4	5.5	1.8	(1.7)	10.3	2.3	(8.6)
Return On Assets (%)	18.0	13.9	1.2	23.4	9.4	2.0	12.8	3.4	(1.5)	7.2	1.8	(7.6)
Return On Nw (%)	120.7	27.4	9.6	56.6	22.6	6.2	22.7	5.3	(2.0)	17.4	5.7	(3.8)

SIC 4812 RDIO TELPHON COMM
(NO BREAKDOWN)
2013 (14 Establishments)

	$	%
Cash	786,801	20.6
Accounts Receivable	798,259	20.9
Notes Receivable	0	0.0
Inventory	389,581	10.2
Other Current	198,609	5.2
Total Current	**2,173,250**	**56.9**
Fixed Assets	893,744	23.4
Other Non-current	752,426	19.7
Total Assets	**3,819,420**	**100.0**
Accounts Payable	1,042,702	27.3
Bank Loans	0	0.0
Notes Payable	656,940	17.2
Other Current	2,597,206	68.0
Total Current	**4,296,848**	**112.5**
Other Long Term	599,649	15.7
Deferred Credits	3,819	0.1
Net Worth	(1,080,896)	(28.3)
Total Liab & Net Worth	**3,819,420**	**100.0**
Net Sales	2,362,041	100.0
Gross Profit	1,093,625	46.3
Net Profit After Tax	18,896	0.8
Working Capital	(2,123,598)	---

RATIOS	UQ	MED	LQ
SOLVENCY			
Quick Ratio (times)	3.8	1.3	0.5
Current Ratio (times)	4.8	2.0	1.2
Curr Liab To Nw (%)	14.8	27.5	98.1
Curr Liab To Inv (%)	147.7	166.4	577.4
Total Liab To Nw (%)	15.5	84.8	145.5
Fixed Assets To Nw (%)	15.8	40.8	83.4
EFFICIENCY			
Coll Period (days)	24.5	52.6	62.8
Sales To Inv (times)	29.4	19.3	15.0
Assets To Sales (%)	38.0	161.7	236.8
Sales To Nwc (times)	8.3	4.6	2.3
Acct Pay To Sales (%)	0.9	4.7	10.3
PROFITABILITY			
Return On Sales (%)	3.4	1.9	(319.6)
Return On Assets (%)	9.8	2.1	(22.9)
Return On Nw (%)	19.9	5.8	(12.9)

SIC 4813 TEL COMM,EXC RDIO
(NO BREAKDOWN)
2013 (122 Establishments)

	$	%
Cash	13,458,753	18.4
Accounts Receivable	8,996,884	12.3
Notes Receivable	1,097,181	1.5
Inventory	2,706,380	3.7
Other Current	6,217,358	8.5
Total Current	**32,476,556**	**44.4**
Fixed Assets	24,211,126	33.1
Other Non-current	16,457,715	22.5
Total Assets	**73,145,397**	**100.0**
Accounts Payable	9,362,611	12.8
Bank Loans	877,745	1.2
Notes Payable	55,078,484	75.3
Other Current	31,671,956	43.3
Total Current	**96,990,796**	**132.6**
Other Long Term	24,064,836	32.9
Deferred Credits	1,170,326	1.6
Net Worth	(49,080,561)	(67.1)
Total Liab & Net Worth	**73,145,397**	**100.0**
Net Sales	51,839,403	100.0
Gross Profit	24,520,038	47.3
Net Profit After Tax	1,036,788	2.0
Working Capital	(64,514,240)	---

RATIOS	UQ	MED	LQ
SOLVENCY			
Quick Ratio (times)	1.8	0.9	0.5
Current Ratio (times)	2.6	1.4	0.8
Curr Liab To Nw (%)	17.9	40.5	102.5
Curr Liab To Inv (%)	391.3	851.5	999.9
Total Liab To Nw (%)	38.9	142.1	359.5
Fixed Assets To Nw (%)	21.0	90.6	190.1
EFFICIENCY			
Coll Period (days)	17.2	34.3	50.0
Sales To Inv (times)	77.2	31.0	15.5
Assets To Sales (%)	55.6	141.1	247.7
Sales To Nwc (times)	16.9	4.7	2.6
Acct Pay To Sales (%)	3.0	6.1	11.0
PROFITABILITY			
Return On Sales (%)	8.6	1.5	(9.3)
Return On Assets (%)	6.7	1.7	(7.6)
Return On Nw (%)	18.3	4.9	(6.3)

SIC 4833 TEL BRDCSTG STNS
(NO BREAKDOWN)
2013 (19 Establishments)

	$	%
Cash	3,513,267	8.2
Accounts Receivable	2,527,838	5.9
Notes Receivable	0	0.0
Inventory	128,534	0.3
Other Current	3,384,732	7.9
Total Current	**9,554,371**	**22.3**
Fixed Assets	11,696,607	27.3
Other Non-current	21,593,737	50.4
Total Assets	**42,844,715**	**100.0**
Accounts Payable	3,856,024	9.0
Bank Loans	0	0.0
Notes Payable	42,845	0.1
Other Current	5,098,521	11.9
Total Current	**8,997,390**	**21.0**
Other Long Term	19,194,432	44.8
Deferred Credits	471,292	1.1
Net Worth	14,181,601	33.1
Total Liab & Net Worth	**42,844,715**	**100.0**
Net Sales	22,973,038	100.0
Gross Profit	12,382,467	53.9
Net Profit After Tax	895,948	3.9
Working Capital	556,981	---

RATIOS	UQ	MED	LQ
SOLVENCY			
Quick Ratio (times)	1.8	1.1	0.8
Current Ratio (times)	3.6	2.1	1.5
Curr Liab To Nw (%)	8.0	25.1	41.3
Curr Liab To Inv (%)	544.9	787.1	999.9
Total Liab To Nw (%)	26.3	89.1	302.6
Fixed Assets To Nw (%)	35.5	46.5	121.8
EFFICIENCY			
Coll Period (days)	14.8	67.7	81.0
Sales To Inv (times)	476.8	30.3	19.8
Assets To Sales (%)	172.6	186.5	327.2
Sales To Nwc (times)	7.4	4.3	2.3
Acct Pay To Sales (%)	1.8	2.4	4.4
PROFITABILITY			
Return On Sales (%)	14.7	(3.1)	(5.5)
Return On Assets (%)	7.9	(2.1)	(2.2)
Return On Nw (%)	16.4	3.8	(2.1)

SIC 4899 COMMNCTN SVCS,NEC
(NO BREAKDOWN)
2013 (17 Establishments)

	$	%
Cash	10,284,054	12.5
Accounts Receivable	13,245,862	16.1
Notes Receivable	0	0.0
Inventory	5,100,891	6.2
Other Current	9,625,874	11.7
Total Current	**38,256,681**	**46.5**
Fixed Assets	23,036,281	28.0
Other Non-current	20,979,470	25.5
Total Assets	**82,272,432**	**100.0**
Accounts Payable	119,377,299	145.1
Bank Loans	0	0.0
Notes Payable	58,824,789	71.5
Other Current	45,085,292	54.8
Total Current	**223,287,380**	**271.4**
Other Long Term	49,610,277	60.3
Deferred Credits	5,512,253	6.7
Net Worth	(196,137,478)	(238.4)
Total Liab & Net Worth	**82,272,432**	**100.0**
Net Sales	63,189,272	100.0
Gross Profit	29,698,958	47.0
Net Profit After Tax	(6,002,981)	(9.5)
Working Capital	(185,030,699)	---

RATIOS	UQ	MED	LQ
SOLVENCY			
Quick Ratio (times)	2.3	1.1	0.3
Current Ratio (times)	2.4	1.6	0.6
Curr Liab To Nw (%)	12.3	33.9	51.1
Curr Liab To Inv (%)	299.9	400.5	999.9
Total Liab To Nw (%)	108.2	139.3	161.4
Fixed Assets To Nw (%)	48.9	98.3	162.6
EFFICIENCY			
Coll Period (days)	19.7	41.3	69.0
Sales To Inv (times)	28.4	20.6	14.3
Assets To Sales (%)	24.4	130.2	436.1
Sales To Nwc (times)	13.8	3.4	2.0
Acct Pay To Sales (%)	3.5	5.9	11.5
PROFITABILITY			
Return On Sales (%)	4.8	(3.1)	(24.6)
Return On Assets (%)	1.8	2.1	(16.3)
Return On Nw (%)	4.6	1.4	(28.5)

	SIC 49 ELEC,GAS,SANITARY SV (NO BREAKDOWN) 2013 (445 Establishments) $	%	SIC 4911 ELECTRIC SERVICES (NO BREAKDOWN) 2013 (218 Establishments) $	%	SIC 4941 WATER SUPPLY (NO BREAKDOWN) 2013 (41 Establishments) $	%	SIC 4952 SEWERAGE SYSTEMS (NO BREAKDOWN) 2013 (16 Establishments) $	%
Cash	25,471,657	6.3	40,317,530	4.4	12,983,845	7.4	3,668,777	5.0
Accounts Receivable	26,684,593	6.6	35,735,993	3.9	2,982,775	1.7	1,100,633	1.5
Notes Receivable	404,312	0.1	916,308	0.1	0	0.0	0	0.0
Inventory	8,490,552	2.1	18,326,150	2.0	877,287	0.5	73,376	0.1
Other Current	25,471,659	6.3	50,396,912	5.5	12,632,930	7.2	10,272,575	14.0
Total Current	**86,522,773**	**21.4**	**145,692,893**	**15.9**	**29,476,837**	**16.8**	**15,115,361**	**20.6**
Fixed Assets	256,333,822	63.4	633,168,483	69.1	120,188,295	68.5	52,316,761	71.3
Other Non-current	61,455,427	15.2	137,446,124	15.0	25,792,233	14.7	5,943,419	8.1
Total Assets	**404,312,022**	**100.0**	**916,307,500**	**100.0**	**175,457,365**	**100.0**	**73,375,541**	**100.0**
Accounts Payable	26,684,593	6.6	55,894,758	6.1	1,579,116	0.9	1,981,140	2.7
Bank Loans	808,624	0.2	1,832,615	0.2	0	0.0	0	0.0
Notes Payable	7,277,616	1.8	19,242,458	2.1	0	0.0	0	0.0
Other Current	48,113,132	11.9	93,463,364	10.2	9,123,783	5.2	4,989,536	6.8
Total Current	**82,883,965**	**20.5**	**170,433,195**	**18.6**	**10,702,899**	**6.1**	**6,970,676**	**9.5**
Other Long Term	169,002,425	41.8	443,492,829	48.4	75,095,753	42.8	26,635,322	36.3
Deferred Credits	5,660,368	1.4	15,577,228	1.7	175,457	0.1	0	0.0
Net Worth	146,765,264	36.3	286,804,248	31.3	89,483,256	51.0	39,769,543	54.2
Total Liab & Net Worth	**404,312,022**	**100.0**	**916,307,500**	**100.0**	**175,457,365**	**100.0**	**73,375,541**	**100.0**
Net Sales	145,018,659	100.0	329,015,260	100.0	29,518,399	100.0	10,657,304	100.0
Gross Profit	60,472,781	41.7	134,896,257	41.0	17,091,153	57.9	2,994,702	28.1
Net Profit After Tax	9,861,269	6.8	20,069,931	6.1	3,512,689	11.9	1,182,961	11.1
Working Capital	3,638,808	---	(24,740,302)	---	18,773,938	---	8,144,685	---

RATIOS	UQ	MED	LQ	UQ	MED	LQ	UQ	MED	LQ	UQ	MED	LQ
SOLVENCY												
Quick Ratio (times)	1.2	0.6	0.3	0.9	0.5	0.3	3.4	1.4	0.5	2.3	1.5	0.4
Current Ratio (times)	2.2	1.3	0.9	1.6	1.2	0.9	5.3	3.0	1.5	3.4	2.6	1.6
Curr Liab To Nw (%)	14.3	24.5	40.8	17.4	25.4	37.7	5.7	8.4	18.2	3.8	6.3	25.1
Curr Liab To Inv (%)	343.1	648.7	999.9	331.1	611.9	999.9	558.5	999.9	999.9	999.9	999.9	999.9
Total Liab To Nw (%)	83.7	167.8	227.2	122.2	187.7	235.2	53.0	93.3	195.4	21.8	61.8	181.9
Fixed Assets To Nw (%)	109.6	185.2	239.7	149.9	217.1	251.0	95.0	140.6	223.3	93.8	132.5	233.2
EFFICIENCY												
Coll Period (days)	26.3	36.3	48.2	25.2	32.9	46.4	27.7	38.0	51.8	34.9	39.1	53.1
Sales To Inv (times)	54.6	25.0	13.0	49.7	20.8	12.4	84.9	57.8	26.5	122.7	72.9	70.6
Assets To Sales (%)	179.3	278.8	388.9	213.0	278.5	361.3	386.9	594.4	989.3	550.7	688.5	957.3
Sales To Nwc (times)	16.1	7.2	3.0	18.8	10.1	4.7	3.2	1.4	0.7	4.0	2.1	1.0
Acct Pay To Sales (%)	5.3	8.0	10.3	6.6	8.3	10.3	2.4	4.5	9.1	1.9	2.4	4.0
PROFITABILITY												
Return On Sales (%)	11.4	7.0	3.1	10.4	7.1	4.1	19.4	12.0	(0.5)	21.0	11.4	1.5
Return On Assets (%)	3.9	2.7	1.3	3.4	2.6	1.6	3.3	2.0	0.1	3.5	1.9	0.1
Return On Nw (%)	10.3	7.6	3.3	9.8	7.6	5.1	7.9	3.4	(0.1)	7.7	3.2	0.2

Balance Sheet

	SIC 4953 REFUSE SYSTEMS (NO BREAKDOWN) 2013 (35 Establishments) $	%	SIC 4959 SANITARY SVCS,NEC (NO BREAKDOWN) 2013 (15 Establishments) $	%	SIC 50 WHOLESALE TRADE (NO BREAKDOWN) 2013 (2036 Establishments) $	%	SIC 5012 AUTO,OTHR MTR VHCLS (NO BREAKDOWN) 2013 (31 Establishments) $	%
Cash	2,364,988	16.2	491,298	16.1	524,757	15.2	574,732	13.0
Accounts Receivable	2,978,133	20.4	851,380	27.9	939,039	27.2	729,467	16.5
Notes Receivable	29,197	0.2	39,670	1.3	10,357	0.3	8,842	0.2
Inventory	686,138	4.7	97,649	3.2	1,166,894	33.8	1,812,615	41.0
Other Current	905,120	6.2	430,268	14.1	234,760	6.8	265,260	6.0
Total Current	**6,963,576**	**47.7**	**1,910,265**	**62.6**	**2,875,807**	**83.3**	**3,390,916**	**76.7**
Fixed Assets	4,802,969	32.9	762,885	25.0	369,401	10.7	579,153	13.1
Other Non-current	2,832,146	19.4	378,391	12.4	207,141	6.0	450,943	10.2
Total Assets	**14,598,691**	**100.0**	**3,051,541**	**100.0**	**3,452,349**	**100.0**	**4,421,012**	**100.0**
Accounts Payable	3,240,909	22.2	369,236	12.1	807,850	23.4	366,944	8.3
Bank Loans	102,191	0.7	91,546	3.0	27,619	0.8	8,842	0.2
Notes Payable	583,948	4.0	183,092	6.0	124,285	3.6	526,100	11.9
Other Current	6,248,240	42.8	454,681	14.9	890,705	25.8	977,044	22.1
Total Current	**10,175,288**	**69.7**	**1,098,555**	**36.0**	**1,850,459**	**53.6**	**1,878,930**	**42.5**
Other Long Term	4,146,028	28.4	353,979	11.6	386,664	11.2	450,943	10.2
Deferred Credits	14,599	0.1	0	0.0	3,452	0.1	0	0.0
Net Worth	262,776	1.8	1,599,007	52.4	1,211,774	35.1	2,091,139	47.3
Total Liab & Net Worth	**14,598,691**	**100.0**	**3,051,541**	**100.0**	**3,452,349**	**100.0**	**4,421,012**	**100.0**
Net Sales	15,481,115	100.0	7,146,466	100.0	9,484,475	100.0	12,453,555	100.0
Gross Profit	4,272,788	27.6	2,465,531	34.5	2,646,169	27.9	3,325,099	26.7
Net Profit After Tax	46,443	0.3	643,182	9.0	284,534	3.0	398,514	3.2
Working Capital	(3,211,712)	---	811,710	---	1,025,348	---	1,511,986	---

RATIOS

	SIC 4953 UQ	MED	LQ	SIC 4959 UQ	MED	LQ	SIC 50 UQ	MED	LQ	SIC 5012 UQ	MED	LQ
SOLVENCY												
Quick Ratio (times)	2.1	1.0	0.6	3.3	1.0	0.6	2.1	1.1	0.6	1.5	0.6	0.3
Current Ratio (times)	2.5	1.3	0.9	3.7	1.6	1.2	4.2	2.2	1.4	2.9	1.7	1.3
Curr Liab To Nw (%)	16.6	52.3	75.5	24.5	49.6	142.1	25.9	69.7	159.5	51.0	106.0	146.6
Curr Liab To Inv (%)	231.7	999.9	999.9	650.5	812.4	999.9	58.1	102.0	206.9	60.3	108.0	214.5
Total Liab To Nw (%)	51.6	118.7	227.2	35.2	132.7	186.5	32.7	88.2	195.0	70.7	132.9	225.7
Fixed Assets To Nw (%)	22.7	65.0	114.1	9.6	45.2	101.7	5.0	13.7	32.4	4.9	15.6	72.0
EFFICIENCY												
Coll Period (days)	29.2	41.6	59.7	25.9	40.3	84.0	23.7	35.8	50.0	4.4	18.3	37.2
Sales To Inv (times)	190.5	52.2	24.5	110.7	90.6	45.7	16.7	8.2	4.6	15.3	6.0	4.0
Assets To Sales (%)	32.8	94.3	181.2	29.3	42.7	56.2	25.7	36.4	51.8	25.7	35.5	53.6
Sales To Nwc (times)	17.8	8.0	4.1	12.1	7.0	4.0	12.0	6.6	3.9	14.9	7.6	5.9
Acct Pay To Sales (%)	3.8	6.4	11.6	2.3	4.1	6.6	2.9	5.2	8.7	1.6	3.2	5.2
PROFITABILITY												
Return On Sales (%)	10.3	2.4	(1.6)	15.9	5.7	1.7	4.6	1.9	0.5	3.6	1.5	0.4
Return On Assets (%)	10.7	3.2	(3.2)	32.0	24.6	4.2	12.3	5.0	1.3	12.9	3.7	1.3
Return On Nw (%)	25.5	7.5	(1.7)	73.6	44.0	8.5	27.8	10.9	3.1	22.1	10.0	4.6

Balance Sheet ($ and %)

	SIC 5013 MTR VHCL SPLS, PRTS (NO BREAKDOWN) 2013 (68 Establishments) $	%	SIC 5014 TIRES AND TUBES (NO BREAKDOWN) 2013 (26 Establishments) $	%	SIC 5021 FURNITURE (NO BREAKDOWN) 2013 (67 Establishments) $	%	SIC 5023 HOMEFURNISHINGS (NO BREAKDOWN) 2013 (43 Establishments) $	%
Cash	573,682	13.6	547,904	8.6	531,921	18.4	337,722	15.6
Accounts Receivable	750,849	17.8	1,140,405	17.9	1,089,860	37.7	610,497	28.2
Notes Receivable	16,873	0.4	114,678	1.8	0	0.0	2,165	0.1
Inventory	1,995,233	47.3	3,121,779	49.0	604,193	20.9	738,225	34.1
Other Current	257,313	6.1	229,355	3.6	239,943	8.3	207,829	9.6
Total Current	**3,593,950**	**85.2**	**5,154,121**	**80.9**	**2,465,917**	**85.3**	**1,896,438**	**87.6**
Fixed Assets	459,789	10.9	834,598	13.1	219,707	7.6	205,664	9.5
Other Non-current	164,512	3.9	382,259	6.0	205,252	7.1	62,781	2.9
Total Assets	**4,218,251**	**100.0**	**6,370,978**	**100.0**	**2,890,876**	**100.0**	**2,164,883**	**100.0**
Accounts Payable	733,976	17.4	1,732,906	27.2	549,266	19.0	368,030	17.0
Bank Loans	8,437	0.2	127,420	2.0	8,673	0.3	25,979	1.2
Notes Payable	59,056	1.4	324,920	5.1	37,581	1.3	233,807	10.8
Other Current	797,248	18.9	828,227	13.0	800,773	27.7	573,694	26.5
Total Current	**1,598,717**	**37.9**	**3,013,473**	**47.3**	**1,396,293**	**48.3**	**1,201,510**	**55.5**
Other Long Term	316,369	7.5	796,372	12.5	202,361	7.0	151,542	7.0
Deferred Credits	0	0.0	38,226	0.6	2,891	0.1	2,165	0.1
Net Worth	2,303,165	54.6	2,522,907	39.6	1,289,331	44.6	809,666	37.4
Total Liab & Net Worth	**4,218,251**	**100.0**	**6,370,978**	**100.0**	**2,890,876**	**100.0**	**2,164,883**	**100.0**
Net Sales	9,674,888	100.0	19,909,306	100.0	10,287,815	100.0	5,652,436	100.0
Gross Profit	2,854,092	29.5	4,917,599	24.7	2,448,500	23.8	1,740,950	30.8
Net Profit After Tax	261,222	2.7	238,912	1.2	195,468	1.9	282,622	5.0
Working Capital	1,995,233	--	2,140,648	--	1,069,624		694,928	--

RATIOS

	SIC 5013 UQ	MED	LQ	SIC 5014 UQ	MED	LQ	SIC 5021 UQ	MED	LQ	SIC 5023 UQ	MED	LQ
SOLVENCY												
Quick Ratio (times)	1.7	0.7	0.4	0.7	0.5	0.4	1.9	1.0	0.8	3.3	1.2	0.5
Current Ratio (times)	4.1	2.4	1.6	1.9	1.7	1.4	2.6	1.7	1.3	5.7	2.3	1.3
Curr Liab To Nw (%)	30.6	56.1	143.5	76.1	143.7	195.1	64.2	126.4	266.7	16.4	68.2	286.9
Curr Liab To Inv (%)	44.3	76.7	116.9	79.2	99.6	129.4	90.0	273.3	706.6	51.6	112.1	195.2
Total Liab To Nw (%)	40.1	77.1	180.9	92.5	174.3	269.3	73.0	155.9	305.5	17.9	123.5	351.3
Fixed Assets To Nw (%)	6.5	14.7	28.4	21.3	29.1	40.2	4.2	14.2	36.3	4.3	9.8	33.6
EFFICIENCY												
Coll Period (days)	17.9	27.9	39.1	18.1	27.0	34.2	23.6	35.0	53.5	28.7	46.4	68.5
Sales To Inv (times)	8.1	4.9	3.2	7.8	6.6	5.3	42.4	18.8	9.3	27.0	7.6	3.5
Assets To Sales (%)	31.4	43.6	66.1	25.5	32.0	41.5	19.7	28.1	38.7	26.8	38.3	56.4
Sales To Nwc (times)	10.5	5.0	3.3	13.0	10.5	5.8	21.0	11.0	7.5	13.8	8.3	4.3
Acct Pay To Sales (%)	3.5	6.6	12.8	5.8	8.9	12.4	2.6	5.0	6.9	2.4	4.4	8.1
PROFITABILITY												
Return On Sales (%)	4.6	2.0	0.6	2.8	0.9	0.2	3.8	1.8	0.5	3.8	1.5	0.4
Return On Assets (%)	10.5	4.3	1.7	7.1	3.0	0.6	16.4	5.6	1.8	13.1	3.1	1.2
Return On Nw (%)	21.8	9.8	3.2	20.0	8.2	2.7	42.6	13.9	4.3	26.6	11.9	2.9

	SIC 5031 LBR,PLYWD,MILLWRK (NO BREAKDOWN) 2013 (111 Establishments)		SIC 5032 BRCK,STN,RLTD MTRLS (NO BREAKDOWN) 2013 (26 Establishments)		SIC 5033 RFNG,SIDNG,INSULTN (NO BREAKDOWN) 2013 (17 Establishments)		SIC 5039 CONSTR MTRLS, NEC (NO BREAKDOWN) 2013 (15 Establishments)	
	$	%	$	%	$	%	$	%
Cash	348,068	10.4	461,463	16.6	440,166	11.5	266,405	17.0
Accounts Receivable	973,922	29.1	767,251	27.6	780,816	20.4	443,486	28.3
Notes Receivable	20,081	0.6	27,799	1.0	3,828	0.1	40,744	2.6
Inventory	1,084,367	32.4	658,835	23.7	1,550,148	40.5	159,843	10.2
Other Current	190,769	5.7	152,895	5.5	68,895	1.8	340,057	21.7
Total Current	**2,617,207**	**78.2**	**2,068,243**	**74.4**	**2,843,853**	**74.3**	**1,250,535**	**79.8**
Fixed Assets	491,981	14.7	522,620	18.8	635,369	16.6	300,881	19.2
Other Non-current	237,624	7.1	189,033	6.8	348,305	9.1	15,671	1.0
Total Assets	**3,346,812**	**100.0**	**2,779,896**	**100.0**	**3,827,527**	**100.0**	**1,567,087**	**100.0**
Accounts Payable	391,577	11.7	644,936	23.2	539,681	14.1	236,630	15.1
Bank Loans	43,509	1.3	0	0.0	0	0.0	0	0.0
Notes Payable	103,751	3.1	11,120	0.4	133,963	3.5	12,537	0.8
Other Current	548,877	16.4	366,946	13.2	673,646	17.6	222,526	14.2
Total Current	**1,087,714**	**32.5**	**1,023,002**	**36.8**	**1,347,290**	**35.2**	**471,693**	**30.1**
Other Long Term	284,479	8.5	503,161	18.1	516,716	13.5	141,038	9.0
Deferred Credits	0	0.0	0	0.0	0	0.0	0	0.0
Net Worth	1,974,619	59.0	1,253,733	45.1	1,963,521	51.3	954,356	60.9
Total Liab & Net Worth	**3,346,812**	**100.0**	**2,779,896**	**100.0**	**3,827,527**	**100.0**	**1,567,087**	**100.0**
Net Sales	9,672,867	100.0	6,915,164	100.0	9,568,818	100.0	3,553,485	100.0
Gross Profit	2,234,432	23.1	1,984,652	28.7	2,411,342	25.2	1,083,813	30.5
Net Profit After Tax	222,476	2.3	325,013	4.7	287,065	3.0	67,516	1.9
Working Capital	1,529,493	---	1,045,241	---	1,496,563	---	778,842	---

RATIOS	UQ	MED	LQ	UQ	MED	LQ	UQ	MED	LQ	UQ	MED	LQ
SOLVENCY												
Quick Ratio (times)	3.1	1.5	0.8	3.9	1.5	0.6	1.8	1.2	0.5	3.9	1.8	0.9
Current Ratio (times)	5.7	3.1	1.7	4.6	2.2	1.4	3.5	2.2	1.6	5.4	2.9	1.7
Curr Liab To Nw (%)	15.9	41.0	107.9	23.8	49.3	138.1	24.1	54.8	152.1	15.5	53.5	115.2
Curr Liab To Inv (%)	35.1	80.5	156.0	60.0	133.1	558.2	63.4	90.3	128.2	98.0	277.7	999.9
Total Liab To Nw (%)	19.4	63.0	156.6	25.3	97.5	200.3	44.1	94.9	190.2	20.6	59.7	147.5
Fixed Assets To Nw (%)	5.4	20.2	40.7	6.3	35.0	65.4	14.4	25.0	55.6	11.6	17.8	98.5
EFFICIENCY												
Coll Period (days)	25.6	33.6	44.5	27.0	36.0	57.7	20.1	27.0	35.8	37.2	46.8	76.7
Sales To Inv (times)	14.5	8.4	5.4	47.4	8.2	4.6	8.9	7.5	4.3	60.5	22.9	11.3
Assets To Sales (%)	24.7	34.6	45.0	25.2	40.2	69.6	29.1	40.0	51.0	33.6	44.1	53.2
Sales To Nwc (times)	12.6	6.0	4.1	21.5	7.4	2.6	12.3	8.2	4.4	8.3	6.1	3.5
Acct Pay To Sales (%)	1.9	3.4	5.9	4.1	6.0	9.6	4.2	5.5	8.2	1.1	4.1	10.6
PROFITABILITY												
Return On Sales (%)	3.2	1.1	0.2	6.5	3.1	0.6	5.2	3.5	1.8	2.0	1.4	0.6
Return On Assets (%)	10.2	3.9	0.5	16.4	5.6	2.6	13.1	9.7	4.0	8.2	4.0	1.8
Return On Nw (%)	18.0	8.0	0.9	35.7	21.7	4.8	37.3	22.3	9.6	15.3	8.2	2.4

SIC 5044 OFFICE EQUIPMENT (NO BREAKDOWN) — 2013 (26 Establishments)
SIC 5045 CMPTRS,PERIPH SFTWR (NO BREAKDOWN) — 2013 (112 Establishments)
SIC 5046 CMMRCL EQUIP, NEC (NO BREAKDOWN) — 2013 (28 Establishments)
SIC 5047 MEDICAL HOSP EQUIP (NO BREAKDOWN) — 2013 (61 Establishments)

	SIC 5044 $	%	SIC 5045 $	%	SIC 5046 $	%	SIC 5047 $	%
Cash	255,794	15.5	777,838	23.6	295,732	14.7	395,944	16.5
Accounts Receivable	442,276	26.8	1,324,961	40.2	679,982	33.8	683,904	28.5
Notes Receivable	0	0.0	3,296	0.1	8,047	0.4	0	0.0
Inventory	465,380	28.2	477,909	14.5	541,169	26.9	621,512	25.9
Other Current	85,815	5.2	326,295	9.9	142,837	7.1	191,973	8.0
Total Current	**1,249,265**	**75.7**	**2,910,299**	**88.3**	**1,667,767**	**82.9**	**1,893,333**	**78.9**
Fixed Assets	234,340	14.2	161,500	4.9	211,237	10.5	319,155	13.3
Other Non-current	166,679	10.1	224,123	6.8	132,778	6.6	187,174	7.8
Total Assets	**1,650,284**	**100.0**	**3,295,922**	**100.0**	**2,011,782**	**100.0**	**2,399,662**	**100.0**
Accounts Payable	265,696	16.1	926,154	28.1	432,533	21.5	907,072	37.8
Bank Loans	8,251	0.5	6,592	0.2	0	0.0	4,799	0.2
Notes Payable	39,607	2.4	92,286	2.8	22,130	1.1	11,998	0.5
Other Current	496,735	30.1	1,001,960	30.4	527,087	26.2	1,219,029	50.8
Total Current	**810,289**	**49.1**	**2,026,992**	**61.5**	**981,750**	**48.8**	**2,142,898**	**89.3**
Other Long Term	191,434	11.6	148,316	4.5	215,260	10.7	508,729	21.2
Deferred Credits	6,601	0.4	6,592	0.2	0	0.0	0	0.0
Net Worth	641,960	38.9	1,114,022	33.8	814,772	40.5	(251,965)	(10.5)
Total Liab & Net Worth	**1,650,284**	**100.0**	**3,295,922**	**100.0**	**2,011,782**	**100.0**	**2,399,662**	**100.0**
Net Sales	3,883,021	100.0	12,437,442	100.0	5,917,006	100.0	7,016,556	100.0
Gross Profit	1,611,454	41.5	3,470,046	27.9	1,834,272	31.0	2,799,606	39.9
Net Profit After Tax	155,321	4.0	211,437	1.7	278,099	4.7	385,911	5.5
Working Capital	438,976	—	883,307	—	686,017	—	(249,565)	—

RATIOS	5044 UQ	MED	LQ	5045 UQ	MED	LQ	5046 UQ	MED	LQ	5047 UQ	MED	LQ
SOLVENCY												
Quick Ratio (times)	1.2	0.7	0.5	2.1	1.2	0.8	1.6	1.2	0.8	2.4	1.1	0.7
Current Ratio (times)	2.5	1.4	1.0	2.8	1.5	1.1	2.8	1.9	1.4	3.5	1.8	1.2
Curr Liab To Nw (%)	59.3	147.5	191.0	55.6	139.2	285.6	38.2	112.4	224.7	31.4	73.7	171.9
Curr Liab To Inv (%)	101.1	179.1	302.8	154.7	403.0	999.9	92.7	145.6	273.4	65.0	141.6	358.7
Total Liab To Nw (%)	66.4	159.5	303.3	55.6	154.6	305.1	43.1	132.3	334.5	43.7	101.4	227.7
Fixed Assets To Nw (%)	5.7	21.8	71.0	1.8	7.8	19.5	4.6	12.8	39.7	9.2	21.9	44.4
EFFICIENCY												
Coll Period (days)	24.5	32.9	42.3	24.8	40.9	55.1	25.9	42.2	51.5	25.2	41.6	50.4
Sales To Inv (times)	16.2	11.7	5.1	91.6	22.7	12.0	14.0	10.1	7.3	35.4	13.3	6.7
Assets To Sales (%)	27.2	42.5	48.0	18.5	26.5	40.8	28.3	34.0	42.9	21.8	34.2	45.1
Sales To Nwc (times)	23.4	7.7	4.4	20.6	11.3	5.6	13.5	8.3	5.2	18.7	8.9	4.6
Acct Pay To Sales (%)	2.9	4.9	8.7	2.8	7.3	12.6	4.1	5.4	9.7	2.4	6.9	9.0
PROFITABILITY												
Return On Sales (%)	6.6	2.6	0.2	3.6	1.0	(0.1)	5.8	2.1	0.7	7.4	2.7	0.9
Return On Assets (%)	15.0	6.0	0.7	14.5	3.9	(0.7)	14.2	6.1	2.4	20.9	7.8	2.3
Return On Nw (%)	44.7	18.4	3.0	36.7	10.7	0.2	28.9	15.0	3.5	60.9	18.0	5.3

SIC 5049 PRFSSNL EQUIP,NEC (NO BREAKDOWN) 2013 (31 Establishments) — SIC 5051 METLS SVC CNTRS,OFF (NO BREAKDOWN) 2013 (91 Establishments) — SIC 5063 ELEC APPRATUS,EQUIP (NO BREAKDOWN) 2013 (162 Establishments) — SIC 5064 ELEC APPL,TEL,RADIO (NO BREAKDOWN) 2013 (17 Establishments)

	SIC 5049 $	%	SIC 5051 $	%	SIC 5063 $	%	SIC 5064 $	%
Cash	380,983	24.3	1,381,799	16.4	645,025	15.4	295,655	11.7
Accounts Receivable	418,611	26.7	1,853,633	22.0	1,315,181	31.4	664,592	26.3
Notes Receivable	4,703	0.3	25,277	0.3	4,188	0.1	17,689	0.7
Inventory	388,822	24.8	3,193,304	37.9	1,457,589	34.8	952,667	37.7
Other Current	103,477	6.6	328,599	3.9	217,802	5.2	308,290	12.2
Total Current	**1,296,596**	**82.7**	**6,782,612**	**80.5**	**3,639,785**	**86.9**	**2,238,893**	**88.6**
Fixed Assets	131,698	8.4	1,095,329	13.0	322,513	7.7	214,792	8.5
Other Non-current	139,537	8.9	547,664	6.5	226,177	5.4	73,282	2.9
Total Assets	**1,567,831**	**100.0**	**8,425,605**	**100.0**	**4,188,475**	**100.0**	**2,526,967**	**100.0**
Accounts Payable	272,803	17.4	943,668	11.2	887,957	21.2	525,609	20.8
Bank Loans	15,678	1.0	109,533	1.3	29,319	0.7	42,958	1.7
Notes Payable	3,136	0.2	176,938	2.1	138,220	3.3	0	0.0
Other Current	349,626	22.3	2,106,401	25.0	586,386	14.0	540,772	21.4
Total Current	**641,243**	**40.9**	**3,336,540**	**39.6**	**1,641,882**	**39.2**	**1,109,339**	**43.9**
Other Long Term	243,014	15.5	733,027	8.7	305,759	7.3	90,970	3.6
Deferred Credits	0	0.0	0	0.0	4,188	0.1	0	0.0
Net Worth	683,574	43.6	4,356,038	51.7	2,236,646	53.4	1,326,658	52.5
Total Liab & Net Worth	**1,567,831**	**100.0**	**8,425,605**	**100.0**	**4,188,475**	**100.0**	**2,526,967**	**100.0**
Net Sales	5,025,099	100.0	17,265,584	100.0	11,475,274	100.0	7,872,171	100.0
Gross Profit	1,472,354	29.3	4,230,068	24.5	3,098,324	27.0	1,786,983	22.7
Net Profit After Tax	155,778	3.1	690,623	4.0	298,357	2.6	204,676	2.6
Working Capital	655,353	—	3,446,072	—	1,997,903	—	1,129,554	—

RATIOS	SIC 5049 UQ	MED	LQ	SIC 5051 UQ	MED	LQ	SIC 5063 UQ	MED	LQ	SIC 5064 UQ	MED	LQ
SOLVENCY												
Quick Ratio (times)	2.2	1.4	1.0	3.5	1.6	0.7	2.3	1.3	0.8	1.6	1.1	0.4
Current Ratio (times)	3.4	2.5	1.5	7.4	3.3	1.6	4.3	2.5	1.8	4.8	2.7	1.3
Curr Liab To Nw (%)	30.8	49.0	107.7	12.5	36.5	104.5	24.6	57.7	108.8	20.1	46.7	140.3
Curr Liab To Inv (%)	48.0	195.9	472.2	31.8	62.0	113.7	55.3	105.9	163.0	75.8	108.7	140.7
Total Liab To Nw (%)	36.5	69.2	144.4	15.9	52.2	145.8	29.3	75.8	165.9	20.1	47.2	150.9
Fixed Assets To Nw (%)	3.0	8.9	26.0	5.1	13.4	33.3	5.1	9.8	19.7	0.9	3.8	28.7
EFFICIENCY												
Coll Period (days)	19.4	33.1	50.7	28.5	38.7	46.7	30.3	42.3	53.5	19.4	28.7	59.9
Sales To Inv (times)	24.7	16.5	9.0	8.6	5.3	3.3	12.5	7.2	5.0	10.9	8.6	6.3
Assets To Sales (%)	18.9	31.2	53.3	36.4	48.8	66.1	27.7	36.5	51.3	20.4	32.1	39.8
Sales To Nwc (times)	9.0	6.5	4.2	9.0	4.4	2.5	9.4	5.4	3.5	10.4	7.4	5.1
Acct Pay To Sales (%)	2.4	3.9	9.8	2.9	4.6	7.3	3.6	6.2	8.9	3.1	4.5	8.8
PROFITABILITY												
Return On Sales (%)	5.6	2.3	0.5	4.4	2.5	0.6	4.1	2.1	0.5	3.4	1.5	0.4
Return On Assets (%)	14.4	6.7	1.5	12.4	5.3	1.9	11.7	4.6	1.4	9.4	4.9	1.6
Return On Nw (%)	48.9	12.0	1.8	20.6	9.3	4.6	24.6	8.3	2.4	16.8	10.8	3.1

Balance Sheet Items

	SIC 5065 ELEC PARTS, EQUIP (NO BREAKDOWN) 2013 (124 Establishments) $	%	SIC 5072 HARDWARE (NO BREAKDOWN) 2013 (59 Establishments) $	%	SIC 5074 PLMBG HDRNC,HTG SUP (NO BREAKDOWN) 2013 (86 Establishments) $	%	SIC 5075 WRM AIR HTG,AC (NO BREAKDOWN) 2013 (58 Establishments) $	%
Cash	592,911	19.4	427,555	13.4	290,529	11.7	329,794	10.1
Accounts Receivable	907,704	29.7	823,202	25.8	521,462	21.0	1,165,707	35.7
Notes Receivable	6,112	0.2	0	0.0	19,865	0.8	13,061	0.4
Inventory	776,286	25.4	1,266,711	39.7	933,664	37.6	1,208,156	37.0
Other Current	265,894	8.7	178,679	5.6	253,281	10.2	173,061	5.3
Total Current	**2,548,907**	**83.4**	**2,696,147**	**84.5**	**2,018,801**	**81.3**	**2,889,779**	**88.5**
Fixed Assets	275,062	9.0	303,117	9.5	268,180	10.8	277,549	8.5
Other Non-current	232,275	7.6	191,443	6.0	196,169	7.9	97,959	3.0
Total Assets	**3,056,244**	**100.0**	**3,190,707**	**100.0**	**2,483,150**	**100.0**	**3,265,287**	**100.0**
Accounts Payable	1,198,048	39.2	443,508	13.9	337,708	13.6	656,323	20.1
Bank Loans	42,787	1.4	19,144	0.6	14,899	0.6	71,836	2.2
Notes Payable	192,543	6.3	54,242	1.7	52,146	2.1	39,183	1.2
Other Current	2,585,583	84.6	443,509	13.9	389,855	15.7	721,629	22.1
Total Current	**4,018,961**	**131.5**	**960,403**	**30.1**	**794,608**	**32.0**	**1,488,971**	**45.6**
Other Long Term	290,344	9.5	283,972	8.9	148,989	6.0	241,631	7.4
Deferred Credits	6,112	0.2	3,191	0.1	0	0.0	3,265	0.1
Net Worth	(1,259,173)	(41.2)	1,943,141	60.9	1,539,553	62.0	1,531,420	46.9
Total Liab & Net Worth	**3,056,244**	**100.0**	**3,190,707**	**100.0**	**2,483,150**	**100.0**	**3,265,287**	**100.0**
Net Sales	8,237,854	100.0	8,037,045	100.0	6,302,411	100.0	10,300,590	100.0
Gross Profit	2,232,458	27.1	2,740,632	34.1	1,928,538	30.6	2,842,963	27.6
Net Profit After Tax	288,325	3.5	249,148	3.1	144,955	2.3	247,214	2.4
Working Capital	(1,470,054)	—	1,735,744	—	1,224,193	—	1,400,808	—

RATIOS

	5065 UQ	MED	LQ	5072 UQ	MED	LQ	5074 UQ	MED	LQ	5075 UQ	MED	LQ
SOLVENCY												
Quick Ratio (times)	2.8	1.2	0.6	2.9	1.5	0.8	2.2	1.3	0.6	1.5	1.1	0.7
Current Ratio (times)	4.5	1.9	1.3	5.1	3.4	2.2	5.7	2.9	1.7	3.2	1.9	1.4
Curr Liab To Nw (%)	24.2	73.0	170.6	19.5	41.9	82.9	18.0	37.3	102.9	42.4	99.1	192.9
Curr Liab To Inv (%)	75.8	179.1	295.1	45.2	74.5	108.4	38.5	76.9	140.9	56.4	110.3	352.5
Total Liab To Nw (%)	26.6	92.7	188.2	20.5	56.9	126.0	25.8	57.1	119.1	48.1	131.0	209.0
Fixed Assets To Nw (%)	3.3	10.7	25.8	4.3	11.3	22.7	5.2	11.3	26.3	5.0	11.3	25.2
EFFICIENCY												
Coll Period (days)	22.6	38.7	55.1	27.6	39.3	51.7	25.9	34.0	48.6	30.0	38.3	55.7
Sales To Inv (times)	22.7	9.9	6.5	11.3	6.3	4.3	10.1	6.2	3.6	25.0	8.1	4.9
Assets To Sales (%)	24.4	37.1	52.2	31.0	39.7	54.0	29.3	39.4	69.7	26.3	31.7	41.8
Sales To Nwc (times)	13.1	6.4	3.6	6.7	4.9	3.7	8.2	4.9	2.5	14.3	7.2	4.8
Acct Pay To Sales (%)	3.1	6.4	10.9	3.6	5.4	7.1	3.5	5.9	7.8	3.8	6.6	10.3
PROFITABILITY												
Return On Sales (%)	4.9	1.5	0.3	4.3	2.0	0.5	3.6	1.8	0.3	3.9	1.3	0.4
Return On Assets (%)	12.5	4.2	0.7	11.0	5.9	0.8	7.9	3.1	0.5	11.6	4.1	1.4
Return On Nw (%)	37.6	14.4	2.2	21.3	9.9	1.9	16.2	6.6	1.1	24.7	9.7	3.7

	SIC 5078 RFGTN EQUIP.SPPLS (NO BREAKDOWN) 2013 (11 Establishments) $	%	SIC 5082 CONSTR, MINNG MACH (NO BREAKDOWN) 2013 (57 Establishments) $	%	SIC 5083 FARM,GRDN MACH (NO BREAKDOWN) 2013 (107 Establishments) $	%	SIC 5084 INDL MCHNRY.EQPT (NO BREAKDOWN) 2013 (240 Establishments) $	%
Cash	789,328	18.5	554,280	8.8	421,998	8.0	582,596	17.2
Accounts Receivable	857,595	20.1	1,203,039	19.1	527,498	10.0	1,009,381	29.8
Notes Receivable	29,866	0.7	94,479	1.5	15,825	0.3	10,162	0.3
Inventory	1,318,392	30.9	2,550,946	40.5	3,492,036	66.2	995,833	29.4
Other Current	699,729	16.4	623,565	9.9	221,549	4.2	142,261	4.2
Total Current	**3,694,910**	**86.6**	**5,026,309**	**79.8**	**4,678,906**	**88.7**	**2,740,233**	**80.9**
Fixed Assets	396,798	9.3	825,121	13.1	453,648	8.6	430,173	12.7
Other Non-current	174,932	4.1	447,203	7.1	142,425	2.7	216,780	6.4
Total Assets	**4,266,640**	**100.0**	**6,298,633**	**100.0**	**5,274,979**	**100.0**	**3,387,186**	**100.0**
Accounts Payable	3,844,243	90.1	799,926	12.7	691,022	13.1	623,242	18.4
Bank Loans	230,399	5.4	94,479	1.5	5,275	0.1	13,549	0.4
Notes Payable	115,199	2.7	283,438	4.5	564,423	10.7	54,195	1.6
Other Current	11,690,593	274.0	1,423,492	22.6	1,535,019	29.1	775,666	22.9
Total Current	**15,880,434**	**372.2**	**2,601,335**	**41.3**	**2,795,739**	**53.0**	**1,466,652**	**43.3**
Other Long Term	18,611,084	436.2	900,705	14.3	480,023	9.1	355,654	10.5
Deferred Credits	0	0.0	6,299	0.1	0	0.0	3,387	0.1
Net Worth	(30,224,878)	(708.4)	2,790,294	44.3	1,999,217	37.9	1,561,493	46.1
Total Liab & Net Worth	**4,266,640**	**100.0**	**6,298,633**	**100.0**	**5,274,979**	**100.0**	**3,387,186**	**100.0**
Net Sales	8,833,623	100.0	12,136,094	100.0	12,238,930	100.0	8,984,578	100.0
Gross Profit	2,252,574	25.5	2,876,254	23.7	2,521,220	20.6	2,713,343	30.2
Net Profit After Tax	194,340	2.2	364,083	3.0	257,018	2.1	296,491	3.3
Working Capital	(12,185,524)	—	2,424,974	—	1,883,167	—	1,273,581	—

RATIOS	5078 UQ	MED	LQ	5082 UQ	MED	LQ	5083 UQ	MED	LQ	5084 UQ	MED	LQ
SOLVENCY												
Quick Ratio (times)	1.7	0.6	0.4	1.7	0.7	0.3	0.7	0.3	0.1	2.2	1.3	0.7
Current Ratio (times)	2.8	1.6	1.3	3.3	1.7	1.3	2.6	1.6	1.3	4.0	2.2	1.6
Curr Liab To Nw (%)	49.0	65.1	143.3	41.9	98.7	148.0	65.7	167.8	274.8	28.7	64.1	128.7
Curr Liab To Inv (%)	104.2	137.3	459.9	65.6	93.5	146.7	63.1	79.1	92.2	66.3	118.1	237.5
Total Liab To Nw (%)	51.1	68.7	177.1	65.9	127.4	270.7	87.9	196.6	301.2	35.5	86.0	160.3
Fixed Assets To Nw (%)	2.6	8.1	40.5	7.0	19.1	53.1	8.7	16.3	30.1	7.1	17.4	39.3
EFFICIENCY												
Coll Period (days)	25.2	31.3	67.2	21.9	32.9	53.0	4.4	11.9	24.5	25.2	37.6	50.2
Sales To Inv (times)	40.2	5.5	4.6	8.2	4.7	2.6	5.9	3.4	2.4	20.2	10.2	5.7
Assets To Sales (%)	30.7	48.3	52.9	36.4	51.9	68.2	34.2	43.1	50.4	23.7	37.7	53.2
Sales To Nwc (times)	14.3	6.4	4.3	9.9	5.3	2.8	12.0	7.7	4.8	11.2	6.6	4.1
Acct Pay To Sales (%)	3.3	8.5	11.3	1.9	4.2	8.0	1.3	3.1	6.6	3.2	5.3	7.6
PROFITABILITY												
Return On Sales (%)	3.1	1.2	0.5	4.7	2.5	1.3	3.6	1.5	0.6	5.4	2.3	0.8
Return On Assets (%)	6.9	4.1	1.0	10.2	5.1	2.4	9.1	3.7	1.6	13.1	6.6	2.4
Return On Nw (%)	21.1	6.4	3.1	30.1	13.5	5.8	22.7	9.1	4.0	26.3	11.7	4.9

SIC 5085 INDUSTRIAL SUPPLIES
(NO BREAKDOWN)
2013 (143 Establishments)

	$	%
Cash	388,858	13.9
Accounts Receivable	819,679	29.3
Notes Receivable	5,595	0.2
Inventory	923,188	33.0
Other Current	207,019	7.4
Total Current	**2,344,339**	**83.8**
Fixed Assets	313,324	11.2
Other Non-current	139,877	5.0
Total Assets	**2,797,540**	**100.0**
Accounts Payable	442,011	15.8
Bank Loans	19,583	0.7
Notes Payable	81,129	2.9
Other Current	444,809	15.9
Total Current	**987,532**	**35.3**
Other Long Term	218,208	7.8
Deferred Credits	0	0.0
Net Worth	1,591,800	56.9
Total Liab & Net Worth	**2,797,540**	**100.0**
Net Sales	8,156,093	100.0
Gross Profit	2,397,891	29.4
Net Profit After Tax	277,307	3.4
Working Capital	1,356,807	---

RATIOS	UQ	MED	LQ
SOLVENCY			
Quick Ratio (times)	2.2	1.3	0.8
Current Ratio (times)	4.5	2.6	1.8
Curr Liab To Nw (%)	21.5	54.8	104.7
Curr Liab To Inv (%)	53.4	90.8	177.9
Total Liab To Nw (%)	23.4	65.8	138.6
Fixed Assets To Nw (%)	4.6	12.7	34.1
EFFICIENCY			
Coll Period (days)	32.2	39.3	47.9
Sales To Inv (times)	15.1	9.0	5.1
Assets To Sales (%)	25.3	34.3	49.7
Sales To Nwc (times)	10.2	5.8	3.4
Acct Pay To Sales (%)	2.7	4.5	6.6
PROFITABILITY			
Return On Sales (%)	4.9	2.2	0.6
Return On Assets (%)	16.3	6.6	1.6
Return On Nw (%)	30.1	12.3	3.2

SIC 5087 SVC ESTBLSHMNT EQPT
(NO BREAKDOWN)
2013 (39 Establishments)

	$	%
Cash	319,839	16.0
Accounts Receivable	585,705	29.3
Notes Receivable	0	0.0
Inventory	667,663	33.4
Other Current	151,923	7.6
Total Current	**1,725,130**	**86.3**
Fixed Assets	175,911	8.8
Other Non-current	97,951	4.9
Total Assets	**1,998,992**	**100.0**
Accounts Payable	395,800	19.8
Bank Loans	47,976	2.4
Notes Payable	25,987	1.3
Other Current	357,820	17.9
Total Current	**827,583**	**41.4**
Other Long Term	99,949	5.0
Deferred Credits	0	0.0
Net Worth	1,071,460	53.6
Total Liab & Net Worth	**1,998,992**	**100.0**
Net Sales	7,515,008	100.0
Gross Profit	2,269,532	30.2
Net Profit After Tax	157,815	2.1
Working Capital	897,547	---

RATIOS	UQ	MED	LQ
SOLVENCY			
Quick Ratio (times)	1.9	1.1	0.6
Current Ratio (times)	3.5	2.1	1.6
Curr Liab To Nw (%)	34.9	87.1	140.3
Curr Liab To Inv (%)	61.9	102.4	182.9
Total Liab To Nw (%)	38.7	88.2	164.3
Fixed Assets To Nw (%)	4.5	14.2	28.2
EFFICIENCY			
Coll Period (days)	21.9	28.3	40.6
Sales To Inv (times)	17.9	10.1	7.4
Assets To Sales (%)	22.4	26.6	34.5
Sales To Nwc (times)	13.1	8.1	5.9
Acct Pay To Sales (%)	3.5	4.8	8.2
PROFITABILITY			
Return On Sales (%)	3.2	1.3	0.4
Return On Assets (%)	12.4	4.4	1.9
Return On Nw (%)	25.0	11.2	4.1

SIC 5088 TRNSPRTN EQPT.SUPPL
(NO BREAKDOWN)
2013 (39 Establishments)

	$	%
Cash	592,834	19.8
Accounts Receivable	760,504	25.4
Notes Receivable	5,988	0.2
Inventory	1,173,692	39.2
Other Current	185,635	6.2
Total Current	**2,718,653**	**90.8**
Fixed Assets	176,653	5.9
Other Non-current	98,805	3.3
Total Assets	**2,994,111**	**100.0**
Accounts Payable	862,304	28.8
Bank Loans	68,865	2.3
Notes Payable	697,628	23.3
Other Current	700,621	23.4
Total Current	**2,329,418**	**77.8**
Other Long Term	122,759	4.1
Deferred Credits	0	0.0
Net Worth	541,934	18.1
Total Liab & Net Worth	**2,994,111**	**100.0**
Net Sales	8,991,324	100.0
Gross Profit	2,625,467	29.2
Net Profit After Tax	512,505	5.7
Working Capital	389,235	---

RATIOS	UQ	MED	LQ
SOLVENCY			
Quick Ratio (times)	2.2	0.9	0.6
Current Ratio (times)	4.2	2.4	1.7
Curr Liab To Nw (%)	22.5	55.5	116.7
Curr Liab To Inv (%)	50.6	93.6	165.1
Total Liab To Nw (%)	28.4	63.9	120.1
Fixed Assets To Nw (%)	2.2	4.2	20.8
EFFICIENCY			
Coll Period (days)	17.2	30.7	49.6
Sales To Inv (times)	13.2	6.6	4.2
Assets To Sales (%)	23.3	33.3	51.1
Sales To Nwc (times)	12.2	5.4	3.3
Acct Pay To Sales (%)	2.4	4.9	9.0
PROFITABILITY			
Return On Sales (%)	7.1	3.9	1.2
Return On Assets (%)	20.1	8.6	3.8
Return On Nw (%)	45.2	15.0	7.5

SIC 5091 SPTG,RECRTNL GOODS
(NO BREAKDOWN)
2013 (38 Establishments)

	$	%
Cash	334,076	22.4
Accounts Receivable	319,162	21.4
Notes Receivable	4,474	0.3
Inventory	524,977	35.2
Other Current	68,605	4.6
Total Current	**1,251,294**	**83.9**
Fixed Assets	134,227	9.0
Other Non-current	105,890	7.1
Total Assets	**1,491,411**	**100.0**
Accounts Payable	259,506	17.4
Bank Loans	0	0.0
Notes Payable	76,062	5.1
Other Current	483,217	32.4
Total Current	**818,785**	**54.9**
Other Long Term	116,330	7.8
Deferred Credits	0	0.0
Net Worth	556,296	37.3
Total Liab & Net Worth	**1,491,411**	**100.0**
Net Sales	4,285,664	100.0
Gross Profit	1,268,557	29.6
Net Profit After Tax	175,712	4.1
Working Capital	432,509	---

RATIOS	UQ	MED	LQ
SOLVENCY			
Quick Ratio (times)	1.6	1.1	0.6
Current Ratio (times)	4.7	2.2	1.4
Curr Liab To Nw (%)	24.4	62.8	143.0
Curr Liab To Inv (%)	41.8	99.3	216.9
Total Liab To Nw (%)	26.8	62.8	208.6
Fixed Assets To Nw (%)	5.8	13.9	29.1
EFFICIENCY			
Coll Period (days)	14.2	28.5	50.7
Sales To Inv (times)	17.3	7.1	4.9
Assets To Sales (%)	22.3	34.8	58.4
Sales To Nwc (times)	12.4	6.8	3.3
Acct Pay To Sales (%)	3.7	6.3	10.3
PROFITABILITY			
Return On Sales (%)	5.1	2.9	0.7
Return On Assets (%)	20.7	8.3	2.4
Return On Nw (%)	35.6	13.8	3.8

SIC 5092 TOYS,HBBY GDS,SUPPL (NO BREAKDOWN) 2013 (15 Establishments) | SIC 5093 SCRAP,WASTE MTRLS (NO BREAKDOWN) 2013 (29 Establishments) | SIC 5094 JWLRY,PRCIOUS STNS (NO BREAKDOWN) 2013 (22 Establishments) | SIC 5099 DURABLE GOODS, NEC (NO BREAKDOWN) 2013 (26 Establishments)

	SIC 5092 $	%	SIC 5093 $	%	SIC 5094 $	%	SIC 5099 $	%
Cash	408,891	11.9	1,638,173	14.5	578,615	7.9	220,099	12.1
Accounts Receivable	876,196	25.5	3,027,795	26.8	1,611,333	22.0	671,211	36.9
Notes Receivable	20,616	0.6	22,595	0.2	0	0.0	0	0.0
Inventory	1,267,907	36.9	2,259,548	20.0	3,969,739	54.2	531,148	29.2
Other Current	481,048	14.0	666,567	5.9	468,751	6.4	130,968	7.2
Total Current	**3,054,658**	**88.9**	**7,614,678**	**67.4**	**6,628,438**	**90.5**	**1,553,426**	**85.4**
Fixed Assets	147,751	4.3	2,937,413	26.0	366,212	5.0	165,529	9.1
Other Non-current	233,652	6.8	745,651	6.6	329,591	4.5	100,045	5.5
Total Assets	**3,436,061**	**100.0**	**11,297,742**	**100.0**	**7,324,241**	**100.0**	**1,819,000**	**100.0**
Accounts Payable	3,233,333	94.1	1,412,218	12.5	1,508,794	20.6	225,556	12.4
Bank Loans	99,646	2.9	0	0.0	197,755	2.7	5,457	0.3
Notes Payable	123,698	3.6	158,168	1.4	29,297	0.4	36,380	2.0
Other Current	6,349,841	184.8	2,429,015	21.5	1,325,687	18.1	392,904	21.6
Total Current	**9,806,518**	**285.4**	**3,999,401**	**35.4**	**3,061,533**	**41.8**	**660,297**	**36.3**
Other Long Term	30,925	0.9	892,521	7.9	556,642	7.6	167,348	9.2
Deferred Credits	0	0.0	11,298	0.1	0	0.0	0	0.0
Net Worth	(6,401,382)	(186.3)	6,394,522	56.6	3,706,066	50.6	991,355	54.5
Total Liab & Net Worth	**3,436,061**	**100.0**	**11,297,742**	**100.0**	**7,324,241**	**100.0**	**1,819,000**	**100.0**
Net Sales	8,878,711	100.0	36,210,712	100.0	11,851,523	100.0	6,687,500	100.0
Gross Profit	3,258,487	36.7	5,866,135	16.2	2,583,632	21.8	1,992,875	29.8
Net Profit After Tax	399,542	4.5	651,793	1.8	142,218	1.2	247,438	3.7
Working Capital	(6,751,860)	---	3,615,277	---	3,566,905	---	893,129	---

RATIOS	SIC 5092 UQ	MED	LQ	SIC 5093 UQ	MED	LQ	SIC 5094 UQ	MED	LQ	SIC 5099 UQ	MED	LQ
SOLVENCY												
Quick Ratio (times)	1.1	0.6	0.5	2.4	1.3	0.7	1.9	0.9	0.4	2.2	1.6	0.8
Current Ratio (times)	3.7	2.1	1.3	3.0	2.2	1.3	4.9	2.6	1.5	4.8	2.3	1.7
Curr Liab To Nw (%)	32.2	72.7	314.2	16.3	50.0	113.5	20.4	85.6	290.3	24.5	61.5	107.0
Curr Liab To Inv (%)	39.3	111.1	262.6	68.3	100.2	220.0	33.0	82.8	132.5	68.1	113.5	279.2
Total Liab To Nw (%)	32.2	73.2	347.8	28.4	79.5	144.0	31.5	92.8	395.2	32.4	78.0	148.6
Fixed Assets To Nw (%)	8.3	11.2	16.8	9.3	35.5	106.3	1.0	6.8	14.2	4.7	10.2	25.2
EFFICIENCY												
Coll Period (days)	13.2	52.6	75.6	23.0	29.9	37.6	23.0	50.6	82.9	28.5	36.9	43.8
Sales To Inv (times)	8.5	6.1	4.1	35.7	17.6	9.0	4.6	2.6	1.9	28.4	13.7	8.1
Assets To Sales (%)	24.8	38.7	49.3	21.8	31.2	41.0	33.4	61.8	76.8	22.5	27.2	42.4
Sales To Nwc (times)	17.9	7.1	5.7	15.7	10.4	6.2	8.1	6.1	2.4	10.5	7.4	4.3
Acct Pay To Sales (%)	4.8	12.6	17.9	2.0	3.3	5.5	3.4	9.4	15.9	2.6	3.2	4.7
PROFITABILITY												
Return On Sales (%)	5.4	3.8	0.7	5.4	1.3	0.5	1.3	0.7	0.1	5.3	3.0	0.7
Return On Assets (%)	20.9	11.9	1.6	11.0	5.3	1.5	3.0	0.9	0.1	16.2	5.8	2.8
Return On Nw (%)	91.1	38.4	4.8	25.2	7.3	2.7	7.4	4.4	0.5	34.4	13.4	4.0

Balance Sheet

	SIC 51 WHLE TRD NONDURBL GDS (NO BREAKDOWN) 2013 (1303 Establishments) $	%	SIC 5112 STNRY,OFFC SUPPL (NO BREAKDOWN) 2013 (22 Establishments) $	%	SIC 5113 INDL,PRSNL SVC PPR (NO BREAKDOWN) 2013 (36 Establishments) $	%	SIC 5122 DRGS,PRPRTRS,SNDRS (NO BREAKDOWN) 2013 (51 Establishments) $	%
Cash	803,998	13.2	418,258	26.4	419,142	15.0	1,380,288	15.8
Accounts Receivable	1,626,269	26.7	660,657	41.7	874,610	31.3	2,157,792	24.7
Notes Receivable	24,364	0.4	1,584	0.1	2,794	0.1	17,472	0.2
Inventory	1,571,451	25.8	236,062	14.9	888,581	31.8	2,909,088	33.3
Other Current	517,727	8.5	82,385	5.2	97,801	3.5	463,008	5.3
Total Current	**4,543,809**	**74.6**	**1,398,946**	**88.3**	**2,282,928**	**81.7**	**6,927,648**	**79.3**
Fixed Assets	1,023,271	16.8	71,294	4.5	332,519	11.9	847,392	9.7
Other Non-current	523,817	8.6	114,070	7.2	178,834	6.4	960,960	11.0
Total Assets	**6,090,897**	**100.0**	**1,584,310**	**100.0**	**2,794,281**	**100.0**	**8,736,000**	**100.0**
Accounts Payable	1,364,361	22.4	370,729	23.4	357,668	12.8	2,236,416	25.6
Bank Loans	36,545	0.6	0	0.0	5,589	0.2	61,152	0.7
Notes Payable	401,999	6.6	107,733	6.8	36,326	1.3	384,384	4.4
Other Current	1,193,816	19.6	264,579	16.7	486,204	17.4	3,791,424	43.4
Total Current	**2,996,721**	**49.2**	**743,041**	**46.9**	**885,787**	**31.7**	**6,473,376**	**74.1**
Other Long Term	669,999	11.0	72,879	4.6	315,753	11.3	1,022,112	11.7
Deferred Credits	6,091	0.1	0	0.0	5,589	0.2	8,736	0.1
Net Worth	2,418,086	39.7	768,390	48.5	1,587,152	56.8	1,231,776	14.1
Total Liab & Net Worth	**6,090,897**	**100.0**	**1,584,310**	**100.0**	**2,794,281**	**100.0**	**8,736,000**	**100.0**
Net Sales	22,727,228	100.0	5,933,745	100.0	10,465,472	100.0	26,634,146	100.0
Gross Profit	4,159,083	18.3	1,880,997	31.7	2,815,212	26.9	7,164,585	26.9
Net Profit After Tax	499,999	2.2	172,079	2.9	313,964	3.0	(745,756)	(2.8)
Working Capital	1,547,088	---	655,905	---	1,397,141	---	454,272	---

RATIOS

	SIC 51 UQ	MED	LQ	SIC 5112 UQ	MED	LQ	SIC 5113 UQ	MED	LQ	SIC 5122 UQ	MED	LQ
SOLVENCY												
Quick Ratio (times)	1.6	0.9	0.5	3.1	1.9	0.9	3.4	1.7	0.8	1.1	0.8	0.6
Current Ratio (times)	2.9	1.7	1.3	3.8	2.4	1.4	5.0	3.4	1.6	2.3	1.6	1.2
Curr Liab To Nw (%)	34.7	83.0	173.3	28.6	59.2	142.0	20.0	35.5	108.2	52.9	116.6	235.2
Curr Liab To Inv (%)	85.0	146.0	296.2	165.2	253.4	739.0	50.9	89.3	153.8	88.4	141.7	240.9
Total Liab To Nw (%)	47.5	111.7	228.3	38.2	59.2	192.4	20.0	47.5	155.0	94.2	136.5	294.2
Fixed Assets To Nw (%)	8.7	30.4	62.0	3.0	5.8	15.5	3.8	16.7	31.5	3.4	19.1	35.5
EFFICIENCY												
Coll Period (days)	12.1	22.3	36.5	27.4	32.9	46.4	23.7	31.0	35.8	23.4	34.3	45.7
Sales To Inv (times)	36.7	14.4	7.5	120.3	23.7	10.4	16.9	11.8	7.7	14.5	8.0	5.3
Assets To Sales (%)	15.3	26.8	43.8	17.3	26.7	42.4	21.2	26.7	37.4	23.8	32.8	55.7
Sales To Nwc (times)	26.5	12.8	6.4	19.2	7.0	4.4	14.3	8.8	4.7	15.5	8.6	5.0
Acct Pay To Sales (%)	2.0	3.8	7.0	3.7	4.9	6.8	2.6	3.7	7.8	4.4	8.0	12.2
PROFITABILITY												
Return On Sales (%)	3.2	1.2	0.3	0.9	0.9	0.1	2.5	1.7	0.3	2.9	1.1	0.1
Return On Assets (%)	10.8	5.0	1.4	11.5	3.0	0.3	11.7	5.9	1.8	8.3	2.6	(0.3)
Return On Nw (%)	23.7	11.8	3.9	21.5	6.8	1.0	21.4	13.8	7.2	21.7	10.2	0.7

SIC 5131 PCE GDS,NOTIONS
(NO BREAKDOWN)
2013 (21 Establishments)

	$	%
Cash	240,872	14.3
Accounts Receivable	353,728	21.0
Notes Receivable	40,426	2.4
Inventory	715,877	42.5
Other Current	70,745	4.2
Total Current	**1,421,648**	**84.4**
Fixed Assets	144,860	8.6
Other Non-current	117,909	7.0
Total Assets	**1,684,417**	**100.0**
Accounts Payable	175,179	10.4
Bank Loans	0	0.0
Notes Payable	32,004	1.9
Other Current	370,572	22.0
Total Current	**577,755**	**34.3**
Other Long Term	96,012	5.7
Deferred Credits	0	0.0
Net Worth	1,010,650	60.0
Total Liab & Net Worth	**1,684,417**	**100.0**
Net Sales	4,148,810	100.0
Gross Profit	1,269,536	30.6
Net Profit After Tax	132,762	3.2
Working Capital	843,893	—

RATIOS	UQ	MED	LQ
SOLVENCY			
Quick Ratio (times)	1.7	1.0	0.7
Current Ratio (times)	3.8	2.9	1.9
Curr Liab To Nw (%)	30.7	53.5	88.9
Curr Liab To Inv (%)	38.7	62.4	168.4
Total Liab To Nw (%)	27.7	53.5	122.2
Fixed Assets To Nw (%)	5.3	10.0	15.9
EFFICIENCY			
Coll Period (days)	19.4	27.4	36.5
Sales To Inv (times)	21.3	6.1	4.0
Assets To Sales (%)	27.7	40.6	52.1
Sales To Nwc (times)	10.8	5.8	3.5
Acct Pay To Sales (%)	2.6	4.0	9.7
PROFITABILITY			
Return On Sales (%)	5.9	1.0	0.4
Return On Assets (%)	19.1	4.2	0.7
Return On Nw (%)	26.1	7.4	1.1

SIC 5136 MENS,BOYS CLOTHING
(NO BREAKDOWN)
2013 (19 Establishments)

	$	%
Cash	396,860	20.6
Accounts Receivable	387,227	20.1
Notes Receivable	0	0.0
Inventory	631,893	32.8
Other Current	173,385	9.0
Total Current	**1,589,365**	**82.5**
Fixed Assets	281,269	14.6
Other Non-current	55,869	2.9
Total Assets	**1,926,503**	**100.0**
Accounts Payable	300,534	15.6
Bank Loans	9,633	0.5
Notes Payable	28,898	1.5
Other Current	924,721	48.0
Total Current	**1,263,786**	**65.6**
Other Long Term	48,163	2.5
Deferred Credits	0	0.0
Net Worth	614,554	31.9
Total Liab & Net Worth	**1,926,503**	**100.0**
Net Sales	4,368,488	100.0
Gross Profit	1,336,757	30.6
Net Profit After Tax	218,424	5.0
Working Capital	325,579	—

RATIOS	UQ	MED	LQ
SOLVENCY			
Quick Ratio (times)	4.1	1.4	0.7
Current Ratio (times)	5.7	3.4	1.7
Curr Liab To Nw (%)	18.2	26.3	89.9
Curr Liab To Inv (%)	65.6	90.0	157.6
Total Liab To Nw (%)	18.2	26.3	97.5
Fixed Assets To Nw (%)	1.9	16.5	22.8
EFFICIENCY			
Coll Period (days)	19.0	32.7	43.8
Sales To Inv (times)	11.7	10.1	6.9
Assets To Sales (%)	32.7	44.1	48.5
Sales To Nwc (times)	8.0	4.6	2.7
Acct Pay To Sales (%)	3.5	5.0	6.9
PROFITABILITY			
Return On Sales (%)	10.6	2.4	0.0
Return On Assets (%)	19.7	5.9	(0.1)
Return On Nw (%)	22.9	7.4	0.7

SIC 5137 WMNS,CLDRNS CLTHNG
(NO BREAKDOWN)
2013 (20 Establishments)

	$	%
Cash	218,350	11.5
Accounts Receivable	436,701	23.0
Notes Receivable	3,797	0.2
Inventory	867,705	45.7
Other Current	131,010	6.9
Total Current	**1,657,563**	**87.3**
Fixed Assets	140,504	7.4
Other Non-current	100,631	5.3
Total Assets	**1,898,698**	**100.0**
Accounts Payable	421,511	22.2
Bank Loans	37,974	2.0
Notes Payable	(22,784)	(1.2)
Other Current	729,100	38.4
Total Current	**1,165,801**	**61.4**
Other Long Term	45,568	2.4
Deferred Credits	0	0.0
Net Worth	687,329	36.2
Total Liab & Net Worth	**1,898,698**	**100.0**
Net Sales	5,736,248	100.0
Gross Profit	1,680,721	29.3
Net Profit After Tax	229,450	4.0
Working Capital	491,762	—

RATIOS	UQ	MED	LQ
SOLVENCY			
Quick Ratio (times)	2.0	0.7	0.3
Current Ratio (times)	4.9	2.8	1.6
Curr Liab To Nw (%)	23.1	42.0	130.2
Curr Liab To Inv (%)	32.4	61.2	202.7
Total Liab To Nw (%)	23.1	42.0	130.5
Fixed Assets To Nw (%)	2.8	4.9	18.1
EFFICIENCY			
Coll Period (days)	9.5	23.7	34.3
Sales To Inv (times)	16.1	8.7	4.8
Assets To Sales (%)	15.9	33.1	40.8
Sales To Nwc (times)	14.5	6.1	3.7
Acct Pay To Sales (%)	1.7	3.7	6.5
PROFITABILITY			
Return On Sales (%)	6.6	2.7	0.5
Return On Assets (%)	36.5	10.8	3.4
Return On Nw (%)	50.9	26.6	8.8

SIC 5139 FOOTWEAR
(NO BREAKDOWN)
2013 (10 Establishments)

	$	%
Cash	512,130	11.1
Accounts Receivable	1,278,019	27.7
Notes Receivable	0	0.0
Inventory	1,670,191	36.2
Other Current	207,620	4.5
Total Current	**3,667,960**	**79.5**
Fixed Assets	447,537	9.7
Other Non-current	498,289	10.8
Total Assets	**4,613,786**	**100.0**
Accounts Payable	622,861	13.5
Bank Loans	0	0.0
Notes Payable	55,365	1.2
Other Current	622,862	13.5
Total Current	**1,301,088**	**28.2**
Other Long Term	835,095	18.1
Deferred Credits	0	0.0
Net Worth	2,477,603	53.7
Total Liab & Net Worth	**4,613,786**	**100.0**
Net Sales	8,941,446	100.0
Gross Profit	3,031,150	33.9
Net Profit After Tax	473,897	5.3
Working Capital	2,366,872	—

RATIOS	UQ	MED	LQ
SOLVENCY			
Quick Ratio (times)	4.7	1.7	0.7
Current Ratio (times)	10.1	3.0	2.0
Curr Liab To Nw (%)	20.1	56.1	82.0
Curr Liab To Inv (%)	31.0	80.2	117.4
Total Liab To Nw (%)	49.5	82.1	114.7
Fixed Assets To Nw (%)	3.4	13.6	31.1
EFFICIENCY			
Coll Period (days)	40.2	43.1	58.8
Sales To Inv (times)	5.9	5.2	4.8
Assets To Sales (%)	43.1	51.6	71.5
Sales To Nwc (times)	4.4	3.0	2.4
Acct Pay To Sales (%)	4.1	6.4	9.7
PROFITABILITY			
Return On Sales (%)	8.7	5.1	1.7
Return On Assets (%)	16.9	6.8	1.8
Return On Nw (%)	25.2	10.4	4.7

SIC 5141 GROCERIES,GNRL LNE (NO BREAKDOWN) 2013 (69 Establishments)

	$	%
Cash	675,747	11.9
Accounts Receivable	1,720,600	30.3
Notes Receivable	11,357	0.2
Inventory	1,624,064	28.6
Other Current	391,820	6.9
Total Current	**4,423,588**	**77.9**
Fixed Assets	823,389	14.5
Other Non-current	431,570	7.6
Total Assets	**5,678,547**	**100.0**
Accounts Payable	1,203,852	21.2
Bank Loans	22,714	0.4
Notes Payable	102,214	1.8
Other Current	1,135,709	20.0
Total Current	**2,464,489**	**43.4**
Other Long Term	539,462	9.5
Deferred Credits	0	0.0
Net Worth	2,674,596	47.1
Total Liab & Net Worth	**5,678,547**	**100.0**
Net Sales	23,859,441	100.0
Gross Profit	3,984,527	16.7
Net Profit After Tax	71,578	0.3
Working Capital	1,959,099	---

RATIOS	UQ	MED	LQ
SOLVENCY			
Quick Ratio (times)	1.7	0.9	0.6
Current Ratio (times)	3.6	1.7	1.3
Curr Liab To Nw (%)	22.7	94.1	210.3
Curr Liab To Inv (%)	59.2	119.2	171.2
Total Liab To Nw (%)	33.7	132.9	275.7
Fixed Assets To Nw (%)	5.3	21.6	60.0
EFFICIENCY			
Coll Period (days)	12.3	21.9	37.8
Sales To Inv (times)	24.8	13.9	8.9
Assets To Sales (%)	14.9	23.8	36.0
Sales To Nwc (times)	27.2	15.5	6.7
Acct Pay To Sales (%)	2.0	4.6	7.3
PROFITABILITY			
Return On Sales (%)	2.4	1.0	0.1
Return On Assets (%)	9.8	4.2	0.7
Return On Nw (%)	20.1	9.9	2.3

SIC 5142 PCKGD FROZEN GOODS (NO BREAKDOWN) 2013 (10 Establishments)

	$	%
Cash	622,781	4.2
Accounts Receivable	3,425,297	23.1
Notes Receivable	88,969	0.6
Inventory	5,619,859	37.9
Other Current	326,218	2.2
Total Current	**10,083,124**	**68.0**
Fixed Assets	3,454,953	23.3
Other Non-current	1,290,047	8.7
Total Assets	**14,828,124**	**100.0**
Accounts Payable	2,832,172	19.1
Bank Loans	0	0.0
Notes Payable	0	0.0
Other Current	2,921,140	19.7
Total Current	**5,753,312**	**38.8**
Other Long Term	2,847,000	19.2
Deferred Credits	0	0.0
Net Worth	6,227,812	42.0
Total Liab & Net Worth	**14,828,124**	**100.0**
Net Sales	55,328,821	100.0
Gross Profit	7,137,418	12.9
Net Profit After Tax	(55,329)	(0.1)
Working Capital	4,329,812	---

RATIOS	UQ	MED	LQ
SOLVENCY			
Quick Ratio (times)	1.6	0.7	0.5
Current Ratio (times)	3.8	1.8	1.3
Curr Liab To Nw (%)	23.4	88.3	289.7
Curr Liab To Inv (%)	54.3	94.0	138.4
Total Liab To Nw (%)	126.8	153.0	320.8
Fixed Assets To Nw (%)	3.8	62.2	129.4
EFFICIENCY			
Coll Period (days)	16.8	21.0	34.7
Sales To Inv (times)	15.9	7.4	5.7
Assets To Sales (%)	21.8	26.8	77.3
Sales To Nwc (times)	15.2	9.1	6.7
Acct Pay To Sales (%)	2.0	7.0	10.9
PROFITABILITY			
Return On Sales (%)	1.3	0.4	0.1
Return On Assets (%)	1.8	1.2	1.0
Return On Nw (%)	5.4	3.7	1.2

SIC 5144 PLTRY,PLTRY PRDTS (NO BREAKDOWN) 2013 (11 Establishments)

	$	%
Cash	391,323	6.6
Accounts Receivable	2,419,085	40.8
Notes Receivable	65,220	1.1
Inventory	1,179,897	19.9
Other Current	747,071	12.6
Total Current	**4,802,596**	**81.0**
Fixed Assets	794,504	13.4
Other Non-current	332,031	5.6
Total Assets	**5,929,131**	**100.0**
Accounts Payable	1,369,629	23.1
Bank Loans	0	0.0
Notes Payable	260,882	4.4
Other Current	616,630	10.4
Total Current	**2,247,141**	**37.9**
Other Long Term	669,991	11.3
Deferred Credits	0	0.0
Net Worth	3,011,999	50.8
Total Liab & Net Worth	**5,929,131**	**100.0**
Net Sales	36,599,574	100.0
Gross Profit	4,355,349	11.9
Net Profit After Tax	475,794	1.3
Working Capital	2,555,455	---

RATIOS	UQ	MED	LQ
SOLVENCY			
Quick Ratio (times)	2.8	1.9	0.8
Current Ratio (times)	5.9	2.1	1.3
Curr Liab To Nw (%)	35.8	95.0	140.4
Curr Liab To Inv (%)	85.5	131.6	289.5
Total Liab To Nw (%)	54.0	141.6	228.6
Fixed Assets To Nw (%)	12.3	21.5	42.5
EFFICIENCY			
Coll Period (days)	16.8	23.0	30.7
Sales To Inv (times)	46.1	27.5	16.1
Assets To Sales (%)	12.7	16.2	24.4
Sales To Nwc (times)	21.8	13.5	10.3
Acct Pay To Sales (%)	2.6	4.0	4.7
PROFITABILITY			
Return On Sales (%)	2.4	1.1	0.2
Return On Assets (%)	11.8	4.9	1.3
Return On Nw (%)	21.0	12.0	3.4

SIC 5145 CONFECTIONERY (NO BREAKDOWN) 2013 (19 Establishments)

	$	%
Cash	275,042	13.4
Accounts Receivable	550,084	26.8
Notes Receivable	0	0.0
Inventory	621,923	30.3
Other Current	77,996	3.8
Total Current	**1,525,045**	**74.3**
Fixed Assets	428,983	20.9
Other Non-current	98,523	4.8
Total Assets	**2,052,551**	**100.0**
Accounts Payable	330,461	16.1
Bank Loans	8,210	0.4
Notes Payable	51,314	2.5
Other Current	330,460	16.1
Total Current	**720,445**	**35.1**
Other Long Term	346,881	16.9
Deferred Credits	10,263	0.5
Net Worth	974,962	47.5
Total Liab & Net Worth	**2,052,551**	**100.0**
Net Sales	8,343,703	100.0
Gross Profit	2,035,864	24.4
Net Profit After Tax	358,779	4.3
Working Capital	804,600	---

RATIOS	UQ	MED	LQ
SOLVENCY			
Quick Ratio (times)	3.0	1.1	0.6
Current Ratio (times)	3.9	2.5	1.6
Curr Liab To Nw (%)	29.6	71.7	145.1
Curr Liab To Inv (%)	66.9	99.5	149.4
Total Liab To Nw (%)	49.3	112.4	341.0
Fixed Assets To Nw (%)	19.6	38.6	75.1
EFFICIENCY			
Coll Period (days)	13.9	24.5	33.6
Sales To Inv (times)	18.2	9.6	6.7
Assets To Sales (%)	17.2	24.6	38.7
Sales To Nwc (times)	15.4	10.2	6.0
Acct Pay To Sales (%)	2.2	3.0	6.1
PROFITABILITY			
Return On Sales (%)	2.9	1.3	0.5
Return On Assets (%)	14.7	6.0	0.8
Return On Nw (%)	31.3	13.5	3.8

SIC 5146 FISH AND SEAFOODS (NO BREAKDOWN) 2013 (17 Establishments)

	$	%
Cash	466,982	9.7
Accounts Receivable	1,347,991	28.0
Notes Receivable	24,071	0.5
Inventory	1,468,347	30.5
Other Current	621,039	12.9
Total Current	**3,928,430**	**81.6**
Fixed Assets	770,280	16.0
Other Non-current	115,542	2.4
Total Assets	**4,814,252**	**100.0**
Accounts Payable	1,319,105	27.4
Bank Loans	19,257	0.4
Notes Payable	101,099	2.1
Other Current	977,294	20.3
Total Current	**2,416,755**	**50.2**
Other Long Term	414,025	8.6
Deferred Credits	0	0.0
Net Worth	1,983,472	41.2
Total Liab & Net Worth	**4,814,252**	**100.0**
Net Sales	16,833,049	100.0
Gross Profit	1,902,135	11.3
Net Profit After Tax	235,663	1.4
Working Capital	1,511,675	—

RATIOS	UQ	MED	LQ
SOLVENCY			
Quick Ratio (times)	0.9	0.8	0.6
Current Ratio (times)	1.9	1.6	1.2
Curr Liab To Nw (%)	37.6	101.7	257.5
Curr Liab To Inv (%)	104.4	142.5	252.7
Total Liab To Nw (%)	66.0	135.3	257.5
Fixed Assets To Nw (%)	3.3	35.8	77.9
EFFICIENCY			
Coll Period (days)	17.2	29.0	56.8
Sales To Inv (times)	19.1	11.9	7.0
Assets To Sales (%)	16.8	28.6	46.7
Sales To Nwc (times)	21.9	11.9	9.5
Acct Pay To Sales (%)	4.3	5.4	12.3
PROFITABILITY			
Return On Sales (%)	2.4	0.7	0.6
Return On Assets (%)	7.1	3.6	1.5
Return On Nw (%)	29.1	8.6	5.3

SIC 5147 MEATS, MEAT PRDTS (NO BREAKDOWN) 2013 (44 Establishments)

	$	%
Cash	666,897	20.8
Accounts Receivable	1,090,120	34.0
Notes Receivable	3,206	0.1
Inventory	705,371	22.0
Other Current	182,755	5.7
Total Current	**2,648,349**	**82.6**
Fixed Assets	538,647	16.8
Other Non-current	19,238	0.6
Total Assets	**3,206,234**	**100.0**
Accounts Payable	830,415	25.9
Bank Loans	70,537	2.2
Notes Payable	105,806	3.3
Other Current	609,184	19.0
Total Current	**1,615,942**	**50.4**
Other Long Term	176,343	5.5
Deferred Credits	0	0.0
Net Worth	1,413,949	44.1
Total Liab & Net Worth	**3,206,234**	**100.0**
Net Sales	19,791,568	100.0
Gross Profit	2,770,820	14.0
Net Profit After Tax	395,831	2.0
Working Capital	1,032,407	—

RATIOS	UQ	MED	LQ
SOLVENCY			
Quick Ratio (times)	2.8	1.1	0.7
Current Ratio (times)	4.7	1.5	1.2
Curr Liab To Nw (%)	21.5	101.0	284.5
Curr Liab To Inv (%)	58.7	162.0	257.9
Total Liab To Nw (%)	24.8	132.6	346.9
Fixed Assets To Nw (%)	3.8	22.0	89.4
EFFICIENCY			
Coll Period (days)	12.8	18.3	25.6
Sales To Inv (times)	42.5	27.3	17.5
Assets To Sales (%)	13.0	16.2	26.9
Sales To Nwc (times)	37.3	18.4	7.0
Acct Pay To Sales (%)	1.4	2.3	4.6
PROFITABILITY			
Return On Sales (%)	3.2	0.7	0.1
Return On Assets (%)	15.4	5.5	1.0
Return On Nw (%)	31.9	13.7	3.7

SIC 5148 FRSH FRTS, VGTBLES (NO BREAKDOWN) 2013 (122 Establishments)

	$	%
Cash	649,531	17.8
Accounts Receivable	1,514,355	41.5
Notes Receivable	21,894	0.6
Inventory	237,188	6.5
Other Current	332,064	9.1
Total Current	**2,755,032**	**75.5**
Fixed Assets	572,901	15.7
Other Non-current	321,116	8.8
Total Assets	**3,649,049**	**100.0**
Accounts Payable	912,262	25.0
Bank Loans	10,947	0.3
Notes Payable	32,841	0.9
Other Current	795,494	21.8
Total Current	**1,751,544**	**48.0**
Other Long Term	266,380	7.3
Deferred Credits	7,298	0.2
Net Worth	1,623,827	44.5
Total Liab & Net Worth	**3,649,049**	**100.0**
Net Sales	22,524,994	100.0
Gross Profit	4,031,974	17.9
Net Profit After Tax	518,075	2.3
Working Capital	1,003,488	—

RATIOS	UQ	MED	LQ
SOLVENCY			
Quick Ratio (times)	1.9	1.3	0.8
Current Ratio (times)	2.6	1.5	1.1
Curr Liab To Nw (%)	40.6	111.5	221.7
Curr Liab To Inv (%)	322.1	542.9	999.9
Total Liab To Nw (%)	51.2	140.4	294.7
Fixed Assets To Nw (%)	5.9	29.3	63.7
EFFICIENCY			
Coll Period (days)	17.0	24.8	33.4
Sales To Inv (times)	153.5	84.5	49.2
Assets To Sales (%)	11.5	16.2	23.6
Sales To Nwc (times)	46.6	23.0	11.3
Acct Pay To Sales (%)	1.8	4.5	7.1
PROFITABILITY			
Return On Sales (%)	2.7	1.1	0.2
Return On Assets (%)	14.6	5.7	1.0
Return On Nw (%)	35.8	16.5	3.5

SIC 5149 GRCRS, RLTD PRDS, NEC (NO BREAKDOWN) 2013 (66 Establishments)

	$	%
Cash	429,190	15.2
Accounts Receivable	686,139	24.3
Notes Receivable	2,824	0.1
Inventory	869,674	30.8
Other Current	172,241	6.1
Total Current	**2,160,068**	**76.5**
Fixed Assets	369,894	13.1
Other Non-current	293,656	10.4
Total Assets	**2,823,618**	**100.0**
Accounts Payable	832,967	29.5
Bank Loans	22,589	0.8
Notes Payable	327,540	11.6
Other Current	1,620,757	57.4
Total Current	**2,803,853**	**99.3**
Other Long Term	279,538	9.9
Deferred Credits	0	0.0
Net Worth	(259,773)	(9.2)
Total Liab & Net Worth	**2,823,618**	**100.0**
Net Sales	9,443,538	100.0
Gross Profit	2,398,659	25.4
Net Profit After Tax	226,645	2.4
Working Capital	(643,785)	—

RATIOS	UQ	MED	LQ
SOLVENCY			
Quick Ratio (times)	1.8	1.0	0.5
Current Ratio (times)	3.5	1.8	1.3
Curr Liab To Nw (%)	20.1	70.4	136.3
Curr Liab To Inv (%)	54.9	138.2	229.8
Total Liab To Nw (%)	36.8	107.3	237.4
Fixed Assets To Nw (%)	3.3	15.5	54.1
EFFICIENCY			
Coll Period (days)	19.9	26.7	45.8
Sales To Inv (times)	17.5	10.3	4.9
Assets To Sales (%)	21.6	29.9	63.9
Sales To Nwc (times)	18.9	10.1	5.0
Acct Pay To Sales (%)	2.2	4.9	12.7
PROFITABILITY			
Return On Sales (%)	4.3	1.7	0.2
Return On Assets (%)	11.4	4.4	0.4
Return On Nw (%)	28.1	12.0	2.7

SIC 5153 GRAIN,FIELD BEANS
(NO BREAKDOWN)
2013 (126 Establishments)

	$	%
Cash	2,502,558	10.2
Accounts Receivable	2,428,953	9.9
Notes Receivable	73,605	0.3
Inventory	7,630,348	31.1
Other Current	3,115,930	12.7
Total Current	**15,751,394**	**64.2**
Fixed Assets	5,961,976	24.3
Other Non-current	2,821,512	11.5
Total Assets	**24,534,882**	**100.0**
Accounts Payable	2,085,465	8.5
Bank Loans	0	0.0
Notes Payable	1,668,372	6.8
Other Current	7,090,581	28.9
Total Current	**10,844,418**	**44.2**
Other Long Term	2,625,232	10.7
Deferred Credits	0	0.0
Net Worth	11,065,232	45.1
Total Liab & Net Worth	**24,534,882**	**100.0**
Net Sales	74,801,470	100.0
Gross Profit	5,460,507	7.3
Net Profit After Tax	1,570,831	2.1
Working Capital	4,906,976	---

RATIOS	UQ	MED	LQ
SOLVENCY			
Quick Ratio (times)	0.7	0.4	0.2
Current Ratio (times)	1.7	1.4	1.2
Curr Liab To Nw (%)	57.7	103.0	146.5
Curr Liab To Inv (%)	104.5	134.0	201.9
Total Liab To Nw (%)	80.8	130.5	207.7
Fixed Assets To Nw (%)	36.5	53.6	67.4
EFFICIENCY			
Coll Period (days)	5.1	9.1	15.5
Sales To Inv (times)	19.1	9.9	5.8
Assets To Sales (%)	24.0	32.8	47.1
Sales To Nwc (times)	24.2	17.2	11.5
Acct Pay To Sales (%)	1.0	1.8	3.8
PROFITABILITY			
Return On Sales (%)	3.0	1.9	1.0
Return On Assets (%)	8.5	5.5	3.1
Return On Nw (%)	17.5	12.6	8.5

SIC 5162 PLSTCS MTRLS,B SHPS
(NO BREAKDOWN)
2013 (16 Establishments)

	$	%
Cash	1,059,701	9.7
Accounts Receivable	4,632,096	42.4
Notes Receivable	152,947	1.4
Inventory	3,168,179	29.0
Other Current	666,410	6.1
Total Current	**9,679,333**	**88.6**
Fixed Assets	382,366	3.5
Other Non-current	863,056	7.9
Total Assets	**10,924,755**	**100.0**
Accounts Payable	2,228,650	20.4
Bank Loans	76,473	0.7
Notes Payable	775,658	7.1
Other Current	2,250,499	20.6
Total Current	**5,331,280**	**48.8**
Other Long Term	1,988,306	18.2
Deferred Credits	0	0.0
Net Worth	3,605,169	33.0
Total Liab & Net Worth	**10,924,755**	**100.0**
Net Sales	27,940,550	100.0
Gross Profit	5,532,229	19.8
Net Profit After Tax	1,704,374	6.1
Working Capital	4,348,053	---

RATIOS	UQ	MED	LQ
SOLVENCY			
Quick Ratio (times)	2.0	1.0	0.7
Current Ratio (times)	3.8	1.8	1.2
Curr Liab To Nw (%)	44.7	170.1	314.0
Curr Liab To Inv (%)	83.5	152.7	357.8
Total Liab To Nw (%)	74.7	173.7	346.3
Fixed Assets To Nw (%)	0.4	3.6	12.6
EFFICIENCY			
Coll Period (days)	46.4	74.1	191.6
Sales To Inv (times)	10.0	7.6	6.6
Assets To Sales (%)	27.1	39.1	85.3
Sales To Nwc (times)	17.6	11.7	5.3
Acct Pay To Sales (%)	4.7	12.7	19.2
PROFITABILITY			
Return On Sales (%)	2.6	1.9	1.3
Return On Assets (%)	8.0	3.2	0.6
Return On Nw (%)	22.0	12.5	3.6

SIC 5169 CHEM,ALLD PRDTS,NEC
(NO BREAKDOWN)
2013 (64 Establishments)

	$	%
Cash	1,023,005	15.7
Accounts Receivable	1,661,569	25.5
Notes Receivable	0	0.0
Inventory	1,492,154	22.9
Other Current	983,908	15.1
Total Current	**5,160,636**	**79.2**
Fixed Assets	1,023,005	15.7
Other Non-current	332,314	5.1
Total Assets	**6,515,955**	**100.0**
Accounts Payable	2,521,675	38.7
Bank Loans	19,548	0.3
Notes Payable	195,479	3.0
Other Current	1,628,988	25.0
Total Current	**4,365,690**	**67.0**
Other Long Term	1,042,553	16.0
Deferred Credits	0	0.0
Net Worth	1,107,712	17.0
Total Liab & Net Worth	**6,515,955**	**100.0**
Net Sales	20,110,972	100.0
Gross Profit	5,932,737	29.5
Net Profit After Tax	945,216	4.7
Working Capital	794,946	---

RATIOS	UQ	MED	LQ
SOLVENCY			
Quick Ratio (times)	1.9	1.2	0.7
Current Ratio (times)	2.9	2.0	1.5
Curr Liab To Nw (%)	36.3	81.3	137.9
Curr Liab To Inv (%)	91.3	124.5	222.1
Total Liab To Nw (%)	41.5	100.5	150.5
Fixed Assets To Nw (%)	4.3	26.7	52.3
EFFICIENCY			
Coll Period (days)	28.1	35.0	43.6
Sales To Inv (times)	17.5	13.1	7.8
Assets To Sales (%)	25.6	32.4	52.9
Sales To Nwc (times)	13.6	7.8	4.6
Acct Pay To Sales (%)	4.1	6.5	8.0
PROFITABILITY			
Return On Sales (%)	7.2	4.4	1.2
Return On Assets (%)	21.1	8.0	3.2
Return On Nw (%)	44.8	17.0	5.8

SIC 5171 PETRO BLK STNS,TMNL
(NO BREAKDOWN)
2013 (76 Establishments)

	$	%
Cash	1,219,260	14.8
Accounts Receivable	2,487,950	30.2
Notes Receivable	41,191	0.5
Inventory	1,252,213	15.2
Other Current	527,249	6.4
Total Current	**5,527,863**	**67.1**
Fixed Assets	1,968,941	23.9
Other Non-current	741,442	9.0
Total Assets	**8,238,246**	**100.0**
Accounts Payable	1,820,652	22.1
Bank Loans	32,953	0.4
Notes Payable	148,288	1.8
Other Current	1,408,741	17.1
Total Current	**3,410,634**	**41.4**
Other Long Term	1,120,402	13.6
Deferred Credits	16,476	0.2
Net Worth	3,690,734	44.8
Total Liab & Net Worth	**8,238,246**	**100.0**
Net Sales	66,437,468	100.0
Gross Profit	6,377,997	9.6
Net Profit After Tax	1,660,937	2.5
Working Capital	2,117,229	---

RATIOS	UQ	MED	LQ
SOLVENCY			
Quick Ratio (times)	1.4	0.9	0.7
Current Ratio (times)	2.0	1.6	1.2
Curr Liab To Nw (%)	50.8	94.1	189.2
Curr Liab To Inv (%)	168.8	257.0	449.7
Total Liab To Nw (%)	71.8	130.3	239.7
Fixed Assets To Nw (%)	24.5	45.5	104.3
EFFICIENCY			
Coll Period (days)	10.6	13.9	21.9
Sales To Inv (times)	96.9	55.4	26.7
Assets To Sales (%)	8.2	12.4	22.3
Sales To Nwc (times)	66.3	33.8	13.3
Acct Pay To Sales (%)	2.3	2.9	3.9
PROFITABILITY			
Return On Sales (%)	1.7	0.5	0.2
Return On Assets (%)	9.1	4.3	1.8
Return On Nw (%)	18.6	12.4	4.8

	SIC 5172 PETRO PRDTS.NEC (NO BREAKDOWN) 2013 (124 Establishments)		SIC 5181 BEER AND ALE (NO BREAKDOWN) 2013 (21 Establishments)		SIC 5191 FARM SUPPLIES (NO BREAKDOWN) 2013 (154 Establishments)		SIC 5193 FLWRS,FLRSTS SPPLS (NO BREAKDOWN) 2013 (23 Establishments)	
	$	%	$	%	$	%	$	%
Cash	1,343,646	11.0	1,872,693	12.8	945,066	10.1	396,581	8.0
Accounts Receivable	4,006,509	32.8	1,097,281	7.5	1,693,633	18.1	936,923	18.9
Notes Receivable	109,935	0.9	0	0.0	46,785	0.5	19,829	0.4
Inventory	2,088,759	17.1	3,101,647	21.2	3,022,339	32.3	1,858,975	37.5
Other Current	696,252	5.7	1,155,803	7.9	823,424	8.8	247,864	5.0
Total Current	**8,245,101**	**67.5**	**7,227,424**	**49.4**	**6,531,247**	**69.8**	**3,460,172**	**69.8**
Fixed Assets	2,797,227	22.9	2,721,257	18.6	1,946,274	20.8	1,110,428	22.4
Other Non-current	1,172,637	9.6	4,681,731	32.0	879,566	9.4	386,666	7.8
Total Assets	**12,214,965**	**100.0**	**14,630,412**	**100.0**	**9,357,087**	**100.0**	**4,957,266**	**100.0**
Accounts Payable	5,582,239	45.7	1,272,846	8.7	1,328,706	14.2	550,257	11.1
Bank Loans	97,720	0.8	248,717	1.7	46,785	0.5	54,530	1.1
Notes Payable	4,214,163	34.5	219,456	1.5	430,426	4.6	138,803	2.8
Other Current	(3,725,565)	(30.5)	1,931,214	13.2	2,021,132	21.6	698,974	14.1
Total Current	**6,168,557**	**50.5**	**3,672,233**	**25.1**	**3,827,049**	**40.9**	**1,442,564**	**29.1**
Other Long Term	1,893,320	15.5	2,531,062	17.3	945,066	10.1	738,633	14.9
Deferred Credits	24,430	0.2	0	0.0	37,428	0.4	0	0.0
Net Worth	4,128,658	33.8	8,427,117	57.6	4,547,544	48.6	2,776,069	56.0
Total Liab & Net Worth	**12,214,965**	**100.0**	**14,630,412**	**100.0**	**9,357,087**	**100.0**	**4,957,266**	**100.0**
Net Sales	95,429,414	100.0	49,933,147	100.0	24,367,414	100.0	9,514,906	100.0
Gross Profit	8,111,500	8.5	13,382,083	26.8	4,142,460	17.0	3,216,038	33.8
Net Profit After Tax	1,049,724	1.1	1,897,460	3.8	682,288	2.8	161,753	1.7
Working Capital	2,076,544	---	3,555,191	---	2,704,198	---	2,017,608	---

RATIOS	UQ	MED	LQ	UQ	MED	LQ	UQ	MED	LQ	UQ	MED	LQ
SOLVENCY												
Quick Ratio (times)	1.5	1.0	0.6	1.4	0.7	0.4	1.1	0.6	0.4	1.3	0.8	0.3
Current Ratio (times)	2.2	1.5	1.1	3.8	2.2	1.2	2.4	1.7	1.3	5.1	2.7	1.4
Curr Liab To Nw (%)	51.5	111.5	198.7	17.4	33.7	55.0	38.4	78.6	160.0	16.7	40.8	86.0
Curr Liab To Inv (%)	144.7	302.3	633.0	46.5	119.5	182.5	89.5	135.2	212.5	31.0	72.1	146.9
Total Liab To Nw (%)	80.4	154.1	252.4	30.9	63.1	178.3	47.2	99.5	208.0	19.6	49.4	134.9
Fixed Assets To Nw (%)	21.7	51.4	87.3	13.0	26.9	43.5	19.4	36.6	66.7	16.2	33.6	64.3
EFFICIENCY												
Coll Period (days)	9.0	16.5	24.9	1.9	2.9	20.8	12.4	21.7	38.0	10.4	24.1	44.2
Sales To Inv (times)	114.0	52.2	25.3	21.9	17.8	14.1	15.5	10.1	5.7	8.2	4.1	1.9
Assets To Sales (%)	7.9	12.8	21.7	20.1	29.3	46.7	27.9	38.4	49.9	24.5	52.1	92.6
Sales To Nwc (times)	69.4	32.0	14.4	20.9	11.6	5.7	18.7	10.4	6.2	12.6	5.7	2.0
Acct Pay To Sales (%)	2.0	2.9	3.8	1.8	3.0	5.0	2.7	4.4	7.0	3.1	4.6	7.1
PROFITABILITY												
Return On Sales (%)	1.2	0.5	0.2	5.7	2.2	1.2	4.5	1.9	0.8	4.7	2.7	(0.5)
Return On Assets (%)	7.3	4.4	1.6	19.5	7.6	2.6	9.7	5.1	2.3	8.2	3.7	(0.5)
Return On Nw (%)	21.9	10.1	4.7	31.9	22.2	6.5	18.2	12.7	5.4	19.2	4.7	(0.1)

	SIC 5194 TBCCO,TBCCO PRDTS (NO BREAKDOWN) 2013 (29 Establishments) $	%	SIC 5198 PNTS,VRNSHS,SUPPL (NO BREAKDOWN) 2013 (11 Establishments) $	%	SIC 5199 NNDRBL GDS,NEC (NO BREAKDOWN) 2013 (79 Establishments) $	%	SIC 52 BLD MTLS HDW GDN SUP (NO BREAKDOWN) 2013 (474 Establishments) $	%
Cash	500,751	8.7	153,882	9.3	250,428	11.9	267,256	12.1
Accounts Receivable	2,026,026	35.2	368,987	22.3	627,121	29.8	346,770	15.7
Notes Receivable	0	0.0	0	0.0	6,313	0.3	11,044	0.5
Inventory	2,060,561	35.8	673,443	40.7	551,361	26.2	885,700	40.1
Other Current	374,125	6.5	114,171	6.9	292,516	13.9	123,688	5.6
Total Current	**4,961,463**	**86.2**	**1,310,483**	**79.2**	**1,727,739**	**82.1**	**1,634,458**	**74.0**
Fixed Assets	633,133	11.0	271,363	16.4	204,130	9.7	373,275	16.9
Other Non-current	161,161	2.8	72,804	4.4	172,564	8.2	200,994	9.1
Total Assets	**5,755,757**	**100.0**	**1,654,650**	**100.0**	**2,104,433**	**100.0**	**2,208,727**	**100.0**
Accounts Payable	627,378	10.9	372,296	22.5	395,633	18.8	269,465	12.2
Bank Loans	0	0.0	0	0.0	33,671	1.6	8,835	0.4
Notes Payable	259,009	4.5	9,928	0.6	92,595	4.4	64,053	2.9
Other Current	915,165	15.9	162,156	9.8	479,811	22.8	395,362	17.9
Total Current	**1,801,552**	**31.3**	**544,380**	**32.9**	**1,001,710**	**47.6**	**737,715**	**33.4**
Other Long Term	627,377	10.9	168,774	10.2	229,383	10.9	234,125	10.6
Deferred Credits	0	0.0	0	0.0	0	0.0	2,209	0.1
Net Worth	3,326,828	57.8	941,496	56.9	873,340	41.5	1,234,678	55.9
Total Liab & Net Worth	**5,755,757**	**100.0**	**1,654,650**	**100.0**	**2,104,433**	**100.0**	**2,208,727**	**100.0**
Net Sales	50,489,096	100.0	4,714,103	100.0	6,576,353	100.0	5,387,139	100.0
Gross Profit	3,382,769	6.7	1,730,076	36.7	1,907,142	29.0	1,551,496	28.8
Net Profit After Tax	252,445	0.5	296,988	6.3	131,527	2.0	113,130	2.1
Working Capital	3,159,911	---	766,103	---	726,029	---	896,743	---

RATIOS	UQ	MED	LQ	UQ	MED	LQ	UQ	MED	LQ	UQ	MED	LQ
SOLVENCY												
Quick Ratio (times)	2.4	1.1	0.9	1.6	1.1	0.8	2.1	1.1	0.5	2.2	0.9	0.4
Current Ratio (times)	4.4	2.9	2.0	4.4	2.9	1.9	4.1	2.1	1.4	5.2	2.7	1.7
Curr Liab To Nw (%)	27.0	53.6	114.8	19.9	53.2	137.8	22.5	64.1	181.3	17.4	40.0	84.7
Curr Liab To Inv (%)	47.9	72.5	137.6	43.3	85.2	128.1	50.7	118.7	259.0	36.5	64.7	107.0
Total Liab To Nw (%)	32.4	77.8	124.6	28.8	57.6	222.4	24.0	75.6	181.3	21.7	55.2	141.3
Fixed Assets To Nw (%)	8.2	15.8	24.8	18.8	27.6	44.9	2.7	12.3	27.4	8.2	22.3	53.3
EFFICIENCY												
Coll Period (days)	10.1	12.5	21.6	21.9	25.0	36.4	29.8	40.9	54.4	10.4	23.0	35.2
Sales To Inv (times)	31.1	23.7	15.5	8.8	7.4	5.9	15.6	9.2	4.1	9.6	5.8	4.2
Assets To Sales (%)	8.8	11.4	16.7	27.2	35.1	41.3	21.8	32.0	49.0	31.7	41.0	57.1
Sales To Nwc (times)	25.6	20.4	11.4	8.6	7.0	5.1	12.5	6.8	4.2	8.9	5.3	3.6
Acct Pay To Sales (%)	0.7	1.0	1.9	2.7	8.1	10.9	2.8	4.9	9.7	2.7	3.9	6.4
PROFITABILITY												
Return On Sales (%)	0.5	0.3	0.1	10.1	3.6	0.4	4.9	1.7	(0.1)	3.3	1.5	0.4
Return On Assets (%)	6.6	3.1	0.7	30.2	9.2	1.0	15.7	4.7	(0.1)	7.5	3.6	1.0
Return On Nw (%)	11.1	6.5	0.9	66.7	30.5	4.3	45.8	12.8	1.6	15.9	5.7	1.7

	SIC 5211 LMBR,BLDNG MTRLS (NO BREAKDOWN) 2013 (269 Establishments)		SIC 5231 PNT,GLS,WLPR STRS (NO BREAKDOWN) 2013 (11 Establishments)		SIC 5251 HARDWARE STORES (NO BREAKDOWN) 2013 (125 Establishments)		SIC 5261 RET NSRS,GDN STRS (NO BREAKDOWN) 2013 (63 Establishments)	
	$	%	$	%	$	%	$	%
Cash	332,002	11.6	120,829	18.7	202,150	12.5	222,900	11.5
Accounts Receivable	575,279	20.1	181,567	28.1	140,696	8.7	180,258	9.3
Notes Receivable	14,310	0.5	7,108	1.1	11,320	0.7	1,938	0.1
Inventory	1,021,764	35.7	124,706	19.3	734,207	45.4	994,328	51.3
Other Current	174,586	6.1	59,446	9.2	76,008	4.7	100,791	5.2
Total Current	**2,117,941**	**74.0**	**493,656**	**76.4**	**1,164,381**	**72.0**	**1,500,215**	**77.4**
Fixed Assets	506,589	17.7	109,199	16.9	240,962	14.9	343,072	17.7
Other Non-current	237,553	8.3	43,292	6.7	211,853	13.1	94,975	4.9
Total Assets	**2,862,083**	**100.0**	**646,147**	**100.0**	**1,617,196**	**100.0**	**1,938,262**	**100.0**
Accounts Payable	346,312	12.1	89,168	13.8	168,188	10.4	327,566	16.9
Bank Loans	20,035	0.7	1,292	0.2	0	0.0	0	0.0
Notes Payable	88,725	3.1	14,215	2.2	24,258	1.5	98,851	5.1
Other Current	518,036	18.1	87,231	13.5	236,111	14.6	439,986	22.7
Total Current	**973,108**	**34.0**	**191,906**	**29.7**	**428,557**	**26.5**	**866,403**	**44.7**
Other Long Term	260,450	9.1	104,675	16.2	208,618	12.9	203,518	10.5
Deferred Credits	5,724	0.2	0	0.0	0	0.0	0	0.0
Net Worth	1,622,801	56.7	349,566	54.1	980,021	60.6	868,341	44.8
Total Liab & Net Worth	**2,862,083**	**100.0**	**646,147**	**100.0**	**1,617,196**	**100.0**	**1,938,262**	**100.0**
Net Sales	7,101,943	100.0	1,969,960	100.0	3,369,158	100.0	5,008,429	100.0
Gross Profit	1,803,894	25.4	860,873	43.7	1,172,467	34.8	1,467,470	29.3
Net Profit After Tax	142,039	2.0	43,339	2.2	74,121	2.2	140,236	2.8
Working Capital	1,144,833	---	301,750	---	735,824	---	633,812	---

RATIOS	UQ	MED	LQ	UQ	MED	LQ	UQ	MED	LQ	UQ	MED	LQ
SOLVENCY												
Quick Ratio (times)	2.5	1.0	0.6	5.3	1.2	0.9	1.8	0.9	0.3	1.0	0.3	0.1
Current Ratio (times)	5.4	3.0	1.9	7.0	4.2	1.3	5.8	3.3	2.0	2.4	1.7	1.3
Curr Liab To Nw (%)	16.1	36.1	70.8	19.6	29.6	117.2	14.9	32.4	77.4	45.3	93.9	227.4
Curr Liab To Inv (%)	36.9	68.0	114.7	33.5	266.4	449.2	30.4	50.4	77.3	63.7	80.2	100.1
Total Liab To Nw (%)	18.0	45.1	107.2	20.2	73.7	217.0	18.6	54.4	146.8	54.4	125.3	254.7
Fixed Assets To Nw (%)	10.3	21.8	48.5	13.8	27.9	64.3	5.0	15.6	51.2	11.0	40.0	79.7
EFFICIENCY												
Coll Period (days)	19.7	29.2	39.1	20.4	23.9	38.0	6.6	13.5	24.8	3.9	8.4	16.1
Sales To Inv (times)	10.5	6.7	4.8	34.8	21.0	10.5	6.5	4.7	3.4	9.7	5.3	3.5
Assets To Sales (%)	31.5	40.3	55.1	23.0	32.8	35.9	34.5	48.0	62.2	27.6	38.7	50.5
Sales To Nwc (times)	8.1	5.2	3.5	16.2	9.5	4.3	6.6	4.8	3.4	16.4	9.0	4.9
Acct Pay To Sales (%)	2.9	4.1	5.7	1.7	4.4	6.7	2.4	3.5	7.2	2.0	3.5	8.7
PROFITABILITY												
Return On Sales (%)	3.2	1.3	0.3	3.3	1.5	(0.2)	3.8	1.9	0.6	2.4	1.3	0.5
Return On Assets (%)	7.5	3.5	0.6	14.3	5.6	(2.2)	7.6	3.8	1.3	7.3	3.8	1.2
Return On Nw (%)	14.6	5.2	1.2	26.4	14.4	(10.3)	15.5	6.4	2.5	18.3	6.1	3.0

SIC 53 GEN MERCHANDISE (NO BREAKDOWN) — 2013 (84 Establishments)
SIC 5311 DEPARTMENT STORES (NO BREAKDOWN) — 2013 (53 Establishments)
SIC 5331 VARIETY STORES (NO BREAKDOWN) — 2013 (18 Establishments)
SIC 5399 MISC GNRL MRCH STRS (NO BREAKDOWN) — 2013 (13 Establishments)

	SIC 53 $	SIC 53 %	SIC 5311 $	SIC 5311 %	SIC 5331 $	SIC 5331 %	SIC 5399 $	SIC 5399 %
Cash	510,416	14.3	629,684	13.4	692,602	14.3	353,322	18.0
Accounts Receivable	124,927	3.5	173,868	3.7	24,217	0.5	127,589	6.5
Notes Receivable	0	0.0	0	0.0	0	0.0	0	0.0
Inventory	1,684,730	47.2	2,250,886	47.9	2,305,446	47.6	861,714	43.9
Other Current	207,023	5.8	220,859	4.7	319,663	6.6	188,438	9.6
Total Current	**2,527,096**	**70.8**	**3,275,297**	**69.7**	**3,341,928**	**69.0**	**1,531,063**	**78.0**
Fixed Assets	785,256	22.0	1,188,881	25.3	799,157	16.5	310,138	15.8
Other Non-current	256,992	7.2	234,957	5.0	702,289	14.5	121,700	6.2
Total Assets	**3,569,344**	**100.0**	**4,699,135**	**100.0**	**4,843,374**	**100.0**	**1,962,901**	**100.0**
Accounts Payable	453,307	12.7	620,286	13.2	581,205	12.0	221,808	11.3
Bank Loans	0	0.0	0	0.0	0	0.0	0	0.0
Notes Payable	28,555	0.8	51,690	1.1	19,373	0.4	0	0.0
Other Current	553,248	15.5	512,206	10.9	1,244,747	25.7	398,469	20.3
Total Current	**1,035,110**	**29.0**	**1,184,182**	**25.2**	**1,845,325**	**38.1**	**620,277**	**31.6**
Other Long Term	403,336	11.3	549,799	11.7	576,362	11.9	176,661	9.0
Deferred Credits	3,569	0.1	4,699	0.1	14,530	0.3	0	0.0
Net Worth	2,127,329	59.6	2,960,455	63.0	2,407,157	49.7	1,165,963	59.4
Total Liab & Net Worth	**3,569,344**	**100.0**	**4,699,135**	**100.0**	**4,843,374**	**100.0**	**1,962,901**	**100.0**
Net Sales	7,514,408	100.0	8,866,292	100.0	13,269,518	100.0	4,461,139	100.0
Gross Profit	2,690,158	35.8	3,129,801	35.3	5,467,041	41.2	1,298,191	29.1
Net Profit After Tax	210,403	2.8	221,657	2.5	291,929	2.2	218,596	4.9
Working Capital	1,491,986	—	2,091,115	—	1,496,603	—	910,786	—

RATIOS	SIC 53 UQ	SIC 53 MED	SIC 53 LQ	SIC 5311 UQ	SIC 5311 MED	SIC 5311 LQ	SIC 5331 UQ	SIC 5331 MED	SIC 5331 LQ	SIC 5399 UQ	SIC 5399 MED	SIC 5399 LQ
SOLVENCY												
Quick Ratio (times)	1.2	0.5	0.2	1.3	0.5	0.2	0.8	0.3	0.1	1.5	1.2	0.3
Current Ratio (times)	4.7	2.8	1.7	5.1	3.1	1.7	4.5	2.1	1.6	3.8	3.0	1.9
Curr Liab To Nw (%)	22.2	38.9	82.7	19.3	38.9	61.4	23.8	34.9	94.4	27.2	44.3	111.4
Curr Liab To Inv (%)	31.5	54.3	108.8	31.2	50.3	105.0	46.9	64.1	100.7	25.4	76.7	167.9
Total Liab To Nw (%)	26.7	53.3	131.0	27.5	45.3	105.5	26.6	65.1	142.4	27.2	63.6	162.2
Fixed Assets To Nw (%)	7.4	22.0	72.0	8.0	26.6	89.1	9.9	25.5	50.3	4.6	9.3	38.4
EFFICIENCY												
Coll Period (days)	1.5	4.4	11.6	2.2	4.8	9.5	0.4	0.7	1.8	2.9	12.5	64.2
Sales To Inv (times)	7.6	5.1	3.5	5.7	4.2	2.9	8.3	7.1	5.3	9.2	4.4	3.6
Assets To Sales (%)	32.0	47.5	67.0	35.2	53.0	68.6	25.2	36.5	53.0	28.3	44.0	72.4
Sales To Nwc (times)	9.9	5.5	2.8	9.0	3.7	2.7	11.8	9.3	6.3	7.2	5.5	3.1
Acct Pay To Sales (%)	2.7	6.6	9.1	4.3	7.1	9.7	1.7	4.1	6.9	1.9	4.4	8.3
PROFITABILITY												
Return On Sales (%)	5.1	2.4	0.2	5.1	3.1	0.3	4.8	1.3	0.1	8.8	3.0	0.7
Return On Assets (%)	8.9	5.2	0.5	8.4	5.8	0.7	10.6	4.1	0.2	17.0	7.4	0.5
Return On Nw (%)	16.9	9.3	1.2	16.7	8.8	1.0	19.1	6.9	2.2	21.3	11.2	0.8

	SIC 54 FOOD STORES (NO BREAKDOWN) 2013 (122 Establishments) $	%	SIC 5411 GROCERY STORES (NO BREAKDOWN) 2013 (95 Establishments) $	%	SIC 55 AUTO DEALER SVC STATN (NO BREAKDOWN) 2013 (389 Establishments) $	%	SIC 5511 NEW/USED CAR DLRS (NO BREAKDOWN) 2013 (166 Establishments) $	%
Cash	886,672	18.3	1,132,879	15.9	925,485	12.4	1,288,794	10.6
Accounts Receivable	411,842	8.5	377,626	5.3	619,478	8.3	522,813	4.3
Notes Receivable	14,536	0.3	28,500	0.4	14,927	0.2	24,317	0.2
Inventory	1,085,325	22.4	1,759,881	24.7	3,724,331	49.9	7,343,694	60.4
Other Current	324,628	6.7	434,628	6.1	500,060	6.7	1,130,733	9.3
Total Current	**2,723,003**	**56.2**	**3,733,514**	**52.4**	**5,784,281**	**77.5**	**10,310,351**	**84.8**
Fixed Assets	1,468,096	30.3	2,358,384	33.1	1,224,029	16.4	1,313,111	10.8
Other Non-current	654,102	13.5	1,033,128	14.5	455,279	6.1	534,971	4.4
Total Assets	**4,845,201**	**100.0**	**7,125,026**	**100.0**	**7,463,589**	**100.0**	**12,158,433**	**100.0**
Accounts Payable	726,780	15.0	1,018,879	14.3	820,995	11.0	547,129	4.5
Bank Loans	14,536	0.3	21,375	0.3	44,782	0.6	48,634	0.4
Notes Payable	213,189	4.4	363,376	5.1	970,267	13.0	2,905,865	23.9
Other Current	1,603,761	33.1	1,603,131	22.5	2,731,672	36.6	7,282,902	59.9
Total Current	**2,558,266**	**52.8**	**3,006,761**	**42.2**	**4,567,716**	**61.2**	**10,784,530**	**88.7**
Other Long Term	978,731	20.2	1,389,380	19.5	783,677	10.5	1,021,308	8.4
Deferred Credits	0	0.0	7,125	0.1	14,927	0.2	0	0.0
Net Worth	1,308,204	27.0	2,721,760	38.2	2,097,269	28.1	352,595	2.9
Total Liab & Net Worth	**4,845,201**	**100.0**	**7,125,026**	**100.0**	**7,463,589**	**100.0**	**12,158,433**	**100.0**
Net Sales	22,747,423	100.0	34,926,598	100.0	23,544,445	100.0	40,126,842	100.0
Gross Profit	5,800,593	25.5	7,404,439	21.2	4,661,800	19.8	5,617,758	14.0
Net Profit After Tax	636,928	2.8	593,752	1.7	423,800	1.8	682,156	1.7
Working Capital	164,737	—	726,753	—	1,216,565	—	(474,179)	—

RATIOS	UQ	MED	LQ	UQ	MED	LQ	UQ	MED	LQ	UQ	MED	LQ
SOLVENCY												
Quick Ratio (times)	1.7	0.7	0.4	1.4	0.7	0.4	0.9	0.3	0.1	0.3	0.2	0.1
Current Ratio (times)	3.5	2.1	1.3	3.0	2.1	1.3	2.2	1.4	1.2	1.5	1.2	1.1
Curr Liab To Nw (%)	20.8	40.1	96.9	22.0	39.0	79.6	49.9	147.7	332.4	153.7	278.7	568.1
Curr Liab To Inv (%)	74.1	115.9	210.8	72.7	104.4	185.2	79.7	102.0	134.5	93.9	108.1	126.1
Total Liab To Nw (%)	29.9	57.9	187.0	31.6	54.5	158.6	72.9	191.1	393.4	165.2	318.3	630.4
Fixed Assets To Nw (%)	20.4	47.8	98.7	27.6	53.7	108.5	10.7	33.9	81.8	11.6	34.8	82.8
EFFICIENCY												
Coll Period (days)	0.9	3.5	7.9	0.7	3.3	6.9	2.6	8.0	16.4	3.5	7.3	14.1
Sales To Inv (times)	39.0	22.1	14.5	37.1	21.8	15.5	11.1	6.4	3.8	7.2	5.8	4.3
Assets To Sales (%)	14.1	21.3	38.3	13.9	20.4	36.4	23.1	31.7	44.4	24.5	30.3	37.1
Sales To Nwc (times)	35.5	16.1	9.9	35.2	17.0	11.9	26.5	13.2	6.5	35.5	18.7	10.8
Acct Pay To Sales (%)	1.7	2.7	4.1	1.7	2.7	4.0	0.8	1.5	3.9	0.6	0.9	1.5
PROFITABILITY												
Return On Sales (%)	3.1	1.1	0.2	2.5	1.1	0.2	2.9	1.4	0.4	2.4	1.3	0.6
Return On Assets (%)	13.0	5.8	1.2	12.3	5.5	1.2	8.7	4.4	1.4	7.9	4.3	2.1
Return On Nw (%)	22.5	11.7	3.3	20.5	11.4	3.3	26.2	13.3	4.5	32.5	19.2	10.4

SIC 5531 AUTO,HOME SPPL STRS (NO BREAKDOWN) 2013 (74 Establishments)

	$	%
Cash	278,584	14.4
Accounts Receivable	297,930	15.4
Notes Receivable	0	0.0
Inventory	804,799	41.6
Other Current	83,189	4.3
Total Current	**1,464,502**	**75.7**
Fixed Assets	357,903	18.5
Other Non-current	112,208	5.8
Total Assets	**1,934,613**	**100.0**
Accounts Payable	468,176	24.2
Bank Loans	1,935	0.1
Notes Payable	48,365	2.5
Other Current	216,677	11.2
Total Current	**735,153**	**38.0**
Other Long Term	253,434	13.1
Deferred Credits	5,804	0.3
Net Worth	940,222	48.6
Total Liab & Net Worth	**1,934,613**	**100.0**
Net Sales	6,301,671	100.0
Gross Profit	1,991,328	31.6
Net Profit After Tax	157,542	2.5
Working Capital	729,349	---

RATIOS	UQ	MED	LQ
SOLVENCY			
Quick Ratio (times)	1.7	0.9	0.3
Current Ratio (times)	4.1	2.1	1.4
Curr Liab To Nw (%)	25.5	54.0	173.5
Curr Liab To Inv (%)	45.0	91.7	141.9
Total Liab To Nw (%)	34.1	78.8	206.7
Fixed Assets To Nw (%)	8.5	32.8	68.5
EFFICIENCY			
Coll Period (days)	8.0	15.3	26.7
Sales To Inv (times)	11.8	8.2	5.8
Assets To Sales (%)	19.6	30.7	39.4
Sales To Nwc (times)	13.9	8.4	4.9
Acct Pay To Sales (%)	3.9	7.0	10.5
PROFITABILITY			
Return On Sales (%)	3.8	1.9	0.6
Return On Assets (%)	11.4	5.9	1.6
Return On Nw (%)	25.8	11.5	3.4

SIC 5541 GASLNE SVC STATIONS (NO BREAKDOWN) 2013 (64 Establishments)

	$	%
Cash	1,284,435	15.4
Accounts Receivable	1,292,776	15.5
Notes Receivable	16,681	0.2
Inventory	1,417,883	17.0
Other Current	400,344	4.8
Total Current	**4,412,119**	**52.9**
Fixed Assets	2,969,214	35.6
Other Non-current	959,156	11.5
Total Assets	**8,340,489**	**100.0**
Accounts Payable	1,484,607	17.8
Bank Loans	0	0.0
Notes Payable	200,172	2.4
Other Current	1,117,625	13.4
Total Current	**2,802,404**	**33.6**
Other Long Term	1,176,009	14.1
Deferred Credits	50,043	0.6
Net Worth	4,312,033	51.7
Total Liab & Net Worth	**8,340,489**	**100.0**
Net Sales	53,809,606	100.0
Gross Profit	7,640,964	14.2
Net Profit After Tax	860,954	1.6
Working Capital	1,609,715	---

RATIOS	UQ	MED	LQ
SOLVENCY			
Quick Ratio (times)	1.6	1.0	0.6
Current Ratio (times)	2.5	1.5	1.2
Curr Liab To Nw (%)	26.4	60.7	112.7
Curr Liab To Inv (%)	126.9	195.3	297.1
Total Liab To Nw (%)	40.4	88.0	189.6
Fixed Assets To Nw (%)	37.0	67.9	115.4
EFFICIENCY			
Coll Period (days)	2.8	5.8	17.4
Sales To Inv (times)	63.6	40.3	29.7
Assets To Sales (%)	9.4	15.5	30.5
Sales To Nwc (times)	47.8	29.7	15.4
Acct Pay To Sales (%)	2.3	3.0	3.9
PROFITABILITY			
Return On Sales (%)	2.6	0.7	0.1
Return On Assets (%)	9.6	4.8	1.1
Return On Nw (%)	18.2	10.1	2.5

SIC 5551 BOAT DEALERS (NO BREAKDOWN) 2013 (22 Establishments)

	$	%
Cash	318,653	11.0
Accounts Receivable	118,771	4.1
Notes Receivable	2,897	0.1
Inventory	1,685,966	58.2
Other Current	121,668	4.2
Total Current	**2,247,955**	**77.6**
Fixed Assets	417,146	14.4
Other Non-current	231,748	8.0
Total Assets	**2,896,849**	**100.0**
Accounts Payable	295,479	10.2
Bank Loans	66,628	2.3
Notes Payable	78,215	2.7
Other Current	770,561	26.6
Total Current	**1,210,883**	**41.8**
Other Long Term	399,765	13.8
Deferred Credits	0	0.0
Net Worth	1,286,201	44.4
Total Liab & Net Worth	**2,896,849**	**100.0**
Net Sales	4,812,042	100.0
Gross Profit	1,241,507	25.8
Net Profit After Tax	(9,624)	(0.2)
Working Capital	1,037,072	---

RATIOS	UQ	MED	LQ
SOLVENCY			
Quick Ratio (times)	1.6	0.3	0.1
Current Ratio (times)	5.0	1.9	1.4
Curr Liab To Nw (%)	34.7	72.0	208.6
Curr Liab To Inv (%)	27.6	70.0	96.2
Total Liab To Nw (%)	38.9	194.7	334.2
Fixed Assets To Nw (%)	14.4	26.6	45.2
EFFICIENCY			
Coll Period (days)	1.7	6.6	15.2
Sales To Inv (times)	3.4	2.8	2.2
Assets To Sales (%)	44.4	60.2	104.9
Sales To Nwc (times)	6.9	4.5	2.3
Acct Pay To Sales (%)	1.1	1.8	5.9
PROFITABILITY			
Return On Sales (%)	3.8	2.3	0.6
Return On Assets (%)	6.4	2.2	1.1
Return On Nw (%)	21.4	7.1	2.8

SIC 5561 RCRTNL VHCLE DLRS (NO BREAKDOWN) 2013 (21 Establishments)

	$	%
Cash	528,437	15.1
Accounts Receivable	34,996	1.0
Notes Receivable	0	0.0
Inventory	2,439,207	69.7
Other Current	62,992	1.8
Total Current	**3,065,632**	**87.6**
Fixed Assets	409,451	11.7
Other Non-current	24,497	0.7
Total Assets	**3,499,580**	**100.0**
Accounts Payable	62,992	1.8
Bank Loans	55,993	1.6
Notes Payable	720,913	20.6
Other Current	1,116,367	31.9
Total Current	**1,956,265**	**55.9**
Other Long Term	143,483	4.1
Deferred Credits	3,500	0.1
Net Worth	1,396,332	39.9
Total Liab & Net Worth	**3,499,580**	**100.0**
Net Sales	7,811,563	100.0
Gross Profit	1,718,544	22.0
Net Profit After Tax	156,231	2.0
Working Capital	1,109,367	---

RATIOS	UQ	MED	LQ
SOLVENCY			
Quick Ratio (times)	0.7	0.1	0.1
Current Ratio (times)	2.2	1.3	1.2
Curr Liab To Nw (%)	71.5	166.3	313.5
Curr Liab To Inv (%)	71.2	87.3	93.9
Total Liab To Nw (%)	71.8	202.5	313.5
Fixed Assets To Nw (%)	6.3	30.8	44.4
EFFICIENCY			
Coll Period (days)	0.4	1.1	1.8
Sales To Inv (times)	3.9	3.0	2.3
Assets To Sales (%)	35.7	44.8	56.4
Sales To Nwc (times)	13.5	7.5	5.5
Acct Pay To Sales (%)	0.3	0.6	1.0
PROFITABILITY			
Return On Sales (%)	3.1	1.4	0.3
Return On Assets (%)	6.8	3.7	0.7
Return On Nw (%)	13.1	10.4	1.5

	SIC 5571 MOTORCYCLE DEALERS (NO BREAKDOWN) 2013 (21 Establishments)		SIC 5599 ATMTVE DLRS,NEC (NO BREAKDOWN) 2013 (13 Establishments)		SIC 56 APPAREL ACCES STORES (NO BREAKDOWN) 2013 (311 Establishments)		SIC 5611 MNS,BYS CLTHNG STRS (NO BREAKDOWN) 2013 (83 Establishments)	
	$	%	$	%	$	%	$	%
Cash	411,053	12.1	380,683	10.7	162,641	16.4	113,099	14.8
Accounts Receivable	74,737	2.2	569,246	16.0	48,594	4.9	45,087	5.9
Notes Receivable	0	0.0	35,578	1.0	2,975	0.3	1,528	0.2
Inventory	2,286,271	67.3	1,764,661	49.6	499,824	50.4	388,204	50.8
Other Current	244,594	7.2	128,080	3.6	53,553	5.4	52,728	6.9
Total Current	**3,016,655**	**88.8**	**2,878,248**	**80.9**	**767,587**	**77.4**	**600,646**	**78.6**
Fixed Assets	214,019	6.3	370,010	10.4	146,774	14.8	93,994	12.3
Other Non-current	166,460	4.9	309,527	8.7	77,354	7.8	69,541	9.1
Total Assets	**3,397,134**	**100.0**	**3,557,785**	**100.0**	**991,715**	**100.0**	**764,181**	**100.0**
Accounts Payable	322,728	9.5	366,452	10.3	114,047	11.5	77,946	10.2
Bank Loans	3,397	0.1	177,889	5.0	4,959	0.5	6,113	0.8
Notes Payable	220,814	6.5	56,925	1.6	9,917	1.0	4,585	0.6
Other Current	1,263,733	37.2	917,908	25.8	161,649	16.3	134,497	17.6
Total Current	**1,810,672**	**53.3**	**1,519,174**	**42.7**	**290,572**	**29.3**	**223,141**	**29.2**
Other Long Term	356,699	10.5	170,774	4.8	83,304	8.4	60,370	7.9
Deferred Credits	0	0.0	3,558	0.1	992	0.1	764	0.1
Net Worth	1,229,763	36.2	1,864,279	52.4	616,847	62.2	479,906	62.8
Total Liab & Net Worth	**3,397,134**	**100.0**	**3,557,785**	**100.0**	**991,715**	**100.0**	**764,181**	**100.0**
Net Sales	6,835,280	100.0	10,312,420	100.0	2,203,811	100.0	1,444,577	100.0
Gross Profit	1,572,114	23.0	2,908,102	28.2	943,231	42.8	678,951	47.0
Net Profit After Tax	143,541	2.1	247,498	2.4	66,114	3.0	36,114	2.5
Working Capital	1,205,983	---	1,359,074	---	477,015	---	377,505	---

RATIOS	UQ	MED	LQ	UQ	MED	LQ	UQ	MED	LQ	UQ	MED	LQ
SOLVENCY												
Quick Ratio (times)	0.5	0.2	0.1	2.8	0.9	0.3	2.1	0.7	0.2	2.3	0.7	0.2
Current Ratio (times)	2.0	1.5	1.2	3.7	1.7	1.3	6.9	3.0	1.7	7.1	4.0	2.0
Curr Liab To Nw (%)	72.9	105.5	320.1	28.6	82.8	271.5	14.2	34.1	79.5	11.6	26.5	70.4
Curr Liab To Inv (%)	57.2	81.6	92.5	65.0	90.2	144.4	24.3	53.4	89.9	23.1	43.9	79.5
Total Liab To Nw (%)	73.3	164.3	441.1	34.7	131.7	272.1	15.4	49.3	114.5	15.0	37.7	110.3
Fixed Assets To Nw (%)	4.7	10.3	23.2	7.7	12.7	22.2	5.3	15.2	44.9	6.0	12.6	32.5
EFFICIENCY												
Coll Period (days)	0.7	1.3	3.7	7.2	15.0	38.4	1.5	4.8	17.5	1.5	7.3	20.8
Sales To Inv (times)	4.0	3.0	2.3	12.3	6.7	3.4	8.2	4.9	3.0	6.2	4.0	2.7
Assets To Sales (%)	33.4	49.7	60.8	27.7	34.5	52.0	31.7	45.0	63.5	38.8	52.9	71.9
Sales To Nwc (times)	12.3	9.3	4.8	13.4	10.4	5.7	8.7	4.8	2.8	5.6	3.6	2.5
Acct Pay To Sales (%)	0.8	1.4	3.8	1.1	1.6	5.4	2.9	4.7	7.5	3.0	4.4	6.6
PROFITABILITY												
Return On Sales (%)	2.6	1.8	0.1	4.1	2.2	0.3	5.1	1.7	0.0	4.2	1.6	(0.9)
Return On Assets (%)	8.4	2.9	0.2	14.3	5.4	0.8	11.5	3.8	(0.1)	9.1	2.8	(1.3)
Return On Nw (%)	21.0	7.9	0.2	17.4	12.4	3.3	17.9	7.4	0.3	14.2	4.4	(1.3)

	SIC 5621 WOMENS CLTHNG STRS (NO BREAKDOWN) 2013 (78 Establishments) $	%	SIC 5632 WMNS ACCY.SPCTY STR (NO BREAKDOWN) 2013 (12 Establishments) $	%	SIC 5651 FMLY CLTHNG STRS (NO BREAKDOWN) 2013 (35 Establishments) $	%	SIC 5661 SHOE STORES (NO BREAKDOWN) 2013 (56 Establishments) $	%
Cash	233,616	18.8	533,191	16.5	256,079	15.7	142,301	16.2
Accounts Receivable	58,404	4.7	177,730	5.5	48,932	3.0	19,325	2.2
Notes Receivable	0	0.0	0	0.0	1,631	0.1	0	0.0
Inventory	533,093	42.9	1,347,520	41.7	861,208	52.8	553,394	63.0
Other Current	100,654	8.1	177,731	5.5	63,612	3.9	27,231	3.1
Total Current	**925,767**	**74.5**	**2,236,172**	**69.2**	**1,231,462**	**75.5**	**742,251**	**84.5**
Fixed Assets	229,888	18.5	542,886	16.8	275,652	16.9	84,327	9.6
Other Non-current	86,985	7.0	452,405	14.0	123,962	7.6	51,825	5.9
Total Assets	**1,242,640**	**100.0**	**3,231,463**	**100.0**	**1,631,076**	**100.0**	**878,403**	**100.0**
Accounts Payable	127,992	10.3	487,951	15.1	163,108	10.0	122,098	13.9
Bank Loans	4,971	0.4	0	0.0	0	0.0	6,149	0.7
Notes Payable	9,941	0.8	58,166	1.8	1,631	0.1	14,933	1.7
Other Current	173,969	14.0	594,589	18.4	256,079	15.7	144,936	16.5
Total Current	**316,873**	**25.5**	**1,140,706**	**35.3**	**420,818**	**25.8**	**288,116**	**32.8**
Other Long Term	94,441	7.6	681,839	21.1	215,302	13.2	41,286	4.7
Deferred Credits	0	0.0	25,852	0.8	0	0.0	878	0.1
Net Worth	831,326	66.9	1,383,066	42.8	994,956	61.0	548,123	62.4
Total Liab & Net Worth	**1,242,640**	**100.0**	**3,231,463**	**100.0**	**1,631,076**	**100.0**	**878,403**	**100.0**
Net Sales	3,186,256	100.0	6,803,080	100.0	3,288,460	100.0	1,947,678	100.0
Gross Profit	1,366,904	42.9	3,224,660	47.4	1,236,461	37.6	773,228	39.7
Net Profit After Tax	82,843	2.6	605,474	8.9	101,942	3.1	54,535	2.8
Working Capital	608,894	---	1,095,466	---	810,644	---	454,135	---

RATIOS	UQ	MED	LQ	UQ	MED	LQ	UQ	MED	LQ	UQ	MED	LQ
SOLVENCY												
Quick Ratio (times)	2.4	0.9	0.4	1.6	0.7	0.3	1.7	0.5	0.3	1.9	0.4	0.2
Current Ratio (times)	6.6	2.9	1.7	3.3	1.6	1.3	11.2	2.9	2.0	7.2	3.1	2.0
Curr Liab To Nw (%)	14.5	32.2	83.9	34.2	86.9	157.1	7.9	34.1	80.5	13.8	35.0	71.6
Curr Liab To Inv (%)	23.3	67.0	115.4	62.1	106.4	148.2	14.6	38.5	80.8	21.9	49.1	64.7
Total Liab To Nw (%)	16.6	47.4	97.5	34.2	142.3	209.7	9.0	72.5	136.8	13.8	39.5	81.4
Fixed Assets To Nw (%)	7.6	21.1	54.4	9.9	34.4	53.7	5.3	18.1	72.8	3.4	9.6	28.1
EFFICIENCY												
Coll Period (days)	2.2	4.0	13.1	4.4	6.9	33.6	1.1	4.4	6.2	0.6	2.8	9.3
Sales To Inv (times)	12.3	7.2	4.7	10.2	7.3	3.9	7.8	3.7	2.1	5.7	3.7	2.5
Assets To Sales (%)	28.7	39.0	48.8	34.1	47.5	70.1	32.1	49.6	77.3	35.6	45.1	60.8
Sales To Nwc (times)	11.6	6.5	3.7	14.3	10.9	7.2	8.4	3.9	1.5	6.6	3.6	2.7
Acct Pay To Sales (%)	2.4	3.8	6.6	4.9	6.5	7.2	2.4	3.5	8.2	3.9	6.3	10.3
PROFITABILITY												
Return On Sales (%)	5.5	1.9	0.3	13.1	0.9	(0.3)	6.1	2.3	0.3	4.8	1.4	0.0
Return On Assets (%)	12.6	5.8	0.7	16.7	4.2	(0.6)	11.6	3.7	0.3	10.3	2.8	0.0
Return On Nw (%)	18.8	9.6	1.1	21.1	10.3	(2.0)	38.8	7.6	0.7	15.4	4.9	0.4

	SIC 5699 MISC APPRL.ACCY STR (NO BREAKDOWN) 2013 (38 Establishments)		SIC 57 FURN.HOME FURNISHGS (NO BREAKDOWN) 2013 (464 Establishments)		SIC 5712 FURNITURE STORES (NO BREAKDOWN) 2013 (217 Establishments)		SIC 5713 FLR CVRNG STRS (NO BREAKDOWN) 2013 (73 Establishments)	
	$	%	$	%	$	%	$	%
Cash	168,595	15.9	230,292	17.1	197,619	14.4	129,159	15.4
Accounts Receivable	77,405	7.3	232,985	17.3	207,225	15.1	194,577	23.2
Notes Receivable	16,965	1.6	6,734	0.5	9,606	0.7	3,355	0.4
Inventory	520,628	49.1	523,880	38.9	585,995	42.7	273,414	32.6
Other Current	19,087	1.8	78,111	5.8	85,087	6.2	62,900	7.5
Total Current	**802,680**	**75.7**	**1,072,002**	**79.6**	**1,085,532**	**79.1**	**663,405**	**79.1**
Fixed Assets	192,982	18.2	206,051	15.3	225,066	16.4	124,126	14.8
Other Non-current	64,681	6.1	68,683	5.1	61,756	4.5	51,161	6.1
Total Assets	**1,060,343**	**100.0**	**1,346,736**	**100.0**	**1,372,354**	**100.0**	**838,692**	**100.0**
Accounts Payable	156,931	14.8	199,317	14.8	155,076	11.3	115,739	13.8
Bank Loans	7,422	0.7	6,734	0.5	6,862	0.5	4,193	0.5
Notes Payable	20,147	1.9	22,895	1.7	15,096	1.1	17,613	2.1
Other Current	178,137	16.8	315,135	23.4	327,992	23.9	197,932	23.6
Total Current	**362,637**	**34.2**	**544,081**	**40.4**	**505,026**	**36.8**	**335,477**	**40.0**
Other Long Term	83,767	7.9	118,513	8.8	105,672	7.7	84,708	10.1
Deferred Credits	2,121	0.2	1,347	0.1	0	0.0	0	0.0
Net Worth	611,818	57.7	682,795	50.7	761,656	55.5	418,507	49.9
Total Liab & Net Worth	**1,060,343**	**100.0**	**1,346,736**	**100.0**	**1,372,354**	**100.0**	**838,692**	**100.0**
Net Sales	2,718,828	100.0	3,679,607	100.0	3,042,914	100.0	2,852,694	100.0
Gross Profit	1,117,438	41.1	1,394,571	37.9	1,250,638	41.1	921,420	32.3
Net Profit After Tax	92,440	3.4	88,311	2.4	69,987	2.3	54,201	1.9
Working Capital	440,043	---	527,921	---	580,506	---	327,928	---

RATIOS	UQ	MED	LQ	UQ	MED	LQ	UQ	MED	LQ	UQ	MED	LQ
SOLVENCY												
Quick Ratio (times)	1.5	0.8	0.2	2.0	0.8	0.3	2.0	0.8	0.2	2.4	1.0	0.4
Current Ratio (times)	4.3	2.3	1.4	4.2	2.3	1.4	4.4	2.6	1.5	4.5	2.1	1.3
Curr Liab To Nw (%)	29.1	46.9	74.8	22.7	52.8	125.9	17.5	41.3	105.8	21.3	50.1	114.7
Curr Liab To Inv (%)	44.2	71.6	85.6	46.3	80.0	150.9	38.7	72.4	121.9	57.1	91.6	162.8
Total Liab To Nw (%)	29.1	53.3	140.6	28.0	68.3	162.1	20.8	55.0	130.7	21.3	54.2	129.4
Fixed Assets To Nw (%)	7.3	26.7	52.3	7.5	21.0	44.7	7.2	22.1	45.8	6.2	21.1	37.1
EFFICIENCY												
Coll Period (days)	1.1	9.1	25.2	5.1	17.5	37.4	2.2	15.7	38.3	13.9	25.9	38.7
Sales To Inv (times)	9.3	5.4	3.3	12.2	6.6	4.2	8.2	5.0	3.4	16.8	10.8	7.0
Assets To Sales (%)	31.1	39.0	57.2	25.1	36.6	54.8	31.2	45.1	65.5	23.8	29.4	37.5
Sales To Nwc (times)	9.3	6.2	4.2	12.1	5.8	3.4	10.1	4.6	3.0	17.6	6.6	4.4
Acct Pay To Sales (%)	3.5	4.7	7.8	2.3	4.3	6.6	2.4	4.0	5.8	2.1	4.1	6.5
PROFITABILITY												
Return On Sales (%)	5.6	3.0	1.2	3.7	1.5	0.2	4.1	1.8	0.1	3.3	1.4	0.3
Return On Assets (%)	12.6	6.3	2.4	10.1	3.9	0.6	9.2	3.6	0.4	11.0	4.0	0.9
Return On Nw (%)	23.1	11.0	3.8	23.3	7.2	1.5	17.2	6.2	0.8	25.2	9.1	1.3

Balance Sheet

	SIC 5719 MISC HMFRNSHNGS STR (NO BREAKDOWN) 2013 (25 Establishments) $	%	SIC 5722 HSHLD APPLNCE STRS (NO BREAKDOWN) 2013 (44 Establishments) $	%	SIC 5731 RDO,TV,ELECTRNC STR (NO BREAKDOWN) 2013 (33 Establishments) $	%	SIC 5734 COMPTR,SOFTWRE STRS (NO BREAKDOWN) 2013 (52 Establishments) $	%
Cash	510,533	22.8	277,234	15.4	265,254	20.7	426,166	27.4
Accounts Receivable	109,720	4.9	205,225	11.4	203,745	15.9	527,264	33.9
Notes Receivable	2,239	0.1	1,800	0.1	19,221	1.5	0	0.0
Inventory	1,009,869	45.1	948,717	52.7	431,838	33.7	250,412	16.1
Other Current	60,458	2.7	45,006	2.5	78,167	6.1	88,656	5.7
Total Current	**1,692,819**	**75.6**	**1,477,982**	**82.1**	**998,225**	**77.9**	**1,292,498**	**83.1**
Fixed Assets	436,640	19.5	214,226	11.9	189,650	14.8	194,419	12.5
Other Non-current	109,719	4.9	108,014	6.0	93,543	7.3	68,435	4.4
Total Assets	**2,239,178**	**100.0**	**1,800,222**	**100.0**	**1,281,418**	**100.0**	**1,555,352**	**100.0**
Accounts Payable	270,941	12.1	307,838	17.1	331,887	25.9	363,952	23.4
Bank Loans	0	0.0	1,800	0.1	7,689	0.6	13,998	0.9
Notes Payable	8,957	0.4	43,205	2.4	14,096	1.1	37,328	2.4
Other Current	461,270	20.6	406,851	22.6	287,037	22.4	402,837	25.9
Total Current	**741,168**	**33.1**	**759,694**	**42.2**	**640,709**	**50.0**	**818,115**	**52.6**
Other Long Term	259,745	11.6	187,223	10.4	148,645	11.6	88,655	5.7
Deferred Credits	0	0.0	0	0.0	10,251	0.8	0	0.0
Net Worth	1,238,265	55.3	853,305	47.4	481,813	37.6	648,582	41.7
Total Liab & Net Worth	**2,239,178**	**100.0**	**1,800,222**	**100.0**	**1,281,418**	**100.0**	**1,555,352**	**100.0**
Net Sales	4,899,733	100.0	5,921,783	100.0	3,520,379	100.0	6,704,103	100.0
Gross Profit	1,989,292	40.6	1,776,535	30.0	1,334,224	37.9	2,312,916	34.5
Net Profit After Tax	122,493	2.5	65,140	1.1	63,367	1.8	274,868	4.1
Working Capital	951,651	---	718,288	---	357,516	---	474,383	---

RATIOS

	SIC 5719 UQ	MED	LQ	SIC 5722 UQ	MED	LQ	SIC 5731 UQ	MED	LQ	SIC 5734 UQ	MED	LQ
SOLVENCY												
Quick Ratio (times)	1.1	0.7	0.4	1.8	0.7	0.2	2.2	0.8	0.3	2.0	1.3	0.7
Current Ratio (times)	4.3	2.4	1.4	4.7	2.0	1.5	3.5	2.4	1.4	2.6	1.7	1.1
Curr Liab To Nw (%)	22.8	40.1	85.3	28.5	71.0	129.1	23.2	53.9	98.1	61.0	103.6	232.7
Curr Liab To Inv (%)	37.1	78.7	118.9	46.2	75.0	121.0	58.6	88.1	164.5	138.6	243.6	971.2
Total Liab To Nw (%)	24.2	53.9	112.4	31.3	90.5	180.9	33.7	64.6	142.9	61.0	142.1	269.8
Fixed Assets To Nw (%)	10.2	18.1	35.4	6.3	16.6	40.0	11.9	20.4	48.0	5.0	21.2	43.6
EFFICIENCY												
Coll Period (days)	3.5	6.9	15.9	5.0	9.0	20.6	5.1	20.1	43.3	16.5	24.8	46.6
Sales To Inv (times)	9.0	6.0	4.0	8.2	6.8	4.5	11.2	7.1	4.7	98.5	28.9	12.2
Assets To Sales (%)	26.9	45.7	59.2	23.4	30.4	39.8	25.8	36.4	65.5	15.4	23.2	35.7
Sales To Nwc (times)	11.5	5.7	4.2	13.7	7.3	3.8	12.1	5.7	4.6	32.8	11.8	5.4
Acct Pay To Sales (%)	2.8	4.3	6.6	1.9	4.5	9.2	4.1	5.2	9.2	2.2	4.3	7.0
PROFITABILITY												
Return On Sales (%)	5.6	2.3	0.0	2.6	0.9	0.2	3.1	1.1	(1.0)	4.7	2.0	0.5
Return On Assets (%)	11.0	4.6	0.0	6.5	3.1	0.6	7.8	2.6	(2.1)	23.3	7.6	2.4
Return On Nw (%)	23.9	7.8	(0.2)	13.9	5.7	1.8	37.6	6.2	1.4	61.2	19.4	5.4

	SIC 5736 MSCL INSTRMNT STRS (NO BREAKDOWN) 2013 (13 Establishments)		SIC 58 EATING,DRINKG PLACES (NO BREAKDOWN) 2013 (112 Establishments)		SIC 5812 EATING PLACES (NO BREAKDOWN) 2013 (106 Establishments)		SIC 59 MISC RETAIL STORES (NO BREAKDOWN) 2013 (671 Establishments)	
	$	%	$	%	$	%	$	%
Cash	113,000	9.4	3,067,980	14.7	3,363,018	14.7	411,996	19.3
Accounts Receivable	70,925	5.9	834,824	4.0	915,107	4.0	296,723	13.9
Notes Receivable	0	0.0	83,482	0.4	114,388	0.5	2,135	0.1
Inventory	647,946	53.9	980,919	4.7	1,075,251	4.7	785,568	36.8
Other Current	80,543	6.7	1,711,390	8.2	1,830,214	8.0	140,890	6.6
Total Current	**912,414**	**75.9**	**6,678,595**	**32.0**	**7,297,978**	**31.9**	**1,637,312**	**76.7**
Fixed Assets	223,596	18.6	10,998,811	52.7	11,804,880	51.6	318,070	14.9
Other Non-current	66,117	5.5	3,193,204	15.3	3,774,817	16.5	179,314	8.4
Total Assets	**1,202,127**	**100.0**	**20,870,610**	**100.0**	**22,877,675**	**100.0**	**2,134,696**	**100.0**
Accounts Payable	147,862	12.3	1,419,201	6.8	1,578,560	6.9	708,719	33.2
Bank Loans	12,021	1.0	187,835	0.9	228,777	1.0	10,673	0.5
Notes Payable	34,862	2.9	250,447	1.2	297,410	1.3	241,221	11.3
Other Current	217,585	18.1	4,967,206	23.8	5,422,008	23.7	196,392	9.2
Total Current	**412,330**	**34.3**	**6,824,689**	**32.7**	**7,526,755**	**32.9**	**1,157,005**	**54.2**
Other Long Term	187,531	15.6	6,386,407	30.6	6,748,914	29.5	256,163	12.0
Deferred Credits	0	0.0	20,871	0.1	22,878	0.1	2,135	0.1
Net Worth	602,266	50.1	7,638,643	36.6	8,579,128	37.5	719,393	33.7
Total Liab & Net Worth	**1,202,127**	**100.0**	**20,870,610**	**100.0**	**22,877,675**	**100.0**	**2,134,696**	**100.0**
Net Sales	2,329,703	100.0	34,668,787	100.0	38,193,114	100.0	5,707,743	100.0
Gross Profit	1,032,058	44.3	19,137,170	55.2	20,624,282	54.0	1,997,710	35.0
Net Profit After Tax	109,496	4.7	1,421,420	4.1	1,451,338	3.8	148,401	2.6
Working Capital	500,084	—	(146,094)	—	(228,777)	—	480,307	—

RATIOS	UQ	MED	LQ	UQ	MED	LQ	UQ	MED	LQ	UQ	MED	LQ
SOLVENCY												
Quick Ratio (times)	0.6	0.4	0.2	1.3	0.5	0.3	1.3	0.6	0.2	2.0	0.8	0.3
Current Ratio (times)	3.1	2.5	1.5	1.9	1.0	0.6	1.9	1.0	0.6	4.0	2.1	1.4
Curr Liab To Nw (%)	40.3	56.2	223.3	23.0	43.9	71.8	23.0	44.8	76.0	20.5	53.3	137.8
Curr Liab To Inv (%)	38.1	46.5	95.8	393.2	816.0	999.9	392.5	792.7	999.9	52.2	91.2	185.3
Total Liab To Nw (%)	40.3	82.6	225.7	46.7	82.1	261.5	47.3	75.4	268.9	27.1	70.6	161.7
Fixed Assets To Nw (%)	19.7	25.1	82.4	61.9	101.6	180.5	61.6	100.7	181.4	7.2	20.2	48.0
EFFICIENCY												
Coll Period (days)	6.1	10.5	18.1	2.2	5.5	10.2	2.4	5.5	10.8	4.6	14.6	31.4
Sales To Inv (times)	5.3	4.5	3.4	124.4	77.6	47.5	124.7	79.3	46.0	18.7	8.6	4.0
Assets To Sales (%)	30.6	51.6	56.1	34.0	60.2	80.3	33.2	59.9	79.7	23.8	37.4	59.4
Sales To Nwc (times)	8.1	4.9	3.6	34.5	16.1	5.5	34.6	18.6	7.0	13.2	7.0	3.8
Acct Pay To Sales (%)	3.1	5.1	10.4	1.8	2.7	3.9	1.8	2.7	3.9	2.4	4.4	8.2
PROFITABILITY												
Return On Sales (%)	3.5	2.6	1.0	5.9	3.2	0.6	5.6	3.1	0.6	4.5	1.7	0.2
Return On Assets (%)	6.8	4.7	1.4	11.2	5.4	1.3	11.2	5.3	1.2	11.0	4.5	0.5
Return On Nw (%)	25.8	9.0	4.3	25.4	13.1	4.1	25.6	13.0	2.4	23.2	9.7	2.1

Balance Sheet

	SIC 5912 DRG STRS,PRPRTRY ST (48 Establishments)		SIC 5932 USED MERCH STRES (11 Establishments)		SIC 5941 SPTG GDS,BCYLE SHPS (76 Establishments)		SIC 5942 BOOK STORES (25 Establishments)	
	$	%	$	%	$	%	$	%
Cash	303,873	22.0	2,825,492	23.3	262,206	16.6	891,898	19.5
Accounts Receivable	187,849	13.6	1,346,050	11.1	135,842	8.6	187,527	4.1
Notes Receivable	2,762	0.2	0	0.0	6,318	0.4	0	0.0
Inventory	506,915	36.7	1,382,430	11.4	862,437	54.6	1,632,860	35.7
Other Current	98,069	7.1	2,401,062	19.8	77,398	4.9	292,727	6.4
Total Current	**1,099,468**	**79.6**	**7,955,034**	**65.6**	**1,344,201**	**85.1**	**3,005,012**	**65.7**
Fixed Assets	196,136	14.2	1,406,683	11.6	148,478	9.4	1,198,346	26.2
Other Non-current	85,637	6.2	2,764,859	22.8	86,876	5.5	370,480	8.1
Total Assets	**1,381,241**	**100.0**	**12,126,576**	**100.0**	**1,579,555**	**100.0**	**4,573,838**	**100.0**
Accounts Payable	250,005	18.1	873,113	7.2	328,547	20.8	475,679	10.4
Bank Loans	1,381	0.1	0	0.0	6,318	0.4	0	0.0
Notes Payable	12,431	0.9	12,127	0.1	18,955	1.2	4,574	0.1
Other Current	212,711	15.4	3,128,657	25.8	290,638	18.4	612,894	13.4
Total Current	**476,528**	**34.5**	**4,013,897**	**33.1**	**644,458**	**40.8**	**1,093,147**	**23.9**
Other Long Term	143,649	10.4	1,394,556	11.5	126,365	8.0	676,928	14.8
Deferred Credits	4,144	0.3	0	0.0	0	0.0	0	0.0
Net Worth	756,920	54.8	6,718,123	55.4	808,732	51.2	2,803,763	61.3
Total Liab & Net Worth	**1,381,241**	**100.0**	**12,126,576**	**100.0**	**1,579,555**	**100.0**	**4,573,838**	**100.0**
Net Sales	5,755,171	100.0	29,362,169	100.0	4,538,951	100.0	8,038,380	100.0
Gross Profit	1,692,020	29.4	18,292,631	62.3	1,525,088	33.6	2,877,740	35.8
Net Profit After Tax	74,817	1.3	58,724	0.2	99,857	2.2	32,154	0.4
Working Capital	622,940	---	3,941,137	---	699,743	---	1,911,865	---

RATIOS

	SIC 5912			SIC 5932			SIC 5941			SIC 5942		
	UQ	MED	LQ	UQ	MED	LQ	UQ	MED	LQ	UQ	MED	LQ
SOLVENCY												
Quick Ratio (times)	3.4	1.5	0.8	4.9	1.4	0.4	1.3	0.5	0.2	2.1	1.1	0.4
Current Ratio (times)	6.0	3.4	1.8	6.5	4.9	2.7	3.3	2.0	1.5	5.9	3.1	1.8
Curr Liab To Nw (%)	14.6	31.2	52.3	7.7	12.0	16.6	33.1	68.2	160.9	10.1	22.8	83.0
Curr Liab To Inv (%)	35.5	68.4	105.5	72.6	98.5	361.2	51.6	77.5	103.7	26.1	56.7	110.5
Total Liab To Nw (%)	15.1	35.7	90.4	12.0	34.7	59.0	37.6	84.0	200.5	15.5	41.2	139.7
Fixed Assets To Nw (%)	2.9	10.6	22.7	3.0	13.3	25.1	5.8	17.3	38.1	13.1	35.0	81.9
EFFICIENCY												
Coll Period (days)	5.7	11.0	22.8	1.5	10.2	19.7	2.6	5.3	27.7	2.4	5.1	13.1
Sales To Inv (times)	14.7	11.9	9.3	65.3	15.1	8.0	7.4	4.9	3.8	7.0	5.1	4.6
Assets To Sales (%)	18.8	24.0	31.6	22.3	41.3	99.7	28.8	34.8	47.6	41.3	56.9	67.4
Sales To Nwc (times)	11.3	7.0	5.2	5.0	3.6	2.7	12.8	6.0	4.0	6.0	5.0	3.1
Acct Pay To Sales (%)	1.6	3.1	4.3	2.3	4.9	7.9	4.0	8.7	11.8	2.0	4.1	5.3
PROFITABILITY												
Return On Sales (%)	4.1	1.9	0.5	12.7	5.9	1.7	3.8	1.8	0.3	3.3	0.4	(1.8)
Return On Assets (%)	18.1	6.6	1.7	36.1	10.5	2.9	10.3	4.1	0.7	4.6	0.7	(3.8)
Return On Nw (%)	30.8	12.7	3.1	39.6	14.4	8.5	21.4	9.8	1.7	12.6	2.2	(4.6)

All breakdowns marked (NO BREAKDOWN), 2013.

	SIC 5943 STATIONERY STORES (NO BREAKDOWN) 2013 (26 Establishments)		SIC 5944 JEWELRY STORES (NO BREAKDOWN) 2013 (61 Establishments)		SIC 5945 HOBBY,TOY,GME SHPS (NO BREAKDOWN) 2013 (11 Establishments)		SIC 5947 GFT,NVLTY,SVENR SHP (NO BREAKDOWN) 2013 (25 Establishments)	
	$	%	$	%	$	%	$	%
Cash	394,767	22.1	336,723	13.8	4,257,805	16.1	304,394	26.4
Accounts Receivable	530,524	29.7	214,722	8.8	3,252,857	12.3	39,202	3.4
Notes Receivable	0	0.0	0	0.0	0	0.0	0	0.0
Inventory	344,751	19.3	1,395,691	57.2	9,361,881	35.4	446,214	38.7
Other Current	87,527	4.9	107,361	4.4	1,480,975	5.6	129,137	11.2
Total Current	**1,357,569**	**76.0**	**2,054,497**	**84.2**	**18,353,518**	**69.4**	**918,947**	**79.7**
Fixed Assets	294,735	16.5	229,362	9.4	4,654,494	17.6	185,634	16.1
Other Non-current	133,971	7.5	156,161	6.4	3,437,979	13.0	48,426	4.2
Total Assets	**1,786,275**	**100.0**	**2,440,020**	**100.0**	**26,445,991**	**100.0**	**1,153,007**	**100.0**
Accounts Payable	362,614	20.3	351,363	14.4	3,332,195	12.6	183,328	15.9
Bank Loans	0	0.0	0	0.0	0	0.0	0	0.0
Notes Payable	19,649	1.1	21,960	0.9	264,460	1.0	0	0.0
Other Current	273,300	15.3	29,280	1.2	5,156,968	19.5	282,487	24.5
Total Current	**655,563**	**36.7**	**758,846**	**31.1**	**8,753,623**	**33.1**	**465,815**	**40.4**
Other Long Term	130,398	7.3	148,841	6.1	6,849,512	25.9	94,546	8.2
Deferred Credits	0	0.0	4,880	0.2	0	0.0	0	0.0
Net Worth	1,000,314	56.0	1,527,453	62.6	10,842,856	41.0	592,646	51.4
Total Liab & Net Worth	**1,786,275**	**100.0**	**2,440,020**	**100.0**	**26,445,991**	**100.0**	**1,153,007**	**100.0**
Net Sales	7,173,795	100.0	3,697,000	100.0	56,751,054	100.0	2,868,177	100.0
Gross Profit	2,317,136	32.3	1,574,922	42.6	20,941,139	36.9	1,399,670	48.8
Net Profit After Tax	129,128	1.8	107,213	2.9	681,013	1.2	192,168	6.7
Working Capital	702,006	---	1,295,651	---	9,599,895	---	453,132	---

RATIOS	5943 UQ	MED	LQ	5944 UQ	MED	LQ	5945 UQ	MED	LQ	5947 UQ	MED	LQ
SOLVENCY												
Quick Ratio (times)	2.8	1.7	0.9	1.8	0.8	0.2	1.1	0.5	0.3	2.2	0.9	0.4
Current Ratio (times)	4.2	2.1	1.5	7.3	3.5	1.6	3.7	1.4	1.4	4.6	2.6	1.8
Curr Liab To Nw (%)	23.4	72.5	141.2	13.1	29.3	108.2	19.6	57.9	106.4	10.5	52.4	110.5
Curr Liab To Inv (%)	97.0	190.9	341.3	18.3	38.7	82.2	59.1	100.0	133.1	42.7	62.2	92.0
Total Liab To Nw (%)	23.4	89.1	155.6	13.4	39.2	133.9	19.6	60.8	130.6	25.5	54.1	114.2
Fixed Assets To Nw (%)	12.6	20.7	38.6	3.8	8.5	26.5	1.3	18.9	60.3	8.9	28.7	47.1
EFFICIENCY												
Coll Period (days)	26.3	32.7	36.1	3.3	13.1	27.4	3.7	10.3	24.1	0.0	0.0	3.7
Sales To Inv (times)	32.4	19.5	10.3	4.5	2.4	1.8	8.2	6.8	4.2	10.8	6.8	3.7
Assets To Sales (%)	20.5	24.9	47.3	54.2	66.0	89.4	30.2	46.6	58.6	24.7	40.2	51.6
Sales To Nwc (times)	18.4	9.5	5.1	5.1	2.5	1.8	18.4	11.8	6.9	10.4	5.9	3.5
Acct Pay To Sales (%)	2.8	4.3	7.8	2.9	6.5	11.4	3.6	7.2	9.5	2.7	4.0	11.3
PROFITABILITY												
Return On Sales (%)	3.3	1.2	0.0	5.1	1.9	0.0	2.8	1.2	(0.2)	5.8	1.1	0.1
Return On Assets (%)	11.0	6.1	0.0	7.8	2.6	0.2	10.5	2.5	(0.4)	9.3	1.5	0.1
Return On Nw (%)	30.1	8.0	0.1	13.5	4.8	0.4	8.8	7.0	(0.8)	39.6	10.2	0.8

	SIC 5961 CTLG,ML-ORDER HSES (NO BREAKDOWN) 2013 (55 Establishments)		SIC 5962 MERCH MCHNE OPRTRS (NO BREAKDOWN) 2013 (11 Establishments)		SIC 5963 DRCT SLLNG ESTBMNTS (NO BREAKDOWN) 2013 (11 Establishments)		SIC 5983 FUEL OIL DEALERS (NO BREAKDOWN) 2013 (49 Establishments)	
	$	%	$	%	$	%	$	%
Cash	2,381,855	28.3	281,398	28.4	227,522	19.0	526,075	26.3
Accounts Receivable	1,127,804	13.4	65,395	6.6	268,236	22.4	612,087	30.6
Notes Receivable	0	0.0	1,982	0.2	0	0.0	2,000	0.1
Inventory	2,365,022	28.1	143,672	14.5	238,299	19.9	270,038	13.5
Other Current	816,395	9.7	31,707	3.2	111,367	9.3	72,010	3.6
Total Current	**6,691,076**	**79.5**	**524,154**	**52.9**	**845,424**	**70.6**	**1,482,210**	**74.1**
Fixed Assets	673,316	8.0	299,233	30.2	192,795	16.1	326,046	16.3
Other Non-current	1,052,056	12.5	167,452	16.9	159,265	13.3	192,028	9.6
Total Assets	**8,416,448**	**100.0**	**990,839**	**100.0**	**1,197,484**	**100.0**	**2,000,284**	**100.0**
Accounts Payable	3,391,829	40.3	757,001	76.4	247,879	20.7	356,051	17.8
Bank Loans	42,082	0.5	0	0.0	0	0.0	6,001	0.3
Notes Payable	210,411	2.5	5,945	0.6	110,169	9.2	44,006	2.2
Other Current	3,223,500	38.3	3,540,268	357.3	352,060	29.4	436,062	21.8
Total Current	**6,867,822**	**81.6**	**4,303,214**	**434.3**	**710,108**	**59.3**	**842,120**	**42.1**
Other Long Term	2,407,104	28.6	136,736	13.8	135,316	11.3	158,022	7.9
Deferred Credits	16,833	0.2	0	0.0	0	0.0	10,001	0.5
Net Worth	(875,311)	(10.4)	(3,449,111)	(348.1)	352,060	29.4	990,141	49.5
Total Liab & Net Worth	**8,416,448**	**100.0**	**990,839**	**100.0**	**1,197,484**	**100.0**	**2,000,284**	**100.0**
Net Sales	24,046,994	100.0	3,206,599	100.0	3,542,852	100.0	9,853,616	100.0
Gross Profit	9,234,046	38.4	1,600,093	49.9	1,257,712	35.5	1,428,774	14.5
Net Profit After Tax	937,833	3.9	128,264	4.0	(74,400)	(2.1)	98,536	1.0
Working Capital	(176,746)	---	(3,779,060)	---	135,316	---	640,090	---

RATIOS	UQ	MED	LQ	UQ	MED	LQ	UQ	MED	LQ	UQ	MED	LQ
SOLVENCY												
Quick Ratio (times)	2.1	1.0	0.5	1.0	0.9	0.7	1.2	1.0	0.8	2.4	1.4	0.9
Current Ratio (times)	4.0	1.9	1.3	1.9	1.4	1.1	2.1	1.6	1.2	3.2	1.7	1.3
Curr Liab To Nw (%)	25.9	69.0	124.7	33.5	79.1	154.6	56.0	108.7	173.0	41.0	73.8	167.6
Curr Liab To Inv (%)	62.7	130.4	259.5	138.7	177.2	220.9	100.5	224.3	367.2	195.9	409.2	582.6
Total Liab To Nw (%)	28.6	84.2	157.0	50.0	128.8	154.6	58.6	113.4	366.8	42.5	94.7	214.4
Fixed Assets To Nw (%)	5.7	14.6	31.9	49.8	78.6	93.4	4.5	18.7	37.4	9.9	23.0	52.1
EFFICIENCY												
Coll Period (days)	2.6	12.8	28.1	3.7	5.5	6.9	17.9	21.9	36.5	13.5	17.6	31.4
Sales To Inv (times)	17.4	10.2	6.6	22.8	21.6	18.4	17.9	14.1	9.9	85.8	46.4	27.0
Assets To Sales (%)	25.1	35.0	63.8	18.0	30.9	37.4	23.0	33.8	48.6	14.2	20.3	26.7
Sales To Nwc (times)	15.6	7.5	3.2	34.0	18.0	9.4	32.4	10.0	7.5	23.1	14.3	8.9
Acct Pay To Sales (%)	3.9	6.9	10.7	1.7	3.7	5.6	2.5	3.1	7.3	2.1	3.0	4.6
PROFITABILITY												
Return On Sales (%)	6.5	2.4	(0.6)	7.2	0.7	(0.4)	4.7	1.2	(0.2)	1.4	0.6	0.0
Return On Assets (%)	17.5	7.0	(2.0)	8.5	2.1	(3.4)	16.2	2.7	0.3	8.1	3.9	0.3
Return On Nw (%)	45.8	14.6	2.8	50.6	10.2	(5.1)	85.4	16.6	6.8	19.1	8.6	1.3

	SIC 5984 LQFD PETRO GAS DLRS (NO BREAKDOWN) 2013 (26 Establishments) $	%	SIC 5999 MISC RTL STRS,NEC (NO BREAKDOWN) 2013 (206 Establishments) $	%	SIC 61 CREDIT AGENC EX BANK (NO BREAKDOWN) 2013 (28 Establishments) $	%	SIC 6162 MTG BKRS,CORRSPNDNT (NO BREAKDOWN) 2013 (11 Establishments) $	%
Cash	461,275	18.7	397,494	16.3	5,999,418	18.5	9,395,592	27.6
Accounts Receivable	372,474	15.1	356,037	14.6	2,172,762	6.7	1,668,058	4.9
Notes Receivable	0	0.0	4,877	0.2	129,717	0.4	306,378	0.9
Inventory	303,406	12.3	982,761	40.3	97,288	0.3	0	0.0
Other Current	192,403	7.8	165,826	6.8	12,128,554	37.4	10,212,600	30.0
Total Current	**1,329,558**	**53.9**	**1,906,995**	**78.2**	**20,527,739**	**63.3**	**21,582,628**	**63.4**
Fixed Assets	769,614	31.2	365,792	15.0	3,437,504	10.6	1,736,142	5.1
Other Non-current	367,540	14.9	165,826	6.8	8,464,044	26.1	10,723,230	31.5
Total Assets	**2,466,712**	**100.0**	**2,438,613**	**100.0**	**32,429,287**	**100.0**	**34,042,000**	**100.0**
Accounts Payable	244,204	9.9	1,519,256	62.3	5,285,974	16.3	1,361,680	4.0
Bank Loans	0	0.0	24,386	1.0	0	0.0	0	0.0
Notes Payable	32,067	1.3	816,935	33.5	4,280,666	13.2	0	0.0
Other Current	431,675	17.5	(824,251)	(33.8)	16,441,648	50.7	11,642,364	34.2
Total Current	**707,946**	**28.7**	**1,536,326**	**63.0**	**26,008,288**	**80.2**	**13,004,044**	**38.2**
Other Long Term	419,341	17.0	280,441	11.5	7,069,585	21.8	12,901,918	37.9
Deferred Credits	0	0.0	4,877	0.2	0	0.0	0	0.0
Net Worth	1,339,425	54.3	616,969	25.3	(648,586)	(2.0)	8,136,038	23.9
Total Liab & Net Worth	**2,466,712**	**100.0**	**2,438,613**	**100.0**	**32,429,287**	**100.0**	**34,042,000**	**100.0**
Net Sales	5,065,117	100.0	6,205,122	100.0	20,537,864	100.0	24,793,882	100.0
Gross Profit	1,701,879	33.6	2,128,357	34.3	9,529,569	46.4	9,595,232	38.7
Net Profit After Tax	187,409	3.7	192,359	3.1	2,094,862	10.2	2,157,068	8.7
Working Capital	621,612	—	370,669	—	(5,480,549)	—	8,578,584	—

RATIOS	UQ	MED	LQ	UQ	MED	LQ	UQ	MED	LQ	UQ	MED	LQ
SOLVENCY												
Quick Ratio (times)	2.5	0.9	0.5	1.6	0.6	0.2	1.5	0.7	0.1	1.9	1.2	0.7
Current Ratio (times)	2.8	1.5	0.9	3.3	1.8	1.3	2.4	1.6	1.1	2.2	1.8	1.4
Curr Liab To Nw (%)	20.7	44.7	125.3	27.8	67.2	181.4	23.7	82.6	258.3	19.9	83.4	237.2
Curr Liab To Inv (%)	154.8	292.1	388.2	61.6	89.6	162.4	352.7	676.3	999.9	—	—	—
Total Liab To Nw (%)	43.8	79.8	178.1	37.7	90.9	205.6	68.3	178.0	380.0	19.9	207.6	359.5
Fixed Assets To Nw (%)	33.4	70.9	118.6	7.5	21.8	53.7	2.8	7.6	22.5	3.1	5.3	14.2
EFFICIENCY												
Coll Period (days)	15.3	24.3	34.7	5.5	17.2	35.4	3.1	33.6	44.0	2.8	8.3	40.0
Sales To Inv (times)	33.0	19.8	11.7	14.4	7.5	3.5	12.1	6.1	0.0	—	—	—
Assets To Sales (%)	31.7	48.7	72.8	26.7	39.3	58.2	52.6	157.9	414.2	37.0	137.3	192.9
Sales To Nwc (times)	24.6	11.8	2.6	12.2	7.9	4.3	14.7	3.0	1.1	16.3	5.3	2.5
Acct Pay To Sales (%)	2.4	3.7	6.3	2.2	4.1	7.4	1.6	3.5	12.2	1.3	2.3	3.0
PROFITABILITY												
Return On Sales (%)	6.8	3.9	0.4	4.6	2.0	0.5	17.2	10.1	0.5	17.3	12.5	0.3
Return On Assets (%)	13.7	5.9	1.4	11.9	5.0	1.2	6.2	2.9	(0.8)	11.0	5.7	(5.7)
Return On Nw (%)	20.4	14.8	2.8	26.6	10.9	4.1	25.7	11.4	4.5	56.2	14.2	4.4

Balance Sheet

	SIC 62 SEC.COM BROKERS.SVS (NO BREAKDOWN) 2013 (36 Establishments) $	%	SIC 6211 SECURITY BRKRS.DLRS (NO BREAKDOWN) 2013 (14 Establishments) $	%	SIC 6282 INVESTMENT ADVICE (NO BREAKDOWN) 2013 (13 Establishments) $	%	SIC 65 REAL ESTATE (NO BREAKDOWN) 2013 (149 Establishments) $	%
Cash	9,635,158	24.9	29,100,026	24.5	3,014,528	30.5	1,286,812	18.0
Accounts Receivable	4,759,536	12.3	14,846,952	12.5	770,928	7.8	336,001	4.7
Notes Receivable	0	0.0	0	0.0	0	0.0	121,532	1.7
Inventory	1,625,207	4.2	6,532,659	5.5	0	0.0	264,511	3.7
Other Current	8,512,991	22.0	34,801,255	29.3	2,085,460	21.1	786,385	11.0
Total Current	**24,532,892**	**63.4**	**85,280,892**	**71.8**	**5,870,916**	**59.4**	**2,795,241**	**39.1**
Fixed Assets	3,637,369	9.4	17,103,689	14.4	800,579	8.1	3,138,391	43.9
Other Non-current	10,525,153	27.2	16,391,034	13.8	3,212,202	32.5	1,215,322	17.0
Total Assets	**38,695,414**	**100.0**	**118,775,615**	**100.0**	**9,883,697**	**100.0**	**7,148,954**	**100.0**
Accounts Payable	4,798,231	12.4	23,517,572	19.8	731,394	7.4	800,683	11.2
Bank Loans	193,477	0.5	1,662,859	1.4	0	0.0	28,596	0.4
Notes Payable	270,868	0.7	0	0.0	118,604	1.2	521,874	7.3
Other Current	27,667,221	71.5	172,462,192	145.2	2,124,995	21.5	8,492,957	118.8
Total Current	**32,929,797**	**85.1**	**197,642,623**	**166.4**	**2,974,993**	**30.1**	**9,844,110**	**137.7**
Other Long Term	6,462,135	16.7	21,023,284	17.7	1,087,206	11.0	2,058,898	28.8
Deferred Credits	116,086	0.3	0	0.0	69,186	0.7	57,192	0.8
Net Worth	(812,604)	(2.1)	(99,890,292)	(84.1)	5,752,312	58.2	(4,811,246)	(67.3)
Total Liab & Net Worth	**38,695,414**	**100.0**	**118,775,615**	**100.0**	**9,883,697**	**100.0**	**7,148,954**	**100.0**
Net Sales	36,505,108	100.0	121,696,327	100.0	7,644,004	100.0	2,440,749	100.0
Gross Profit	14,200,487	38.9	39,916,395	32.8	4,143,050	54.2	1,056,844	43.3
Net Profit After Tax	2,372,832	6.5	10,830,973	8.9	787,332	10.3	85,426	3.5
Working Capital	(8,396,905)	—	(112,361,731)	—	2,895,923	—	(7,048,869)	—

RATIOS

	SIC 62 UQ	MED	LQ	SIC 6211 UQ	MED	LQ	SIC 6282 UQ	MED	LQ	SIC 65 UQ	MED	LQ
SOLVENCY												
Quick Ratio (times)	1.7	1.0	0.4	1.5	0.6	0.1	4.1	1.5	0.7	2.4	0.7	0.2
Current Ratio (times)	3.2	1.7	1.1	2.5	1.8	1.3	4.4	2.4	1.1	4.2	1.7	0.7
Curr Liab To Nw (%)	22.8	44.4	210.9	26.6	60.4	245.5	13.1	39.9	90.2	8.3	29.1	87.5
Curr Liab To Inv (%)	77.1	178.0	604.5	32.8	85.1	270.8	—	—	—	82.6	526.1	999.9
Total Liab To Nw (%)	66.6	97.5	253.4	72.7	94.5	340.4	57.2	86.1	169.8	19.4	101.5	258.0
Fixed Assets To Nw (%)	3.7	7.1	16.0	4.7	7.0	11.3	2.0	6.6	23.3	24.8	80.9	188.0
EFFICIENCY												
Coll Period (days)	12.1	39.5	72.6	5.5	37.6	321.6	9.9	34.4	86.3	3.9	18.5	52.0
Sales To Inv (times)	67.5	33.3	6.4	59.7	6.8	6.4	—	—	—	102.0	16.8	4.6
Assets To Sales (%)	31.4	106.0	367.5	25.7	97.6	311.6	52.8	129.3	307.4	83.2	292.9	640.1
Sales To Nwc (times)	8.8	3.7	2.3	5.0	2.4	0.9	9.2	2.8	1.3	11.2	3.4	1.1
Acct Pay To Sales (%)	1.3	4.1	10.6	1.9	6.3	10.3	0.4	0.9	12.7	1.4	3.7	11.6
PROFITABILITY												
Return On Sales (%)	14.5	2.9	0.7	11.3	2.9	1.5	18.9	1.2	(1.0)	12.5	3.9	(7.7)
Return On Assets (%)	13.4	4.0	0.1	14.2	5.3	0.6	9.8	4.4	(0.5)	7.0	2.2	(1.9)
Return On Nw (%)	25.5	9.9	2.1	25.4	10.5	5.1	17.5	10.0	(0.5)	21.9	4.9	(2.5)

SIC 6512 NRSDNTL BLDG OPRTRS (NO BREAKDOWN) 2013 (30 Establishments)
SIC 6513 APMNT BLDG OPRTRS (NO BREAKDOWN) 2013 (25 Establishments)
SIC 6531 RL ESTE AGNTS,MGRS (NO BREAKDOWN) 2013 (61 Establishments)
SIC 6552 SBDVDRS,DVLPRS,NEC (NO BREAKDOWN) 2013 (21 Establishments)

	6512 $	6512 %	6513 $	6513 %	6531 $	6531 %	6552 $	6552 %
Cash	2,282,142	12.1	1,082,750	16.4	989,139	20.0	3,692,534	22.4
Accounts Receivable	1,452,272	7.7	369,719	5.6	212,665	4.3	65,938	0.4
Notes Receivable	150,885	0.8	0	0.0	113,751	2.3	642,897	3.9
Inventory	169,746	0.9	46,215	0.7	281,905	5.7	989,072	6.0
Other Current	2,263,283	12.0	798,858	12.1	459,948	9.3	1,796,814	10.9
Total Current	**6,318,328**	**33.5**	**2,297,542**	**34.8**	**2,057,408**	**41.6**	**7,187,255**	**43.6**
Fixed Assets	9,901,858	52.5	3,551,948	53.8	1,834,852	37.1	6,049,822	36.7
Other Non-current	2,640,495	14.0	752,643	11.4	1,053,433	21.3	3,247,452	19.7
Total Assets	**18,860,681**	**100.0**	**6,602,133**	**100.0**	**4,945,693**	**100.0**	**16,484,529**	**100.0**
Accounts Payable	3,753,276	19.9	72,623	1.1	331,361	6.7	4,648,637	28.2
Bank Loans	94,303	0.5	0	0.0	34,620	0.7	0	0.0
Notes Payable	56,582	0.3	0	0.0	133,534	2.7	6,445,451	39.1
Other Current	11,146,662	59.1	1,723,157	26.1	1,409,522	28.5	104,462,460	633.7
Total Current	**15,050,823**	**79.8**	**1,795,780**	**27.2**	**1,909,037**	**38.6**	**115,556,548**	**701.0**
Other Long Term	3,583,530	19.0	2,871,928	43.5	1,191,912	24.1	7,764,214	47.1
Deferred Credits	56,582	0.3	125,441	1.9	4,946	0.1	98,907	0.6
Net Worth	169,746	0.9	1,808,984	27.4	1,839,798	37.2	(106,935,140)	(648.7)
Total Liab & Net Worth	**18,860,681**	**100.0**	**6,602,133**	**100.0**	**4,945,693**	**100.0**	**16,484,529**	**100.0**
Net Sales	5,287,547	100.0	1,982,623	100.0	3,801,455	100.0	5,463,881	100.0
Gross Profit	2,321,233	43.9	888,215	44.8	1,809,493	47.6	(994,426)	(18.2)
Net Profit After Tax	380,703	7.2	144,731	7.3	125,448	3.3	(1,005,354)	(18.4)
Working Capital	(8,732,495)	—	501,762	—	148,371	—	(108,369,293)	—

RATIOS	6512 UQ	6512 MED	6512 LQ	6513 UQ	6513 MED	6513 LQ	6531 UQ	6531 MED	6531 LQ	6552 UQ	6552 MED	6552 LQ
SOLVENCY												
Quick Ratio (times)	2.4	0.9	0.2	4.2	1.1	0.4	1.7	0.7	0.2	3.7	0.5	0.0
Current Ratio (times)	3.8	1.8	1.1	4.2	2.2	0.5	3.6	1.3	0.7	6.2	1.6	0.2
Curr Liab To Nw (%)	9.6	18.6	43.6	8.2	28.4	72.2	13.2	46.8	124.9	3.1	13.3	72.0
Curr Liab To Inv (%)	313.6	508.1	983.4	886.6	999.9	999.9	74.7	465.8	567.2	89.3	697.8	767.5
Total Liab To Nw (%)	17.8	70.6	141.5	55.8	155.2	530.9	18.9	103.7	262.7	62.5	113.7	199.9
Fixed Assets To Nw (%)	34.4	78.5	138.1	72.8	130.9	332.8	12.5	70.9	158.3	25.8	57.5	97.8
EFFICIENCY												
Coll Period (days)	17.2	28.3	64.6	0.7	3.3	11.7	4.4	18.6	51.8	0.9	7.2	77.1
Sales To Inv (times)	394.8	26.1	5.9	999.9	208.9	21.9	17.1	13.2	3.7	55.6	29.8	1.8
Assets To Sales (%)	98.5	356.7	799.1	179.2	333.0	500.7	34.8	130.1	378.5	107.0	301.7	999.9
Sales To Nwc (times)	9.0	3.5	1.5	2.5	1.3	0.7	20.0	8.1	2.9	4.5	1.2	0.7
Acct Pay To Sales (%)	2.7	6.2	11.8	2.2	4.3	8.6	1.0	2.2	8.0	1.3	5.3	14.9
PROFITABILITY												
Return On Sales (%)	15.6	5.3	0.2	16.0	10.9	(10.4)	8.7	(3.1)	(6.5)	5.9	(3.1)	(90.4)
Return On Assets (%)	6.1	1.8	0.3	6.6	3.4	(0.6)	9.4	(3.2)	(1.6)	1.0	(3.2)	(73.7)
Return On Nw (%)	16.0	4.0	0.5	31.0	9.2	(10.5)	32.0	(4.7)	(1.5)	2.1	(4.7)	(8.2)

SIC 67 HOLDG,RE INVESTM COS
(NO BREAKDOWN)
2013 (139 Establishments)

	$	%
Cash	962,186	39.5
Accounts Receivable	187,565	7.7
Notes Receivable	4,872	0.2
Inventory	112,052	4.6
Other Current	348,336	14.3
Total Current	**1,615,011**	**66.3**
Fixed Assets	302,053	12.4
Other Non-current	518,850	21.3
Total Assets	**2,435,914**	**100.0**
Accounts Payable	13,037,012	535.2
Bank Loans	9,744	0.4
Notes Payable	3,032,713	124.5
Other Current	10,111,478	415.1
Total Current	**26,190,947**	**75.2**
Other Long Term	891,545	36.6
Deferred Credits	0	0.0
Net Worth	(24,646,578)	(11.8)
Total Liab & Net Worth	**2,435,914**	**100.0**
Net Sales	1,985,260	100.0
Gross Profit	1,032,335	52.0
Net Profit After Tax	152,865	7.7
Working Capital	(24,575,936)	---

RATIOS	UQ	MED	LQ
SOLVENCY			
Quick Ratio (times)	3.3	0.9	0.1
Current Ratio (times)	4.8	1.4	0.1
Curr Liab To Nw (%)	6.1	19.2	48.1
Curr Liab To Inv (%)	214.6	778.6	999.9
Total Liab To Nw (%)	11.2	40.7	171.0
Fixed Assets To Nw (%)	1.9	11.5	58.5
EFFICIENCY			
Coll Period (days)	12.3	36.9	68.9
Sales To Inv (times)	133.9	27.0	8.5
Assets To Sales (%)	48.6	122.7	359.7
Sales To Nwc (times)	8.5	4.5	1.8
Acct Pay To Sales (%)	2.6	6.4	16.3
PROFITABILITY			
Return On Sales (%)	10.2	(0.1)	(109.9)
Return On Assets (%)	3.1	(29.2)	(564.5)
Return On Nw (%)	16.2	(0.3)	(36.2)

SIC 6719 HOLDING COS,NEC
(NO BREAKDOWN)
2013 (25 Establishments)

	$	%
Cash	10,672,057	14.4
Accounts Receivable	7,707,597	10.4
Notes Receivable	74,112	0.1
Inventory	5,780,698	7.8
Other Current	8,226,377	11.1
Total Current	**32,460,841**	**43.8**
Fixed Assets	12,376,622	16.7
Other Non-current	29,274,047	39.5
Total Assets	**74,111,510**	**100.0**
Accounts Payable	229,004,566	309.0
Bank Loans	0	0.0
Notes Payable	3,335,018	4.5
Other Current	327,721,097	442.2
Total Current	**560,060,681**	**755.7**
Other Long Term	18,231,432	24.6
Deferred Credits	0	0.0
Net Worth	(504,180,603)	(680.3)
Total Liab & Net Worth	**74,111,510**	**100.0**
Net Sales	83,271,360	100.0
Gross Profit	33,891,444	40.7
Net Profit After Tax	1,748,699	2.1
Working Capital	(527,599,840)	---

RATIOS	UQ	MED	LQ
Quick Ratio (times)	1.1	1.0	0.3
Current Ratio (times)	2.2	2.0	0.7
Curr Liab To Nw (%)	20.2	27.4	48.1
Curr Liab To Inv (%)	128.0	386.2	999.9
Total Liab To Nw (%)	28.0	81.2	126.1
Fixed Assets To Nw (%)	4.1	30.0	64.7
Coll Period (days)	27.4	40.9	71.0
Sales To Inv (times)	60.4	11.2	7.3
Assets To Sales (%)	60.0	89.0	165.3
Sales To Nwc (times)	7.7	5.4	3.3
Acct Pay To Sales (%)	3.0	8.2	14.2
Return On Sales (%)	4.5	(0.1)	(130.7)
Return On Assets (%)	4.3	(2.8)	(59.0)
Return On Nw (%)	7.4	(1.5)	(33.7)

SIC 6794 PATENT OWNERS,LESSO
(NO BREAKDOWN)
2013 (34 Establishments)

	$	%
Cash	2,771,994	29.7
Accounts Receivable	821,332	8.8
Notes Receivable	18,667	0.2
Inventory	457,332	4.9
Other Current	1,922,662	20.6
Total Current	**5,991,987**	**64.2**
Fixed Assets	382,666	4.1
Other Non-current	2,958,660	31.7
Total Assets	**9,333,313**	**100.0**
Accounts Payable	4,451,990	47.7
Bank Loans	0	0.0
Notes Payable	2,529,328	27.1
Other Current	3,294,660	35.3
Total Current	**10,275,978**	**110.1**
Other Long Term	5,683,988	60.9
Deferred Credits	9,333	0.1
Net Worth	(6,635,986)	(71.1)
Total Liab & Net Worth	**9,333,313**	**100.0**
Net Sales	6,513,128	100.0
Gross Profit	5,015,109	77.0
Net Profit After Tax	872,759	13.4
Working Capital	(4,283,991)	---

RATIOS	UQ	MED	LQ
Quick Ratio (times)	5.9	2.3	0.8
Current Ratio (times)	8.3	3.5	1.3
Curr Liab To Nw (%)	6.5	13.6	48.5
Curr Liab To Inv (%)	222.0	999.9	999.9
Total Liab To Nw (%)	10.1	28.2	100.5
Fixed Assets To Nw (%)	1.0	3.5	12.1
Coll Period (days)	9.3	31.8	78.0
Sales To Inv (times)	191.0	95.8	8.9
Assets To Sales (%)	67.7	143.3	530.6
Sales To Nwc (times)	6.2	2.9	0.5
Acct Pay To Sales (%)	2.2	4.9	90.2
Return On Sales (%)	12.7	(1.6)	(409.0)
Return On Assets (%)	20.1	(3.8)	(64.3)
Return On Nw (%)	31.7	3.3	(39.7)

SIC 6798 RL EST INVSTMNT TRST
(NO BREAKDOWN)
2013 (10 Establishments)

	$	%
Cash	1,512,845	15.0
Accounts Receivable	393,340	3.9
Notes Receivable	121,028	1.2
Inventory	50,428	0.5
Other Current	191,627	1.9
Total Current	**2,269,268**	**22.5**
Fixed Assets	6,283,350	62.3
Other Non-current	1,533,016	15.2
Total Assets	**10,085,634**	**100.0**
Accounts Payable	18,658,423	185.0
Bank Loans	0	0.0
Notes Payable	10,086	0.1
Other Current	1,260,704	12.5
Total Current	**19,929,213**	**197.6**
Other Long Term	3,469,458	34.4
Deferred Credits	10,086	0.1
Net Worth	(13,323,123)	(132.1)
Total Liab & Net Worth	**10,085,634**	**100.0**
Net Sales	4,973,192	100.0
Gross Profit	1,675,966	33.7
Net Profit After Tax	303,365	6.1
Working Capital	(17,659,945)	---

RATIOS	UQ	MED	LQ
Quick Ratio (times)	1.6	1.1	0.1
Current Ratio (times)	2.0	1.7	0.7
Curr Liab To Nw (%)	6.1	21.8	32.1
Curr Liab To Inv (%)	599.4	999.9	999.9
Total Liab To Nw (%)	48.9	110.0	210.9
Fixed Assets To Nw (%)	120.8	165.5	168.7
Coll Period (days)	15.9	23.7	44.9
Sales To Inv (times)	500.2	196.9	18.4
Assets To Sales (%)	118.5	202.8	402.4
Sales To Nwc (times)	15.2	9.0	7.9
Acct Pay To Sales (%)	1.9	2.8	3.6
Return On Sales (%)	20.1	11.8	3.7
Return On Assets (%)	4.0	2.0	(0.2)
Return On Nw (%)	16.5	7.4	0.6

SIC 6799 INVESTORS, NEC (NO BREAKDOWN) 2013 (64 Establishments)

	$	%
Cash	84,868	56.5
Accounts Receivable	9,764	6.5
Notes Receivable	150	0.1
Inventory	5,708	3.8
Other Current	23,132	15.4
Total Current	**123,622**	**82.3**
Fixed Assets	12,317	8.2
Other Non-current	14,270	9.5
Total Assets	**150,209**	**100.0**
Accounts Payable	1,482,413	986.9
Bank Loans	1,051	0.7
Notes Payable	381,681	254.1
Other Current	1,058,823	704.9
Total Current	**2,923,968**	**946.6**
Other Long Term	47,617	31.7
Deferred Credits	0	0.0
Net Worth	(2,821,376)	(878.3)
Total Liab & Net Worth	**150,209**	**100.0**
Net Sales	221,221	100.0
Gross Profit	77,206	34.9
Net Profit After Tax	(23,671)	(10.7)
Working Capital	(2,800,346)	---

RATIOS	UQ	MED	LQ
SOLVENCY			
Quick Ratio (times)	3.1	0.1	0.0
Current Ratio (times)	4.9	0.5	0.0
Curr Liab To Nw (%)	3.1	7.2	38.4
Curr Liab To Inv (%)	310.3	999.9	999.9
Total Liab To Nw (%)	5.8	22.6	267.8
Fixed Assets To Nw (%)	0.6	13.2	53.0
EFFICIENCY			
Coll Period (days)	14.1	60.2	71.0
Sales To Inv (times)	72.9	39.9	4.4
Assets To Sales (%)	23.8	67.9	186.3
Sales To Nwc (times)	12.9	3.2	1.9
Acct Pay To Sales (%)	6.7	11.3	19.8
PROFITABILITY			
Return On Sales (%)	1.4	(15.3)	(124.4)
Return On Assets (%)	(22.6)	)(347.0	(999.9)
Return On Nw (%)	3.2	(12.3)	(44.4)

SIC 70 HOTELS,RE LODGG PLA (NO BREAKDOWN) 2013 (64 Establishments)

	$	%
Cash	3,587,005	12.5
Accounts Receivable	1,348,714	4.7
Notes Receivable	0	0.0
Inventory	602,617	2.1
Other Current	1,262,625	4.4
Total Current	**6,800,961**	**23.7**
Fixed Assets	14,606,283	50.9
Other Non-current	7,288,794	25.4
Total Assets	**28,696,038**	**100.0**
Accounts Payable	2,266,987	7.9
Bank Loans	889,577	3.1
Notes Payable	344,352	1.2
Other Current	33,143,925	115.5
Total Current	**36,644,841**	**127.7**
Other Long Term	10,474,054	36.5
Deferred Credits	86,088	0.3
Net Worth	(18,508,945)	(64.5)
Total Liab & Net Worth	**28,696,038**	**100.0**
Net Sales	20,497,170	100.0
Gross Profit	12,831,228	62.6
Net Profit After Tax	1,373,310	6.7
Working Capital	(29,843,880)	---

RATIOS	UQ	MED	LQ
SOLVENCY			
Quick Ratio (times)	1.4	0.7	0.4
Current Ratio (times)	1.8	1.0	0.6
Curr Liab To Nw (%)	15.4	38.1	122.6
Curr Liab To Inv (%)	596.3	999.9	999.9
Total Liab To Nw (%)	38.1	152.1	286.0
Fixed Assets To Nw (%)	61.4	118.3	278.7
EFFICIENCY			
Coll Period (days)	3.9	7.7	24.7
Sales To Inv (times)	148.8	75.2	22.1
Assets To Sales (%)	47.3	140.0	201.5
Sales To Nwc (times)	19.5	12.2	5.1
Acct Pay To Sales (%)	1.8	3.2	5.3
PROFITABILITY			
Return On Sales (%)	15.2	4.9	0.3
Return On Assets (%)	14.0	2.9	(0.1)
Return On Nw (%)	87.0	12.3	2.4

SIC 7011 HOTELS AND MOTELS (NO BREAKDOWN) 2013 (56 Establishments)

	$	%
Cash	6,111,496	12.6
Accounts Receivable	1,600,630	3.3
Notes Receivable	0	0.0
Inventory	1,067,087	2.2
Other Current	2,134,172	4.4
Total Current	**10,913,385**	**22.5**
Fixed Assets	24,834,015	51.2
Other Non-current	12,756,535	26.3
Total Assets	**48,503,935**	**100.0**
Accounts Payable	4,074,331	8.4
Bank Loans	1,697,638	3.5
Notes Payable	582,047	1.2
Other Current	62,376,060	128.6
Total Current	**68,730,076**	**141.7**
Other Long Term	19,547,086	40.3
Deferred Credits	145,512	0.3
Net Worth	(39,918,739)	(82.3)
Total Liab & Net Worth	**48,503,935**	**100.0**
Net Sales	34,645,668	100.0
Gross Profit	20,925,983	60.4
Net Profit After Tax	2,182,677	6.3
Working Capital	(57,816,691)	---

RATIOS	UQ	MED	LQ
SOLVENCY			
Quick Ratio (times)	1.3	0.7	0.3
Current Ratio (times)	1.5	1.0	0.6
Curr Liab To Nw (%)	18.2	47.2	116.2
Curr Liab To Inv (%)	596.3	999.9	999.9
Total Liab To Nw (%)	43.8	162.1	313.0
Fixed Assets To Nw (%)	63.6	126.1	315.6
EFFICIENCY			
Coll Period (days)	3.5	7.7	24.7
Sales To Inv (times)	147.8	75.2	22.0
Assets To Sales (%)	50.2	140.0	199.9
Sales To Nwc (times)	19.8	13.8	7.7
Acct Pay To Sales (%)	1.8	3.3	5.3
PROFITABILITY			
Return On Sales (%)	14.6	4.8	0.0
Return On Assets (%)	12.0	2.9	(0.1)
Return On Nw (%)	86.5	10.8	3.0

SIC 72 PERSONAL SERVICES (NO BREAKDOWN) 2013 (51 Establishments)

	$	%
Cash	500,758	17.0
Accounts Receivable	444,791	15.1
Notes Receivable	32,402	1.1
Inventory	162,010	5.5
Other Current	229,760	7.8
Total Current	**1,369,721**	**46.5**
Fixed Assets	830,670	28.2
Other Non-current	745,246	25.3
Total Assets	**2,945,637**	**100.0**
Accounts Payable	232,705	7.9
Bank Loans	41,239	1.4
Notes Payable	250,379	8.5
Other Current	913,148	31.0
Total Current	**1,437,471**	**48.8**
Other Long Term	597,964	20.3
Deferred Credits	0	0.0
Net Worth	910,202	30.9
Total Liab & Net Worth	**2,945,637**	**100.0**
Net Sales	5,434,755	100.0
Gross Profit	2,896,724	53.3
Net Profit After Tax	467,389	8.6
Working Capital	(67,750)	---

RATIOS	UQ	MED	LQ
SOLVENCY			
Quick Ratio (times)	1.8	0.9	0.4
Current Ratio (times)	3.2	1.7	0.7
Curr Liab To Nw (%)	13.2	35.5	96.5
Curr Liab To Inv (%)	210.4	464.0	999.9
Total Liab To Nw (%)	26.9	62.2	184.0
Fixed Assets To Nw (%)	15.3	37.5	85.8
EFFICIENCY			
Coll Period (days)	8.0	28.8	38.0
Sales To Inv (times)	70.5	40.7	14.0
Assets To Sales (%)	27.0	54.2	112.7
Sales To Nwc (times)	10.6	7.6	4.1
Acct Pay To Sales (%)	1.0	3.1	6.7
PROFITABILITY			
Return On Sales (%)	13.9	6.5	2.1
Return On Assets (%)	24.3	8.7	1.7
Return On Nw (%)	44.8	15.7	5.0

	SIC 7217 CRPT,UPHLSTRY CLNG (NO BREAKDOWN) 2013 (10 Establishments)		SIC 7299 MISC PRSNL SVCS,NEC (NO BREAKDOWN) 2013 (14 Establishments)		SIC 73 MISC BUSINESS SVS (NO BREAKDOWN) 2013 (1495 Establishments)		SIC 7311 ADVRTSNG AGENCIES (NO BREAKDOWN) 2013 (61 Establishments)	
	$	%	$	%	$	%	$	%
Cash	166,746	15.7	3,279,859	22.3	830,379	24.0	804,326	25.2
Accounts Receivable	252,774	23.8	2,397,385	16.3	968,776	28.0	1,139,462	35.7
Notes Receivable	5,310	0.5	0	0.0	13,840	0.4	0	0.0
Inventory	71,159	6.7	191,203	1.3	134,937	3.9	73,411	2.3
Other Current	29,738	2.8	2,176,767	14.8	411,729	11.9	271,299	8.5
Total Current	**525,727**	**49.5**	**8,045,214**	**54.7**	**2,359,661**	**68.2**	**2,288,498**	**71.7**
Fixed Assets	484,306	45.6	1,117,799	7.6	467,088	13.5	335,136	10.5
Other Non-current	52,041	4.9	5,544,873	37.7	633,164	18.3	568,135	17.8
Total Assets	**1,062,074**	**100.0**	**14,707,886**	**100.0**	**3,459,913**	**100.0**	**3,191,769**	**100.0**
Accounts Payable	70,097	6.6	1,029,552	7.0	1,269,788	36.7	1,225,639	38.4
Bank Loans	72,221	6.8	14,708	0.1	31,139	0.9	35,109	1.1
Notes Payable	12,745	1.2	4,397,658	29.9	332,152	9.6	22,342	0.7
Other Current	300,567	28.3	5,839,031	39.7	2,771,390	80.1	1,391,612	43.6
Total Current	**455,630**	**42.9**	**11,280,949**	**76.7**	**4,404,469**	**127.3**	**2,674,702**	**83.8**
Other Long Term	49,917	4.7	2,647,419	18.0	826,920	23.9	536,218	16.8
Deferred Credits	0	0.0	0	0.0	27,679	0.8	0	0.0
Net Worth	556,527	52.4	779,518	5.3	(1,799,155)	(52.0)	(19,151)	(0.6)
Total Liab & Net Worth	**1,062,074**	**100.0**	**14,707,886**	**100.0**	**3,459,913**	**100.0**	**3,191,769**	**100.0**
Net Sales	3,437,133	100.0	22,183,840	100.0	7,345,887	100.0	10,262,923	100.0
Gross Profit	2,024,471	58.9	13,487,775	60.8	3,511,334	47.8	4,279,639	41.7
Net Profit After Tax	230,288	6.7	1,663,788	7.5	257,106	3.5	(51,315)	(0.5)
Working Capital	70,097	—	(3,235,735)	—	(2,044,808)	—	(386,204)	—

RATIOS	UQ	MED	LQ	UQ	MED	LQ	UQ	MED	LQ	UQ	MED	LQ
SOLVENCY												
Quick Ratio (times)	5.7	2.2	1.2	1.8	0.9	0.5	2.6	1.3	0.7	1.9	1.1	0.8
Current Ratio (times)	5.8	2.6	1.8	2.7	1.0	0.7	3.5	1.8	1.1	2.3	1.3	1.0
Curr Liab To Nw (%)	11.6	38.0	42.0	11.7	31.4	87.7	22.7	55.0	142.1	26.8	133.6	374.0
Curr Liab To Inv (%)	197.6	298.5	464.0	508.0	922.3	999.9	184.8	570.6	999.9	645.3	999.9	999.9
Total Liab To Nw (%)	28.8	45.2	72.0	16.4	31.4	127.9	29.6	78.8	200.3	32.3	145.9	398.3
Fixed Assets To Nw (%)	32.1	62.5	84.6	4.8	9.9	23.6	4.9	14.0	38.9	5.7	16.5	30.1
EFFICIENCY												
Coll Period (days)	5.0	28.8	34.5	7.9	28.0	80.7	28.1	48.4	70.8	31.3	52.2	87.8
Sales To Inv (times)	124.5	30.1	12.9	528.2	49.3	24.9	109.6	33.8	12.2	274.0	38.2	13.4
Assets To Sales (%)	23.1	30.9	49.7	33.3	66.3	130.3	24.9	47.1	114.5	21.2	31.1	97.7
Sales To Nwc (times)	11.0	9.8	6.2	17.9	4.8	2.1	13.3	6.9	3.3	22.8	10.4	3.8
Acct Pay To Sales (%)	0.9	1.9	2.3	0.5	2.4	7.5	1.4	3.5	7.9	3.0	8.6	15.4
PROFITABILITY												
Return On Sales (%)	13.1	3.9	1.8	12.9	8.7	(3.8)	8.9	2.7	(0.6)	6.7	0.9	(2.7)
Return On Assets (%)	29.2	19.8	5.4	15.9	7.6	(35.0)	18.4	5.7	(1.5)	13.6	3.0	(2.5)
Return On Nw (%)	41.0	33.9	12.2	28.6	13.0	(8.7)	41.6	14.2	1.1	40.2	5.1	(3.2)

	SIC 7322 ADJSTMNT.CLCTN SVCS (NO BREAKDOWN) 2013 (11 Establishments) $	%	SIC 7334 PHTCPYNG,DPLCTNG SV (NO BREAKDOWN) 2013 (12 Establishments) $	%	SIC 7336 COMMRCL ART.GR DSGN (NO BREAKDOWN) 2013 (20 Establishments) $	%	SIC 7342 DSNFCTNG,PST CNTRL (NO BREAKDOWN) 2013 (16 Establishments) $	%
Cash	3,280,611	27.8	370,420	19.5	376,561	29.1	151,281	22.5
Accounts Receivable	1,392,489	11.8	455,901	24.0	451,614	34.9	121,697	18.1
Notes Receivable	35,402	0.3	0	0.0	1,294	0.1	4,034	0.6
Inventory	11,801	0.1	163,365	8.6	37,527	2.9	47,065	7.0
Other Current	2,301,148	19.5	113,975	6.0	182,457	14.1	47,739	7.1
Total Current	**7,021,451**	**59.5**	**1,103,661**	**58.1**	**1,049,453**	**81.1**	**371,816**	**55.3**
Fixed Assets	1,557,700	13.2	402,713	21.2	194,104	15.0	203,053	30.2
Other Non-current	3,221,607	27.3	393,215	20.7	50,467	3.9	97,492	14.5
Total Assets	**11,800,758**	**100.0**	**1,899,589**	**100.0**	**1,294,024**	**100.0**	**672,361**	**100.0**
Accounts Payable	448,429	3.8	237,449	12.5	461,967	35.7	43,031	6.4
Bank Loans	11,801	0.1	0	0.0	62,113	4.8	0	0.0
Notes Payable	1,038,467	8.8	11,398	0.6	446,438	34.5	0	0.0
Other Current	2,029,730	17.2	419,808	22.1	1,820,692	140.7	276,340	41.1
Total Current	**3,528,427**	**29.9**	**668,655**	**35.2**	**2,791,210**	**215.7**	**319,371**	**47.5**
Other Long Term	1,274,482	10.8	237,449	12.5	32,350	2.5	116,991	17.4
Deferred Credits	0	0.0	0	0.0	0	0.0	0	0.0
Net Worth	6,997,849	59.3	993,485	52.3	(1,529,536)	(118.2)	235,999	35.1
Total Liab & Net Worth	**11,800,758**	**100.0**	**1,899,589**	**100.0**	**1,294,024**	**100.0**	**672,361**	**100.0**
Net Sales	9,433,060	100.0	5,247,483	100.0	3,140,835	100.0	1,971,733	100.0
Gross Profit	5,631,537	59.7	2,093,746	39.9	1,686,628	53.7	1,455,139	73.8
Net Profit After Tax	1,065,936	11.3	110,197	2.1	157,042	5.0	145,908	7.4
Working Capital	3,493,024	---	435,006	---	(1,741,757)	---	52,445	---

RATIOS	UQ	MED	LQ	UQ	MED	LQ	UQ	MED	LQ	UQ	MED	LQ
SOLVENCY												
Quick Ratio (times)	3.2	1.5	0.9	2.6	1.2	0.7	2.8	1.9	1.1	4.1	1.5	0.4
Current Ratio (times)	3.7	1.8	1.4	3.3	2.0	1.0	4.7	2.0	1.2	7.2	1.8	0.9
Curr Liab To Nw (%)	15.5	29.2	91.9	23.6	64.2	251.7	18.9	60.4	221.4	11.1	39.6	106.1
Curr Liab To Inv (%)	999.9	999.9	999.9	174.1	771.4	999.9	572.4	999.9	999.9	73.5	491.5	999.9
Total Liab To Nw (%)	27.6	74.9	104.2	25.3	95.3	376.3	18.9	66.5	221.4	28.1	68.7	106.5
Fixed Assets To Nw (%)	6.1	9.7	31.8	15.3	26.7	60.3	10.6	18.6	39.2	26.6	30.9	63.8
EFFICIENCY												
Coll Period (days)	9.5	15.0	104.8	23.4	28.8	36.4	15.7	45.6	88.5	19.7	25.6	29.9
Sales To Inv (times)	38.9	38.9	38.9	81.8	58.9	18.7	245.9	86.5	51.4	93.2	57.5	25.2
Assets To Sales (%)	54.4	125.1	178.7	30.2	36.2	90.4	30.5	41.2	54.9	22.7	34.1	46.0
Sales To Nwc (times)	11.8	3.1	2.5	14.2	9.5	5.1	11.2	4.8	2.9	12.6	6.3	5.4
Acct Pay To Sales (%)	0.8	1.0	8.1	1.6	3.7	9.5	1.8	3.5	10.9	1.1	2.1	3.8
PROFITABILITY												
Return On Sales (%)	19.3	15.3	8.1	5.6	2.8	0.7	8.0	3.1	0.1	11.7	5.7	1.5
Return On Assets (%)	31.7	17.7	4.6	9.1	3.3	1.9	26.8	5.1	0.2	33.6	15.0	5.5
Return On Nw (%)	33.5	27.2	15.6	19.6	7.7	3.3	37.1	9.9	1.6	68.9	28.1	10.6

Balance Sheet

	SIC 7349 BLDNG MAINT SVC,NEC (NO BREAKDOWN) 2013 (46 Establishments) $	%	SIC 7353 HVY CONST EQPT RNTL (NO BREAKDOWN) 2013 (32 Establishments) $	%	SIC 7359 EQPT RNTL,LSING,NEC (NO BREAKDOWN) 2013 (60 Establishments) $	%	SIC 7361 EMPLOYMENT AGENCIES (NO BREAKDOWN) 2013 (47 Establishments) $	%
Cash	294,325	23.9	889,862	9.9	425,399	13.9	420,396	23.2
Accounts Receivable	337,427	27.4	1,528,046	17.0	498,849	16.3	790,055	43.6
Notes Receivable	7,389	0.6	0	0.0	21,423	0.7	0	0.0
Inventory	30,787	2.5	862,896	9.6	419,278	13.7	0	0.0
Other Current	147,777	12.0	323,586	3.6	358,070	11.7	251,875	13.9
Total Current	**817,705**	**66.4**	**3,604,390**	**40.1**	**1,723,019**	**56.3**	**1,462,326**	**80.7**
Fixed Assets	251,223	20.4	4,844,804	53.9	1,092,571	35.7	137,716	7.6
Other Non-current	162,556	13.2	539,310	6.0	244,834	8.0	212,010	11.7
Total Assets	**1,231,484**	**100.0**	**8,988,504**	**100.0**	**3,060,424**	**100.0**	**1,812,052**	**100.0**
Accounts Payable	112,065	9.1	629,195	7.0	223,411	7.3	416,772	23.0
Bank Loans	11,083	0.9	17,977	0.2	3,060	0.1	28,993	1.6
Notes Payable	44,333	3.6	359,540	4.0	70,390	2.3	106,911	5.9
Other Current	371,909	30.2	1,420,184	15.8	566,179	18.5	838,980	46.3
Total Current	**539,390**	**43.8**	**2,426,896**	**27.0**	**863,040**	**28.2**	**1,391,656**	**76.8**
Other Long Term	140,390	11.4	3,532,482	39.3	596,783	19.5	181,205	10.0
Deferred Credits	3,694	0.3	0	0.0	9,181	0.3	1,812	0.1
Net Worth	548,010	44.5	3,029,126	33.7	1,591,420	52.0	237,379	13.1
Total Liab & Net Worth	**1,231,484**	**100.0**	**8,988,504**	**100.0**	**3,060,424**	**100.0**	**1,812,052**	**100.0**
Net Sales	4,320,996	100.0	9,228,444	100.0	4,873,287	100.0	9,901,923	100.0
Gross Profit	1,961,732	45.4	3,820,576	41.4	2,402,530	49.3	2,990,381	30.2
Net Profit After Tax	302,470	7.0	932,073	10.1	282,651	5.8	277,254	2.8
Working Capital	278,315	—	1,177,494	—	859,979	—	70,670	—

Ratios

RATIOS	UQ	MED	LQ	UQ	MED	LQ	UQ	MED	LQ	UQ	MED	LQ
SOLVENCY												
Quick Ratio (times)	3.4	1.6	0.9	2.1	1.5	0.5	3.3	0.9	0.5	4.0	1.6	0.8
Current Ratio (times)	4.1	2.0	1.1	3.4	1.9	1.0	4.9	2.1	1.2	4.2	1.9	1.0
Curr Liab To Nw (%)	9.3	56.2	100.3	17.4	34.2	65.4	12.4	34.3	102.1	21.8	68.8	184.8
Curr Liab To Inv (%)	330.3	945.4	999.9	114.0	163.7	516.2	77.8	185.1	466.0	—	—	—
Total Liab To Nw (%)	21.1	71.0	148.2	34.1	159.1	370.9	19.2	71.4	189.8	25.1	86.7	222.7
Fixed Assets To Nw (%)	8.8	24.1	74.5	52.9	125.7	268.3	21.8	61.7	135.5	1.2	5.7	24.4
EFFICIENCY												
Coll Period (days)	28.5	39.8	54.8	26.9	39.8	55.3	11.4	40.4	57.1	15.7	33.2	50.4
Sales To Inv (times)	420.8	146.4	37.4	36.2	11.9	5.9	18.6	10.4	6.3	—	—	—
Assets To Sales (%)	15.8	28.5	49.0	52.7	97.4	121.4	39.8	62.8	105.6	11.7	18.3	37.6
Sales To Nwc (times)	23.8	11.4	5.6	9.6	5.8	3.2	10.9	6.3	3.4	35.0	12.3	8.0
Acct Pay To Sales (%)	0.8	2.6	4.4	2.4	4.4	6.7	1.2	2.3	5.9	0.3	0.8	2.7
PROFITABILITY												
Return On Sales (%)	8.9	2.4	0.2	16.2	6.9	1.7	10.4	4.4	0.8	3.9	1.4	(0.9)
Return On Assets (%)	26.4	9.0	0.3	18.6	5.7	1.9	14.6	5.4	0.7	34.0	5.7	(2.6)
Return On Nw (%)	63.4	16.6	2.8	33.2	22.6	7.7	29.1	11.1	3.3	70.5	20.9	(4.1)

	SIC 7363 HELP SUPPLY SVCS (44 Establishments) $	%	SIC 7371 CSTM CMPTR PRGMG SV (217 Establishments) $	%	SIC 7372 PREPACKAGED SFTWARE (190 Establishments) $	%	SIC 7373 CPTR INTGTD SYS DGN (143 Establishments) $	%
Cash	988,950	18.4	1,033,619	32.7	10,394,065	25.2	1,264,357	26.4
Accounts Receivable	2,225,137	41.4	932,470	29.5	6,351,929	15.4	1,661,863	34.7
Notes Receivable	37,623	0.7	22,126	0.7	82,493	0.2	9,578	0.2
Inventory	5,375	0.1	34,770	1.1	824,926	2.0	172,412	3.6
Other Current	526,724	9.8	385,632	12.2	6,021,957	14.6	550,762	11.5
Total Current	**3,783,809**	**70.4**	**2,408,617**	**76.2**	**23,675,370**	**57.4**	**3,658,972**	**76.4**
Fixed Assets	779,336	14.5	202,299	6.4	4,000,890	9.7	373,560	7.8
Other Non-current	811,583	15.1	549,999	17.4	13,570,029	32.9	756,698	15.8
Total Assets	**5,374,728**	**100.0**	**3,160,915**	**100.0**	**41,246,289**	**100.0**	**4,789,230**	**100.0**
Accounts Payable	252,612	4.7	1,738,503	55.0	42,854,894	103.9	737,541	15.4
Bank Loans	0	0.0	31,609	1.0	0	0.0	38,314	0.8
Notes Payable	0	0.0	63,218	2.0	21,943,026	53.2	19,157	0.4
Other Current	1,768,286	32.9	768,103	24.3	110,705,040	268.4	3,462,613	72.3
Total Current	**2,020,898**	**37.6**	**2,601,433**	**82.3**	**175,502,960**	**425.5**	**4,257,625**	**88.9**
Other Long Term	1,241,562	23.1	546,839	17.3	23,922,848	58.0	718,385	15.0
Deferred Credits	26,874	0.5	28,448	0.9	907,418	2.2	47,892	1.0
Net Worth	2,085,394	38.8	(15,805)	(0.5)	(159,086,937)	(385.7)	(234,672)	(4.9)
Total Liab & Net Worth	**5,374,728**	**100.0**	**3,160,915**	**100.0**	**41,246,289**	**100.0**	**4,789,230**	**100.0**
Net Sales	20,672,031	100.0	6,222,274	100.0	30,919,257	100.0	11,035,092	100.0
Gross Profit	4,940,615	23.9	3,422,251	55.0	19,231,778	62.2	5,043,037	45.7
Net Profit After Tax	372,097	1.8	286,225	4.6	(587,466)	(1.9)	132,421	1.2
Working Capital	1,762,911	—	(192,816)	—	(151,827,590)	—	(598,653)	—

RATIOS	UQ	MED	LQ	UQ	MED	LQ	UQ	MED	LQ	UQ	MED	LQ
SOLVENCY												
Quick Ratio (times)	4.3	1.8	1.0	3.6	1.7	0.8	1.9	1.0	0.5	2.7	1.5	0.9
Current Ratio (times)	4.5	2.4	1.3	4.4	2.4	1.2	2.6	1.3	0.8	3.4	2.1	1.3
Curr Liab To Nw (%)	19.3	51.8	115.7	21.3	52.8	132.4	25.0	49.9	101.0	28.6	55.7	128.7
Curr Liab To Inv (%)	321.4	666.7	999.9	185.0	874.4	999.9	356.7	999.9	999.9	367.2	779.9	999.9
Total Liab To Nw (%)	21.5	78.7	161.9	24.9	62.3	201.7	39.1	83.8	166.9	33.6	66.7	165.0
Fixed Assets To Nw (%)	3.2	9.4	23.4	3.0	8.3	19.7	5.5	11.3	26.2	3.9	7.6	22.6
EFFICIENCY												
Coll Period (days)	33.6	51.1	61.0	37.6	57.1	74.1	37.1	57.7	82.0	36.0	55.5	72.3
Sales To Inv (times)	999.9	331.6	72.2	269.1	40.2	14.2	182.6	48.8	14.8	98.6	35.6	19.7
Assets To Sales (%)	17.8	26.0	40.2	23.6	50.8	122.0	65.1	133.4	212.2	24.2	43.4	93.0
Sales To Nwc (times)	20.2	9.8	6.7	11.6	4.6	2.3	9.4	3.5	1.6	11.1	5.7	3.3
Acct Pay To Sales (%)	0.5	1.2	2.7	1.1	2.6	6.3	2.2	4.8	9.9	2.3	4.2	7.1
PROFITABILITY												
Return On Sales (%)	4.2	2.4	(0.5)	10.5	3.9	0.0	9.4	(0.9)	(29.0)	10.4	2.9	(0.3)
Return On Assets (%)	15.7	6.7	(0.5)	23.6	7.0	(0.9)	6.7	(1.6)	(29.3)	23.7	8.1	(0.4)
Return On Nw (%)	33.3	14.9	5.7	39.4	14.6	0.5	15.3	4.3	(22.5)	49.9	15.0	2.4

(NO BREAKDOWN) 2013

Balance Sheet

	SIC 7374 DATA PROC,PRPRTN (NO BREAKDOWN) 2013 (49 Establishments)		SIC 7375 INFRMTN RTRVL SVCS (NO BREAKDOWN) 2013 (25 Establishments)		SIC 7378 COMP MAINT,REPAIR (NO BREAKDOWN) 2013 (16 Establishments)		SIC 7379 COMP RLTD SVCS,NEC (NO BREAKDOWN) 2013 (155 Establishments)	
	$	%	$	%	$	%	$	%
Cash	3,869,448	26.4	6,914,342	31.4	239,940	25.3	540,075	22.7
Accounts Receivable	3,503,023	23.9	2,796,565	12.7	256,062	27.0	1,006,395	42.3
Notes Receivable	14,657	0.1	0	0.0	20,864	2.2	11,896	0.5
Inventory	117,256	0.8	22,020	0.1	119,496	12.6	42,825	1.8
Other Current	1,612,271	11.0	3,567,272	16.2	12,329	1.3	318,810	13.4
Total Current	**9,116,655**	**62.2**	**13,300,199**	**60.4**	**648,691**	**68.4**	**1,920,001**	**80.7**
Fixed Assets	1,700,212	11.6	1,519,394	6.9	200,108	21.1	173,680	7.3
Other Non-current	3,840,134	26.2	7,200,604	32.7	99,580	10.5	285,503	12.0
Total Assets	**14,657,001**	**100.0**	**22,020,197**	**100.0**	**948,379**	**100.0**	**2,379,184**	**100.0**
Accounts Payable	6,111,969	41.7	5,747,271	26.1	102,425	10.8	433,011	18.2
Bank Loans	351,768	2.4	44,040	0.2	31,297	3.3	33,309	1.4
Notes Payable	73,285	0.5	110,101	0.5	21,813	2.3	49,963	2.1
Other Current	22,088,101	150.7	15,458,179	70.2	325,293	34.3	2,526,693	106.2
Total Current	**28,625,123**	**195.3**	**21,359,591**	**97.0**	**480,828**	**50.7**	**3,042,976**	**127.9**
Other Long Term	1,817,468	12.4	34,527,669	156.8	82,509	8.7	180,819	7.6
Deferred Credits	219,855	1.5	110,101	0.5	9,484	1.0	19,033	0.8
Net Worth	(16,005,445)	(109.2)	(33,977,164)	(154.3)	375,558	39.6	(863,644)	(36.3)
Total Liab & Net Worth	**14,657,001**	**100.0**	**22,020,197**	**100.0**	**948,379**	**100.0**	**2,379,184**	**100.0**
Net Sales	18,230,101	100.0	11,762,926	100.0	3,499,554	100.0	7,625,590	100.0
Gross Profit	9,151,511	50.2	6,693,105	56.9	1,662,288	47.5	2,928,227	38.4
Net Profit After Tax	565,133	3.1	(423,465)	(3.6)	139,982	4.0	465,161	6.1
Working Capital	(19,508,468)	---	(8,059,392)	---	167,863	---	(1,122,975)	---

Ratios

RATIOS	UQ	MED	LQ	UQ	MED	LQ	UQ	MED	LQ	UQ	MED	LQ
SOLVENCY												
Quick Ratio (times)	2.8	1.6	1.0	2.6	1.6	0.4	1.6	1.2	0.8	2.8	1.5	1.0
Current Ratio (times)	3.4	2.1	1.2	3.8	2.0	1.0	2.2	1.4	0.9	4.0	1.7	1.2
Curr Liab To Nw (%)	20.3	40.2	65.9	12.8	30.1	79.3	57.3	95.5	197.6	25.9	77.7	177.5
Curr Liab To Inv (%)	583.4	950.0	999.9	999.9	999.9	999.9	170.6	554.7	894.4	345.8	999.9	999.9
Total Liab To Nw (%)	26.3	55.6	142.2	26.6	65.5	157.4	57.3	96.1	203.1	27.6	102.7	220.6
Fixed Assets To Nw (%)	6.8	12.0	24.2	5.8	8.1	19.9	23.7	29.4	78.1	2.3	9.1	22.7
EFFICIENCY												
Coll Period (days)	27.7	45.8	67.2	31.6	52.9	82.0	16.4	30.9	52.2	30.3	50.7	73.7
Sales To Inv (times)	864.2	253.9	39.3	19.9	19.9	19.9	84.2	30.4	10.9	268.4	84.2	29.2
Assets To Sales (%)	35.4	80.4	160.6	106.6	187.2	389.3	23.2	27.1	42.0	20.4	31.2	48.3
Sales To Nwc (times)	9.5	6.4	2.8	4.6	3.4	0.7	13.4	9.1	6.6	17.6	8.6	5.4
Acct Pay To Sales (%)	1.2	3.3	7.7	3.0	4.7	15.5	1.7	3.6	6.7	1.3	3.5	8.2
PROFITABILITY												
Return On Sales (%)	9.5	2.8	(2.5)	6.3	2.1	(57.9)	5.7	3.9	1.5	8.6	4.3	1.3
Return On Assets (%)	12.4	3.1	(2.7)	8.4	0.8	(19.2)	19.9	13.5	5.2	31.4	11.3	3.6
Return On Nw (%)	25.2	7.7	(3.7)	20.3	4.0	(5.9)	73.6	33.0	11.3	63.9	33.8	11.3

	SIC 7381 DTCTV.ARMRD CAR SVC (NO BREAKDOWN) 2013 (14 Establishments) $	%	SIC 7382 SECURITY SYS SVCS (NO BREAKDOWN) 2013 (33 Establishments) $	%	SIC 7389 BUS SERVICES, NEC (NO BREAKDOWN) 2013 (246 Establishments) $	%	SIC 75 AUTO REPAIR,SVS,GAR (NO BREAKDOWN) 2013 (105 Establishments) $	%
Cash	327,964	16.5	537,735	16.6	415,547	20.2	290,149	19.7
Accounts Receivable	826,867	41.6	994,486	30.7	479,319	23.3	226,817	15.4
Notes Receivable	0	0.0	0	0.0	6,171	0.3	1,473	0.1
Inventory	11,926	0.6	226,756	7.0	172,802	8.4	313,714	21.3
Other Current	141,123	7.1	379,005	11.7	263,316	12.8	86,897	5.9
Total Current	**1,307,880**	**65.8**	**2,137,982**	**66.0**	**1,337,155**	**65.0**	**919,050**	**62.4**
Fixed Assets	260,383	13.1	356,330	11.0	372,346	18.1	480,145	32.6
Other Non-current	419,397	21.1	745,055	23.0	347,661	16.9	73,642	5.0
Total Assets	**1,987,660**	**100.0**	**3,239,367**	**100.0**	**2,057,162**	**100.0**	**1,472,837**	**100.0**
Accounts Payable	115,284	5.8	327,176	10.1	285,946	13.9	222,398	15.1
Bank Loans	47,704	2.4	42,112	1.3	18,514	0.9	23,565	1.6
Notes Payable	89,445	4.5	29,154	0.9	43,200	2.1	82,479	5.6
Other Current	687,730	34.6	1,153,215	35.6	631,549	30.7	298,987	20.3
Total Current	**940,163**	**47.3**	**1,551,657**	**47.9**	**979,209**	**47.6**	**627,429**	**42.6**
Other Long Term	222,618	11.2	476,186	14.7	368,233	17.9	263,637	17.9
Deferred Credits	0	0.0	48,591	1.5	6,171	0.3	1,473	0.1
Net Worth	824,879	41.5	1,162,933	35.9	703,549	34.2	580,298	39.4
Total Liab & Net Worth	**1,987,660**	**100.0**	**3,239,367**	**100.0**	**2,057,162**	**100.0**	**1,472,837**	**100.0**
Net Sales	9,202,130	100.0	7,042,102	100.0	4,851,797	100.0	4,975,801	100.0
Gross Profit	3,266,756	35.5	3,302,746	46.9	2,037,755	42.0	1,915,683	38.5
Net Profit After Tax	358,883	3.9	112,674	1.6	242,590	5.0	208,984	4.2
Working Capital	367,717	—	586,325	—	357,946	—	291,621	—

RATIOS	UQ	MED	LQ	UQ	MED	LQ	UQ	MED	LQ	UQ	MED	LQ
SOLVENCY												
Quick Ratio (times)	2.3	1.4	0.8	1.8	1.1	0.8	2.5	1.2	0.6	2.0	0.9	0.4
Current Ratio (times)	2.3	1.6	0.8	2.3	1.6	1.2	3.4	1.8	1.2	2.9	1.6	0.9
Curr Liab To Nw (%)	49.2	122.5	214.2	39.0	74.9	132.0	19.9	49.7	146.1	22.0	59.5	200.2
Curr Liab To Inv (%)	577.1	999.9	999.9	221.7	535.8	807.1	116.3	364.7	999.9	94.4	166.2	443.5
Total Liab To Nw (%)	55.1	129.4	223.0	47.4	87.6	242.5	29.6	78.4	193.8	27.3	74.7	327.2
Fixed Assets To Nw (%)	6.9	12.9	20.9	11.1	21.9	34.2	7.4	24.6	60.9	16.4	55.9	120.2
EFFICIENCY												
Coll Period (days)	25.6	41.6	52.9	40.2	54.0	73.0	18.6	36.0	59.3	6.2	18.6	37.2
Sales To Inv (times)	770.4	316.0	70.7	33.8	29.0	18.8	83.1	22.9	8.2	51.6	18.0	8.5
Assets To Sales (%)	17.2	21.6	46.6	29.9	46.0	115.2	25.4	42.4	89.1	20.0	29.6	41.6
Sales To Nwc (times)	17.4	12.5	10.8	14.8	7.6	4.2	17.2	8.6	4.3	21.7	11.2	4.9
Acct Pay To Sales (%)	1.1	2.1	5.3	1.4	3.4	6.0	1.4	3.7	7.6	1.6	3.3	6.3
PROFITABILITY												
Return On Sales (%)	6.1	2.5	0.4	7.6	2.5	0.1	8.4	2.8	0.1	6.8	2.2	0.8
Return On Assets (%)	15.4	3.8	2.1	16.3	7.0	(0.1)	19.1	5.8	0.3	22.7	7.2	2.2
Return On Nw (%)	31.2	22.4	8.7	32.3	17.4	1.1	41.7	15.5	2.9	39.4	19.8	5.5

SIC 7513 TRCK RNTL, NO DRVRS
(NO BREAKDOWN)
2013 (10 Establishments)

	$	%
Cash	4,304,071	13.1
Accounts Receivable	4,402,638	13.4
Notes Receivable	0	0.0
Inventory	1,839,908	5.6
Other Current	4,238,360	12.9
Total Current	**14,784,977**	**45.0**
Fixed Assets	17,479,129	53.2
Other Non-current	591,399	1.8
Total Assets	**32,855,505**	**100.0**
Accounts Payable	1,807,053	5.5
Bank Loans	0	0.0
Notes Payable	1,675,631	5.1
Other Current	6,702,523	20.4
Total Current	**10,185,207**	**31.0**
Other Long Term	8,542,430	26.0
Deferred Credits	32,856	0.1
Net Worth	14,095,012	42.9
Total Liab & Net Worth	**32,855,505**	**100.0**
Net Sales	41,327,679	100.0
Gross Profit	14,382,032	34.8
Net Profit After Tax	4,422,062	10.7
Working Capital	4,599,770	—

RATIOS	UQ	MED	LQ
SOLVENCY			
Quick Ratio (times)	1.1	0.9	0.4
Current Ratio (times)	2.1	1.3	0.8
Curr Liab To Nw (%)	38.1	62.2	235.5
Curr Liab To Inv (%)	406.6	999.9	999.9
Total Liab To Nw (%)	38.1	210.9	380.0
Fixed Assets To Nw (%)	44.7	147.5	375.6
EFFICIENCY			
Coll Period (days)	13.0	44.2	48.2
Sales To Inv (times)	99.8	45.4	11.0
Assets To Sales (%)	33.2	79.5	201.1
Sales To Nwc (times)	15.2	6.3	6.2
Acct Pay To Sales (%)	0.8	3.0	6.3
PROFITABILITY			
Return On Sales (%)	10.3	3.6	1.4
Return On Assets (%)	10.8	2.9	0.9
Return On Nw (%)	23.7	12.5	4.6

SIC 7532 TP,BDY RPR,PNT SHPS
(NO BREAKDOWN)
2013 (16 Establishments)

	$	%
Cash	63,829	15.0
Accounts Receivable	90,637	21.3
Notes Receivable	0	0.0
Inventory	97,871	23.0
Other Current	22,552	5.3
Total Current	**274,889**	**64.6**
Fixed Assets	116,594	27.4
Other Non-current	34,042	8.0
Total Assets	**425,525**	**100.0**
Accounts Payable	133,189	31.3
Bank Loans	6,808	1.6
Notes Payable	14,893	3.5
Other Current	84,681	19.9
Total Current	**239,571**	**56.3**
Other Long Term	93,615	22.0
Deferred Credits	0	0.0
Net Worth	92,339	21.7
Total Liab & Net Worth	**425,525**	**100.0**
Net Sales	2,227,880	100.0
Gross Profit	922,342	41.4
Net Profit After Tax	75,748	3.4
Working Capital	35,318	—

RATIOS	UQ	MED	LQ
SOLVENCY			
Quick Ratio (times)	1.2	0.9	0.4
Current Ratio (times)	2.1	1.5	0.9
Curr Liab To Nw (%)	41.2	74.7	409.5
Curr Liab To Inv (%)	172.9	283.8	597.7
Total Liab To Nw (%)	47.2	77.9	471.7
Fixed Assets To Nw (%)	16.7	46.0	136.8
EFFICIENCY			
Coll Period (days)	4.2	11.7	24.5
Sales To Inv (times)	61.4	49.3	6.4
Assets To Sales (%)	13.3	19.1	29.9
Sales To Nwc (times)	19.5	12.4	6.8
Acct Pay To Sales (%)	1.6	4.3	7.1
PROFITABILITY			
Return On Sales (%)	5.8	2.5	0.9
Return On Assets (%)	28.4	12.8	4.3
Return On Nw (%)	105.5	40.5	20.3

SIC 7538 GNRL ATMTVE RPR SHP
(NO BREAKDOWN)
2013 (28 Establishments)

	$	%
Cash	382,015	23.4
Accounts Receivable	277,532	17.0
Notes Receivable	0	0.0
Inventory	551,799	33.8
Other Current	66,934	4.1
Total Current	**1,278,280**	**78.3**
Fixed Assets	346,099	21.2
Other Non-current	8,162	0.5
Total Assets	**1,632,541**	**100.0**
Accounts Payable	269,369	16.5
Bank Loans	60,404	3.7
Notes Payable	78,362	4.8
Other Current	372,220	22.8
Total Current	**780,355**	**47.8**
Other Long Term	230,188	14.1
Deferred Credits	0	0.0
Net Worth	621,998	38.1
Total Liab & Net Worth	**1,632,541**	**100.0**
Net Sales	5,610,107	100.0
Gross Profit	1,901,826	33.9
Net Profit After Tax	168,303	3.0
Working Capital	497,925	—

RATIOS	UQ	MED	LQ
SOLVENCY			
Quick Ratio (times)	2.0	1.4	0.5
Current Ratio (times)	3.5	2.3	1.3
Curr Liab To Nw (%)	31.7	70.1	281.8
Curr Liab To Inv (%)	74.9	114.7	144.2
Total Liab To Nw (%)	36.8	74.1	379.3
Fixed Assets To Nw (%)	9.6	37.8	64.6
EFFICIENCY			
Coll Period (days)	9.1	17.5	34.3
Sales To Inv (times)	22.0	10.7	6.3
Assets To Sales (%)	19.6	29.1	37.3
Sales To Nwc (times)	17.8	10.1	4.5
Acct Pay To Sales (%)	2.4	2.9	6.3
PROFITABILITY			
Return On Sales (%)	6.5	1.6	0.1
Return On Assets (%)	17.9	5.2	0.3
Return On Nw (%)	30.4	14.2	1.2

SIC 7539 ATMTVE RPR SHPS,NEC
(NO BREAKDOWN)
2013 (15 Establishments)

	$	%
Cash	195,281	22.9
Accounts Receivable	99,772	11.7
Notes Receivable	853	0.1
Inventory	280,557	32.9
Other Current	32,405	3.8
Total Current	**608,868**	**71.4**
Fixed Assets	237,066	27.8
Other Non-current	6,822	0.8
Total Assets	**852,756**	**100.0**
Accounts Payable	158,613	18.6
Bank Loans	853	0.1
Notes Payable	166,287	19.5
Other Current	167,993	19.7
Total Current	**493,746**	**57.9**
Other Long Term	98,919	11.6
Deferred Credits	0	0.0
Net Worth	260,091	30.5
Total Liab & Net Worth	**852,756**	**100.0**
Net Sales	3,424,723	100.0
Gross Profit	1,226,051	35.8
Net Profit After Tax	133,564	3.9
Working Capital	115,122	—

RATIOS	UQ	MED	LQ
SOLVENCY			
Quick Ratio (times)	2.2	0.6	0.3
Current Ratio (times)	4.0	1.5	0.8
Curr Liab To Nw (%)	17.7	123.5	216.1
Curr Liab To Inv (%)	45.5	90.7	215.0
Total Liab To Nw (%)	20.9	123.5	331.0
Fixed Assets To Nw (%)	21.0	64.7	145.2
EFFICIENCY			
Coll Period (days)	6.6	21.4	24.5
Sales To Inv (times)	51.6	9.8	8.0
Assets To Sales (%)	14.8	24.9	32.2
Sales To Nwc (times)	24.4	16.7	5.3
Acct Pay To Sales (%)	3.0	4.3	8.4
PROFITABILITY			
Return On Sales (%)	5.8	3.4	1.9
Return On Assets (%)	15.9	8.8	6.5
Return On Nw (%)	67.0	18.1	12.9

	SIC 7549 ATMTVE SVCS.NEC (NO BREAKDOWN) 2013 (10 Establishments) $	%	SIC 76 MISC REPAIR SERVICE (NO BREAKDOWN) 2013 (189 Establishments) $	%	SIC 7622 RADIO,TV REPAIR (NO BREAKDOWN) 2013 (13 Establishments) $	%	SIC 7623 RFRGRTN SVC.RPR (NO BREAKDOWN) 2013 (20 Establishments) $	%
Cash	662,153	30.2	338,986	23.3	298,894	26.1	247,122	32.6
Accounts Receivable	311,343	14.2	321,527	22.1	255,377	22.3	213,010	28.1
Notes Receivable	4,385	0.2	10,184	0.7	0	0.0	0	0.0
Inventory	142,516	6.5	312,798	21.5	239,345	20.9	113,706	15.0
Other Current	225,834	10.3	120,755	8.3	51,533	4.5	73,531	9.7
Total Current	**1,346,231**	**61.4**	**1,104,250**	**75.9**	**845,149**	**73.8**	**647,369**	**85.4**
Fixed Assets	526,214	24.0	261,878	18.0	250,796	21.9	94,755	12.5
Other Non-current	320,113	14.6	88,747	6.1	49,244	4.3	15,919	2.1
Total Assets	**2,192,558**	**100.0**	**1,454,875**	**100.0**	**1,145,189**	**100.0**	**758,043**	**100.0**
Accounts Payable	295,995	13.5	132,394	9.1	137,423	12.0	87,175	11.5
Bank Loans	48,236	2.2	13,094	0.9	0	0.0	12,887	1.7
Notes Payable	6,578	0.3	46,556	3.2	17,178	1.5	2,274	0.3
Other Current	315,729	14.4	315,707	21.7	287,442	25.1	122,803	16.2
Total Current	**666,538**	**30.4**	**507,751**	**34.9**	**442,043**	**38.6**	**225,139**	**29.7**
Other Long Term	620,494	28.3	162,946	11.2	83,599	7.3	92,481	12.2
Deferred Credits	0	0.0	0	0.0	1,145	0.1	0	0.0
Net Worth	905,526	41.3	784,178	53.9	618,402	54.0	440,423	58.1
Total Liab & Net Worth	**2,192,558**	**100.0**	**1,454,875**	**100.0**	**1,145,189**	**100.0**	**758,043**	**100.0**
Net Sales	9,330,034	100.0	3,711,416	100.0	2,688,237	100.0	2,406,486	100.0
Gross Profit	4,030,575	43.2	1,477,144	39.8	1,010,777	37.6	861,522	35.8
Net Profit After Tax	(167,941)	(1.8)	163,302	4.4	67,206	2.5	60,162	2.5
Working Capital	679,693	---	596,499	---	403,106	---	422,230	---

RATIOS	UQ	MED	LQ	UQ	MED	LQ	UQ	MED	LQ	UQ	MED	LQ
SOLVENCY												
Quick Ratio (times)	2.1	0.9	0.7	3.6	1.6	0.8	4.8	2.8	0.9	8.3	2.6	1.1
Current Ratio (times)	2.7	1.7	1.3	6.8	2.9	1.6	8.7	3.3	1.5	13.0	3.5	1.9
Curr Liab To Nw (%)	8.8	45.1	63.1	15.1	37.2	87.1	7.3	30.1	93.8	12.3	28.5	70.4
Curr Liab To Inv (%)	246.8	306.8	716.1	56.7	122.5	254.4	40.0	178.0	489.6	65.3	104.8	281.8
Total Liab To Nw (%)	46.5	60.2	81.0	19.8	52.4	121.6	18.8	47.9	128.1	24.1	54.9	95.6
Fixed Assets To Nw (%)	30.0	66.8	89.9	6.5	21.0	51.0	19.0	36.7	50.6	4.9	21.0	36.8
EFFICIENCY												
Coll Period (days)	1.8	12.1	81.0	19.8	32.9	46.2	14.8	24.1	38.9	25.2	27.4	40.9
Sales To Inv (times)	176.4	64.1	16.8	29.6	11.6	6.1	42.5	12.4	10.0	60.3	14.6	6.9
Assets To Sales (%)	11.3	23.5	38.7	28.3	39.2	55.2	27.7	42.6	56.5	27.0	31.5	37.4
Sales To Nwc (times)	89.2	19.4	6.1	9.7	5.1	3.2	9.1	4.5	2.2	8.1	5.8	3.3
Acct Pay To Sales (%)	1.7	3.3	7.7	1.5	2.9	5.5	2.3	3.3	4.2	1.4	3.8	6.3
PROFITABILITY												
Return On Sales (%)	4.2	0.6	(2.9)	6.2	2.5	0.9	3.5	1.8	1.0	4.8	1.0	0.2
Return On Assets (%)	14.0	4.6	(26.8)	14.5	6.0	2.2	11.3	7.8	2.0	14.5	3.6	0.7
Return On Nw (%)	27.1	11.9	(36.2)	28.5	11.1	4.3	25.8	12.0	4.5	22.4	11.6	2.9

SIC 7629 ELECTL RPR SHPS,NEC (NO BREAKDOWN) 2013 (32 Establishments)

	$	%
Cash	402,405	26.9
Accounts Receivable	390,438	26.1
Notes Receivable	5,984	0.4
Inventory	297,690	19.9
Other Current	79,285	5.3
Total Current	**1,175,802**	**78.6**
Fixed Assets	252,812	16.9
Other Non-current	67,317	4.5
Total Assets	**1,495,931**	**100.0**
Accounts Payable	166,048	11.1
Bank Loans	4,488	0.3
Notes Payable	61,333	4.1
Other Current	399,414	26.7
Total Current	**631,283**	**42.2**
Other Long Term	154,081	10.3
Deferred Credits	0	0.0
Net Worth	710,567	47.5
Total Liab & Net Worth	**1,495,931**	**100.0**
Net Sales	3,825,910	100.0
Gross Profit	1,626,012	42.5
Net Profit After Tax	118,603	3.1
Working Capital	544,519	---

RATIOS	UQ	MED	LQ
SOLVENCY			
Quick Ratio (times)	3.9	1.8	0.7
Current Ratio (times)	6.2	2.6	1.5
Curr Liab To Nw (%)	17.1	39.9	102.6
Curr Liab To Inv (%)	109.8	152.6	231.0
Total Liab To Nw (%)	17.1	51.8	147.3
Fixed Assets To Nw (%)	11.3	17.7	53.2
EFFICIENCY			
Coll Period (days)	26.8	38.7	48.4
Sales To Inv (times)	19.8	10.5	7.3
Assets To Sales (%)	28.1	39.1	53.8
Sales To Nwc (times)	11.3	6.0	3.6
Acct Pay To Sales (%)	1.5	3.6	7.2
PROFITABILITY			
Return On Sales (%)	7.3	2.5	0.3
Return On Assets (%)	13.7	5.8	0.9
Return On Nw (%)	28.8	12.4	2.6

SIC 7692 WELDING REPAIR (NO BREAKDOWN) 2013 (11 Establishments)

	$	%
Cash	466,283	29.5
Accounts Receivable	275,028	17.4
Notes Receivable	1,581	0.1
Inventory	365,124	23.1
Other Current	105,902	6.7
Total Current	**1,213,918**	**76.8**
Fixed Assets	309,802	19.6
Other Non-current	56,902	3.6
Total Assets	**1,580,622**	**100.0**
Accounts Payable	88,515	5.6
Bank Loans	0	0.0
Notes Payable	41,096	2.6
Other Current	159,643	10.1
Total Current	**289,254**	**18.3**
Other Long Term	158,062	10.0
Deferred Credits	0	0.0
Net Worth	1,133,306	71.7
Total Liab & Net Worth	**1,580,622**	**100.0**
Net Sales	2,797,561	100.0
Gross Profit	892,422	31.9
Net Profit After Tax	25,178	0.9
Working Capital	924,664	---

RATIOS	UQ	MED	LQ
SOLVENCY			
Quick Ratio (times)	7.5	3.4	1.2
Current Ratio (times)	13.0	7.0	3.3
Curr Liab To Nw (%)	8.0	16.9	45.7
Curr Liab To Inv (%)	42.0	56.0	65.3
Total Liab To Nw (%)	9.8	31.8	80.4
Fixed Assets To Nw (%)	2.6	29.6	50.9
EFFICIENCY			
Coll Period (days)	33.4	52.9	54.6
Sales To Inv (times)	15.4	6.1	4.8
Assets To Sales (%)	38.3	56.5	67.1
Sales To Nwc (times)	3.9	2.7	1.8
Acct Pay To Sales (%)	1.7	2.1	4.0
PROFITABILITY			
Return On Sales (%)	2.0	1.7	1.0
Return On Assets (%)	5.3	3.2	1.8
Return On Nw (%)	5.5	3.6	1.9

SIC 7694 ARMTRE REWNDNG SHPS (NO BREAKDOWN) 2013 (17 Establishments)

	$	%
Cash	162,193	19.5
Accounts Receivable	189,641	22.8
Notes Receivable	0	0.0
Inventory	238,715	28.7
Other Current	64,876	7.8
Total Current	**655,425**	**78.8**
Fixed Assets	166,352	20.0
Other Non-current	9,981	1.2
Total Assets	**831,758**	**100.0**
Accounts Payable	123,932	14.9
Bank Loans	12,476	1.5
Notes Payable	9,149	1.1
Other Current	113,951	13.7
Total Current	**259,508**	**31.2**
Other Long Term	92,326	11.1
Deferred Credits	0	0.0
Net Worth	479,924	57.7
Total Liab & Net Worth	**831,758**	**100.0**
Net Sales	1,970,991	100.0
Gross Profit	752,919	38.2
Net Profit After Tax	43,362	2.2
Working Capital	395,917	---

RATIOS	UQ	MED	LQ
SOLVENCY			
Quick Ratio (times)	5.8	1.2	0.9
Current Ratio (times)	9.4	2.8	1.7
Curr Liab To Nw (%)	6.0	34.5	82.0
Curr Liab To Inv (%)	29.5	73.2	253.9
Total Liab To Nw (%)	6.0	41.1	120.4
Fixed Assets To Nw (%)	5.8	35.6	65.1
EFFICIENCY			
Coll Period (days)	22.3	30.0	42.3
Sales To Inv (times)	15.2	9.5	6.1
Assets To Sales (%)	31.0	42.2	50.8
Sales To Nwc (times)	9.8	4.6	3.0
Acct Pay To Sales (%)	1.9	3.8	6.2
PROFITABILITY			
Return On Sales (%)	4.6	1.9	0.7
Return On Assets (%)	11.3	4.9	2.4
Return On Nw (%)	16.2	9.7	3.3

SIC 7699 REPAIR SVCS,NEC (NO BREAKDOWN) 2013 (93 Establishments)

	$	%
Cash	449,428	19.7
Accounts Receivable	447,147	19.6
Notes Receivable	29,658	1.3
Inventory	504,181	22.1
Other Current	230,418	10.1
Total Current	**1,660,832**	**72.8**
Fixed Assets	424,333	18.6
Other Non-current	196,197	8.6
Total Assets	**2,281,362**	**100.0**
Accounts Payable	159,695	7.0
Bank Loans	25,095	1.1
Notes Payable	95,817	4.2
Other Current	531,558	23.3
Total Current	**812,165**	**35.6**
Other Long Term	282,889	12.4
Deferred Credits	0	0.0
Net Worth	1,186,308	52.0
Total Liab & Net Worth	**2,281,362**	**100.0**
Net Sales	5,646,936	100.0
Gross Profit	2,247,481	39.8
Net Profit After Tax	316,228	5.6
Working Capital	848,667	---

RATIOS	UQ	MED	LQ
SOLVENCY			
Quick Ratio (times)	2.8	1.4	0.6
Current Ratio (times)	5.0	2.8	1.6
Curr Liab To Nw (%)	18.0	40.0	87.0
Curr Liab To Inv (%)	57.9	128.2	273.3
Total Liab To Nw (%)	23.5	56.3	123.6
Fixed Assets To Nw (%)	5.6	19.4	50.7
EFFICIENCY			
Coll Period (days)	15.7	32.9	45.6
Sales To Inv (times)	38.6	12.8	5.0
Assets To Sales (%)	29.4	40.4	58.8
Sales To Nwc (times)	10.4	5.9	3.7
Acct Pay To Sales (%)	1.4	2.6	5.3
PROFITABILITY			
Return On Sales (%)	6.8	3.3	1.4
Return On Assets (%)	16.6	6.1	3.2
Return On Nw (%)	34.1	12.0	5.9

	SIC 78 MOTION PICTURES (NO BREAKDOWN) 2013 (36 Establishments) $	%	SIC 7812 MTN PCTRE,VDEO PROD (NO BREAKDOWN) 2013 (19 Establishments) $	%	SIC 79 AMUSE RECREATION SVCS (NO BREAKDOWN) 2013 (136 Establishments) $	%	SIC 7922 THTRCL PRDCRS,SVCS (NO BREAKDOWN) 2013 (41 Establishments) $	%
Cash	1,577,763	23.3	492,706	30.0	564,413	24.1	284,162	29.8
Accounts Receivable	690,695	10.2	203,652	12.4	86,653	3.7	31,468	3.3
Notes Receivable	0	0.0	1,642	0.1	2,342	0.1	0	0.0
Inventory	47,401	0.7	11,496	0.7	72,601	3.1	6,675	0.7
Other Current	846,439	12.5	307,120	18.7	262,299	11.2	174,502	18.3
Total Current	**3,162,298**	**46.7**	**1,016,616**	**61.9**	**988,308**	**42.2**	**496,807**	**52.1**
Fixed Assets	2,193,971	32.4	415,515	25.3	990,650	42.3	275,580	28.9
Other Non-current	1,415,246	20.9	210,221	12.8	363,004	15.5	181,177	19.0
Total Assets	**6,771,515**	**100.0**	**1,642,352**	**100.0**	**2,341,962**	**100.0**	**953,564**	**100.0**
Accounts Payable	13,258,626	195.8	6,012,651	366.1	800,951	34.2	58,167	6.1
Bank Loans	74,487	1.1	0	0.0	4,684	0.2	4,768	0.5
Notes Payable	54,172	0.8	11,496	0.7	72,601	3.1	77,239	8.1
Other Current	(7,103,319)	(104.9)	(3,467,005)	(211.1)	1,777,549	75.9	398,590	41.8
Total Current	**6,283,966**	**92.8**	**2,557,142**	**155.7**	**2,655,785**	**113.4**	**538,764**	**56.5**
Other Long Term	(521,406)	(7.7)	(786,687)	(47.9)	435,605	18.6	58,167	6.1
Deferred Credits	108,344	1.6	0	0.0	35,129	1.5	6,675	0.7
Net Worth	900,611	13.3	(128,103)	(7.8)	(784,557)	(33.5)	349,958	36.7
Total Liab & Net Worth	**6,771,515**	**100.0**	**1,642,352**	**100.0**	**2,341,962**	**100.0**	**953,564**	**100.0**
Net Sales	7,211,411	100.0	4,299,351	100.0	1,738,650	100.0	1,172,895	100.0
Gross Profit	3,785,991	52.5	1,913,211	44.5	1,091,872	62.8	399,957	34.1
Net Profit After Tax	57,691	0.8	159,076	3.7	102,580	5.9	114,944	9.8
Working Capital	(3,121,668)	—	(1,540,526)	—	(1,667,477)	—	(41,957)	—

RATIOS	UQ	MED	LQ	UQ	MED	LQ	UQ	MED	LQ	UQ	MED	LQ
SOLVENCY												
Quick Ratio (times)	2.8	1.3	0.2	4.3	1.3	0.2	3.5	1.1	0.5	3.9	1.3	0.4
Current Ratio (times)	3.4	1.8	0.8	4.8	1.8	1.4	5.0	1.6	0.9	4.2	1.5	0.8
Curr Liab To Nw (%)	25.2	38.5	65.4	19.6	42.9	69.8	6.5	14.9	43.3	4.5	16.5	68.5
Curr Liab To Inv (%)	886.7	999.9	999.9	303.0	999.9	999.9	287.8	740.3	999.9	483.9	999.9	999.9
Total Liab To Nw (%)	31.8	92.7	192.6	28.0	66.1	136.2	12.2	39.7	93.8	6.5	33.2	91.1
Fixed Assets To Nw (%)	18.6	45.8	103.8	19.8	38.7	57.4	16.2	69.3	106.3	13.0	30.4	75.7
EFFICIENCY												
Coll Period (days)	11.0	34.7	61.3	12.1	39.4	71.9	2.2	10.2	30.7	0.7	7.7	21.9
Sales To Inv (times)	186.0	129.1	10.5	176.7	10.3	9.9	108.4	50.3	25.5	208.1	143.2	25.4
Assets To Sales (%)	36.8	93.9	183.6	17.5	38.2	184.1	46.8	134.7	256.1	18.2	81.3	261.3
Sales To Nwc (times)	15.0	8.0	3.0	19.1	13.8	4.1	11.7	4.5	2.0	15.4	5.2	2.2
Acct Pay To Sales (%)	2.4	4.6	9.6	1.1	1.8	9.4	1.2	2.3	4.7	0.6	1.7	3.7
PROFITABILITY												
Return On Sales (%)	8.1	3.0	(11.0)	8.1	3.0	(0.2)	10.4	3.5	(3.3)	15.2	5.5	(2.8)
Return On Assets (%)	8.1	0.8	(11.4)	15.8	0.8	(4.0)	9.8	3.3	(2.3)	37.3	5.4	(2.1)
Return On Nw (%)	25.2	11.1	(11.0)	41.3	15.6	(2.2)	27.6	6.4	(2.3)	51.1	8.8	(1.2)

	SIC 7929 ENTRS.ENTRTNMNT GRP (NO BREAKDOWN) 2013 (12 Establishments)		SIC 7997 MBRSHP SPT.RCRTN CLB (NO BREAKDOWN) 2013 (22 Establishments)		SIC 7999 AMUSEMENT.RCRTN.NEC (NO BREAKDOWN) 2013 (28 Establishments)		SIC 80 HEALTH SERVICES (NO BREAKDOWN) 2013 (369 Establishments)	
	$	%	$	%	$	%	$	%
Cash	363,939	19.2	687,762	11.3	577,102	23.4	5,123,064	16.1
Accounts Receivable	30,328	1.6	267,801	4.4	120,846	4.9	4,550,299	14.3
Notes Receivable	0	0.0	12,173	0.2	2,466	0.1	95,461	0.3
Inventory	7,582	0.4	109,555	1.8	160,306	6.5	540,945	1.7
Other Current	549,701	29.0	103,468	1.7	254,024	10.3	2,959,284	9.3
Total Current	**951,550**	**50.2**	**1,180,759**	**19.4**	**1,114,744**	**45.2**	**13,269,053**	**41.7**
Fixed Assets	225,567	11.9	4,643,912	76.3	1,023,493	41.5	11,232,556	35.3
Other Non-current	718,401	37.9	261,714	4.3	328,010	13.3	7,318,663	23.0
Total Assets	**1,895,518**	**100.0**	**6,086,385**	**100.0**	**2,466,247**	**100.0**	**31,820,272**	**100.0**
Accounts Payable	20,851	1.1	103,469	1.7	160,306	6.5	2,863,824	9.0
Bank Loans	0	0.0	0	0.0	0	0.0	0	0.0
Notes Payable	13,269	0.7	6,086	0.1	19,730	0.8	700,046	2.2
Other Current	227,461	12.0	645,157	10.6	337,876	13.7	18,583,039	58.4
Total Current	**261,581**	**13.8**	**766,885**	**12.6**	**517,912**	**21.0**	**22,146,909**	**69.6**
Other Long Term	168,701	8.9	2,331,085	38.3	466,121	18.9	6,427,696	20.2
Deferred Credits	115,627	6.1	146,073	2.4	0	0.0	381,843	1.2
Net Worth	1,349,609	71.2	2,842,342	46.7	1,482,214	60.1	2,863,824	9.0
Total Liab & Net Worth	**1,895,518**	**100.0**	**6,086,385**	**100.0**	**2,466,247**	**100.0**	**31,820,272**	**100.0**
Net Sales	1,159,338	100.0	3,510,026	100.0	1,889,844	100.0	31,788,484	100.0
Gross Profit	569,235	49.1	2,372,778	67.6	1,232,178	65.2	15,258,472	48.0
Net Profit After Tax	161,148	13.9	3,510	0.1	153,077	8.1	1,557,636	4.9
Working Capital	689,969	—	413,874	—	596,832	—	(8,877,856)	—

RATIOS	UQ	MED	LQ	UQ	MED	LQ	UQ	MED	LQ	UQ	MED	LQ
SOLVENCY												
Quick Ratio (times)	11.0	2.1	0.5	3.5	1.1	0.5	2.5	1.3	0.9	2.5	1.5	0.9
Current Ratio (times)	20.5	7.0	1.4	4.3	1.3	0.7	12.4	1.9	1.3	3.4	2.1	1.3
Curr Liab To Nw (%)	1.1	18.0	32.5	9.3	16.2	22.1	3.7	10.1	60.1	13.4	23.9	52.1
Curr Liab To Inv (%)	988.8	999.9	999.9	461.5	793.9	999.9	120.4	420.9	999.9	520.1	885.9	999.9
Total Liab To Nw (%)	6.6	28.7	103.4	33.4	51.5	72.2	11.5	32.5	81.1	34.0	66.4	170.1
Fixed Assets To Nw (%)	0.5	6.3	22.7	92.5	113.0	147.9	22.3	73.2	113.3	33.2	65.7	109.7
EFFICIENCY												
Coll Period (days)	0.0	7.9	29.6	14.8	32.2	43.1	2.2	7.5	21.9	28.1	42.3	54.8
Sales To Inv (times)	999.9	999.9	999.9	58.5	44.8	32.8	81.1	36.4	12.8	135.7	58.2	38.6
Assets To Sales (%)	66.5	163.5	327.9	131.5	173.4	232.2	53.8	130.5	291.6	60.5	100.1	163.4
Sales To Nwc (times)	6.0	3.1	1.8	8.6	5.0	2.5	12.3	3.7	1.8	11.1	6.8	3.6
Acct Pay To Sales (%)	0.6	1.4	2.3	1.8	3.3	3.6	1.2	2.3	6.7	1.8	3.2	5.8
PROFITABILITY												
Return On Sales (%)	32.1	7.4	(5.0)	7.9	1.3	(5.1)	7.6	2.7	(0.5)	9.9	3.5	(0.7)
Return On Assets (%)	11.8	9.8	(7.1)	4.2	0.7	(2.3)	9.4	5.0	(0.3)	9.3	3.2	(0.9)
Return On Nw (%)	29.5	11.1	(11.3)	3.0	0.7	(7.2)	25.7	9.0	0.7	20.7	8.5	0.5

	SIC 8011 OFCS,CLNS OF MDL DR (NO BREAKDOWN) 2013 (49 Establishments) $	%	SIC 8051 SKLLD NRSNG CR FCLT (NO BREAKDOWN) 2013 (36 Establishments) $	%	SIC 8059 NRSNG,PRSNL CRE,NEC (NO BREAKDOWN) 2013 (21 Establishments) $	%	SIC 8062 GNL MDL,SRGL HSPTLS (NO BREAKDOWN) 2013 (104 Establishments) $	%
Cash	2,574,337	21.5	4,432,967	8.4	1,930,424	9.5	9,533,916	9.2
Accounts Receivable	1,065,656	8.9	7,493,826	14.2	1,341,136	6.6	14,197,245	13.7
Notes Receivable	11,974	0.1	52,773	0.1	0	0.0	0	0.0
Inventory	191,579	1.6	105,547	0.2	20,320	0.1	1,968,961	1.9
Other Current	1,077,628	9.0	4,063,554	7.7	1,971,064	9.7	9,637,546	9.3
Total Current	**4,921,174**	**41.1**	**16,148,667**	**30.6**	**5,262,944**	**25.9**	**35,337,668**	**34.1**
Fixed Assets	3,819,598	31.9	23,536,946	44.6	9,489,556	46.7	42,902,624	41.4
Other Non-current	3,232,888	27.0	13,087,808	24.8	5,567,749	27.4	25,389,234	24.5
Total Assets	**11,973,660**	**100.0**	**52,773,421**	**100.0**	**20,320,249**	**100.0**	**103,629,526**	**100.0**
Accounts Payable	598,683	5.0	1,319,336	2.5	792,490	3.9	4,352,440	4.2
Bank Loans	11,974	0.1	0	0.0	0	0.0	0	0.0
Notes Payable	203,552	1.7	369,414	0.7	894,091	4.4	0	0.0
Other Current	3,663,940	30.6	8,443,747	16.0	1,524,018	7.5	71,918,891	69.4
Total Current	**4,478,149**	**37.4**	**10,132,497**	**19.2**	**3,210,599**	**15.8**	**76,271,331**	**73.6**
Other Long Term	3,843,545	32.1	31,136,318	59.0	5,913,193	29.1	(11,295,618)	(10.9)
Deferred Credits	0	0.0	1,847,070	3.5	1,259,855	6.2	0	0.0
Net Worth	3,651,966	30.5	9,657,536	18.3	9,936,602	48.9	38,653,813	37.3
Total Liab & Net Worth	**11,973,660**	**100.0**	**52,773,421**	**100.0**	**20,320,249**	**100.0**	**103,629,526**	**100.0**
Net Sales	12,446,632	100.0	37,614,698	100.0	9,774,050	100.0	84,183,206	100.0
Gross Profit	7,555,106	60.7	11,397,253	30.3	8,268,846	84.6	54,634,901	64.9
Net Profit After Tax	1,381,576	11.1	752,294	2.0	781,924	8.0	4,630,076	5.5
Working Capital	443,025	---	6,016,170	---	2,052,345	---	(40,933,663)	---

RATIOS	UQ	MED	LQ	UQ	MED	LQ	UQ	MED	LQ	UQ	MED	LQ
SOLVENCY												
Quick Ratio (times)	4.5	1.9	1.0	2.1	1.0	0.7	1.6	1.2	0.7	2.1	1.5	1.1
Current Ratio (times)	5.9	2.7	1.4	3.0	1.7	1.0	2.8	1.6	1.2	3.1	2.2	1.5
Curr Liab To Nw (%)	5.5	17.5	39.6	13.0	31.5	82.5	8.9	26.0	44.6	14.9	21.6	40.3
Curr Liab To Inv (%)	669.8	999.9	999.9	959.1	999.9	999.9	999.9	999.9	999.9	526.8	757.5	999.9
Total Liab To Nw (%)	7.9	43.1	115.4	47.8	183.6	815.0	36.4	74.7	359.3	50.8	74.8	122.5
Fixed Assets To Nw (%)	30.6	62.4	85.6	59.7	134.3	403.8	51.6	106.4	287.4	52.5	72.8	109.2
EFFICIENCY												
Coll Period (days)	16.4	30.3	46.0	21.5	38.3	45.3	16.8	24.1	35.1	41.6	48.2	59.9
Sales To Inv (times)	219.6	88.9	75.1	400.3	209.0	83.8	400.5	305.5	164.6	67.3	49.7	39.5
Assets To Sales (%)	44.2	96.2	185.7	84.1	140.3	228.0	92.3	207.9	359.9	82.4	123.1	167.0
Sales To Nwc (times)	10.1	5.7	3.5	11.4	7.2	4.2	24.0	8.4	2.3	9.7	6.5	3.5
Acct Pay To Sales (%)	0.6	2.1	3.6	1.9	3.0	4.5	1.7	3.0	4.5	2.8	3.7	6.0
PROFITABILITY												
Return On Sales (%)	12.7	4.9	0.3	8.5	2.6	(3.0)	11.1	2.9	(0.9)	11.1	4.6	(0.2)
Return On Assets (%)	8.8	3.3	0.3	5.7	1.3	(1.3)	5.5	1.8	(0.8)	8.2	4.7	(0.2)
Return On Nw (%)	14.8	8.0	2.3	25.3	6.7	0.9	39.1	5.6	0.0	15.5	9.0	0.4

SIC 8071 MDCL LBRTRS
(NO BREAKDOWN)
2013 (24 Establishments)

	$	%
Cash	11,493,856	24.5
Accounts Receivable	7,177,796	15.3
Notes Receivable	1,501,238	3.2
Inventory	1,125,929	2.4
Other Current	4,738,284	10.1
Total Current	**26,037,103**	**55.5**
Fixed Assets	9,101,258	19.4
Other Non-current	11,775,338	25.1
Total Assets	**46,913,699**	**100.0**
Accounts Payable	5,770,385	12.3
Bank Loans	46,914	0.1
Notes Payable	7,928,415	16.9
Other Current	19,328,444	41.2
Total Current	**33,074,158**	**70.5**
Other Long Term	14,074,109	30.0
Deferred Credits	985,188	2.1
Net Worth	(1,219,756)	(2.6)
Total Liab & Net Worth	**46,913,699**	**100.0**
Net Sales	46,129,498	100.0
Gross Profit	25,140,576	54.5
Net Profit After Tax	(2,675,511)	(5.8)
Working Capital	(7,037,055)	—

RATIOS	UQ	MED	LQ
SOLVENCY			
Quick Ratio (times)	2.7	1.3	0.8
Current Ratio (times)	4.2	1.9	1.1
Curr Liab To Nw (%)	24.1	47.3	69.9
Curr Liab To Inv (%)	270.9	650.0	999.9
Total Liab To Nw (%)	34.8	76.1	182.5
Fixed Assets To Nw (%)	12.6	24.4	29.2
EFFICIENCY			
Coll Period (days)	40.5	45.6	59.1
Sales To Inv (times)	83.8	40.1	10.6
Assets To Sales (%)	59.4	101.7	135.0
Sales To Nwc (times)	12.1	6.6	2.3
Acct Pay To Sales (%)	2.0	6.5	12.9
PROFITABILITY			
Return On Sales (%)	5.3	(1.9)	(39.7)
Return On Assets (%)	9.1	(4.7)	(31.5)
Return On Nw (%)	31.0	8.6	(26.2)

SIC 8082 HME HLTH CRE SVCS
(NO BREAKDOWN)
2013 (30 Establishments)

	$	%
Cash	2,391,591	17.0
Accounts Receivable	3,474,841	24.7
Notes Receivable	14,068	0.1
Inventory	225,091	1.6
Other Current	1,223,932	8.7
Total Current	**7,329,523**	**52.1**
Fixed Assets	2,701,091	19.2
Other Non-current	4,037,568	28.7
Total Assets	**14,068,182**	**100.0**
Accounts Payable	1,069,182	7.6
Bank Loans	14,068	0.1
Notes Payable	70,341	0.5
Other Current	2,644,818	18.8
Total Current	**3,798,409**	**27.0**
Other Long Term	3,306,023	23.5
Deferred Credits	0	0.0
Net Worth	6,963,750	49.5
Total Liab & Net Worth	**14,068,182**	**100.0**
Net Sales	22,837,958	100.0
Gross Profit	9,249,373	40.5
Net Profit After Tax	776,491	3.4
Working Capital	3,531,114	—

RATIOS	UQ	MED	LQ
SOLVENCY			
Quick Ratio (times)	3.5	1.4	0.7
Current Ratio (times)	3.7	2.0	1.2
Curr Liab To Nw (%)	20.2	31.4	57.6
Curr Liab To Inv (%)	413.2	738.5	999.9
Total Liab To Nw (%)	36.1	60.7	147.5
Fixed Assets To Nw (%)	10.5	34.1	59.2
EFFICIENCY			
Coll Period (days)	34.0	47.5	65.3
Sales To Inv (times)	210.9	43.7	24.5
Assets To Sales (%)	35.8	61.6	88.2
Sales To Nwc (times)	13.4	8.5	5.3
Acct Pay To Sales (%)	1.3	3.1	4.6
PROFITABILITY			
Return On Sales (%)	6.0	2.3	(1.7)
Return On Assets (%)	11.7	6.1	(3.4)
Return On Nw (%)	18.4	9.1	(0.3)

SIC 8093 SPTY OTPNT CLNS.NEC
(NO BREAKDOWN)
2013 (48 Establishments)

	$	%
Cash	2,219,054	25.1
Accounts Receivable	1,184,674	13.4
Notes Receivable	8,841	0.1
Inventory	70,727	0.8
Other Current	1,140,470	12.9
Total Current	**4,623,766**	**52.3**
Fixed Assets	3,200,389	36.2
Other Non-current	1,016,698	11.5
Total Assets	**8,840,853**	**100.0**
Accounts Payable	2,528,484	28.6
Bank Loans	0	0.0
Notes Payable	44,204	0.5
Other Current	17,354,595	196.3
Total Current	**19,927,283**	**225.4**
Other Long Term	1,626,716	18.4
Deferred Credits	8,841	0.1
Net Worth	(12,721,987)	(143.9)
Total Liab & Net Worth	**8,840,853**	**100.0**
Net Sales	13,395,232	100.0
Gross Profit	3,670,294	27.4
Net Profit After Tax	575,995	4.3
Working Capital	(15,303,517)	—

RATIOS	UQ	MED	LQ
SOLVENCY			
Quick Ratio (times)	2.9	1.7	1.1
Current Ratio (times)	3.7	2.4	1.6
Curr Liab To Nw (%)	16.8	28.7	45.5
Curr Liab To Inv (%)	682.0	999.9	999.9
Total Liab To Nw (%)	31.5	44.2	104.4
Fixed Assets To Nw (%)	24.6	66.6	90.4
EFFICIENCY			
Coll Period (days)	20.4	34.1	47.8
Sales To Inv (times)	369.1	132.6	48.2
Assets To Sales (%)	35.4	66.0	94.7
Sales To Nwc (times)	11.3	6.6	3.7
Acct Pay To Sales (%)	0.9	1.6	3.1
PROFITABILITY			
Return On Sales (%)	9.8	4.2	0.2
Return On Assets (%)	19.7	4.5	0.2
Return On Nw (%)	50.5	13.1	2.4

SIC 8099 HLTH.ALLD SVCS.NEC
(NO BREAKDOWN)
2013 (21 Establishments)

	$	%
Cash	3,613,565	19.5
Accounts Receivable	5,262,833	28.4
Notes Receivable	37,062	0.2
Inventory	426,215	2.3
Other Current	1,649,268	8.9
Total Current	**10,988,943**	**59.3**
Fixed Assets	4,706,900	25.4
Other Non-current	2,835,259	15.3
Total Assets	**18,531,102**	**100.0**
Accounts Payable	2,909,383	15.7
Bank Loans	0	0.0
Notes Payable	18,531	0.1
Other Current	3,446,785	18.6
Total Current	**6,374,699**	**34.4**
Other Long Term	3,835,938	20.7
Deferred Credits	741,244	4.0
Net Worth	7,579,221	40.9
Total Liab & Net Worth	**18,531,102**	**100.0**
Net Sales	24,774,201	100.0
Gross Profit	9,191,229	37.1
Net Profit After Tax	371,613	1.5
Working Capital	4,614,244	—

RATIOS	UQ	MED	LQ
SOLVENCY			
Quick Ratio (times)	2.6	1.5	1.2
Current Ratio (times)	3.6	2.0	1.3
Curr Liab To Nw (%)	13.4	34.5	129.7
Curr Liab To Inv (%)	274.0	287.4	551.9
Total Liab To Nw (%)	34.3	62.8	289.8
Fixed Assets To Nw (%)	9.1	36.7	61.5
EFFICIENCY			
Coll Period (days)	23.2	46.7	67.6
Sales To Inv (times)	60.2	32.4	22.3
Assets To Sales (%)	44.0	74.8	114.9
Sales To Nwc (times)	9.0	5.8	3.5
Acct Pay To Sales (%)	2.5	5.4	7.8
PROFITABILITY			
Return On Sales (%)	4.6	1.3	(0.5)
Return On Assets (%)	12.2	1.4	(0.7)
Return On Nw (%)	31.4	2.1	(0.3)

SIC 81 — LEGAL SERVICES (NO BREAKDOWN) 2013 (17 Establishments) / SIC 8111 — LEGAL SERVICES (NO BREAKDOWN) 2013 (17 Establishments) / SIC 82 — EDUCATIONAL SERVICE (NO BREAKDOWN) 2013 (254 Establishments) / SIC 8211 — ELMNTRY.SCNDRY SCLS (NO BREAKDOWN) 2013 (82 Establishments)

	SIC 81 $	SIC 81 %	SIC 8111 $	SIC 8111 %	SIC 82 $	SIC 82 %	SIC 8211 $	SIC 8211 %
Cash	1,590,373	43.4	1,590,373	43.4	5,355,746	21.4	3,666,672	22.8
Accounts Receivable	315,143	8.6	315,143	8.6	1,726,853	6.9	369,884	2.3
Notes Receivable	3,664	0.1	3,664	0.1	25,027	0.1	32,164	0.2
Inventory	73,289	2.0	73,289	2.0	300,322	1.2	225,147	1.4
Other Current	567,990	15.5	567,990	15.5	3,153,384	12.6	1,897,662	11.8
Total Current	**2,550,459**	**69.6**	**2,550,459**	**69.6**	**10,561,332**	**42.2**	**6,191,529**	**38.5**
Fixed Assets	791,522	21.6	791,522	21.6	11,011,815	44.0	9,295,334	57.8
Other Non-current	322,472	8.8	322,472	8.8	3,453,705	13.8	595,030	3.7
Total Assets	**3,664,453**	**100.0**	**3,664,453**	**100.0**	**25,026,852**	**100.0**	**16,081,893**	**100.0**
Accounts Payable	4,697,829	128.2	4,697,829	128.2	1,001,074	4.0	192,983	1.2
Bank Loans	7,329	0.2	7,329	0.2	0	0.0	0	0.0
Notes Payable	4,027,234	109.9	4,027,234	109.9	225,242	0.9	112,573	0.7
Other Current	9,340,690	254.9	9,340,690	254.9	4,204,511	16.8	1,913,745	11.9
Total Current	**18,073,082**	**493.2**	**18,073,082**	**493.2**	**5,430,827**	**21.7**	**2,219,301**	**13.8**
Other Long Term	985,738	26.9	985,738	26.9	6,557,035	26.2	6,175,447	38.4
Deferred Credits	0	0.0	0	0.0	150,161	0.6	144,737	0.9
Net Worth	(15,394,367)	(420.1)	(15,394,367)	(420.1)	12,888,829	51.5	7,542,408	46.9
Total Liab & Net Worth	**3,664,453**	**100.0**	**3,664,453**	**100.0**	**25,026,852**	**100.0**	**16,081,893**	**100.0**
Net Sales	23,795,149	100.0	23,795,149	100.0	14,155,459	100.0	10,858,807	100.0
Gross Profit	8,161,736	34.3	8,161,736	34.3	8,719,763	61.6	7,785,765	71.7
Net Profit After Tax	2,070,178	8.7	2,070,178	8.7	962,571	6.8	640,670	5.9
Working Capital	(15,522,623)	—	(15,522,623)	—	5,130,505	—	3,972,228	—

RATIOS

	SIC 81 UQ	SIC 81 MED	SIC 81 LQ	SIC 8111 UQ	SIC 8111 MED	SIC 8111 LQ	SIC 82 UQ	SIC 82 MED	SIC 82 LQ	SIC 8211 UQ	SIC 8211 MED	SIC 8211 LQ
SOLVENCY												
Quick Ratio (times)	3.6	1.5	0.7	3.6	1.5	0.7	3.1	1.4	0.6	3.6	1.5	0.5
Current Ratio (times)	3.2	1.8	1.1	3.2	1.8	1.1	4.7	2.4	1.3	6.3	2.8	1.6
Curr Liab To Nw (%)	7.8	36.8	112.1	7.8	36.8	112.1	9.8	22.8	47.9	6.2	24.5	46.8
Curr Liab To Inv (%)	27.2	175.4	323.6	27.2	175.4	323.6	999.9	999.9	999.9	999.9	999.9	999.9
Total Liab To Nw (%)	32.1	41.7	168.0	32.1	41.7	168.0	24.6	59.6	159.8	28.4	96.6	249.0
Fixed Assets To Nw (%)	6.5	23.0	75.6	6.5	23.0	75.6	41.6	87.8	140.5	74.7	137.4	251.2
EFFICIENCY												
Coll Period (days)	0.0	3.3	22.3	0.0	3.3	22.3	10.1	24.5	48.7	3.3	10.2	12.4
Sales To Inv (times)	44.9	24.4	3.9	44.9	24.4	3.9	401.5	139.0	34.5	999.9	400.4	242.7
Assets To Sales (%)	10.8	15.4	52.6	10.8	15.4	52.6	76.9	176.8	336.1	89.2	148.1	196.8
Sales To Nwc (times)	28.3	15.6	8.2	28.3	15.6	8.2	7.9	3.6	1.6	7.4	4.2	1.9
Acct Pay To Sales (%)	0.7	1.4	2.5	0.7	1.4	2.5	1.3	2.9	6.5	0.7	1.4	3.4
PROFITABILITY												
Return On Sales (%)	9.8	0.4	(0.6)	9.8	0.4	(0.6)	12.2	3.8	(1.6)	12.5	2.0	(2.3)
Return On Assets (%)	38.3	3.8	(2.4)	38.3	3.8	(2.4)	7.2	2.3	(0.6)	6.9	1.6	(1.4)
Return On Nw (%)	77.8	15.7	(0.3)	77.8	15.7	(0.3)	14.4	4.6	(0.8)	18.6	4.6	(6.0)

SIC 8221 COLLEGES,UNVRSTES
(NO BREAKDOWN)
2013 (61 Establishments)

	$	%
Cash	42,994,805	13.6
Accounts Receivable	10,432,563	3.3
Notes Receivable	0	0.0
Inventory	632,277	0.2
Other Current	27,504,029	8.7
Total Current	**81,563,674**	**25.8**
Fixed Assets	160,598,243	50.8
Other Non-current	73,976,356	23.4
Total Assets	**316,138,273**	**100.0**
Accounts Payable	4,109,798	1.3
Bank Loans	0	0.0
Notes Payable	0	0.0
Other Current	34,775,210	11.0
Total Current	**38,885,008**	**12.3**
Other Long Term	83,460,504	26.4
Deferred Credits	0	0.0
Net Worth	193,792,761	61.3
Total Liab & Net Worth	**316,138,273**	**100.0**
Net Sales	111,355,503	100.0
Gross Profit	70,042,611	62.9
Net Profit After Tax	10,021,995	9.0
Working Capital	42,678,666	---

RATIOS	UQ	MED	LQ
SOLVENCY			
Quick Ratio (times)	2.4	1.1	0.6
Current Ratio (times)	3.4	2.2	1.3
Curr Liab To Nw (%)	9.2	16.4	25.5
Curr Liab To Inv (%)	999.9	999.9	999.9
Total Liab To Nw (%)	27.4	53.0	103.3
Fixed Assets To Nw (%)	64.1	82.9	114.3
EFFICIENCY			
Coll Period (days)	12.4	30.9	49.6
Sales To Inv (times)	338.6	139.0	76.4
Assets To Sales (%)	212.7	283.9	518.8
Sales To Nwc (times)	6.1	2.4	1.2
Acct Pay To Sales (%)	3.3	5.4	8.7
PROFITABILITY			
Return On Sales (%)	16.5	8.2	1.5
Return On Assets (%)	5.8	3.1	0.1
Return On Nw (%)	8.1	5.5	0.3

SIC 8222 JUNIOR COLLEGES
(NO BREAKDOWN)
2013 (25 Establishments)

	$	%
Cash	5,574,178	11.2
Accounts Receivable	1,841,470	3.7
Notes Receivable	0	0.0
Inventory	348,386	0.7
Other Current	4,728,098	9.5
Total Current	**12,492,132**	**25.1**
Fixed Assets	29,911,439	60.1
Other Non-current	7,365,878	14.8
Total Assets	**49,769,449**	**100.0**
Accounts Payable	447,925	0.9
Bank Loans	0	0.0
Notes Payable	49,769	0.1
Other Current	4,827,637	9.7
Total Current	**5,325,331**	**10.7**
Other Long Term	14,383,371	28.9
Deferred Credits	0	0.0
Net Worth	30,060,747	60.4
Total Liab & Net Worth	**49,769,449**	**100.0**
Net Sales	12,603,051	100.0
Gross Profit	0	0.0
Net Profit After Tax	718,374	5.7
Working Capital	7,166,801	---

RATIOS	UQ	MED	LQ
SOLVENCY			
Quick Ratio (times)	2.4	1.3	1.1
Current Ratio (times)	3.9	2.5	1.5
Curr Liab To Nw (%)	7.1	21.6	29.7
Curr Liab To Inv (%)	683.2	999.9	999.9
Total Liab To Nw (%)	29.3	78.9	114.7
Fixed Assets To Nw (%)	86.7	99.2	129.0
EFFICIENCY			
Coll Period (days)	31.3	65.7	102.2
Sales To Inv (times)	65.5	25.6	13.6
Assets To Sales (%)	327.3	394.9	828.4
Sales To Nwc (times)	3.6	1.8	0.8
Acct Pay To Sales (%)	2.3	6.9	9.5
PROFITABILITY			
Return On Sales (%)	8.4	(0.4)	(5.2)
Return On Assets (%)	2.2	(0.1)	(1.1)
Return On Nw (%)	3.6	(0.2)	(2.3)

SIC 8249 VOCTNL SCHLS, NEC
(NO BREAKDOWN)
2013 (12 Establishments)

	$	%
Cash	651,884	26.4
Accounts Receivable	207,418	8.4
Notes Receivable	41,977	1.7
Inventory	61,731	2.5
Other Current	627,191	25.4
Total Current	**1,590,201**	**64.4**
Fixed Assets	634,599	25.7
Other Non-current	244,456	9.9
Total Assets	**2,469,256**	**100.0**
Accounts Payable	501,259	20.3
Bank Loans	0	0.0
Notes Payable	0	0.0
Other Current	1,148,204	46.5
Total Current	**1,649,463**	**66.8**
Other Long Term	360,511	14.6
Deferred Credits	0	0.0
Net Worth	459,282	18.6
Total Liab & Net Worth	**2,469,256**	**100.0**
Net Sales	2,975,007	100.0
Gross Profit	2,025,980	68.1
Net Profit After Tax	(29,750)	(1.0)
Working Capital	(59,262)	---

RATIOS	UQ	MED	LQ
SOLVENCY			
Quick Ratio (times)	3.0	1.8	0.8
Current Ratio (times)	4.3	3.0	1.8
Curr Liab To Nw (%)	13.4	22.5	66.8
Curr Liab To Inv (%)	249.6	808.3	999.9
Total Liab To Nw (%)	16.4	44.9	133.7
Fixed Assets To Nw (%)	3.8	53.8	170.0
EFFICIENCY			
Coll Period (days)	10.6	30.7	41.6
Sales To Inv (times)	228.3	61.3	14.6
Assets To Sales (%)	73.8	83.0	154.1
Sales To Nwc (times)	9.3	4.8	1.5
Acct Pay To Sales (%)	2.3	3.6	8.3
PROFITABILITY			
Return On Sales (%)	3.3	1.0	(7.5)
Return On Assets (%)	3.1	0.9	(6.0)
Return On Nw (%)	8.2	3.5	(4.9)

SIC 8299 SCLS,EDCTL SVCS,NEC
(NO BREAKDOWN)
2013 (61 Establishments)

	$	%
Cash	989,890	29.1
Accounts Receivable	500,048	14.7
Notes Receivable	0	0.0
Inventory	68,034	2.0
Other Current	557,876	16.4
Total Current	**2,115,848**	**62.2**
Fixed Assets	707,550	20.8
Other Non-current	578,287	17.0
Total Assets	**3,401,685**	**100.0**
Accounts Payable	268,733	7.9
Bank Loans	0	0.0
Notes Payable	88,444	2.6
Other Current	959,275	28.2
Total Current	**1,316,452**	**38.7**
Other Long Term	476,236	14.0
Deferred Credits	37,419	1.1
Net Worth	1,571,578	46.2
Total Liab & Net Worth	**3,401,685**	**100.0**
Net Sales	6,566,959	100.0
Gross Profit	3,894,207	59.3
Net Profit After Tax	387,451	5.9
Working Capital	799,396	---

RATIOS	UQ	MED	LQ
SOLVENCY			
Quick Ratio (times)	2.3	1.0	0.4
Current Ratio (times)	4.4	1.8	1.0
Curr Liab To Nw (%)	19.2	39.1	135.2
Curr Liab To Inv (%)	277.1	879.6	999.9
Total Liab To Nw (%)	24.5	59.8	154.8
Fixed Assets To Nw (%)	6.1	30.0	71.3
EFFICIENCY			
Coll Period (days)	7.3	25.0	39.4
Sales To Inv (times)	213.8	51.1	22.1
Assets To Sales (%)	23.4	51.8	157.3
Sales To Nwc (times)	14.3	7.3	2.6
Acct Pay To Sales (%)	1.3	2.2	6.5
PROFITABILITY			
Return On Sales (%)	9.2	3.9	0.2
Return On Assets (%)	14.1	6.7	0.8
Return On Nw (%)	40.5	12.6	3.0

SIC 83 SOC SEV
(NO BREAKDOWN)
2013 (395 Establishments)

	$	%
Cash	640,848	25.7
Accounts Receivable	229,409	9.2
Notes Receivable	7,481	0.3
Inventory	39,897	1.6
Other Current	403,958	16.2
Total Current	**1,321,593**	**53.0**
Fixed Assets	842,827	33.8
Other Non-current	329,151	13.2
Total Assets	**2,493,571**	**100.0**
Accounts Payable	124,679	5.0
Bank Loans	2,494	0.1
Notes Payable	17,455	0.7
Other Current	446,348	17.9
Total Current	**590,976**	**23.7**
Other Long Term	321,671	12.9
Deferred Credits	19,949	0.8
Net Worth	1,560,975	62.6
Total Liab & Net Worth	**2,493,571**	**100.0**
Net Sales	3,086,103	100.0
Gross Profit	1,805,370	58.5
Net Profit After Tax	219,113	7.1
Working Capital	730,617	—

RATIOS	UQ	MED	LQ
SOLVENCY			
Quick Ratio (times)	4.6	1.9	0.9
Current Ratio (times)	7.4	3.1	1.4
Curr Liab To Nw (%)	5.9	17.4	47.0
Curr Liab To Inv (%)	118.1	843.1	999.9
Total Liab To Nw (%)	9.5	35.3	102.0
Fixed Assets To Nw (%)	16.7	51.4	91.7
EFFICIENCY			
Coll Period (days)	8.4	23.0	38.0
Sales To Inv (times)	405.6	134.0	15.1
Assets To Sales (%)	35.4	80.8	152.3
Sales To Nwc (times)	13.4	4.9	2.4
Acct Pay To Sales (%)	0.8	1.9	3.7
PROFITABILITY			
Return On Sales (%)	9.8	3.2	0.2
Return On Assets (%)	11.6	4.4	0.2
Return On Nw (%)	21.8	8.2	0.6

SIC 8322 INDVDL,FMLY SVCS
(NO BREAKDOWN)
2013 (199 Establishments)

	$	%
Cash	482,043	28.6
Accounts Receivable	148,321	8.8
Notes Receivable	3,371	0.2
Inventory	35,395	2.1
Other Current	269,675	16.0
Total Current	**938,805**	**55.7**
Fixed Assets	556,204	33.0
Other Non-current	190,457	11.3
Total Assets	**1,685,466**	**100.0**
Accounts Payable	70,790	4.2
Bank Loans	1,685	0.1
Notes Payable	5,056	0.3
Other Current	271,360	16.1
Total Current	**348,891**	**20.7**
Other Long Term	185,402	11.0
Deferred Credits	10,113	0.6
Net Worth	1,141,060	67.7
Total Liab & Net Worth	**1,685,466**	**100.0**
Net Sales	2,169,197	100.0
Gross Profit	1,492,408	68.8
Net Profit After Tax	147,505	6.8
Working Capital	589,914	—

RATIOS	UQ	MED	LQ
SOLVENCY			
Quick Ratio (times)	5.4	2.0	1.0
Current Ratio (times)	8.6	3.3	1.6
Curr Liab To Nw (%)	5.8	14.0	41.8
Curr Liab To Inv (%)	164.8	854.9	999.9
Total Liab To Nw (%)	8.4	26.8	81.3
Fixed Assets To Nw (%)	13.7	43.3	88.8
EFFICIENCY			
Coll Period (days)	8.2	20.1	36.7
Sales To Inv (times)	362.7	144.0	27.8
Assets To Sales (%)	33.6	77.7	133.3
Sales To Nwc (times)	13.0	4.9	2.8
Acct Pay To Sales (%)	0.5	1.6	3.7
PROFITABILITY			
Return On Sales (%)	10.1	3.3	(0.2)
Return On Assets (%)	13.3	5.0	(0.3)
Return On Nw (%)	27.2	8.8	0.1

SIC 8331 JOB TRNNG,RLTD SVCS
(NO BREAKDOWN)
2013 (54 Establishments)

	$	%
Cash	923,617	25.6
Accounts Receivable	429,337	11.9
Notes Receivable	0	0.0
Inventory	111,844	3.1
Other Current	512,319	14.2
Total Current	**1,977,117**	**54.8**
Fixed Assets	1,251,933	34.7
Other Non-current	378,827	10.5
Total Assets	**3,607,877**	**100.0**
Accounts Payable	245,336	6.8
Bank Loans	10,824	0.3
Notes Payable	3,608	0.1
Other Current	523,141	14.5
Total Current	**782,909**	**21.7**
Other Long Term	353,572	9.8
Deferred Credits	3,608	0.1
Net Worth	2,467,788	68.4
Total Liab & Net Worth	**3,607,877**	**100.0**
Net Sales	4,990,148	100.0
Gross Profit	2,425,212	48.6
Net Profit After Tax	94,813	1.9
Working Capital	1,194,208	—

RATIOS	UQ	MED	LQ
SOLVENCY			
Quick Ratio (times)	4.6	2.4	1.0
Current Ratio (times)	6.6	4.1	1.6
Curr Liab To Nw (%)	6.4	16.8	41.5
Curr Liab To Inv (%)	74.4	329.8	999.9
Total Liab To Nw (%)	16.1	26.5	89.3
Fixed Assets To Nw (%)	20.0	45.7	78.0
EFFICIENCY			
Coll Period (days)	12.8	28.1	45.3
Sales To Inv (times)	177.8	51.6	9.4
Assets To Sales (%)	31.3	72.3	111.4
Sales To Nwc (times)	12.2	4.5	2.9
Acct Pay To Sales (%)	0.8	2.2	4.4
PROFITABILITY			
Return On Sales (%)	5.3	2.4	0.4
Return On Assets (%)	10.3	3.4	0.5
Return On Nw (%)	13.9	5.5	0.6

SIC 8351 CHILD DAY CARE SVCS
(NO BREAKDOWN)
2013 (28 Establishments)

	$	%
Cash	390,958	22.8
Accounts Receivable	216,056	12.6
Notes Receivable	0	0.0
Inventory	0	0.0
Other Current	272,642	15.9
Total Current	**879,656**	**51.3**
Fixed Assets	675,604	39.4
Other Non-current	159,470	9.3
Total Assets	**1,714,730**	**100.0**
Accounts Payable	192,050	11.2
Bank Loans	0	0.0
Notes Payable	25,721	1.5
Other Current	372,096	21.7
Total Current	**589,867**	**34.4**
Other Long Term	322,369	18.8
Deferred Credits	0	0.0
Net Worth	802,494	46.8
Total Liab & Net Worth	**1,714,730**	**100.0**
Net Sales	3,528,251	100.0
Gross Profit	815,026	23.1
Net Profit After Tax	194,054	5.5
Working Capital	289,789	—

RATIOS	UQ	MED	LQ
SOLVENCY			
Quick Ratio (times)	2.0	1.1	0.6
Current Ratio (times)	2.7	1.4	1.1
Curr Liab To Nw (%)	17.5	37.5	196.9
Curr Liab To Inv (%)	—	—	—
Total Liab To Nw (%)	22.9	86.2	310.1
Fixed Assets To Nw (%)	40.8	71.3	105.5
EFFICIENCY			
Coll Period (days)	1.1	10.1	48.9
Sales To Inv (times)	—	—	—
Assets To Sales (%)	23.6	48.6	169.7
Sales To Nwc (times)	32.1	17.5	4.2
Acct Pay To Sales (%)	1.0	1.8	3.2
PROFITABILITY			
Return On Sales (%)	7.9	2.4	(1.0)
Return On Assets (%)	8.2	2.6	(4.6)
Return On Nw (%)	70.7	10.8	(3.0)

SIC 8361 RESIDENTIAL CARE (NO BREAKDOWN) 2013 (57 Establishments)

	$	%
Cash	1,508,656	12.6
Accounts Receivable	1,221,293	10.2
Notes Receivable	11,973	0.1
Inventory	23,947	0.2
Other Current	1,724,177	14.4
Total Current	**4,490,046**	**37.5**
Fixed Assets	5,423,976	45.3
Other Non-current	2,059,435	17.2
Total Assets	**11,973,457**	**100.0**
Accounts Payable	395,124	3.3
Bank Loans	0	0.0
Notes Payable	23,947	0.2
Other Current	3,149,019	26.3
Total Current	**3,568,090**	**29.8**
Other Long Term	2,694,028	22.5
Deferred Credits	347,230	2.9
Net Worth	5,364,109	44.8
Total Liab & Net Worth	**11,973,457**	**100.0**
Net Sales	9,296,162	100.0
Gross Profit	7,567,076	81.4
Net Profit After Tax	855,247	9.2
Working Capital	921,956	--

RATIOS	UQ	MED	LQ
SOLVENCY			
Quick Ratio (times)	2.8	1.2	0.7
Current Ratio (times)	4.9	2.5	1.3
Curr Liab To Nw (%)	6.6	19.1	51.3
Curr Liab To Inv (%)	561.9	999.9	999.9
Total Liab To Nw (%)	23.0	57.0	164.3
Fixed Assets To Nw (%)	48.9	73.5	140.4
EFFICIENCY			
Coll Period (days)	10.6	27.4	45.6
Sales To Inv (times)	600.4	227.1	144.8
Assets To Sales (%)	60.6	128.8	277.8
Sales To Nwc (times)	13.3	5.2	2.3
Acct Pay To Sales (%)	1.5	2.1	3.3
PROFITABILITY			
Return On Sales (%)	9.4	3.5	0.9
Return On Assets (%)	8.9	3.1	1.0
Return On Nw (%)	15.5	5.7	1.7

SIC 8399 SOCIAL SVCS,NEC (NO BREAKDOWN) 2013 (57 Establishments)

	$	%
Cash	1,773,125	30.6
Accounts Receivable	289,726	5.0
Notes Receivable	92,712	1.6
Inventory	28,973	0.5
Other Current	1,199,467	20.7
Total Current	**3,384,003**	**58.4**
Fixed Assets	1,240,028	21.4
Other Non-current	1,170,494	20.2
Total Assets	**5,794,525**	**100.0**
Accounts Payable	278,137	4.8
Bank Loans	0	0.0
Notes Payable	162,247	2.8
Other Current	985,069	17.0
Total Current	**1,425,453**	**24.6**
Other Long Term	591,041	10.2
Deferred Credits	17,384	0.3
Net Worth	3,760,647	64.9
Total Liab & Net Worth	**5,794,525**	**100.0**
Net Sales	6,691,137	100.0
Gross Profit	5,219,087	78.0
Net Profit After Tax	736,025	11.0
Working Capital	1,958,550	--

RATIOS	UQ	MED	LQ
SOLVENCY			
Quick Ratio (times)	5.1	2.1	0.9
Current Ratio (times)	8.9	3.6	1.3
Curr Liab To Nw (%)	2.9	17.4	43.8
Curr Liab To Inv (%)	118.1	999.9	999.9
Total Liab To Nw (%)	5.5	34.0	65.7
Fixed Assets To Nw (%)	2.6	12.7	74.4
EFFICIENCY			
Coll Period (days)	7.3	11.4	35.0
Sales To Inv (times)	765.5	225.1	28.0
Assets To Sales (%)	39.6	86.6	248.6
Sales To Nwc (times)	11.3	4.2	1.4
Acct Pay To Sales (%)	0.8	1.2	3.5
PROFITABILITY			
Return On Sales (%)	23.0	3.8	(0.7)
Return On Assets (%)	13.7	7.1	(0.1)
Return On Nw (%)	27.0	10.0	1.8

SIC 84 MUSEUM,BOT,ZOO GARD (NO BREAKDOWN) 2013 (36 Establishments)

	$	%
Cash	971,906	18.5
Accounts Receivable	131,339	2.5
Notes Receivable	0	0.0
Inventory	120,832	2.3
Other Current	478,072	9.1
Total Current	**1,702,149**	**32.4**
Fixed Assets	2,069,897	39.4
Other Non-current	1,481,499	28.2
Total Assets	**5,253,545**	**100.0**
Accounts Payable	68,296	1.3
Bank Loans	0	0.0
Notes Payable	73,550	1.4
Other Current	373,001	7.1
Total Current	**514,847**	**9.8**
Other Long Term	183,875	3.5
Deferred Credits	42,028	0.8
Net Worth	4,512,795	85.9
Total Liab & Net Worth	**5,253,545**	**100.0**
Net Sales	1,591,501	100.0
Gross Profit	1,250,920	78.6
Net Profit After Tax	181,431	11.4
Working Capital	1,187,302	--

RATIOS	UQ	MED	LQ
SOLVENCY			
Quick Ratio (times)	11.0	2.6	0.6
Current Ratio (times)	18.0	5.8	1.4
Curr Liab To Nw (%)	0.9	4.5	18.7
Curr Liab To Inv (%)	110.3	530.2	999.9
Total Liab To Nw (%)	1.4	5.5	33.3
Fixed Assets To Nw (%)	22.3	50.2	78.6
EFFICIENCY			
Coll Period (days)	2.6	5.5	30.5
Sales To Inv (times)	135.7	51.0	9.6
Assets To Sales (%)	88.0	330.1	559.0
Sales To Nwc (times)	6.0	2.8	1.6
Acct Pay To Sales (%)	0.8	2.1	3.3
PROFITABILITY			
Return On Sales (%)	20.3	10.3	(7.2)
Return On Assets (%)	12.2	3.5	(1.9)
Return On Nw (%)	14.1	3.6	(2.4)

SIC 8412 MUSEUMS,ART GALLRS (NO BREAKDOWN) 2013 (34 Establishments)

	$	%
Cash	730,014	19.6
Accounts Receivable	96,839	2.6
Notes Receivable	0	0.0
Inventory	89,390	2.4
Other Current	346,384	9.3
Total Current	**1,262,627**	**33.9**
Fixed Assets	1,448,855	38.9
Other Non-current	1,013,081	27.2
Total Assets	**3,724,563**	**100.0**
Accounts Payable	48,419	1.3
Bank Loans	0	0.0
Notes Payable	55,868	1.5
Other Current	253,271	6.8
Total Current	**357,558**	**9.6**
Other Long Term	134,084	3.6
Deferred Credits	33,521	0.9
Net Worth	3,199,400	85.9
Total Liab & Net Worth	**3,724,563**	**100.0**
Net Sales	1,807,163	100.0
Gross Profit	1,420,430	78.6
Net Profit After Tax	139,152	7.7
Working Capital	905,069	--

RATIOS	UQ	MED	LQ
SOLVENCY			
Quick Ratio (times)	12.2	2.6	0.6
Current Ratio (times)	18.8	5.8	1.6
Curr Liab To Nw (%)	1.2	4.5	15.2
Curr Liab To Inv (%)	71.0	553.7	999.9
Total Liab To Nw (%)	1.5	5.5	29.0
Fixed Assets To Nw (%)	18.4	50.2	80.3
EFFICIENCY			
Coll Period (days)	2.6	5.5	44.9
Sales To Inv (times)	91.4	49.4	9.6
Assets To Sales (%)	87.1	206.1	568.2
Sales To Nwc (times)	5.4	2.7	1.4
Acct Pay To Sales (%)	1.0	2.1	3.2
PROFITABILITY			
Return On Sales (%)	18.7	8.1	(7.8)
Return On Assets (%)	11.2	2.7	(2.0)
Return On Nw (%)	11.9	3.5	(2.8)

	SIC 86 MEMBERSHIP ORGANIZATI (NO BREAKDOWN) 2013 (172 Establishments) $	%	SIC 8611 BUSINESS ASSNS (NO BREAKDOWN) 2013 (40 Establishments) $	%	SIC 8621 PRFSSNL ORGNZTNS (NO BREAKDOWN) 2013 (29 Establishments) $	%	SIC 8641 CIVIC,SOCL ASSNS (NO BREAKDOWN) 2013 (45 Establishments) $	%
Cash	880,489	29.7	898,199	34.9	1,760,617	23.3	740,223	34.1
Accounts Receivable	124,514	4.2	200,744	7.8	188,907	2.5	39,073	1.8
Notes Receivable	5,929	0.2	20,589	0.8	0	0.0	0	0.0
Inventory	65,221	2.2	54,046	2.1	52,894	0.7	28,220	1.3
Other Current	503,983	17.0	496,711	19.3	2,145,990	28.4	267,001	12.3
Total Current	**1,580,136**	**53.3**	**1,670,289**	**64.9**	**4,148,408**	**54.9**	**1,074,517**	**49.5**
Fixed Assets	776,727	26.2	468,402	18.2	1,171,226	15.5	803,174	37.0
Other Non-current	607,745	20.5	434,944	16.9	2,236,664	29.6	293,050	13.5
Total Assets	**2,964,608**	**100.0**	**2,573,635**	**100.0**	**7,556,298**	**100.0**	**2,170,741**	**100.0**
Accounts Payable	100,797	3.4	90,077	3.5	136,013	1.8	115,049	5.3
Bank Loans	2,965	0.1	7,721	0.3	22,669	0.3	0	0.0
Notes Payable	8,894	0.3	10,295	0.4	0	0.0	19,537	0.9
Other Current	729,293	24.6	602,230	23.4	1,775,730	23.5	796,662	36.7
Total Current	**841,949**	**28.4**	**710,323**	**27.6**	**1,934,412**	**25.6**	**931,248**	**42.9**
Other Long Term	296,460	10.0	416,930	16.2	664,955	8.8	130,244	6.0
Deferred Credits	23,717	0.8	18,015	0.7	234,245	3.1	0	0.0
Net Worth	1,802,482	60.8	1,428,367	55.5	4,722,686	62.5	1,109,249	51.1
Total Liab & Net Worth	**2,964,608**	**100.0**	**2,573,635**	**100.0**	**7,556,298**	**100.0**	**2,170,741**	**100.0**
Net Sales	3,034,399	100.0	3,864,317	100.0	6,392,807	100.0	2,228,687	100.0
Gross Profit	1,951,119	64.3	2,048,088	53.0	6,047,595	94.6	900,390	40.4
Net Profit After Tax	297,371	9.8	386,432	10.0	581,745	9.1	82,461	3.7
Working Capital	738,187	---	959,966	---	2,213,996	---	143,269	---

RATIOS	UQ	MED	LQ	UQ	MED	LQ	UQ	MED	LQ	UQ	MED	LQ
SOLVENCY												
Quick Ratio (times)	6.1	1.6	0.6	4.3	1.4	0.9	2.8	1.1	0.5	7.4	1.8	0.7
Current Ratio (times)	10.4	2.8	1.3	6.2	2.5	1.7	7.9	1.9	0.9	14.0	2.9	1.4
Curr Liab To Nw (%)	3.3	15.5	46.7	13.7	31.9	81.3	5.9	17.3	54.3	2.6	8.4	45.2
Curr Liab To Inv (%)	228.6	898.8	999.9	920.2	999.9	999.9	999.9	999.9	999.9	224.9	477.9	999.9
Total Liab To Nw (%)	4.8	29.0	81.1	16.7	62.4	195.0	12.8	32.1	89.9	3.4	22.3	56.3
Fixed Assets To Nw (%)	5.3	22.0	74.4	2.7	15.5	42.4	7.0	15.9	47.8	10.5	53.0	95.9
EFFICIENCY												
Coll Period (days)	2.4	7.7	18.6	2.9	11.0	36.1	2.6	8.8	18.6	1.5	4.8	6.6
Sales To Inv (times)	206.9	63.4	29.1	698.9	187.2	56.7	158.4	72.4	51.2	163.4	62.7	39.0
Assets To Sales (%)	49.0	97.7	206.1	35.6	66.6	133.9	99.6	118.2	171.1	50.2	97.4	176.8
Sales To Nwc (times)	7.2	3.8	1.8	7.4	4.0	2.6	4.1	2.8	1.7	9.8	3.7	1.9
Acct Pay To Sales (%)	1.3	2.6	4.8	1.7	2.8	4.8	1.3	3.4	4.9	0.9	2.3	5.4
PROFITABILITY												
Return On Sales (%)	17.5	5.6	0.1	15.3	7.1	0.3	19.3	6.7	2.2	8.6	4.0	(1.8)
Return On Assets (%)	12.9	5.4	0.0	15.4	5.9	0.0	11.6	5.8	2.8	9.3	4.0	(1.3)
Return On Nw (%)	30.6	8.5	0.5	49.7	11.4	0.3	17.1	12.3	5.8	17.1	5.2	(1.5)

SIC 8661 — RELIGIOUS ORGNZTNS
(NO BREAKDOWN) — 2013 (18 Establishments)

	$	%
Cash	453,129	25.4
Accounts Receivable	89,199	5.0
Notes Receivable	0	0.0
Inventory	37,463	2.1
Other Current	247,972	13.9
Total Current	**827,763**	**46.4**
Fixed Assets	692,182	38.8
Other Non-current	264,028	14.8
Total Assets	**1,783,973**	**100.0**
Accounts Payable	28,544	1.6
Bank Loans	0	0.0
Notes Payable	0	0.0
Other Current	199,805	11.2
Total Current	**228,349**	**12.8**
Other Long Term	132,014	7.4
Deferred Credits	1,784	0.1
Net Worth	1,421,826	79.7
Total Liab & Net Worth	**1,783,973**	**100.0**
Net Sales	865,586	100.0
Gross Profit	693,334	80.1
Net Profit After Tax	90,887	10.5
Working Capital	599,414	---

RATIOS	UQ	MED	LQ
SOLVENCY			
Quick Ratio (times)	15.3	4.9	1.6
Current Ratio (times)	23.7	9.2	2.0
Curr Liab To Nw (%)	1.8	5.1	20.9
Curr Liab To Inv (%)	123.2	365.5	697.9
Total Liab To Nw (%)	2.5	8.8	42.3
Fixed Assets To Nw (%)	13.4	32.1	96.9
EFFICIENCY			
Coll Period (days)	4.0	16.4	28.8
Sales To Inv (times)	104.7	29.1	28.2
Assets To Sales (%)	39.9	206.1	295.9
Sales To Nwc (times)	5.7	1.8	1.1
Acct Pay To Sales (%)	1.1	2.3	2.8
PROFITABILITY			
Return On Sales (%)	12.8	3.6	0.5
Return On Assets (%)	12.4	4.5	0.5
Return On Nw (%)	12.9	6.3	0.5

SIC 8699 — MBRSHP ORGNZTNS.NEC
(NO BREAKDOWN) — 2013 (34 Establishments)

	$	%
Cash	1,738,652	20.0
Accounts Receivable	356,424	4.1
Notes Receivable	17,387	0.2
Inventory	469,436	5.4
Other Current	1,330,068	15.3
Total Current	**3,911,967**	**45.0**
Fixed Assets	2,182,008	25.1
Other Non-current	2,599,285	29.9
Total Assets	**8,693,260**	**100.0**
Accounts Payable	217,332	2.5
Bank Loans	0	0.0
Notes Payable	17,387	0.2
Other Current	1,164,896	13.4
Total Current	**1,399,615**	**16.1**
Other Long Term	799,779	9.2
Deferred Credits	52,160	0.6
Net Worth	6,441,706	74.1
Total Liab & Net Worth	**8,693,260**	**100.0**
Net Sales	7,299,127	100.0
Gross Profit	5,262,671	72.1
Net Profit After Tax	963,485	13.2
Working Capital	2,512,352	---

RATIOS	UQ	MED	LQ
SOLVENCY			
Quick Ratio (times)	4.0	1.5	0.5
Current Ratio (times)	8.6	3.2	1.5
Curr Liab To Nw (%)	2.0	11.1	33.5
Curr Liab To Inv (%)	61.9	294.2	999.9
Total Liab To Nw (%)	2.6	24.5	61.9
Fixed Assets To Nw (%)	1.6	20.7	80.7
EFFICIENCY			
Coll Period (days)	1.1	13.7	21.5
Sales To Inv (times)	54.5	25.6	7.3
Assets To Sales (%)	52.1	119.1	492.7
Sales To Nwc (times)	7.4	4.8	1.8
Acct Pay To Sales (%)	1.4	2.8	3.8
PROFITABILITY			
Return On Sales (%)	33.0	10.3	(0.2)
Return On Assets (%)	13.2	5.3	(0.7)
Return On Nw (%)	26.2	6.7	0.7

SIC 87 — ENGINEERING MGMT SVC
(NO BREAKDOWN) — 2013 (1140 Establishments)

	$	%
Cash	768,638	25.2
Accounts Receivable	1,003,499	32.9
Notes Receivable	12,201	0.4
Inventory	76,254	2.5
Other Current	442,270	14.5
Total Current	**2,302,862**	**75.5**
Fixed Assets	393,469	12.9
Other Non-current	353,818	11.6
Total Assets	**3,050,149**	**100.0**
Accounts Payable	811,340	26.6
Bank Loans	30,501	1.0
Notes Payable	231,811	7.6
Other Current	1,647,081	54.0
Total Current	**2,720,733**	**89.2**
Other Long Term	381,269	12.5
Deferred Credits	9,150	0.3
Net Worth	(61,003)	(2.0)
Total Liab & Net Worth	**3,050,149**	**100.0**
Net Sales	7,587,435	100.0
Gross Profit	3,292,947	43.4
Net Profit After Tax	424,896	5.6
Working Capital	(417,871)	---

RATIOS	UQ	MED	LQ
SOLVENCY			
Quick Ratio (times)	3.0	1.5	0.8
Current Ratio (times)	3.9	2.0	1.3
Curr Liab To Nw (%)	22.4	50.7	121.6
Curr Liab To Inv (%)	182.0	647.3	999.9
Total Liab To Nw (%)	30.9	71.2	161.4
Fixed Assets To Nw (%)	5.0	14.7	38.5
EFFICIENCY			
Coll Period (days)	34.7	57.3	79.9
Sales To Inv (times)	111.7	34.1	11.5
Assets To Sales (%)	26.4	40.2	67.1
Sales To Nwc (times)	11.4	6.0	3.6
Acct Pay To Sales (%)	1.3	3.6	7.6
PROFITABILITY			
Return On Sales (%)	8.8	3.4	0.3
Return On Assets (%)	24.2	7.4	0.1
Return On Nw (%)	50.9	15.8	3.0

SIC 8711 — ENGINEERING SVCS
(NO BREAKDOWN) — 2013 (321 Establishments)

	$	%
Cash	692,291	24.0
Accounts Receivable	1,136,511	39.4
Notes Receivable	8,654	0.3
Inventory	66,345	2.3
Other Current	386,529	13.4
Total Current	**2,290,330**	**79.4**
Fixed Assets	337,492	11.7
Other Non-current	256,724	8.9
Total Assets	**2,884,546**	**100.0**
Accounts Payable	331,723	11.5
Bank Loans	28,845	1.0
Notes Payable	415,375	14.4
Other Current	1,041,321	36.1
Total Current	**1,817,264**	**63.0**
Other Long Term	311,531	10.8
Deferred Credits	5,769	0.2
Net Worth	749,982	26.0
Total Liab & Net Worth	**2,884,546**	**100.0**
Net Sales	7,692,123	100.0
Gross Profit	3,246,076	42.2
Net Profit After Tax	384,606	5.0
Working Capital	473,066	---

RATIOS	UQ	MED	LQ
SOLVENCY			
Quick Ratio (times)	3.1	1.6	1.0
Current Ratio (times)	3.7	2.1	1.4
Curr Liab To Nw (%)	26.2	58.0	123.2
Curr Liab To Inv (%)	201.8	574.9	999.9
Total Liab To Nw (%)	33.0	77.0	158.4
Fixed Assets To Nw (%)	5.6	15.2	36.7
EFFICIENCY			
Coll Period (days)	46.7	63.9	88.5
Sales To Inv (times)	129.2	43.6	16.2
Assets To Sales (%)	26.2	37.5	55.5
Sales To Nwc (times)	10.4	6.1	3.9
Acct Pay To Sales (%)	1.4	3.4	6.7
PROFITABILITY			
Return On Sales (%)	7.8	3.0	0.5
Return On Assets (%)	23.8	7.8	0.8
Return On Nw (%)	45.5	15.6	4.3

	SIC 8712 ARCHITECTURAL SVCS (NO BREAKDOWN) 2013 (70 Establishments) $	%	SIC 8713 SURVEYING SERVICES (NO BREAKDOWN) 2013 (16 Establishments) $	%	SIC 8721 ACCTNG,AUDTNG,BKPNG (NO BREAKDOWN) 2013 (30 Establishments) $	%	SIC 8731 COMMRCL PHYS RSRCH (NO BREAKDOWN) 2013 (110 Establishments) $	%
Cash	418,620	17.4	461,099	22.5	341,805	27.3	6,579,429	40.1
Accounts Receivable	1,085,044	45.1	571,763	27.9	282,959	22.6	2,116,574	12.9
Notes Receivable	9,623	0.4	0	0.0	0	0.0	32,815	0.2
Inventory	60,147	2.5	47,135	2.3	13,772	1.1	410,189	2.5
Other Current	288,704	12.0	352,484	17.2	281,708	22.5	2,411,911	14.7
Total Current	**1,862,138**	**77.4**	**1,432,481**	**69.9**	**920,244**	**73.5**	**11,550,918**	**70.4**
Fixed Assets	319,980	13.3	448,803	21.9	136,471	10.9	2,149,390	13.1
Other Non-current	223,745	9.3	168,045	8.2	195,317	15.6	2,707,246	16.5
Total Assets	**2,405,863**	**100.0**	**2,049,329**	**100.0**	**1,252,032**	**100.0**	**16,407,554**	**100.0**
Accounts Payable	269,457	11.2	75,825	3.7	240,390	19.2	13,667,492	83.3
Bank Loans	134,728	5.6	0	0.0	10,016	0.8	32,815	0.2
Notes Payable	105,858	4.4	6,148	0.3	71,366	5.7	4,216,741	25.7
Other Current	664,018	27.6	338,139	16.5	3,754,844	299.9	20,099,255	122.5
Total Current	**1,174,061**	**48.8**	**420,112**	**20.5**	**4,076,616**	**325.6**	**38,016,303**	**231.7**
Other Long Term	199,687	8.3	291,005	14.2	159,008	12.7	6,218,462	37.9
Deferred Credits	0	0.0	2,049	0.1	0	0.0	114,853	0.7
Net Worth	1,032,115	42.9	1,336,163	65.2	(2,983,592)	(238.3)	(27,942,064)	(170.3)
Total Liab & Net Worth	**2,405,863**	**100.0**	**2,049,329**	**100.0**	**1,252,032**	**100.0**	**16,407,554**	**100.0**
Net Sales	6,450,035	100.0	4,332,619	100.0	3,759,856	100.0	10,229,148	100.0
Gross Profit	3,263,778	50.6	2,083,990	48.1	1,861,129	49.5	4,623,575	45.2
Net Profit After Tax	322,502	5.0	602,234	13.9	552,699	14.7	(593,291)	(5.8)
Working Capital	688,077	—	1,012,369	—	(3,156,372)	—	(26,465,385)	—

RATIOS	UQ	MED	LQ	UQ	MED	LQ	UQ	MED	LQ	UQ	MED	LQ
SOLVENCY												
Quick Ratio (times)	2.6	1.4	1.0	9.4	2.9	1.8	5.1	1.7	0.3	4.3	1.5	0.5
Current Ratio (times)	2.9	1.9	1.2	10.7	3.6	2.6	6.9	2.6	1.0	6.1	2.3	0.9
Curr Liab To Nw (%)	32.5	65.4	140.5	8.2	26.9	52.8	8.2	40.0	99.2	13.6	30.8	66.4
Curr Liab To Inv (%)	187.0	222.8	999.9	114.5	193.2	999.9	221.7	684.9	999.9	266.8	811.1	999.9
Total Liab To Nw (%)	37.5	73.0	165.3	11.8	37.0	96.8	22.6	42.5	169.7	27.7	53.6	108.2
Fixed Assets To Nw (%)	8.8	21.6	37.2	17.6	22.6	39.0	7.5	14.8	40.3	2.6	7.7	33.6
EFFICIENCY												
Coll Period (days)	42.7	60.8	93.1	48.0	56.2	62.3	21.7	31.8	47.1	23.2	50.6	76.5
Sales To Inv (times)	92.0	41.4	14.6	23.6	15.6	7.5	125.2	64.4	14.3	64.1	12.9	5.8
Assets To Sales (%)	26.8	37.3	50.0	36.4	47.3	58.7	19.3	33.3	70.9	60.9	160.4	908.3
Sales To Nwc (times)	15.3	6.4	4.4	7.2	4.5	3.6	12.0	5.6	3.5	4.5	2.1	0.2
Acct Pay To Sales (%)	1.2	4.5	7.7	0.1	0.4	1.5	0.7	1.4	4.9	4.0	12.1	57.2
PROFITABILITY												
Return On Sales (%)	7.6	3.7	0.7	26.7	8.3	4.4	20.1	(23.4)	1.5	3.6	(23.4)	(691.8)
Return On Assets (%)	22.0	8.0	1.8	47.7	21.7	7.9	44.0	(32.0)	3.6	3.0	(32.0)	(93.3)
Return On Nw (%)	37.6	15.3	4.5	69.9	38.8	12.2	82.5	(13.3)	16.8	10.2	(13.3)	(67.0)

SIC 8732 COMMRCL NPHYS RSRCH
(NO BREAKDOWN)
2013 (28 Establishments)

	$	%
Cash	945,658	17.4
Accounts Receivable	1,380,444	25.4
Notes Receivable	0	0.0
Inventory	59,783	1.1
Other Current	934,789	17.2
Total Current	**3,320,674**	**61.1**
Fixed Assets	717,396	13.2
Other Non-current	1,396,748	25.7
Total Assets	**5,434,818**	**100.0**
Accounts Payable	461,960	8.5
Bank Loans	48,913	0.9
Notes Payable	76,087	1.4
Other Current	1,429,357	26.3
Total Current	**2,016,317**	**37.1**
Other Long Term	619,570	11.4
Deferred Credits	21,739	0.4
Net Worth	2,777,192	51.1
Total Liab & Net Worth	**5,434,818**	**100.0**
Net Sales	12,077,373	100.0
Gross Profit	5,857,526	48.5
Net Profit After Tax	2,065,231	17.1
Working Capital	1,304,357	—

RATIOS	UQ	MED	LQ
SOLVENCY			
Quick Ratio (times)	1.8	1.1	0.6
Current Ratio (times)	2.6	1.5	1.0
Curr Liab To Nw (%)	29.3	65.2	181.6
Curr Liab To Inv (%)	237.5	254.4	999.9
Total Liab To Nw (%)	41.6	105.1	219.5
Fixed Assets To Nw (%)	15.2	24.2	63.7
EFFICIENCY			
Coll Period (days)	27.4	55.9	73.7
Sales To Inv (times)	999.9	44.6	1.5
Assets To Sales (%)	26.8	45.0	135.1
Sales To Nwc (times)	10.6	6.8	5.3
Acct Pay To Sales (%)	0.7	3.4	7.1
PROFITABILITY			
Return On Sales (%)	20.5	7.4	2.3
Return On Assets (%)	36.4	10.2	3.8
Return On Nw (%)	100.9	20.2	7.5

SIC 8733 NCMRCL RSCH ORGNZTN
(NO BREAKDOWN)
2013 (41 Establishments)

	$	%
Cash	1,270,460	32.7
Accounts Receivable	524,502	13.5
Notes Receivable	0	0.0
Inventory	11,656	0.3
Other Current	559,468	14.4
Total Current	**2,366,086**	**60.9**
Fixed Assets	773,154	19.9
Other Non-current	745,958	19.2
Total Assets	**3,885,198**	**100.0**
Accounts Payable	1,783,306	45.9
Bank Loans	0	0.0
Notes Payable	0	0.0
Other Current	3,558,841	91.6
Total Current	**5,342,147**	**137.5**
Other Long Term	345,783	8.9
Deferred Credits	7,770	0.2
Net Worth	(1,810,502)	(46.6)
Total Liab & Net Worth	**3,885,198**	**100.0**
Net Sales	4,981,023	100.0
Gross Profit	2,560,246	51.4
Net Profit After Tax	348,672	7.0
Working Capital	(2,976,061)	—

RATIOS	UQ	MED	LQ
SOLVENCY			
Quick Ratio (times)	2.5	1.3	0.6
Current Ratio (times)	3.5	2.1	1.2
Curr Liab To Nw (%)	13.7	42.5	99.1
Curr Liab To Inv (%)	999.9	999.9	999.9
Total Liab To Nw (%)	21.8	56.1	123.7
Fixed Assets To Nw (%)	3.4	12.7	49.0
EFFICIENCY			
Coll Period (days)	30.1	56.2	64.5
Sales To Inv (times)	254.9	102.5	5.6
Assets To Sales (%)	55.4	78.0	207.1
Sales To Nwc (times)	8.6	4.1	2.0
Acct Pay To Sales (%)	1.5	2.7	10.3
PROFITABILITY			
Return On Sales (%)	6.9	2.3	(2.3)
Return On Assets (%)	10.3	0.3	(13.9)
Return On Nw (%)	17.4	4.9	(14.1)

SIC 8734 TESTING LABRTRS
(NO BREAKDOWN)
2013 (19 Establishments)

	$	%
Cash	660,171	20.6
Accounts Receivable	971,029	30.3
Notes Receivable	76,913	2.4
Inventory	64,094	2.0
Other Current	307,653	9.6
Total Current	**2,079,860**	**64.9**
Fixed Assets	721,061	22.5
Other Non-current	403,794	12.6
Total Assets	**3,204,715**	**100.0**
Accounts Payable	262,787	8.2
Bank Loans	0	0.0
Notes Payable	28,842	0.9
Other Current	791,565	24.7
Total Current	**1,083,194**	**33.8**
Other Long Term	810,793	25.3
Deferred Credits	0	0.0
Net Worth	1,310,728	40.9
Total Liab & Net Worth	**3,204,715**	**100.0**
Net Sales	7,137,450	100.0
Gross Profit	3,318,914	46.5
Net Profit After Tax	(64,237)	(0.9)
Working Capital	996,666	—

RATIOS	UQ	MED	LQ
SOLVENCY			
Quick Ratio (times)	3.3	1.7	1.0
Current Ratio (times)	3.6	2.1	1.6
Curr Liab To Nw (%)	23.2	41.4	66.0
Curr Liab To Inv (%)	322.1	551.9	910.8
Total Liab To Nw (%)	23.2	67.8	90.8
Fixed Assets To Nw (%)	12.7	41.5	81.2
EFFICIENCY			
Coll Period (days)	43.8	65.3	76.3
Sales To Inv (times)	561.0	55.2	12.4
Assets To Sales (%)	34.4	44.9	71.2
Sales To Nwc (times)	8.0	5.8	3.7
Acct Pay To Sales (%)	1.7	4.0	5.9
PROFITABILITY			
Return On Sales (%)	4.0	2.2	(0.1)
Return On Assets (%)	12.8	4.2	(0.2)
Return On Nw (%)	13.6	7.8	(0.3)

SIC 8741 MANAGEMENT SERVICES
(NO BREAKDOWN)
2013 (95 Establishments)

	$	%
Cash	1,594,243	22.9
Accounts Receivable	1,837,904	26.4
Notes Receivable	20,885	0.3
Inventory	194,929	2.8
Other Current	1,127,805	16.2
Total Current	**4,775,766**	**68.6**
Fixed Assets	1,267,040	18.2
Other Non-current	918,952	13.2
Total Assets	**6,961,758**	**100.0**
Accounts Payable	3,306,835	47.5
Bank Loans	69,618	1.0
Notes Payable	118,350	1.7
Other Current	2,729,009	39.2
Total Current	**6,223,812**	**89.4**
Other Long Term	(306,318)	(4.4)
Deferred Credits	41,771	0.6
Net Worth	1,002,493	14.4
Total Liab & Net Worth	**6,961,758**	**100.0**
Net Sales	15,334,269	100.0
Gross Profit	5,075,643	33.1
Net Profit After Tax	1,349,416	8.8
Working Capital	(1,448,046)	—

RATIOS	UQ	MED	LQ
SOLVENCY			
Quick Ratio (times)	2.6	1.3	0.6
Current Ratio (times)	3.7	1.7	1.3
Curr Liab To Nw (%)	16.4	47.4	175.0
Curr Liab To Inv (%)	429.5	910.3	999.9
Total Liab To Nw (%)	32.9	88.5	231.1
Fixed Assets To Nw (%)	6.3	28.3	63.2
EFFICIENCY			
Coll Period (days)	21.0	46.0	64.6
Sales To Inv (times)	141.3	72.8	20.3
Assets To Sales (%)	27.7	45.4	106.0
Sales To Nwc (times)	13.0	7.2	3.8
Acct Pay To Sales (%)	1.5	4.4	10.6
PROFITABILITY			
Return On Sales (%)	14.9	3.5	0.7
Return On Assets (%)	24.8	6.9	1.8
Return On Nw (%)	52.7	16.7	5.6

SIC 8742 MNGMNT CNSLTNG SVCS (NO BREAKDOWN) 2013 (198 Establishments)

	$	%
Cash	675,960	26.1
Accounts Receivable	852,072	32.9
Notes Receivable	12,949	0.5
Inventory	77,697	3.0
Other Current	367,763	14.2
Total Current	**1,986,441**	**76.7**
Fixed Assets	222,730	8.6
Other Non-current	380,713	14.7
Total Assets	**2,589,884**	**100.0**
Accounts Payable	813,224	31.4
Bank Loans	23,309	0.9
Notes Payable	28,489	1.1
Other Current	1,351,919	52.2
Total Current	**2,216,941**	**85.6**
Other Long Term	372,943	14.4
Deferred Credits	12,949	0.5
Net Worth	(12,949)	(0.5)
Total Liab & Net Worth	**2,589,884**	**100.0**
Net Sales	7,617,306	100.0
Gross Profit	3,168,799	41.6
Net Profit After Tax	426,569	5.6
Working Capital	(230,500)	---

RATIOS	UQ	MED	LQ
SOLVENCY			
Quick Ratio (times)	2.7	1.3	0.9
Current Ratio (times)	3.5	1.8	1.3
Curr Liab To Nw (%)	27.4	62.1	178.2
Curr Liab To Inv (%)	109.1	553.9	999.9
Total Liab To Nw (%)	40.8	88.8	219.7
Fixed Assets To Nw (%)	3.0	10.6	27.6
EFFICIENCY			
Coll Period (days)	26.7	50.7	77.2
Sales To Inv (times)	67.8	30.0	9.4
Assets To Sales (%)	21.9	34.0	59.8
Sales To Nwc (times)	15.7	7.3	4.4
Acct Pay To Sales (%)	1.1	3.3	6.5
PROFITABILITY			
Return On Sales (%)	8.9	4.0	1.1
Return On Assets (%)	30.5	9.7	2.3
Return On Nw (%)	63.4	26.9	8.3

SIC 8743 PUBLIC RLTNS SVCS (NO BREAKDOWN) 2013 (15 Establishments)

	$	%
Cash	532,195	18.5
Accounts Receivable	1,061,513	36.9
Notes Receivable	2,877	0.1
Inventory	250,275	8.7
Other Current	276,165	9.6
Total Current	**2,123,025**	**73.8**
Fixed Assets	371,098	12.9
Other Non-current	382,605	13.3
Total Assets	**2,876,728**	**100.0**
Accounts Payable	310,687	10.8
Bank Loans	25,891	0.9
Notes Payable	11,507	0.4
Other Current	650,140	22.6
Total Current	**998,225**	**34.7**
Other Long Term	235,891	8.2
Deferred Credits	0	0.0
Net Worth	1,642,612	57.1
Total Liab & Net Worth	**2,876,728**	**100.0**
Net Sales	6,336,405	100.0
Gross Profit	2,705,645	42.7
Net Profit After Tax	931,452	14.7
Working Capital	1,124,800	---

RATIOS	UQ	MED	LQ
SOLVENCY			
Quick Ratio (times)	3.6	1.5	1.0
Current Ratio (times)	5.4	1.9	1.5
Curr Liab To Nw (%)	17.6	44.0	98.3
Curr Liab To Inv (%)	110.3	149.7	174.9
Total Liab To Nw (%)	17.6	54.1	163.7
Fixed Assets To Nw (%)	8.6	20.7	64.2
EFFICIENCY			
Coll Period (days)	26.3	42.0	79.6
Sales To Inv (times)	13.4	6.2	2.5
Assets To Sales (%)	27.9	45.4	66.6
Sales To Nwc (times)	12.9	8.2	4.8
Acct Pay To Sales (%)	1.8	2.7	5.6
PROFITABILITY			
Return On Sales (%)	20.9	4.7	1.5
Return On Assets (%)	39.1	8.3	3.2
Return On Nw (%)	87.7	25.8	6.6

SIC 8744 FCLTS SPPRT SVCS (NO BREAKDOWN) 2013 (16 Establishments)

	$	%
Cash	960,602	20.9
Accounts Receivable	1,884,435	41.0
Notes Receivable	0	0.0
Inventory	147,078	3.2
Other Current	919,236	20.0
Total Current	**3,911,351**	**85.1**
Fixed Assets	413,656	9.0
Other Non-current	271,175	5.9
Total Assets	**4,596,182**	**100.0**
Accounts Payable	615,888	13.4
Bank Loans	50,558	1.1
Notes Payable	133,289	2.9
Other Current	1,305,316	28.4
Total Current	**2,105,051**	**45.8**
Other Long Term	114,905	2.5
Deferred Credits	0	0.0
Net Worth	2,376,226	51.7
Total Liab & Net Worth	**4,596,182**	**100.0**
Net Sales	8,007,286	100.0
Gross Profit	2,498,273	31.2
Net Profit After Tax	272,248	3.4
Working Capital	1,806,300	---

RATIOS	UQ	MED	LQ
SOLVENCY			
Quick Ratio (times)	2.6	1.4	0.9
Current Ratio (times)	3.5	2.6	1.4
Curr Liab To Nw (%)	35.7	53.8	174.1
Curr Liab To Inv (%)	71.1	553.8	999.9
Total Liab To Nw (%)	36.8	53.8	192.5
Fixed Assets To Nw (%)	3.3	9.0	22.4
EFFICIENCY			
Coll Period (days)	49.3	54.0	91.6
Sales To Inv (times)	662.9	165.8	5.1
Assets To Sales (%)	27.2	57.4	90.0
Sales To Nwc (times)	12.6	6.2	2.8
Acct Pay To Sales (%)	0.7	4.2	5.3
PROFITABILITY			
Return On Sales (%)	5.5	3.5	0.2
Return On Assets (%)	27.2	11.4	0.3
Return On Nw (%)	51.0	17.4	0.3

SIC 8748 BUS CNSLTNG,NEC (NO BREAKDOWN) 2013 (181 Establishments)

	$	%
Cash	365,858	22.6
Accounts Receivable	637,823	39.4
Notes Receivable	6,475	0.4
Inventory	42,090	2.6
Other Current	239,589	14.8
Total Current	**1,291,835**	**79.8**
Fixed Assets	221,781	13.7
Other Non-current	105,225	6.5
Total Assets	**1,618,841**	**100.0**
Accounts Payable	234,732	14.5
Bank Loans	8,094	0.5
Notes Payable	17,807	1.1
Other Current	492,128	30.4
Total Current	**752,761**	**46.5**
Other Long Term	153,789	9.5
Deferred Credits	4,857	0.3
Net Worth	707,434	43.7
Total Liab & Net Worth	**1,618,841**	**100.0**
Net Sales	4,935,491	100.0
Gross Profit	2,299,939	46.6
Net Profit After Tax	236,904	4.8
Working Capital	539,074	---

RATIOS	UQ	MED	LQ
SOLVENCY			
Quick Ratio (times)	3.4	1.8	1.0
Current Ratio (times)	4.8	2.3	1.5
Curr Liab To Nw (%)	18.0	42.9	108.7
Curr Liab To Inv (%)	130.6	520.1	999.9
Total Liab To Nw (%)	25.7	58.8	125.5
Fixed Assets To Nw (%)	5.4	14.2	34.4
EFFICIENCY			
Coll Period (days)	33.8	58.4	79.2
Sales To Inv (times)	107.0	39.0	12.6
Assets To Sales (%)	26.3	32.8	51.4
Sales To Nwc (times)	10.6	6.2	3.6
Acct Pay To Sales (%)	1.4	3.2	7.2
PROFITABILITY			
Return On Sales (%)	10.9	4.3	0.6
Return On Assets (%)	29.3	11.2	1.4
Return On Nw (%)	57.5	21.3	4.3

SIC 89
MISC SERVICES
(NO BREAKDOWN)
2013 (15 Establishments)

	$	%
Cash	120,019	26.3
Accounts Receivable	180,256	39.5
Notes Receivable	2,282	0.5
Inventory	19,166	4.2
Other Current	33,770	7.4
Total Current	**355,493**	**77.9**
Fixed Assets	54,305	11.9
Other Non-current	46,547	10.2
Total Assets	**456,345**	**100.0**
Accounts Payable	77,122	16.9
Bank Loans	0	0.0
Notes Payable	24,186	5.3
Other Current	395,652	86.7
Total Current	**496,960**	**108.9**
Other Long Term	140,554	30.8
Deferred Credits	2,282	0.5
Net Worth	(183,451)	(40.2)
Total Liab & Net Worth	**456,345**	**100.0**
Net Sales	916,355	100.0
Gross Profit	425,189	46.4
Net Profit After Tax	85,221	9.3
Working Capital	(141,467)	—

RATIOS	UQ	MED	LQ
SOLVENCY			
Quick Ratio (times)	2.8	2.2	1.5
Current Ratio (times)	3.9	2.8	1.5
Curr Liab To Nw (%)	28.1	34.9	61.4
Curr Liab To Inv (%)	153.0	228.8	858.5
Total Liab To Nw (%)	33.0	39.6	66.2
Fixed Assets To Nw (%)	2.6	8.8	18.6
EFFICIENCY			
Coll Period (days)	62.8	96.2	101.1
Sales To Inv (times)	20.0	14.2	8.3
Assets To Sales (%)	37.3	49.8	56.9
Sales To Nwc (times)	9.1	3.8	3.1
Acct Pay To Sales (%)	0.7	2.4	14.9
PROFITABILITY			
Return On Sales (%)	13.1	8.9	2.8
Return On Assets (%)	30.9	22.1	5.5
Return On Nw (%)	49.3	41.3	16.8